The Business of ⓒreativity

Anthropology and Business: Crossing Boundaries, Innovating Praxis

SERIES EDITOR: Timothy de Waal Malefyt, Fordham School of Business

Both anthropology and business work at the forefront of culture and change. As anthropology brings its concerns with cultural organization and patterns of human behavior to multiple forms of business, a new dynamic of engagement is created. In addition to expanding interest in business as an object of study, anthropologists increasingly hold positions within corporations or work as independent consultants to businesses. In these roles, anthropologists are both redefining the discipline and innovating in industries around the world. These shifts are creating exciting cross-fertilizations and advances in both realms: challenging traditional categories of scholarship and practice, pushing methodological boundaries, and generating new theoretical entanglements. This series advances anthropology's multifaceted work in enterprise, from marketing, design, and technology to user experience research, work practice studies, finance, and many other realms.

The Business of ©reativity
Toward an Anthropology of Worth

▫ ▣ ▫

Brian Moeran

WALNUT CREEK
CALIFORNIA

Left Coast Press, Inc. is committed to preserving ancient forests and natural resources. We elected to print this title on 30% post consumer recycled paper, processed chlorine free. As a result, for this printing, we have saved:

2 Trees (40' tall and 6-8" diameter)
1 Million BTUs of Total Energy
213 Pounds of Greenhouse Gases
1,151 Gallons of Wastewater
77 Pounds of Solid Waste

Left Coast Press, Inc. made this paper choice because our printer, Thomson-Shore, Inc., is a member of Green Press Initiative, a nonprofit program dedicated to supporting authors, publishers, and suppliers in their efforts to reduce their use of fiber obtained from endangered forests.

For more information, visit www.greenpressinitiative.org

Environmental impact estimates were made using the Environmental Defense Paper Calculator. For more information visit: www.papercalculator.org.

Left Coast Press, Inc.
1630 North Main Street, #400
Walnut Creek, CA 94596
www.LCoastPress.com

Copyright © 2014 by Brian Moeran

All rights reserved. No part of this publication may be reproduced, stored in a retrieval system, or transmitted in any form or by any means, electronic, mechanical, photocopying, recording, or otherwise, without the prior permission of the publisher.

ISBN 978-1-61132-911-7 hardback
ISBN 978-1-61132-912-4 paperback
ISBN 978-1-61132-913-1 institutional eBook
ISBN 978-1-61132-914-8 consumer eBook

Library of Congress Cataloging-in-Publication Data on file.

∞ ™ The paper used in this publication meets the minimum requirements of American National Standard for Information Sciences—Permanence of Paper for Printed Library Materials, ANSI/NISO Z39.48–1992.

Cover design by Piper Wallis
Cover images by Brian Moeran
Text design by Margery Cantor

Earlier versions of parts of Chapters 2, 5, and 8 were previously published as "A business anthropology approach to the study of values: evaluative practices in ceramic art" in *Culture and Organization* 18(3):1–16 (2012); "The organization of creativity in Japanese advertising production" in *Human Relations* 62(7):963–85 (2009); "More than just a fashion magazine" in *Current Sociology* 54(5):725–44; and "The *Ursula* faience dinnerware series by Royal Copenhagen" in B. Moeran and B. T. Christensen (eds.), *Exploring Creativity: Evaluative Practices in Innovation, Design, and the Arts* (Cambridge University Press, 2013, pp. 121-45). In addition, some of the ideas developed here first appeared in the introduction to *Exploring Creativity*.

For the stone carver, musician, and artist who are my children

All patterns of creative activity are trivalent:
they can enter the service of humour, discovery, or art.
—Arthur Koestler, *The Act of Creation*

◙

The conclusion of your syllogism, I said lightly,
is fallacious, being based on licensed premises.
—Flann O'Brien, *At Swim-Two-Birds*

◙

The aspects of things that are most important for us are
hidden because of their simplicity and familiarity. (One is
unable to notice something because it is always before our eyes.)
—Ludwig Wittgenstein, *Philosophical Investigations*

◙

I conceive of the art of painting as the science of
juxtaposing colours in such a way that their actual
appearance disappears and lets a poetic image emerge.
—René Magritte

◙

"Divide a loaf by a knife—what's the answer to that?"
—Lewis Carroll, *Through the Looking Glass, and What Alice Found There*

◙

Contents

ACKNOWLEDGEMENTS 11

OVERTURE 13

CHAPTER 1 Circuits of Affordances 35

CHAPTER 2 Putting on a Show 60

CHAPTER 3 Ensemblages of Worth 82

CHAPTER 4 Shooting an Ad Campaign 101

CHAPTER 5 The Organization of Creativity 119

CHAPTER 6 Editing Fashion Magazines 141

CHAPTER 7 Symbolic Markets 162

CHAPTER 8 Designing Ceramics 177

CHAPTER 9 Craftsmanship 200

CHAPTER 10 Judging Artworks 217

CHAPTER 11 The Politics of Evaluation 232

CODA 246

NOTES 255

REFERENCES 277

INDEX 289

ABOUT THE AUTHOR 299

ACKNOWLEDGEMENTS

This book would never have been written had it not been for the friend-ship and hospitality of Gwen and Per Dahlberg who, at a difficult time in my life, invited me for an open-ended stay with them on Lantau Island in Hong Kong. Tania Willis then kindly saved that friendship by allowing me to house-sit her dog, Dotty, while she spent several weeks over Christmas and the New Year with her family back in the United Kingdom. Dotty gra-ciously accepted the intruder and, when not protecting him from a poison-ous snake on the verandah, took him for long walks along the mountain and coastal paths of southern Lantau. This allowed him plenty of time to ruminate on the structure and contents of a book that has turned out somewhat differently from how it was first envisaged. But that is both the instruction and the joy (and, of course, the creativity) of writing.

That the book came to be envisaged in the first place was due to the encouragement of Wong Heung-Wah who, for many years now, has very sweetly insisted that what I have to say is important enough to be published in Chinese, and who has thus taken on the task of having an earlier version of this book translated into that language before it is published in English. Given the difficulties English and American publishers often experience with translation rights in non-European languages, this may well be the way forward for Western scholars in future. Better an audience of thou-sands than the customary few hundred.

Because parts of this book discuss pottery, and because an extremely important part of my life has developed through friendships with potters, I would like here to thank Sandy Brown for introducing me to the name of Bernard Leach, whom I then had the good fortune to meet back in May 1975, and Yasuda Takeshi for pointing me in the direction of Sarayama Onta as a potential field site for my doctoral research in anthropology.

Two others from the world of Japanese pottery whom I cannot, nor would ever wish to, overlook are Sakamoto Shigeki and Kajiwara Jirō. Shigeki took me under his wing when I first went to do fieldwork in Sarayama Onta, opened up his household to me, and assigned himself the role of "older brother" (*aniki*) during the two years that I spent doing research there on the Japanese folk art movement. Jirō did the same when I went over to Koishiwara to see how it compared with Onta. It is hard to

ACKNOWLEDGMENTS

understand why two men, whose lives were—and still are—so different from my own, should have decided to befriend a visiting foreign anthropologist and help him with his research, but the fact that they did so has changed me irrevocably and contributed enormously (although they would never guess) to the particular worldview that I adopt in my scholarly work.

The same may be said of Miyamoto Reisuke who, with his wife Fusa, took me under their wing when I was studying the ceramic art world in Japan. It was Reisuke who, with a wonderful combination of experience, perception, and wicked irony, opened up the black box of sales and marketing, and who revealed a canny knack for strategising that marks the successful entrepreneur. If I have, from time to time, learned to "think aside," it is in large part thanks to Reisuke, whose departure from this world a few years ago was untimely, to say the very least. I miss him, as I will miss Shigeki and Jirō and their families if I have the misfortune to outlast them in the lottery of life.

Someone else with an equally wicked sense of humour and irony, who has reminded me never to think in straight lines, is Malcolm Campbell: once upon a time my publisher, then my business partner, and now a friend with whom I share annual walks in the mountains of Europe, where our "thinking aside" tends to focus on unlikely combinations of actions and attributes that make for hilarious limericks and other verbal distractions. In the publishing world, Malcolm is known as "the Prince of Darkness," but he has spread light in my later life and I love him for it.

At the end of my academic career, I have been lucky enough to have been the doctoral supervisor of a wild, but (unlike her hair) tameable and extremely talented young woman, Ana Alačovska. Ana has taught me much more than she can ever imagine, and I am deeply indebted to her for some of the ideas expressed in this book. My single regret is that she never managed to transfer to my mobile phone her ringtone of a herd of Macedonian sheep baaing up the wrong tree!

So here's to friendships, with many, many thanks.

Pui O and Copenhagen
September, 2012–May, 2013

OVERTURE

This book is about what happens when people set out to be creative in different forms of cultural production. In this respect, it describes creativity as it is practised in different forms of business. *The Business of ©reativity,* then, is about how these people, each brought in because of his or her special skills and professional knowledge, engage with one another and negotiate their different understandings of what it means to be 'creative' as they go about making a film, pop song, fashion collection, animated cartoon, or advertising campaign. For them, creativity is as much in these social engagements and negotiations as it is in the finished product. Creativity is a social and cultural process.

More particularly, this book is about what I like to think of as creativity on the edge. What do I mean by 'on the edge'? Whenever I teach an introductory course on creative industries, I start by pointing out the paradox of the term 'creative industries.' How can an *industry*, which relies on formal organization, rules and routines, be *creative*? Creativity implies individual spontaneity that can only emerge when routines are *not* followed, when rules are broken. This suggests that the term 'creative industries' is little more than an oxymoron.

I then ask my students what *they* think of creativity and how they define it. I get all sorts of answers, of course, and it is often difficult to find any common thread among them (which doesn't make my life as a teacher very easy). But there is one phrase that half a dozen students invariably give in answer to my question every year: creativity is thinking 'out of the box.'

At first glance, this sounds good. It would appear to conform to Arthur Koestler's thesis that the creative act comes about through a "bisociative click" facilitated by "a synthesis of previously unconnected matrices of thought."[1] Still, there's something not quite right about 'thinking out of the box.' This unease stems from the fact that 'out of the box' implies that you are inside a box in the first place, and that you want to get outside it because it's hemming you in in some way or another (almost certainly with the kind of rules and routines that I mentioned above). Fair enough.

But think about what a box is. For a start, it has walls (and sometimes a lid as well). Those walls tend to be quite high. More important, they are generally made of materials that you cannot see through. This means that, when you're in a box, you have no idea what is going on *out*side it, or *who*

14   ▣   **OVERTURE**

is doing *what, why, how, for whom,* and *with what effects.* But the reverse is also true. If you are outside a box, you cannot see what is going on *in*side it.

Thinking 'out of the box,' then, is fine if you happen to be a frog and want to jump out to go and join your friends in a neighbouring rice field (or old pond). But what if you're a human? Suppose you are stuck inside this box, along with a lot of other friends, and you're looking for a way out. And then, one day, quite by chance, when your friends are all asleep, you come across a virtually invisible trap door which opens when you press a crack in the floor, and find your way out of the box. When you try to go back and tell them, however, you find as in children's stories that the door only works one way, like those turnstiles at metro stations, stadiums, or zoos. You are unable, then, to perform a Houdini illusion. When your friends wake up, they immediately realise you're no longer inside the box with them. But they're not quite sure what has happened to you, because they can't see through the walls of the box (and they haven't, of course, spotted the concealed door). Did you manage to get out on your own, or did you get help, or what? How did you do it and what are you up to now? How could they learn from your success?

So, to define creativity as thinking *out* of the box doesn't really make sense. In order to be able to recognize something, or someone, as being 'creative', those left behind in the box have to be able to compare that 'creativity' with what they've been doing before. And you can't do that if one of you is invisible on the other side of a box's wall.

This is why I like to think of creativity as being on the *edge* of the box. If it's on the edge, everyone can see it: both those *out*side and those *in*side the box. They all have the opportunity to judge it and compare it with what has gone on before. Being on the edge allows you to interpret the urn as a profile, material particles as ripples of energy, even cabbages as kings. Being on the edge allows you to bridge the gap between previously unrelated frames of reference and see analogies that nobody has seen before: like Gutenberg's ability to bridge the gap between wine press and seal and so invent the printing press.[2]

But *where* exactly is the edge of a creative box? A plastic, metal, or wooden box has walls whose edges are firmly fixed by their materials. But creativity is not fixed. Indeed, something is 'creative' precisely because it is *not* fixed. A creative box, then, is not a *solid* plastic, metal, or wooden form. Rather, like Alice's Looking-glass, it is *fluid.*

Imagine a box made of some kind of resin that is just solid enough to sustain a form, but which changes its shape every time you touch it. That's creativity on the edge. Creativity on the edge is all about *people* and what they do with *things*. It's about people's *encounters, engagements,* and *negotiations* with, as well as their *evaluations* of, paintings, sculptures, books, music, films, and so on, as they go about conceiving, making, distributing, interpreting, and using them. But it is also about their encounters, engagements, and negotiations with other people—including consumers of the genre with which they are engaged.[3] Because creativity in different forms of cultural production is for the most part collaborative, I am interested in what might be called its 'human chemistry,' 'interactional synchrony,' or 'group flow,'[4] and its potential for '*ensembling*'—a form of expression that can emerge from highly attuned and synchronized interaction among individuals whose actions aspire towards a shared singular purpose (such as a fashion collection, art exhibition, or musical performance).[5] This is what this book is about.

Creativity, then, is not a 'great leap forward' out of the box. It consists of a lot of small steps—with an occasional hop, skip, and jump—to the edge of the box: steps that make something (a fashion collection or chair design) *jut out* from the normal just enough for you to notice it. Put in a slightly more intellectual way, we might say, with Claude Lévi-Strauss, that creativity "lies half-way between scientific knowledge and mythical or magical thought": that is, somewhere between the *reorganization* of elements, neither extending nor renewing them and limited to known transformations, and their *opening up*.[6] Creativity doesn't have to be a 'once in a lifetime' invention. It's just as much in the every day: in everyday things that everyday people make and do in their everyday lives.

Creative Engagements

This book describes and analyses business situations in which people think about, design, manufacture, appraise, and use a variety of products and events they judge to be 'creative.' Its focus is on the *hows*, not *whys*, of creativity. Because it examines creative processes in diverse forms of cultural production, the book is about culture in the making and the accompanying valuative and evaluative processes that come to constitute 'worth.'[7] Since those in charge of cultural production generally demand, secure, and develop rights to the reproduction of specific cultural forms deriving from people's creativity, I have chosen to allude to copyright in the spelling of the book's title. Creativity these days is very much a business.

16 ▣ **OVERTURE**

Before going any further, let me quickly issue a warning to those of you who have picked out this title from among many others on a (virtual) bookstore shelf or as a result of a Google or other Internet search. My interest in the 'hows' of creative practices doesn't mean that this book will provide you with a how-to model of best practice. It doesn't set out to help you improve the creativity of your organization and those working therein by making a product or process in some way 'better.'[8] It doesn't offer any concrete or practical ideas about how to manage creativity, nor does it suggest how creativity might enhance business performance.[9] It doesn't propose, either, that corporate creativity is necessarily a 'good thing.'[10] In short, it doesn't 'celebrate' creativity.[11] It merely explores it.[12]

If, in their explorations, the chapters in this book address collaboration, competence, education, efficiency, entrepreneurship, innovation, knowledge, marketing, or any of those other activities with which creativity has been linked by scholars, they do so coincidentally to its main task, which is to describe and analyse what I like to think of as collaborative *engagements*. Such engagements may or may not lead to the kind of ensembling I mentioned above (and will elaborate on in Chapter 9). They take place on four interlocking levels.

1. Among the different agents assigned to a particular project—an account planner, creative director, art director, copywriter, marketing director, and media buyer, for example, in planning an advertising campaign for the sales manager of a client company—or fashion designer, seamstresses, models, stylists, bookers, buyers, makeup artists, photographer, event manager, fashion house personnel, and so on and so forth, all involved in putting on a fashion show.

2. Between these agents and the institutions by which they are employed, together with their associated hierarchies of power that include both internal positions (CEO, vice president, director, manager, and so on) and external status rankings (Mercedes Benz, BMW, Audi, Volkswagen, and Opel in the German automobile industry, for example).

3. Between agents, institutions, and the materials, tools, and technologies, together with their associated ideals and budgets, with which they all in their different ways engage and negotiate among themselves. And finally,

4. Between all of the above and cultural 'texts' or genres, in the sense that such engagements "employ conventionalised and specialised occupational practices and practical knowledge, work within an institutional context with its own inherent cultural logic and produce a tangible text, product, or performance."[13]

This focus on creative processes calls for an ethnographic approach. In this respect, *The Business of ©reativity* represents what is these days being called business anthropology, or the anthropology of business.[14] It has taken a comparatively long time for anthropologists to recognize and accept that their discipline is extremely well positioned to carry out in-depth ethnographic studies of business organizations and trading relations. Indeed, in this respect, anthropologists working in Japan have very often been ahead of what is now becoming if not a fashion, then at least a trend. Back in the early 1970s, both Ronald Dore and Thomas Rohlen carried out participant-observation in a Japanese factory and bank, respectively, and since then others have followed their example by writing about a Japanese corrugated board manufacturer, advertising agency, and fish market.[15]

This book offers a slightly different take on this strand of scholarship by focusing on the business of creativity: the choices made by different participants in a 'creative world' as they go about conceiving, composing or designing, performing or making, and assessing different cultural products with a view to selling them. It describes practices, rather than prescribes theories, in the sense that its theories are embedded in practices which are themselves necessarily theoretical.[16] Hopefully, the book will show that Einstein's aphorism—"In theory, theory and practice are the same. In practice, they are not"—need not always apply as it tells its stories about the affordances with which creative people have to engage to be 'creative' in the first place. In particular, it addresses the following themes:

1. The formation of *creative worlds* around particular creative products—advertising worlds, for example, or ceramic art worlds, or fashion worlds—and the differences (some greater, some lesser) among them in the organization of creativity.
2. The different values that people in these creative worlds bring to bear during the course of their creative engagements with products, as well as with one another, and their resulting assessments of *worth*.
3. The different *affordances* (usually, but not necessarily, in the form of constraints) that they face when thinking on 'the edge of the box': the materials, aesthetic ideals, genres, situational contexts, personal networks, organizational structures, and budgetary demands that

together influence how different people engage in creative processes and what they come up with as a result.

Because all of these values and affordances are embedded in one another in any creative world—at times one, at times another, singly or in different combinations, illuminating the whole—the social, cultural, economic, and technical may be seen as constituting an 'assemblage'—ideally, because of the collaborative nature of creative work, an *ensemblage*—which frames and embodies what is, and is not, recognized as 'creativity.'[17] It is because such *ensemblages* are made up of evaluations, values, and valuation, as well as group formations of one sort or another and the objects which act upon them, that we may regard business anthropology as an *anthropology of worth*.

Creative Industries

Because both creativity and business are driven by assemblages, this book necessarily engages with those twin theoretical bastions of culture and economy, which lie at the heart of the political discourse that has, since the mid- to late 1990s, dominated national government policies all over the world, from Australia to the United Kingdom, and thence to other parts of Europe and now China, Japan, and the rest of Asia. This snowballing discourse of "economization"[18] has made it fashionable for politicians, corporate executives, civil servants and academics to talk about 'creative industries' (rather than of 'cultural industries' or even 'service industries', as of old),[19] 'creative hubs' (or clusters), 'creative cities', 'creative classes', and so on. By so doing they assign (high) cultural value to commercial activities[20] that are then connected to national interests. Prior to the 2010 general election in the United Kingdom, for example, the website of the Department of Culture, Media and Sport attributed the importance of creative industries to the fact that they accounted for a significant percentage of the country's gross domestic product (GDP); showed greater growth than the economy as a whole; and employed a significant, and increasing, number of people (1.95 million at the last count in 2009). The net result of this discourse is that, like 'military intelligence', the term 'creative industries' is dangerously close to being no more than an oxymoron.

This suspicion is borne out by the fact that, in spite of—or because of—their interest in the economic implications of creativity, those concerned with the promotion of creative industries have rarely gone beyond rudimentary, even banal, definitions[21] of what exactly they mean by 'creative' or 'creativity,' or indeed of related words used in the context of creativity: 'innovation,' 'individuality,' 'spontaneity,' 'originality,' 'difference,' 'genius,' 'merit,' 'talent,' and so on. Instead, they have treated creativity as though it exists in a well-cushioned vacuum. All that is required to nourish it are the right kinds of people gathered in the right kinds of spaces doing the right kinds of creative activity and Bob, whoever he may be, is your uncle. In this sense, most people in the worlds of business, education, and political administration appear to believe in creativity as a form of immaculate conception.[22]

Creativity, like other forms of action, "is not a coherent, controlled, well-rounded and clean-edged affair." It, too, is 'dislocated.'[23] Of course, it doesn't help that creativity is "borrowed, distributed, suggested, influenced, dominated, betrayed, translated,"[24] or that it is used and abused so frequently—"at one moment invoked to praise a specific technical skill, at another uttered in the most vague and casual manner."[25] Moreover, in the Western world at least, "it carries too much Romantic baggage—the mystery of inspiration, the claims of genius"—something that this book questions.[26] Such words tend to rest upon mythic ideas, which themselves often embrace contradictory logics, as Arnold Hauser tellingly remarks:

> Inspiration is sometimes described as the secret origin of an idea for which there appears to be no external cause, sometimes as the effect of a purely external and coincidental happening, or of an experience which is of no consequence in itself but to which the artist relates the genesis of his work in a causal, though hidden, way.[27]

There are three points to keep in mind when talking and thinking about creative industries, especially in the context of non-Western societies, since it is with Japanese forms of cultural production that this book mainly (though not exclusively) deals. In the first place, the very concept of a 'creative' industry rests upon an Anglo-European assumption that creativity is 'individual' (even though most, though not all, forms of cultural production involve a broad range of *collaborative* creative inputs, as Richard Caves noted of what he has called the "motley crew").[28] It also assumes some universalistic notion of 'creativity' (and talent), which, precisely because it is *not* defined, is adopted without question by different governments with different cultural (and creative) traditions in different parts of the world. In this respect, the category of creative industry may be regarded as an intellectually imperialist construct.

20 ▫ OVERTURE

Second, precisely because creative industries have been treated as part of a national (or nationalist) agenda, industries that have been included as 'creative' in some countries are ignored in others, depending on whether they do or do not make a significant contribution to their *economies* (and, note, creativity itself is *not* the issue). Thus, we find that 'tourism' is a creative industry in Indonesia, where a Ministry of Tourism and Creative Economy has been established, but not in the United Kingdom. In some countries, 'fashion' refers to high-end fashion houses with name designers; in others (which have few or no name designers), to *all* clothing manufacturers which design and manufacture (or have manufactured for them) clothes; in yet others (like Hong Kong), the category of 'fashion' until recently didn't exist as a creative industry, even though there are plenty of name designers working there. Similar inconsistencies are to be found among other activities classified by governments as 'creative.' As a result, academics have devoted a lot of discussion to redrafting the rules by which the creative game may be played, and by whom.[29]

This in itself raises a third issue of politics. Some countries like the UK and Hong Kong talk about 'creative' industries; others (the United States, Singapore, Australia, New Zealand) about 'copyright' industries; one or two (such as Japan) about 'contents' industries; and at least one more (Taiwan) about 'cultural creative' industries, depending on the particular characteristics that their governments wish to emphasize. The question then arises: what do those working in these creative, copyright, contents, and cultural creative industries think? My own research suggests that fashion designers, film directors, artists, writers, potters, musicians, architects, and advertising copywriters do not feel a sense of 'community' with one another on the basis of being employed in ostensibly similar kinds of industries that make use of 'creative' personnel. Some may work for a fashion industry, others for a film industry, but not for a commonly shared 'creative' (or copyright and so on) industry. They have no common unions or associations outside their own worlds of fashion, film, art, and so on, other than those set up by governments. Even when something like a 'Creative Industries Council' is formed in the UK, and although its membership includes more than 30 members representing such well-known organizations as Google, the Arts Council, the Advertising Association, BSkyB, the Design Council, ITV, the British Fashion Council, the Publishers Association, and so on (including the odd politician), not one—at the time of writing—is a 'creative' person by occupation or training.

Rather, creative industry personnel's loyalties are more particular: they design clothes, interiors, buildings, or magazine layout; they direct films, paint pictures, write books or advertising copy; they make and fire pots, compose and/or perform music, and so on. In so doing, they communicate with other designers, directors, artists, composers, and musicians in their working worlds. In this respect, 'creative industries' is more a top-down political construct than a bottom-up recognition of a social formation engaged in everyday practice.

Creativity, Improvisation, and Thinking Aside

So what *is* creativity exactly, and how should we go about analyzing it? The cognitive psychologist Mihali Csikszentmihalyi would counter that this is the wrong question to ask, and that we should focus on *where* creativity is to be found. Fair enough, but the "systems model" that he proposes, with its domain of symbolic rules and procedures, field of individuals who act as gatekeepers to the domain, and individual creative persons, is too focused on individual persons for an anthropologist such as myself to accept, even though we may in fact share a number of ideas about where creativity is located and in what it consists.[30] I myself believe that we should locate creativity not in individuals, but in the material, aesthetic, situational, organizational, symbolic, and economic; in short, in the *social*.

There are two problems the social sciences have had to deal with when discussing creative work processes. One is that the relation between inner impulse and actual creative practice is often as obscure to those employed as 'creatives' in the cultural or creative industries as it is to politicians, bureaucrats, corporate managers, academics, and other educationalists. This suggests a need to examine creative processes *in situ* (and not just rely on what people say in interviews): in other words, to make use of the anthropological method of participant observation to see and experience how creative (and other) people actually engage in their work. By building up a series of case studies in different creative industries, we might be able to arrive at a few tentative conclusions about the notion of creativity itself (as well as about how it varies in different industries and between national cultures), and about the products deriving therefrom. This is one aim of the *The Business of ©reativity*.

The other problem derives from the fact that creativity *is* in part inexplicable. Indeed, most creative people I have talked to assert that creativity cannot be totally derived from observable phenomena. In other words, you can't necessarily *see* it. This raises a two-part question:

1. To what extent should we understand creative processes to be founded on *internally* generated drive, talent, inclination, and so on? In other words, is creativity to be attributed to *individual* psychology? And/or
2. How much is creativity conditioned by, and recognized as existing through, *external relationships*? In other words, is creativity *social*?

In a way, the two parts of this question may be rephrased as a distinction between creative *product* and creative *process*, and it is to overcome this distinction that I make use of the concepts of *ensemble* and *ensemblage*. When we talk about an individual's creativity, we are almost invariably considering some*thing* that he or she has invented or made: the hot air balloon by the Montgolfier brothers in 1783, for example, or Google by Larry Page and Sergey Brin during the mid- to late 1990s. Just *how* these products came into existence, however, is not usually that clear, although creative people often post-rationalize and give a simplified account of what they did to come up with their invention. Like many after-the-event explanations, such accounts tend to gloss over messy details (and the same can be said of theatre, music, and other performances which are later judged to be 'creative'). Yet it is precisely out of such messy details that creativity emerges, as people struggle to overcome all sorts of different problems, often over many years.

Anthropologists have also wrestled with creativity and how best to understand and analyse it. John Liep, for example, equates creativity with innovation.[31] This is the way many people (including my students) think. But what exactly *is* 'innovation'? When is something 'new'? And what makes it so?[32] When I make a box out of plastic rather than metal, in the way it used to be, there is an innovation in materials, maybe. But is this innovation particularly 'creative'? After all, all I've done is introduce a different ready-made material with which to manufacture a standard object. I haven't invented plastic as a substance, or anything like that. I've merely improvised.

Another thing about innovation is that you can only gauge it by looking *backwards* at past products. In other words, innovation is in this respect nothing other than a means of *measurement*. This raises the question: can creativity be measured? Governments like to think so and cite endless statistical data relating to turnover and employment figures in different forms of cultural production to prove their point. Others (including myself) beg to disagree. Timothy Ingold and Elizabeth Hallam suggest that we need to focus on *processes* of 'in-the-making,' rather than on the *products* made. At the heart of such processes, they say, is improvisation, which, through small and occasionally surprising changes, may invoke larger implications.[33]

This certainly begins to answer the question of how best to think about and analyse creativity. Improvisation is spur of the moment extemporizing. It consists of people "fabricating and inventing novel responses without a pre-scripted plan and without certainty of outcomes; discovering the future that . . . action creates as it unfolds."[34] In this respect, improvisation is perilous. In different forms of cultural production, it obliges people (fashion designers, film directors, musicians, photographers, and so on) to come up with something whose outcome they cannot necessarily envisage, but which has to be novel and coherent, usually in front of a client or other audience. Precisely because improvisation takes people away from the security of habitual practice and leads them to 'the edge' of the unknown, there is a tendency for them to rely on stock tricks of the trade which have proven effective in the past, rather than to risk failure, even though they know deep down that not to fail is in itself a failure.[35]

Ingold and Hallam argue that it is improvisation, not innovation, which explains 'creativity.' Creativity is *forward-*, not backward-looking.[36] This is a neat distinction, but alas, it doesn't quite work in practice. It is often hard for those working together in collaborative situations to detach improvisation from innovation, process from product. Perhaps this is a characteristic particular to cultural production in the 'creative' industries, which are always conceptualising and manufacturing new products on the basis of past products and experiences. For them, primarily because they are working for the most part with defined genres and brands, the present *is* the past. As a result, we can say that creativity is *product-as-process*, neither one, nor the other, but both together. As Keith Sawyer points out, "improvisation couldn't take place at all without some shared conventions, because otherwise communication would be impossible."[37]

So what more do we need to explain creativity? Creative products in themselves are characterised by what Howard Becker calls a "fundamental indeterminacy."[38] Films, fashion shows, studio shoots, and music gigs vary enormously, even though they may be realised by the same personnel in, for all intents and purposes, the same environments using the same materials and techniques. Yet they are all marked by a series of choices by participants: the choice, for example, of how to shoot a particular scene, or of how to cut and sew a particular material, frame a photo, or phrase a musical idea. The "combination of routine and unusual choices among available possibilities" gives every creative product its character.[39] "Nobody knows" if it will succeed, or not.[40]

What affords such choices, therefore—materials and available technologies, aesthetic ideals, genre and cultural style, personal networks, power relations, money—should be our main concern. As a general rule, creative work moves through many hands before it finally passes from producer to consumer. In so doing, it is subject to all sorts of improvisations and evaluations made by a long series of skilled intermediaries (professional colleagues, clients, performers, managerial staff, and so on) before they arrive at some sort of shared standard of what constitutes both 'creativity' and 'good work.' To understand the meaning of creativity, we need to explore what choices are made by those involved and from what range of possibilities they are selected.[41] In other words, we need to take the sacred relic of creativity out of the crypt and air it in the alley.

I have already suggested that creativity involves moving to the edge of the box. Let me take this suggestion a little further. To be able to move to the edge, you have, necessarily, to be able to "think aside."[42] This is no easy task. As any Zen novice will aver, the harder you try to find the answer to what the sound of one hand clapping might be, the less likely you are to find it. And yet you have to try and try again, because it is when you are beating your head against the wall of the box in frustration that, quite suddenly, a totally unexpected answer is likely to come to mind. Creativity, then, involves thinking aside, and to be able to think aside—as much of the ethnographic material tells us in the chapters that follow—demands preparation, immersion, and incubation before any insight:[43] in other words, discipline, hard work, and patience. Creativity is based on graft, and not on an inexplicable gift from the gods.

Thinking aside is characteristic, as Koestler argues, of humour, science, and art. Each sees analogies which nobody has seen before, whether in a pithy saying ("Statistics are like a bikini. What they reveal is suggestive. What they conceal is vital."), discovery (Kepler's linking of the physical and metaphysical in gravity and the Holy Ghost), or visual image (Meret Oppenheim's *Cup, saucer and spoon in fur*). While people working in different forms of cultural production may not aspire to such Eureka acts, they do, nevertheless, attempt to uncover things that have always been there but "hidden from the eye by the blinkers of habit."[44] They bring together hitherto separate planes of experience to afford 'originality,' which often—like metaphor—consists of no more than a displacement of attention to something that was irrelevant before, but is now made relevant.[45] We will see various examples of this in the chapters that follow.

The aim, then, is to free the mind of those constraints which are necessary for it to maintain a disciplined routine in everyday life, but which at the same time prevent the 'blindingly obvious' from emerging. In Koestler's words:

> Ordered, disciplined thought is a skill governed by set rules of the game, some of which are explicitly stated, others implied and hidden in the code. The creative act, in so far as it depends on unconscious resources, presupposes a relaxing of the controls and a regression to the rules of verbal logic, unperturbed by contradiction, untouched by the dogmas and taboos of so-called common sense. At the decisive stage of discovery the codes of disciplined reasoning are suspended— as they are in the dream, the reverie, the manic flight of thought, when the stream of ideation is free to drift, by its own emotional gravity, as it were, in an apparently 'lawless' fashion.[46]

Editorial Moments

If we accept that creativity is a sort of conversation that emerges out of a series of different kinds of collaborative improvisations made during the *processes* of engaging in cultural production, and that innovation can only be recognized and measured by looking back at past *products*, then we need to ask ourselves how and for what purposes people *evaluate* the work that they do in creative industries. Evaluations consist of what Howard Becker calls "editorial moments,"[47] or the actual choices made by different people at different stages during the performance of creative work: a potter's decision to make *both* stoneware *and* porcelain for an exhibition; an art director's decision to delegate the production of an advertising campaign to a photographer and hairdresser. Such decisions tend to have their knock-on effects: the choice of a particular kind of clay affects both the forms and glazes of pots, influencing their pricing and display at the exhibition; delegation of authority to a hairdresser, rather than to an art director, results in a conflict questioning the relations of trust that underpin all creative work.

During the course of every set of creative processes—whether preparing for a pottery exhibition, shooting an ad campaign, or editing a fashion magazine, as described in later chapters of this book—we find different critical observations about the same product—a ceramic dish, a model's hair, or a magazine page. Does the decoration fit the form? Has the pot been 'properly' fired? Is it 'worth' its price tag? Can a stray wisp of hair be removed by the photographer, thanks to digitization? Or should the studio set be reassembled, so that the hairdresser can 'perfect' the model's look? Should a magazine page's text be similar—in design, colour, or subject matter—to the advertisement on the facing page? Or should it be radically different in order to separate advertising from textual matter?

Different people have different opinions: potter and gallery owner; photographer, hairdresser, and art director; editor, advertising manager, and magazine publisher. These opinions result from their different engagements with the products at hand (pots, advertisements, magazines). They are not competing solutions to particular problems so much as variations that are related in one way or another.[48] Above all, then, editorial moments confirm that creative work is a collaborative venture, and it is creative professionals' involvement with and dependence on such collaborative links that necessarily afford (enable, constrain) the kind of work they produce.[49]

It is easy to make the assumption that *production* primarily makes use of generative creative processes, whereas *consumption* mainly consists of evaluations by critics, reviewers, and consumers. It would, however, be a mistake to do so. Editorial moments constitute evaluations that take place throughout the production-consumption chain, reflecting upon one another in the process. One overarching theme in this book is precisely that evaluative processes take place both during the production of cultural goods (typically by the creator or co-creators) *and* in their consumption afterwards (for example, by critics, reviewers, and consumers).

As such, editorial moments may be separated into two important forms. First, they embrace the ongoing *internal* evaluations made by producers and stakeholders during the creative (and managerial) processes of conceptualizing, designing, and finally making new products. Second, they refer to 'post-production' *external* evaluations that seek to compare and rank cultural producers and goods in a particular domain (fashion, art, design, and so on). Some of these are then picked out and given prizes or awards at regular intervals: the Academy Awards (Oscars) for film, for example; the Michelin Guide for restaurants; the numerous prizes for books and their authors, culminating in the Nobel Prize for Literature; and the Princess Chichibu Cup for ceramic art in Japan (Chapter 10).

In the first form, we find all the nitty-gritty detail of evaluating that, constantly and continuously, takes place as those involved in creative work go about their work and search for that small 'difference' which distinguishes this particular product from all others that have gone before or are currently on the market. To make such an assessment, those working in different forms of cultural production must take into account the following things connected with creativity:

1. *Vision versus actuality:* how the current state of the work-in-progress compares with and adheres to, or differs from, the artist's (composer's, designer's, film director's, potter's, writer's) original vision.
2. *Creative brief:* the criteria and constraints of the task at hand, generally—but not always—stipulated by the client for whom the creative work is being done. Thus, an advertising agency needs to work within the advertiser's overall sales and marketing strategy, as well as to its budget; a fashion designer knows that to survive, he cannot simply design outrageous fashions for a very select few, but must also provide wearable clothes for a more or less mass market.
3. *Creative norms:* the standards and canons of each genre that define creative work—the allegro-andante-rondo tripartite progression of a nineteenth-century piano concerto, for example, or the virtually predictable structure of romance, detective, and travel guide books.[50]

It is the combination, or *ensemblage*, of actuality, norms, and client brief that effectively prevents creative work from ever jumping totally 'out of the box.' In other words, it is often less a matter of a single creator having a 'vision' than it is of a struggle for which of a number of visions to pursue. Informal ongoing conversations among co-creators help them make sense of what is 'good' or 'bad'; what holds promise and what is a dead end; what 'sparkles' and what 'stinks.' They allow them to move to the box's edge in their search for *product difference.*

The main purpose of this form of editorial moment is to guide the creative process ever onwards in fruitful directions to arrive finally at something that is valued as 'different' (and therefore as 'new'). Progress, however, tends to be characterised by fits and starts, rather than by a smooth, continuous flow. Considerable disagreement can arise when key actors make use of differing standards or criteria in their judgements about what is, or is not, 'good.' This then leads to different takes on what the object-in-the-making *should* be, as well as on whether it will succeed or fail.

The second kind of editorial moment mentioned here concerns the practice of evaluating and making decisions in institutions and systems that are external to the actual production of a cultural good. An art world of any kind devotes much of its time to discussing the relative quality and value of individual artworks, which it then compares, ranks, selects, and rewards (as we will see in Chapter 10). The same is true of the world of advertising, film, cuisine, and many other forms of cultural production. Fashion magazine editors, for example, continually evaluate fashion designers, models, celebrities, and others in the fashion world, deciding whose clothing, face, or photograph should be included in this month's issue, and whose should not, as they make provisional decisions on who is in, and who is out of, fashion. But, simultaneously, they compare themselves with other magazine titles, checking on which designers, models, and celebrities *they* select, and on which advertisers *they* have that they themselves have not procured (Chapter 6). The system of differences in which they are engaged is one primarily of *status difference*.

Precisely because they are in many ways repetitive and routine, as well as innovative, and because they involve reflection on past practice as well as on creative solutions to present problems, editorial moments embody an interesting and difficult dilemma for creative professionals. To produce creative products (including performances) that will be of interest to their target audiences, creative workers need ideally to *unlearn* some of what they have learned as the conventionally 'right' way of doing things. Totally conventional pieces appeal to nobody; in the lingo of the market, they become 'product failures' or flops. For a product to be successful, therefore, creative professionals should, to some extent at least, transgress standards and expectations that have been more or less deeply internalized. To this end, they enter into an inner dialogue, within and among themselves, that evaluates not just the materials, forms, and colours of their designs, but the whole world of competing products and organizations. This is the business of creativity.

Structure of This Book

The Business of ©reativity focuses for the most part, though not entirely, on creative practices in Japan. There are three reasons for this. First, as a result of circumstance, I have chosen to specialise in analysing 'things Japanese' during my professional career as an anthropologist. Secondly, because of this ethnographic interest in the 'East,' and because of the undue reverence paid by most members of European and American academia (generally outside anthropology) to theoretical developments in the 'West,' I have often wondered to what extent the latter hold good for societies beyond their own small intellectual worlds, while simultaneously trying to avoid the kind of navel-gazing detail that characterizes what passes for Japanese, and other regional, studies. One underlying aim of this book, then, is to juxtapose Japanese practices with French, other European, and American theories and see how much the latter hold up under the microscope of ethnography. Third, although many Western scholars seem to prefer to ignore the fact, two of the world's three largest economies (including that of Japan) are East Asian. How they go about both business and creativity, therefore, needs to be looked into more than it has been hitherto.

The book is structured into alternating chapters of ethnographic accounts and theoretical propositions. It focuses primarily on pottery, advertising, and fashion magazine publishing, because these are three creative activities that I have researched over many years and know well. I do, of course, suggest how the material that I present in these chapters might be applied to other forms of cultural production—art, fashion, film, publishing, and so on—but I leave it to my readers to make use of their own experiences in these different creative worlds and decide the extent to which what I have to say is, or is not, appropriate and applicable to other creative worlds.

In Chapter 1, I argue that it is the numerous *affordances* by which choices are guided that need to be considered in any discussion of creativity. In previous work, I have located creativity in the context of constraints, because that is how many of my informants have thought of their work. However, the very fact that constraints ultimately *enable* creativity suggests that the term is misleading. The concept of affordance, first developed by Gibson and then taken up by other social scientists, seems better suited to describe and analyse the various ways in which creative processes are both inhibited and enabled in particular social contexts. All industries—not just the so-called creative industries—have to engage with *circuits* of affordances to function effectively. These are techno-material, temporal, spatial, social, representational, and economic affordances. Like circuits of commerce, circuits of affordances are marked by distinctive social relations, shared economic activities, common accounting systems, shared understandings about the meaning of transactions in which they are engaged, and a boundary separating those involved in this social world from other social worlds.[51] Although such an approach is in itself not novel, this chapter builds on previous work by attempting to *systematise* the different affordances constraining, enabling, and otherwise affecting creative choices.

30 ▣ **OVERTURE**

Chapter 2 provides the first of five detailed ethnographic accounts in the book, and focuses on the conception behind, and preparations for, my own pottery exhibition held in a Japanese department store, which, like other stores in Japan, routinely put on cultural events as part of its commercial activities. The account outlines the negotiations that took place between gallery owner (whose idea it was) and department store and media organizations, which have sponsored cultural events of this kind; the strategic packaging that was developed to make the exhibition into an 'event'; pricing and layout mechanisms; and my own struggle with making pots that would be good enough to go on public display. It thus illustrates the ways in which the circuit of affordances comes together and works as an *ensemblage* in a particular situation, while at the same time revealing some of the bisociative strategies that underpin 'thinking aside.'

Affordances give rise to different forms of valuation and evaluation, and Chapter 3 focuses on anthropologists', sociologists', and cultural economists' discussions of values in the context of creative products. In examining the art world of Japanese ceramics, it shows how informants' own evaluations of quality were made up of distinctions between *aesthetic, social,* and *economic* values. These are applied to the ethnographic data from the previous chapter, and three further values are then added: *spatial, temporal,* and *use.* Together these form a system of values in which aesthetic, social, spatial, temporal, and use together constitute a *symbolic exchange* value that has to be equated with *commodity exchange.* I argue further that it should be possible in some situations to calculate the worth of creative goods and services by equating evaluations (qualities) with valuation (quantity, or price). In other words, circuits of affordances give rise to *ensemblages of worth.*

Chapter 4 presents a second ethnographic account of creativity at work, following a production team over three days as it films a television commercial and takes still photos for print magazine advertisements on location in the streets of Tokyo. In spite of what appears to be uncharted chaos, this chapter shows how participants go about their jobs in an orderly fashion according to a predefined creative brief while at the same time being subject to unanticipated interventions (from adverse weather to a bureaucratic policeman) that oblige them to change plans and improvise at a moment's notice.

A production team consists of a number of freelance personnel with different professional skills (photographer, hair stylist, makeup artist, model, art director, studio technician, and so on) who come together to work on a particular project. Because they know one another by reputation only, and do not themselves possess the others' skills, they *assume* that each knows what he or she is doing. This means that *trust* underpins much creative work in the creative industries, and the chapter shows how important trust is to both 'knowledge in the air' and to the potential for *ensembling* in creative collaborations.

Chapter 5 picks up on this theme and examines the organization of creativity. An advertising campaign is in many ways "the deposit of a social relationship," so that what counts is who controls whom, and at what points, during the production of an ad campaign. The initial focus of this chapter is on the broader field of advertising and what Pierre Bourdieu refers to as the "space of possibles" that orients the lines of demarcation between art director, photographer, and client, as the symbolic space of the studio is transformed into a "stake of struggles" in which performers discover whether their vision of how things should be done prevails and, if not, *whose* vision does prevail.

The organization of creativity is complicated by the fact that key personnel are obliged to please two audiences simultaneously: the art director needs to satisfy the client, as well as ensure that the campaign appeals to consumers so that the client's product sells; likewise, the photographer has to satisfy both advertising client and art director, to whom he is subcontracted. Relations of subcontracting freelance personnel, therefore, underpin creativity itself, since these reveal relations of authority based on financial power.

However, such authority is overtly denied so that creativity can take place in a commercial vacuum. In other words, acutely aware of the potential constraints imposed by power relations, people in Japan's advertising world do their best to minimize them in the actual production of advertisements. In this way, they hope, participants will feel free to improvise as they go along, for it is such cultural improvisation that affords numerous, and minute, touches of interactive creativity. It is out of this vacuum that *ensembling* becomes possible.

The third ethnographic account, presented in Chapter 6, focuses on the production of fashion magazines. Picking up on the fact that creativity is never for a single audience, I look at the difficulties faced by magazine editors who (like a photographer subcontracted for an ad campaign) are obliged to appeal to both readers and advertiser when putting together each issue of their publication. However, if they are to be taken seriously, magazine editors know that they must pay attention to a third audience, the fashion world itself.

32 ▣ OVERTURE

The fact that fashion magazines are an integral part of the fashion industry, and that the fashion industry is structured according to two 'seasons' every year, means that their contents, too, tend to be structured in a similar manner, reflecting fashion's trends. This in large part limits each issue's 'creativity,' so that it is to the fashion stories making up each issue's 'fashion well' that personnel devote their attention as they strive to make their magazine 'jut out' and be different from competing titles.

The dialectical relationship between advertisers and readers leads editors to make use of two mechanisms, first noted by Roland Barthes in his analysis of film: *anchorage*, whereby advertisers seek to stop readers and make them pay attention to a particular page on which their products are advertised; and *flow*, where editors do their utmost to arrange textual matter in such a way that readers will consume their magazines effortlessly from cover to cover. The argument is that these two devices are found more generally in other forms of cultural production and form an integral part of every creative product's *genre*.

Chapter 7 starts by pointing out that creative goods are both cultural products and commodities. This means that cultural producers always have to balance those two sides of the equation between symbolic and commodity exchange outlined in the earlier chapter on worth. Second, this balancing act between culture and economy is made apparent both in the play-off between cultural (text, narrative, visual effects) and commercial (advertising, promotions, sponsorship) matter, and in creative industry personnel positions (editor versus publisher; director versus producer; perfumer and fashion designer versus fashion house). Third, creative goods and services frequently are made with an eye to at least two (and sometimes three or more) distinct audiences who reflect the culture-economy dichotomy.

This leads to a discussion of the nature of markets in creative industries, something first picked up on by Bourdieu, who distinguished between the sub-fields of restricted and large-scale production.[52] Although a broad distinction has been made between 'aesthetic' and 'economic' markets, the argument presented here builds on the earlier discussion of affordances and values to suggest that we need to take into account more than just aesthetics when considering the market for creative industries. Given the relevance of material, social, spatial, temporal, and use factors, and the equation between symbolic and commodity exchange outlined in Chapter 3, I suggest that we should see creative industries as operating in *symbolic* markets.

Chapter 8 provides another ethnographic account of pottery, but this time in Denmark, where a renowned potter, Ursula Munch-Petersen, designed a line of faience tableware for the well-known brand Royal Copenhagen. Based on interviews with key personnel involved, the chapter describes in detail the difficulties experienced by the potter and her colleagues in using a new material and associated glazing techniques (thereby picking up on my own pottery experiences related in Chapter 2). But it also brings together the individual creative worker with the larger corporation by which she was employed, and shows how her work had to adapt to a particular concept of *luxury* advocated by Royal Copenhagen, even though Munch-Petersen herself was a *craft* potter. In other words, the focus here is on 'artistic' endeavour and 'commercial' imperative, and on the power of the *brand* (and its associated genre) to influence creativity.

Chapter 9 builds on the work of Richard Sennett and situates creativity in craftsmanship. Craftsmanship of all kinds is founded on highly developed, embodied skills used, in this case, to conceive, make, model, glaze, and fire clay in such a way that the finished product—an oval platter, lidded jug, or cake plate—is appealing in itself, while contributing to a class of other products, in this case tableware manufactured by Royal Copenhagen. While design depends upon endless trial and error, the craftsman has, first and foremost, to learn to imitate. Imitation appears to work against improvisation, thinking aside, and creativity, but the chapter argues that in fact imitation contributes to a crucial link between maker and made, as the latter comes to be seen as imbued with human qualities provided by the former. Because this harks back to nineteenth-century critiques of industrialism, and because creative industries are currently dealing with the ramifications of the digital revolution, I then examine the relationship between craftsmanship, technology, and learning, before picking up once more the concept of 'flow', this time in a group context, and linking it with creativity. The question that remains unanswered, in spite of a conscious association by cognitive psychologists of 'group flow' with 'creativity', is the extent to which it gives rise to 'good' work as recognised by *all* those participating in a creative industry *and* making use of its products.

The final ethnographic account in Chapter 10 takes up the theme of evaluation by describing the selection and awarding of a major prize at the Japan Ceramic Art Exhibition in a Tokyo department store. Based on two days of participant observation, it details how judges went about their selection of pots to be put up for the prize, and then the voting patterns that ensued as they moved towards their final selection. The chapter shows how aesthetic considerations rarely played a part in their voiced deliberations, which hinged instead on potters' established (or not established) reputations, on seemingly unrelated administrative technicalities, and on unspoken hierarchies of personal connections among the different members of the jury. It was these that finally broke a deadlock in the equal number of votes given to first three, then two, contenders.

Chapter 11 looks at the politics of evaluation, focusing in particular on prizes and awards which pick out not 'good' work, but the 'best' among available competitors. Those charged with the responsibility for this task are the critics, whose self-appointed task is to educate the general public in a number of different ways: by developing an aesthetic vocabulary (which was curiously absent in the jurying of the exhibition witnessed), by acting as both guides and teachers to artists and their publics, and by taking on the mantle of high priests in the celebration of 'art.'

The Coda summarizes the arguments presented in this book, before taking up the idea of reputations and arguing that creative industries function in the context of what may be called a *name economy*. The worlds of different creative industries such as those discussed in this book, through both evaluation and valuation, routinely create and make use of the reputations of individual actors, works, genres (often in the form of brands), and organizations. Their names link different fields of cultural production, while simultaneously creating and sustaining 'distinction' in and between different creative industries. They also set in uneasy tension three not-entirely-harmonious principles of beauty, fame, and price, and it is how best to create, sustain, and represent equivalence between them that is the challenge of *The Business of ©reativity*.

CHAPTER 1

Circuits of Affordances

One of the arguments presented in this book is that it is the numerous *affordances*[1] by which choices are guided that need to be considered in any discussion of creative—or, indeed, ordinary work—processes. In earlier writings, I have located creativity in the constraints by which it is hemmed in and acted upon, because that is how most of my informants have thought and talked about their work.[2] However, the very fact that, according to many of my informants, constraints ultimately enable creativity suggests that the term is misleading. The concept of affordance, first developed by Gibson and then taken up by other social scientists—in particular, perhaps, by those interested in human-computer interaction and design[3]—seems better suited to describe and analyse the various ways in which creative processes are both inhibited and enabled—as well as authorized, blocked, encouraged, forbidden, influenced, suggested, and so on—in particular social contexts.[4] In other words, creativity itself is a meaningless concept unless considered in tandem with the enabling and constraining conditions under which it operates.

In different forms of cultural production, affordances help, support, facilitate, enable, and/or constrain the ways in which creative workers think and go about their tasks. Affordances can be physical—like the keyboard, display screen, pointing device, and selection buttons built into a computer system which physically enable something to be done; or they can be perceived, as when a design feature in a device provides a clue about its proper operation, thereby facilitating thinking or knowing about that device. As such, they facilitate functional and sensory understandings.[5]

Take, for example, Richard Sennett's description of the introduction of a mechanical arm into modern bakeries as a means to help bakers manipulate bread while it was baking in the oven.

> Originally just a shovel-like tool to push loaves through the oven, the arm's crudeness meant that some loaves would burn, others half-cook. In the 1980s the technology of the arms improved greatly; bakers could now manipulate the dough during the actual baking process—turned

over, stretched, incised—with the unforeseen result that the machines could now bake many different kinds of bread at the same time.[6]

Improvisation in one aspect of baking thus set in motion a number of other new ways of doing things as material, technical, and social elements coalesced. Improvisation and affordance go hand in hand, together with feedback and constraints, although we would do well to remember that improvisation in itself is not sufficient cause for creativity to emerge. For that we need to be able to display 'originality' by coming up with a new, personal idiom that takes advantage of affordances and deviates from conventional rules.[7]

All industries—not just the so-called creative industries—engage with *circuits of affordances* in order to function effectively. In cultural production, these affordances (whether physical or perceived) are techno-material, temporal, spatial, social, representational, and economic, each of which can feed into and be itself activated by others. Together they form circuits which, like the circuits of commerce analysed by Viviana Zeliger, are marked by the following characteristics:

> **1.** "Distinctive social relations among specific individuals" (for example, in fashion, designers [and their 'muses'], fashion houses, seamstresses and other employees, suppliers, buyers, models [and their agencies], hair stylists, makeup artists, photographers, celebrities, magazine editors, and so on);
>
> **2.** "Shared economic activities carried on by means of those social relations" (advertising and other promotional activities, including preparations for and showing of biannual collections in the 'fashion capitals' of the world);
>
> **3.** "Creation of common accounting systems for evaluating economic exchanges" (including money, credit, and payments in kind, as well as a recognized division of markets [Chapter 7]);
>
> **4.** "Shared understandings concerning the meaning of transactions within the circuit, including their moral valuation" (and evaluation) (trust, solidarity, and shared attitudes towards what constitutes 'fashion'), and
>
> **5.** "A boundary separating members of the circuit from non-members, with some control over transactions crossing the boundary" (the fashion world).[8]

Circuits of affordances exhibit the variable content of exchanges and interpretations of meaning in cultural production, as well as "the dynamic, incessantly negotiated interactions they involve." They thus "define a specific social structure" which includes networks, labour relations, the exploitation and definition of intellectual property rights, and so on, that are found in different forms of cultural production.[9]

The approach that I adopt here is in itself by no means novel.[10] Where it builds on previous work is in its attempt to systematise the different affordances constraining, enabling, and otherwise affecting creative choices. My own preferred take on this kind of discussion starts from Pierre Bourdieu's extended analysis of the relationships between systems of thought, social institutions, and different forms of material and symbolic power.[11] In trying to go beyond the theoretical limitations imposed by the notion of individual actors' free and unrestricted agency on the one hand, and by that of constraints caused by institutions of mechanistic determinism (suggested by structuralism and certain forms of Marxism) on the other, he introduced two concepts: *habitus* and *field*. Habitus was designed to account for the obvious creativity and inventiveness—an overall "disposition"[12]—shown by individual actors in their everyday lives, while at the same time recognizing that their behaviour is to some degree regulated and orchestrated by the social environment in which they live.[13] Field, on the other hand, was developed to account for how individuals do not act in a vacuum, but in concrete social contexts governed by sets of objective social relations.

In general, creative industries—like pottery manufacture, advertising, and fashion magazine publishing described in this book—are good examples of fields of cultural production, where individuals and organizations take up "positions" in "a space of possibles."[14] Each field is hierarchically structured and itself tends to structure interlocking fields hierarchically. Pottery, for example, merges with industry, craft, hobbies (*ikebana* flower arrangement, the Japanese tea ceremony), interior design, and (occasionally, for certain kinds of pottery) luxury goods and art; advertising with media and entertainment (television, radio, newspaper, magazine publishing, music, sports, fashion, film, and so on); and fashion magazines with fashion, music, film, theatre, entertainment, and publishing in general. Different organizations, together with their respective personnel, compete in each field for control of material, ideological, and symbolic resources. These they then convert into different forms of cultural, economic, educational, and symbolic capital. It is the structure of creative fields, together with the positions and dispositions of participants within an overall field of power, which affords the nature of the 'creativity' which does, or does not, take place and which lies at the heart of this book.

Although Bourdieu recognized that products are also integral to positioning and capital conversion (they underpin, after all, the basic strategy of branding), he preferred to focus on individual actors in his research. As a result, the actual contents of a book, film, or music genre, the features of a particular painting, pot, or photograph, have tended to be analysed as variable social phenomena, rather than as constants operating within their own assemblages of ontological, material, and aesthetic properties. This is the contribution of actor-network theory (or ANT), where 'network' (*reseau*) has the meaning of 'connectivity.' Proponents of ANT argue that the social is generated by material practices and that actors, who may or may not be human, constitute 'a network of elements' of which they may not necessarily or fully be aware.[15] They thus analyse ships, sails, and scallops in the same terms of attachment as sailors and scientists.[16] It is this vein of thought that courses through the chapters that follow, as I recount how materials and products generate, assemble, and sustain fashion, advertising, and ceramic art worlds through their accompanying "modalities of valuation."[17]

Two questions that we need to ask ourselves when facing the challenge of creativity are: what choices are being made, by whom, from what range of possibilities, and because of what, in the conception, design, production, marketing, sale, and reception of a 'singular' cultural good? And how are these choices enabled and constrained, or afforded, by the assemblage of relations in which creative work takes place? These in themselves raise another question: is it possible to follow *systematically* "the invention and testing of multiple possibilities" that are "the signature of creative activity"?[18] In other words, is it possible—advisable even—to *manage* creativity?

One way to go about answering these questions is by examining what has been called "the iron cage" of creativity[19] (the 'box' that I talked about at the beginning of the Overture) and by looking at the various ways in which artists and craftsmen, designers and engineers, writers and editors, composers and musicians, copywriters, art directors, and account planners, and others in the creative industries engage with material, technological, financial, social, aesthetic, and other forces around them. In the creative industries, as I have already hinted, there is a continuous, often unresolved, tension between creativity, which we may provisionally define as the ability to push boundaries by bringing together two or more hitherto unassociated frames of expression, and constraints, which maintain them. Just how strong or weak these boundaries are depends on the comparative strength of these interacting forces. In general, though, we make what we make and do what we do because and in spite of the materials and technologies, and their accompanying aesthetic ideologies, available to us; the people and organizations with whom and in which we are, either voluntarily or involuntarily, caught up; and the other, broadly similar, things that others like us have already made or done with the materials and technologies (as well as accompanying aesthetic ideals) available to them among people and organizations by which they, too, have been surrounded. And, all the time, we ignore at our peril what it costs us to make what we make, and for whom, and the financial rewards that accrue therefrom.

In all creative industries, people tend to rely on established conventions (about how a film should be made, a fashion collection shown, or string quartet perform), in order to go about their work. They all make use of standard equipment and materials, which 'afford' both how they work and the finished forms of that work. As becomes clear in the account of my own pottery exhibition in a Japanese department store in the following chapter, it is convention that usually influences what materials are used; what abstractions are best suited to convey ideas or experiences; and the form, or genre, in which materials and abstractions are combined.[20] Conventions arise out of creative people's engagements with a circuit or 'ecosystem' of affordances, and it is these that I will describe in what follows.

Techno-material Affordances

The emergence of conventions may depend upon the presence or absence of particular materials and associated abstractions. Materials 'occur'; they are practically experienced by those working in different forms of cultural production and provide them with "a knowledge born of sensory perception and practical engagement."[21] In so doing, materials afford a "code" that governs cultural producers' "matrices of thought" and the skills that they bring to bear on a particular project.[22] An architect has to learn the mechanical rules of engineering that will prevent his building from collapsing, just as a writer has to learn the grammar and vocabulary of her language, as well as the patterns and rules of the genre (romantic novel, thriller, or scholarly monograph) that she wishes to employ, before she can adequately start to write. In the advertising and fashion magazine industries, copywriters and art directors use particular forms of punctuation and font size for headlines, while selecting from among different typefaces for a 'look' that they feel is best suited to the product advertised, or model illustrated on a magazine issue's cover. Photographers use different camera lenses, apertures, film, and so on to obtain different effects of light, mass, and perspective. Cameramen use freeze frames, soft focus, background music, and other filmic conventions in their preparation of television commercials, which then become recognized as 'commercials' that afford use of such filmic conventions.[23] Materials precede cultural products. Materials afford modes of production, while products afford those of consumption.[24]

Although in almost all cases it does so, a finished work does not *have* to conform to conventions. If it did so in its entirety, all creative work would be stuck in stone (and therefore not 'creative'). Thus, everyday mass-produced materials like drinking straws, toothpicks, or sheets of wrapping paper can be manipulated and used to make giant walls, cubes, or rectangular shapes for display in an art museum, while what Marcel Duchamp (borrowing a term from the clothing industry) called "ready mades"—basketballs, beds, boxes, cages, computers and electronic components, a porcelain urinal, rusty girder, shark, shells, and trash—may also be transformed into objects then designated as 'art.'

Adaptations of one sort or another, therefore, are made in different forms of cultural production, in spite of the hidden persuasion of conventions and codes. The introduction of new technology, together with its availability at affordable prices, can lead to new or change old conventions, and thus alter the final form of creative products. The printing press developed by Gutenberg, for example, was initially based on similar devices already being used to make paper, wine, and textiles, although he also took inspiration from the ways in which playing cards, coins, and seals were made at the time.[25] In other words, there was what Richard Sennett calls a "domain shift" as a tool used for one purpose was applied to a new task.[26] It then served as a prototype for all subsequent screw-type hand-presses until the introduction of power-driven presses nearly four hundred years later.[27] And just as the introduction of the printing press radically changed the dissemination of knowledge (and the costs thereof), so has the more recent adoption of computers and digital technology revolutionised again our ways and means of communication. There was a time, not so many years ago, when a golfer would design a golf course by looking at and walking through a landscape and its undulations, envisaging how particular shots might be made, as he formed a trajectory of the different holes based on his professional golfing skills. Nowadays, however, a designer will take a map of the land, adapt it to a particular computer software programme, and design a course with a slope here, a bend round some trees there, a dip, and a hump, regardless of how the land actually is in its details. He then brings in a bulldozer and does what he wants with the land, rather than allow the land to lend its own affordances to the construction of the course. The affordances now stem from the development of computers and their accompanying software programmes.

Similarly, with digital photography it has become possible to make radical alterations to images. Faces are contorted, bodies twisted, limbs elongated. With a few clicks of a mouse a model can be made to look perfectly proportioned, with a stray wisp of hair here or untimely pimple there removed. Airbrushing is the norm, rather than the exception. Digital technology affords art directors, photographers, and cameramen new ways, and new conventions, of carrying out their work. It also affords the introduction of new materials, such as the use of flat liquid crystal display screens in the work of video artists. Even the layout of buttons on electronic instruments can give a musician unanticipated ideas, so that the industry keeps providing new ways of 'tweaking the knobs,' which then afford new sounds (and the rise of the DJ as 'musician'). In earlier years, the development of industrially manufactured steel frames for guitars, together with amplifying equipment, led to a move away from large musical ensembles and to the formation of small bands, which itself instigated the emergence of the genre of rock music:[28] a genre which is now more or less consigned to small bands. As well as constraining, materials and technologies enable. Yet, in enabling, they also constrain. This is the explanatory power of affordance.

For example, because of the structure of its molecules, a certain kind of earth (clay) is malleable to forming and resistant to breakage under gradually built-up, intense heat. Because the structure is itself never fully consistent (except in mass-produced prepared clays), a potter will know during the kneading process whether a lump of clay will be suitable for making large or small wares (because of the way in which cracks form in the clay as it is kneaded). At the same time, the overall consistency in the clay's molecular structure affords preference for one forming technique (throwing on the wheel, for example) over others previously tried and tested (slabware or use of moulds). Throwing itself affords different techniques ('off the hump,' clay balls, coil-and-throw, and so on)—each of which may be more suitable than the others for particular shapes and sizes of pots to be thrown—and requires the addition of an appropriate amount of water when forming shapes (themselves also afforded by the nature of the clay).

CHAPTER ONE

Because it is, nevertheless, still porous when dry, as well as after firing, clay also affords the development of some form of non-porous covering, depending on the uses to which finished pots are to be put. The covering best suited to functional domestic wares was developed in vitreous glazes. These themselves afford a variety of colours (including transparency) depending on materials used, the temperature at which they are fired, and the presence or absence of air at particular stages in a firing. Firing requires an oven, or kiln, capable of withstanding the necessary intensity of heat. A kiln can be large or small, simple or complex, in structure, affording different production cycles (and thus different labour relations and organizational forms) and, according to the presence or absence of shelving, a range of pottery forms, colours, and decorative styles which themselves reflect back upon the choice of throwing methods, glazes, and so on. Elemental material affordances (clay, water, fire, metals) therefore themselves constitute an ensemblage of technical affordances. It is out of this ensemblage that what we know as a (certain kind of earthenware, porcelain, or stoneware) 'potter' comes into social being.

Spatial Affordances

The description of kiln firing raises the issue of spatial affordances, since the not-entirely-consistent temperatures found in different parts of a climbing kiln, for example, may afford different glaze colours (green at the front of lower shelves, or brown at the back of a chamber). These can be prompted by material and technical properties (the copper in a green glaze needs more heat than the feldspar, wood, and straw ash mix that makes brown glaze). The construction of a climbing kiln used by Japanese potters is such that heat is unpredictably intense at the bottom of each chamber (where pots are engulfed in flames from the wood used to fuel the kiln and raise the temperature of the firing). Small, but not large, surfaces are more likely to withstand direct heat of this kind without breaking. This, together with glaze choices, explains stacking patterns in a chamber (with or without kiln shelves). Large pots can only be placed at the top of a chamber, if they are to avoid breakage. From this it necessarily follows that they can be glazed only in some colours, not others, because of the differences in temperature at the top, bottom, front, and back of the climbing kiln.

Although pots are made to functional size, the same is not necessarily true of painting, which almost invariably diminishes space. The size of the painter's canvas is smaller than the landscape or even portrait waiting to be copied. Adaptations must be made accordingly. But space can also bring about symbolic effects. In a studio shoot for an advertising campaign, different personnel are assigned to work in different areas of the studio and its annexe. The 'set', where the photographer works with the model, tends to be located at the innermost part of the studio. At the outer edge, near the entrance, gather the agency's account manager, art director, client, and others not directly involved in the work at hand. The model herself is tended to by makeup artist and hair stylist in an adjoining annexe. But there is a highly charged common symbolic space in which the two key actors, the art director and photographer, take up their positions and negotiate the work in hand. It is on this point, a photographic stand, that all converge between takes to offer advice or remain silent, and await further directions (Chapter 5).

Spatial affordances also make themselves apparent in the institutions used to display or perform creative work. Theatres are of necessity much smaller than concert halls, because a play of any kind requires that its audience hear actors' voices without the mediation of microphones, and can clearly see their facial and bodily gestures. This is not the case in a concert hall where audibility, not visibility, is paramount (although musicians themselves must be able to see one another to be able to perform, or 'ensemble', together).[29] Similarly, rental costs contribute towards the comparatively small size of art galleries in downtown urban areas. As a result, they tend to exhibit the work of single artists when it comes to special 'one man' exhibitions. Museums of art, however, are able to display much more because of their size and, in the process, to classify artworks into historical periods, styles, and 'schools.' Retail outlets—a jewellery store, for example, or department store gallery—use space to order goods on display: cheap objects are placed in the shop window and near the entrance to entice customers inside; once there, they are steadily drawn in to the most expensive items on display, often placed on plinths or behind glass to signify their value. In this way, retail space in general is symbolically constructed in terms of seduction, awe, revelation, and acquisition on an exterior-interior axis.[30]

Physical location can also be important symbolically, as opposed to technically, in the performance of creative outputs. Acting a part in *Hamlet* in the Shakespeare Theatre in Stratford-on-Avon, for example, can be more inspiring, as well as more anxiety inducing, than playing the same part in a repertory theatre in the north of England. Putting on a fashion show in the palace at Versailles can induce a thrill not experienced, perhaps, in a rundown warehouse in Seoul. Playing a Beethoven piano concerto in the concert hall of the Berlin Philharmoniker can be more uplifting than playing the same piece with a different orchestra at the Wigmore Hall in London. As we know well from our (televisual) participation in football matches and other sporting events, the atmosphere induced by an audience in a particular location often affects actual performance. Better a full house in a small venue than a half-empty concert hall or large lecture theatre.

Spatial and other affordances often combine to affect the appreciation of a cultural product. With oriental carpets, for example, certain combinations of spinning, knotting, or weaving techniques; carpet sizes and colours; stylistic elements (techno-material and representational affordances); and so on are characteristic of a given region and era of production, and affect collectors' appreciation.[31] So, too, with pottery clays, forms, and designs in Japan, at their apex classified as the "six old kilns" (Bizen, Echizen, Seto, Shigaraki, Tamba, and Tokoname).

Probably the best-known example of a spatial condition in this respect is that of *terroir* in the production of French wines, where careful limitation of "the number of appellations and the amount of winegrowing land that can be established in a given territory based on existing reputations,"[32] has established, in contradistinction to the state-organized mass wine market, a limited field of cultural production (economic affordance) of the kind outlined by Pierre Bourdieu.[33] Burgundy, for example, is famous for its huge proliferation of tiny appellations producing Côte d'Or wine, with more than a thousand names recognized within the *terroir*. This, theoretically at least, leads to an extreme example of spatial affordance, for:

> If every grape in Burgundy were harvested by the vine's owner, if every owner bottled his own wine, and if every wine were labeled for the most specific geographic designation to which it is entitled—none of which is the case—there would be less than one case of finished wine made per proprietor per vineyard.[34]

In addition to honouring the *terroir*, wines produced under a designated vineyard, on the one hand explicitly recognize the *savoir faire* of the wine grower and, on the other contribute to the development of regional gastronomic cultures in France,[35] something later exploited elsewhere as Noma in Copenhagen, designated the world's best restaurant, began to source its ingredients from what its owners called the "Nordic *terroir*" to produce "New Nordic Cuisine."[36] The exclusivity and limited production of *terroir* also affords higher prices. As a result, it is not surprising to find that wine-

CIRCUITS OF AFFORDANCES   45

makers in California and Oregon have begun to celebrate the concept of *terroir* by eschewing blending in favour of vineyard-designated bottlings (such as Bien Nacido and Dutton Ranch).[37]

Temporal Affordances

A third set of affordances surrounds the use of *time* in the creative industries. The quality of wines depends on the quality of the grapes from which they are made, and this depends on the weather over time: there is a recognized correlation between sufficient rainfall during the vines' dormant season, followed by a warm and dry season during the growth of the grapes. Day and nighttime temperature differences may also afford the quality of a wine (in addition to types of soils). In addition, wines (and perfumes made from natural oils) must lie and mature before they can be appreciated and used, and age-worthy (but not table) wines tend to increase in value as they get older. Wait too long, though, and they may have peaked and lost the best of their taste (or, with natural perfume, smell). Not waiting long enough can also lead to disaster. Clay, for instance, needs time in its preparation, drying, and subsequent firing. Too little preparation time can lead to loss of plasticity; drying too fast in direct sunshine causes plates to crack at their base; open a kiln too soon and jars and vases will break from the sudden inrush of comparatively cold air.

Generally speaking, as an affordance, time is important in three rather diverse ways. First, there is what Richard Caves refers to as the "time flies" property.[38] *When* a creative product has to be ready for a particular event or the market has a backwards effect on its planning and execution. Deadlines have to be established and met. The fixing of a particular time and date for a fashion show or concert obliges participants to calculate backwards the various tasks that need to be completed—designing, sewing, fitting, and modifying a dress, for example, or musicians' rehearsals and accompanying sound and lighting arrangements—to be properly prepared to go on stage and perform in front of an audience. Such deadlines are more (or less) complex depending on the creative product in question. When holding my own pottery exhibition, I learned rather late in my work schedule that the pots I intended to make had to be ready about one month before the opening of the show because they had to be boxed (and some of them used for promotional purposes). My failure to anticipate this deadline meant that I produced fewer pots than I had originally intended (Chapter 2).

46 ▣ **CHAPTER ONE**

Time affords not just the process of producing a cultural good, but also the practices of evaluating it when finished. A film's release date can help or hinder its chances of being nominated for an Oscar or other film award, while the sequence in which films are shown at a festival may affect their chances of being awarded prizes. A film jury has to operate within very strict time frames, but it is helped by the unstructured time that elapses between viewing a film and discussing it in a plenum session with other jury members. This can lead to individual members influencing others' initial perceptions and views by lobbying for personal favourites, as well as to having their own opinions changed through informal social interaction.[39]

Second, time depends on the medium or communicative channel used. For example, the fact that a fashion show conventionally lasts for an absolute maximum of 20 minutes affects how many items a designer can show, which in itself influences her choice of garments: formal and informal, office and sportswear, evening dress and casual skirt, bridal dress, and so on. The fact that she has a maximum of six months in which to prepare a seasonal collection means that temporal affordance works in reverse and affords how many different articles of clothing, deemed appropriate for display in a 'collection,' can be designed and made in time for the show. Similarly, the convention that a film characteristically lasts longer than 90 minutes but less than two hours affords editing decisions and even storyline (as we know from the alternate 'cuts' of films made available through the introduction of the DVD format). In advertising, a 15-second television commercial offers extremely limited opportunity for an advertiser to include very much more than its own name and the name of the product or service it is promoting, whereas a one-minute radio commercial enables a fast-talking narrator to give information about a product and even to repeat catchy sell-lines. The shorter the time available to broadcast advertising, the more likely it will rely on 'mood' rather than 'information' as its mode of persuasion. Mood products thus invite 15- or 30-second television commercials; information products, longer expositions in the same or different media forms. Like the techniques and materials discussed above, time affords both style and content.

In a documentary series about childhood, producers wanted to include footage from a Muslim country, along with that of families in Brazil, Japan, Russia, and the United States. However, constraints on both programme time and location expense (temporal and economic affordances) meant that they were unable to develop the kind of footage they required in the selected location (Morocco). Rather than portray a Muslim country in a superficial manner, the producers chose in the end to exclude the proposed footage and so to rule Islamic culture out of the series entirely. This decision was influenced both by production expenses and by conventions of documentary presentation (in the form of limited screen time: representational affordance).[40]

Finally, time is important in the sense that every creative product is conceived, made, advertised, distributed, and received in a historical context of all similar products that have preceded it. Ideally, it should differ—if only marginally—from such previous outputs and, ideally, from comparable outputs simultaneously on the market.[41] Creative professionals need to find the right balance between the brand and the 'non-brand' (representational affordance), between something that is recognizable, but not quite recognizable. Thus, a team of young designers working on the Hugo Boss Orange label was required to create something that was new yet "distinctly Orange." The collection had to be different from last year's Orange collection, as well as from competing collections by H&M and other menswear collections.[42] Similarly, all advertising campaigns should, ideally, differ from previous campaigns, both for the product being advertised and for competing products, to mark them off as recognizable, but unrecognizable.

Creative activity, then, ideally "takes apart the structure which was formerly created but restores it in a more complex form and gives to its components a new meaning, a new value, and a new structural role in the totality of the work."[43] Here the field and its circuit of affordances clearly affect not just the positions taken by individual creative individuals or organizations, but the mode of communication that s/he adopts. Every fashion designer, every film director, every rock artist "expresses himself in the language of his predecessors, his models, and his teachers."[44] In other words, the affordance of time in the broader sense of historical continuity means that creative expression is not 'created' so much as 'renewed.' In this sense, creativity is closely patterned on genre or representation.

Representational Affordances

Representational affordances are fundamental to creative practices and products, even though creative people often express an inability to talk about their work, and even though (like the spaces between musical notes) what is *not* said may be as important as what *is*. Indeed, creative work is often assumed to possess 'ineffable qualities' that are seen to characterize 'Art', 'Literature', 'Music', and so on, on the principle that, like a legal adjudication on pornography, you know it when you see, read, or hear it. This is the principle underlying the "ambiguous specificity" of a fashion model's 'look,'[45] or the pinnacle experience of togetherness in musical 'ensembling.'[46]

Representational affordances are primarily aesthetic (or, to use a less loaded term, 'appreciative') and give rise to formal properties based on such concepts as genre, form, and style. But they may also be derived from formal and/or informal material, health, and legal considerations, the last of them often concerning intellectual property rights and interpretations thereof. Because of environmental restrictions on certain natural olfactory materials (for instance, sandalwood and agarwood in South and Southeast Asia), the remote possibility that they will cause allergic reactions, and their potential olfactory instability, the fragrance industry has developed a wide range of synthetic substitutes, which it then represents as exotically 'natural' in its advertising and promotional materials. Other formal constraints on modes of representation can be found in cigarette advertising, for instance, with its large-letter warning of smoking's effect on health. Informally, a recent development in the fashion world has been disapproval, or banning, of 'size zero' models from the catwalks because they are unrealistically thin. Proposals are also being put forward in one or two European countries' parliaments that the current practice of airbrushing female models' blemishes so that they appear to be perfect, be treated in the same way as cigarette advertising: with a warning to that effect. If passed, such proposals will become law and affect the representation of women gracing the pages of fashion magazines, as well, maybe, as that of virtually *all* images in the media.

Different genres tend to encompass distinct representational affordances. Porcelain, faience, stoneware, and earthenware use different clay and glaze materials, affording different skills that result in different appreciative ideals for each end product. Similarly, different genres of music—classical, rock, and jazz—align different instruments together, as well as different ways of playing them. Schönberg's twelve-tone method tells a composer what *not* to do rather than what to do, and "automatically rules out certain kinds of choices, especially those which suggest traditional harmony in any way."[47] In book publishing, literary genres have separate conventions for paper size, title, and cover layout, binding methods (cloth and/or paperback), and so on.[48] Travel guidebook writers, too, are boxed in by stringent rules about word length, detailed stylistic guidelines, extensive product manuals, and meticulous instructions that characterize both the genre of the travel guidebook and the editorial brief given each writer by the publisher.[49] While they take pride in meticulously following instructions (since this may lead to repeat commissions),[50] they also try to move to the edge of the box by providing work that is 'atmospheric,' that has 'an angle,' and that gives a sense of 'being there' for an imagined audience.[51] The merging of genres may pose a particular set of problems for a fashion designer, who has to interpret which of two (or more) sets of representational constraints to adopt, and which to discard, when creating a product that is neither one genre nor another: witness the "funky formal" approach to the Orange clothing line designed by the talent pool for Hugo Boss.[52]

No work that we think of as 'contemporary art,' no film that we see as an 'action film,' no music that we listen to for its 'rock' is ever marked by an aesthetic that is not an essential and accepted characteristic of contemporary art, action film, or rock music. Each carries its own ensemblage of representational conventions—abstract daubs of paint on an unframed canvas, car chases with special effects, and the inevitable quartet of lead singer, drummer, rhythm, and bass guitarists in a rock band—that make the creative product immediately recognizable for what it is. Creative industries are particularly 'generic': think of how hospital dramas, quiz shows, reality TV, sitcoms, and soaps act as our standard television fare,[53] replete with shared conventions, expectations, understandings, and interpretations. This in itself explains both how formulaic they may be while simultaneously making overt claims to 'creativity.' Consider, for example, the following comment about the production of a 'highbrow' educational documentary:

> Genres have a currency and import even prior to the work of production, influencing expectations critical for setting in motion structures of production. A program is developed (planned, funded, scripted), shot, edited, and slotted into a station's schedule with continual attention to genre: what type of program it is, how it coheres with others of this type, and contrasts with different genres, and what textual and contextual features are appropriate, conventional, and effective within that generic class.[54]

In this way, representational affordances end up sustaining different genres. Although they would appear to create that 'iron cage' constraining creativity referred to earlier, in fact they encourage people (like the travel guidebook writers studied by Ana Alačovska) to look continuously over their shoulders and compare what they are doing now with what has been done before. Individual understandings of similarities and differences push those striving to make sense of creative products at different stages in their production, distribution, and reception to come into conflict with one another over proposed innovations, strategies, and the nature of creativity itself. In this respect, 'bisociation' can come about through the clash of different realms of expertise (involving, for example, accounts, marketing, media buying, promotions, and creative in advertising). Precisely because they 'afford' rather than simply constrain, representational affordances come to constitute contested aesthetic and other domains.

Creative people can push the borders of each of these genres, as I've suggested, but only so far, although others will often catch up with them in time. In his ninth piano concerto (K271), Mozart introduced the soloist in the second bar of the opening movement, as he moved to treat piano and orchestra as equals in a musical dialogue. Nothing like this had ever been done before, and it was not tried again until almost 30 years later when Beethoven chose to open his fourth piano concerto with the soloist. While Mozart appears to have been a full generation ahead of his time, Japanese advertising creative directors talk of being just a 'half pace'—no more—ahead of society. If they were a full step ahead, or a half pace behind, they say, nobody would pay attention to their work. Thus, in order to differentiate his client's product (a contact lens) from that of its competitors, an art director decided to colour the lens-cut green, rather than blue (the colour used in all competing ads) because, he said, he sensed the beginning of an environmental trend in Japan.[55] This is being on the edge of the box, rather than outside it.

Just how far borders can be pushed would seem to depend on the personality of the creator; the nature of the product, genre, or communicative style; and the social world of which they are a part. Mozart seems to have had freer rein than the Japanese art director mentioned here. The looser the aesthetic constraints, the easier it is to innovate, and vice versa. In Japan, when the thirteenth-generation enamel overglaze artist Imaizumi Imaemon[56] received a prestigious prize at a national exhibition (discussed in Chapter 10), one of the judges summarised his committee's choice as follows:

Look. The Imaizumi family has been making bowls like this for centuries. Imaemon's father made one just like this, with its floral motif, and so did his grandfather. So did his great grandfather, and probably several other ancestors before him. But Imaemon has produced something different. He has painted the flowers pink rather than red, like everyone before him, and has painted them on a grey, rather than

CIRCUITS OF AFFORDANCES   51

customary blue, background. That's why we gave him the Princess Chichibu Cup. He was stretching tradition to the limit.

This kind of comment reveals the power of judges, critics, and other professional reviewers in aesthetic (and other) evaluations. It is their decisions to award this or that prize that have a ripple effect, not just on the further reception of the creative products in question, but on how similar new products will (or will not) be produced in the future, as art directors, film producers, musicians, 'celebrity' chefs, and so on strive to be noticed in what has become a 'name' economy (Chapter 11 and Coda).

Social Affordances

If there is a single overriding theme in creative people's discussions of their work, it is the role played by other people, specifically by social connections, in the numerous projects that plot their careers. As a result, those working in different forms of cultural production engage in 'strategic friendliness' (politeness and deference) as a means, they hope, of getting what they want.[57] In the world of fashion, for example, models cultivate bookers, bookers cultivate stylists, and stylists cultivate photographers, who themselves cultivate advertisers, editors, and designers. So, too, with film in an ensemblage that includes producers, directors, acting, makeup, styling, set, sound, special effects, and other personnel. My own pottery exhibition described in the following chapter came about because of my friendship with a gallery owner whose own previously established personal networks led to selection of the venue, sponsorship, and timing of the exhibition, while our shared connections decided where and what kind of pots I would make.

One of the most important things characterising a creative industry is that it provides "a supply of interchangeable human parts."[58] This means that, in different forms of cultural production, one can count on replacing people with others just as good, although a lot of attention is paid to who can and cannot work or collaborate with whom. Persons with known animosities towards each other are not placed together in the same design or advertising campaign creative team, for example, while "notorious assholes" are avoided when putting together juries.[59] This in itself encourages a "climate of collaboration" and enables 'creative' work to be carried out in fairly routine ways, although the introduction of new personnel also affords new opportunities as well as constraints (Chapter 10).

52 ▢ CHAPTER ONE

Social affordances may be broadly distinguished into three subsets: those stemming from the fact that most forms of cultural production consist of close contact and communication[60] among networks of cooperating personnel; those connected with the fact that much creative work is commissioned; and those that affect the content of the creative outputs themselves. Each of these highlights, to different degrees, the delicate balance between the unpredictability of individual *habitus* and the structured rules imposed by the field.

First, every creative industry has a pool of skilled personnel on whom it can draw to carry out some specialised task. Some are in more demand than others because of the generally technical nature of their skills; there tends to be an oversupply of those whose roles are thought to contain some element of 'creativity'[61] and thus more than the market can bear.[62] There are two basic organizational principles—one stable, the other discontinuous—underlying the work of the "motley crew"[63] in cultural production. At one extreme, creative personnel are allocated particular tasks because they work for organizations—copywriters for an advertising agency, for example, or stylists for a fashion magazine publisher—and build networks, reputations, and careers through their organizational affiliation. Their work thus tends to follow established practice within the ad agency or magazine publishing house and to be subject to internal politics relating to hierarchy, promotion opportunities, gender, and so on.[64]

At the other extreme, those forming a pool of support personnel are contracted for each task separately: a freelance copywriter for a single ad campaign, or a model and makeup artist for a fashion shoot. For the most part, it is established personal connections that enable one hair stylist or actress, rather than another, to get a particular job. Their professional specialization in a single task, however, can lead to an overemphasis on the importance of their own contribution and to their paying little attention to, or even questioning, other aspects of the creative work in which they are involved. In this sense, cooperation takes place within a spirit of competitiveness. It can also lead to typecasting: this photographer is good for soft-focus images, that one for food; this model for a magazine fashion story, that one for a catalogue (and not vice versa).[65]

In the creative industries social affordances are often organizational, arising from the fact that creative work tends to be commissioned. This is not new. In the art world, patrons have over time had an enormous influence on the selection of an artist's subject matter, materials, size of work, and so on.[66] Collectors of contemporary art still commission work (witness

Charles Saatchi's commissioning of Damien Hirst's infamous stuffed shark).[67] It is their likes and dislikes that determine what will, and what will not, come onto the market. Cultivate a collector and, as an artist, you may make your name; offend one, and you may be doomed to insignificance.

In advertising, too, a client has a major role in the selection of campaign ideas put forward by an agency. It may also make certain demands with regard to choice of model, actress, or celebrity used in the campaign and the clothes she wears, and even interfere with details of the print ads to be run, as well as tell a photographer how to do his work. The client's or creative team's preference for one celebrity over another affects the style of an advertisement, since s/he will bring an already established image to the product being advertised and thus affect its representation.[68]

So, social affordances affect cultural products themselves in a number of different ways. On the one hand, by commissioning work, patrons of one sort or another (advertising clients, collectors, gallery owners, museum curators, and government departments) influence the form it takes; on the other, particular combinations of personnel can lead to particular, and in time predictable, styles of work (representational affordance). Indeed, the more people work together, the more likely they are to develop particular routines (and thus generate genres). Certain film directors (like Pedro Almodovar) work with a 'stable' of actors on whom they draw for each successive work and create a certain style; instrumentalists team up to form groups that then develop a certain sound: the Glenn Miller Band or the Modern Jazz Quartet, the Beatles or the Berlin Philharmoniker.

Economic Affordances

First, the general state of a country's economy almost certainly influences the extent to which a creative industry can or cannot be creative, since the 'bottom line' tends to take on overriding importance in a recession. In times of financial crisis, collectors are loath to commission new artworks by unproven artists, and producers to finance avant-garde films by young directors. In times of prosperity, advertisers are prepared to give creative ideas a chance; in times of hardship, they focus on sales and are not prepared to take risks on 'creativity.' Sometimes, the lack of market demand—when coupled with techno-material and representational affordances—would seem to cripple all hope of original creative work, although at the same time it may well be precisely economic desperation that prompts new ways of representing the same old ideas.

54 ☐ **CHAPTER ONE**

Second, the budget put aside for film, rock concert, fashion show, or advertising campaign has a huge effect on its form in terms of *what* can be done *where* by *whom*. The concert series, or 'spectacular', *This is It,* that Michael Jackson was rehearsing up to the time of his death, allowed for a multipurpose stage with mobile ramp, ejection platforms, and numerous stage effects, including enormous robot machines and pyrotechnics, as well as a giant video screen with especially shot film, backing singers, musicians, dancers, and aerialist choreography. In contrast, a normal rock concert or festival allows for little more than the standard equipment (lighting and sound) that enables a series of rock groups to perform their music on stage in front of an audience.

Similarly, in advertising, a large appropriation affects the style and expression adopted in a campaign since it enables use of a mass medium like television (with all its temporal affordances, as noted earlier). At the same time, a large budget may well enable selection of a foreign (usually exotic), as opposed to domestic, location for filming; a small budget usually means that advertising creativity must be limited to print advertising and function within a studio frame.

A big budget also enables the contracting of (internationally) famous personnel to participate in films, concerts, advertising campaigns, and so on. A budget of $100 million buys more 'star power,' more computerised pyrotechnics, and more exotic locations than one of half that amount. This conversion of economic capital not only gives the finished product a certain cultural cachet; it usually influences its reception by the public. Everyone loves a blockbuster . . . sometimes!

Economic affordances find their most obvious expression in price. An auctioneer relies on prices bid in previous auctions to estimate how much a particular item—a painting by Matisse or an oriental carpet—will fetch at his own auction.[69] Prices are usually fixed according to the cost of materials and labour that go into a product's manufacture. By her own criteria, the ceramist Ursula Munch-Petersen reckoned that the retail prices for items in her *Ursula* range manufactured by Royal Copenhagen were too high (discussed in Chapter 8). In particular, they failed to conform to her aesthetic philosophy that pots should be functional and therefore reasonably priced. But retail prices for Ursula tableware were affected by at least three different factors. One was the ceramist's own perfectionism that required test pieces to be made and remade time and time again. Another came about because the management of Royal Copenhagen decided to discontinue the production of the faience ware in Denmark and outsource it to a Japanese factory, where labour was by no means cheap. Finally, Ursula tableware retail prices were in part affected by the fact that Royal Copenhagen specializes in high-quality porcelain wares. Although faience wares could and should have been cheaper in terms of materials and labour, the company did not wish to detract from its own high-quality image by selling some of its output at a lower price range than porcelain. Here we see how various different ensemblages of affordance function in practice as economic, techno-material, social (organizational), and representational effects come into multifaceted play in different creative contexts in different forms of cultural production.

Circuits of Affordances

Economic affordances are clearly cultural and permit confusion of the two. When Sarah Ferguson presented her host with a Shanghai Tang jacket on *Larry King Live* some years ago, viewers were left wondering whether this was an act of charity (it was King's birthday that evening), a promotional gimmick on behalf of David Tang, who had just opened his new store in Manhattan, or a plug for Sarah Ferguson's clearly stated aspiration to become a television presenter.[70] Cultural production (beyond television shows) invariably comprises interrelated affordances, one or more of which may take on greater importance than others in different creative contexts, so that there is a continuous process of 'entanglement' and 'disentanglement' as those concerned de-contextualize and re-contextualize different aspects of the product or performance in the making, and emphasize now one, now another, affordance, sometimes in the same, sometimes in different, contexts.[71] Yet, in spite of the variation in emphases, it is rare that any of the six affordances outlined here is absent entirely from any form of cultural production.

For example, in the pottery village of Koishiwara, where, as we will see in the following chapter, I used to make pots, the introduction of mechanical means of preparing clay, which previously had been crushed and powdered by water-powered clay pounders fed by the community stream, led to the breakdown of the father-son system of limited household production. Now able to command as much prepared clay as they wished, kiln owners could take on three or four apprentices to assist in production, and at the same time set up new pottery workshops for younger sons who previously had been obliged to leave Koishiwara and seek work elsewhere. This in itself was afforded by the availability of land for new workshops and homes, as well as by the development of a market for folk art pottery and the so-called "*mingei* boom." To meet burgeoning demand, new types of gas kilns were built and fired, in addition to—and often instead of—the old climbing kilns. These gas kilns allowed experimentation with new forms and glazes, so that what constituted 'traditional' Koishiwara wares began to change quite radically, although many of the original potter households and local politicians would promote traditional aspects of Koishiwara's pottery production to the media and the outside world. Thus an innovation in technical affordance led to new social formations fed by an economic affordance, which itself encouraged technical innovations and representational (decorative) changes in the pottery made, as well as recourse to former social formations.

That this series of events was *afforded* and not inevitable can be seen in the example of the neighbouring pottery community of Onta, where a similar method of preparing clay by means of water-power clay crushers is still in existence. As a result, there is just enough clay for one man and his son to work with full-time at the wheel; it is impossible, therefore, to employ apprentices. Second and third sons are still obliged to move elsewhere to seek a living, since there is insufficient land around the community to enable the construction of new houses, workshops, and clay crusher dams. And yet changes have come about as a result of market demand. Some of the potters have broken away from membership of the community's cooperative kiln and have built their own individual household climbing kilns to be able to fire as and when they wish, rather than fall in with the schedule of others. All ten potter households have adapted their wares to market demand by introducing fire-resistant shelves into their kilns (to enable more and smaller pots to be fired at any one time) and an electric motor enabling the wheel to be turned regularly at speed by means of a belt, rather than by foot, but they have not purchased gas or electric kilns to enable more frequent firings. They have also made some, but—in comparison with Koishiwara—not many changes to the kind of pottery they produce: miniaturising large rural storage jars for urban table consumption, for example, and adapting certain forms to a modern lifestyle (like that of the old water jar to umbrella stand). Glazes and decorations, however, have for the most part remained stable.[72]

But there is another representational affordance—in terms of official government designation—which has contributed to this status quo. In the spring of 1995, the Committee for the Preservation of Cultural Properties (*Bunkazai Hozon Shingikai*) in the Agency for Cultural Affairs (*Bunkachō*) announced the selection of Onta pottery as one of Japan's Important Intangible Cultural Properties. This designation has singled out particular materials, technologies, and related skills for 'preservation.' As a result, Onta potters more or less have to adhere to particular decorative techniques and glaze recipes; they *have* to continue using local materials such as clay, slip, and glaze ingredients (feldspar, iron oxide, wood and straw ash); they *have* to fire their pots in climbing kilns; and they *have* to use a particular method of coil and throw on the kick wheel when forming their pots. Several factors, however, militate against such government-preserved traditions. In the first place, new technologies in rice agriculture (in particular, the use of combine harvesting) make it virtually impossible for potters to get rice straw ash. This difficulty is exacerbated by the fact that fewer and fewer farming households in Japan are still growing rice. This means that they are obliged to buy some prepared glaze materials and adapt their glaze recipes accordingly. Second, new environmental laws make it difficult for them to purchase wood ash in the way that they used to because lumber yards now convert wood ends into chip board, rather than burn them as previously. Third, the demand for folk art pottery has declined considerably over the past twenty years. This has affected large pots in particular, but it is in the making of large pots that Onta potters' traditional coil-and-throw method of forming has been used. As a result, very few young potters are able to master the throwing methods cited in the designation of Onta pottery as an Important Intangible Cultural Property.[73]

Other circuits of affordances have more positive endings. What we now know as 'Hollywood' came into being as an assemblage of presences and absences of natural, technical, and social resources. In the early days of filmmaking, when the film camera was not what it is today, electric light was not strong enough to substitute for natural light. As a result, production companies based in New York and Chicago began to seek out sunny locations during the winter season. The presence of a stable climate, a constant supply of natural light, a wide variety of landscape settings, low wages, and proximity to an urban labour supply led to their selecting southern California (specifically Hollywood) as the best place to set up new motion picture companies. The new location afforded an increase in the number of outdoor shootings (spatial affordance), which itself encouraged directors to position their cameras more freely, to split camera 'takes' into more frequent and shorter shots (temporal affordance), and to introduce long shots as they moved actors and animals deeper into available space. From such developments emerged the idea of film as spectacle and the particular genre of the Western,[74] which quickly developed its conventions of chases, battles, gunfights, rugged cowboys, and so on (representational affordance), which themselves were later transferred to a new genre of police detective films.

To take another example of cultural production, an artist normally works with paints on a canvas. But, as Michael Hutter points out: "oil paints cause severe problems for painters: they react with untreated canvas, making it necessary to protect the canvas with a coating that tends to discolour over time, leaving a brownish tint; and they take weeks to dry, making it necessary to structure the workflow around the drying periods."[75] This in part explains modern American artists' embrace of acrylic paints, which use synthetic resins rather than oil as a binder and enable colours to be applied directly to the canvas without leaving signs of a brushstroke. They also dry extremely fast and are cheap enough to be bought by the gallon. In this way, as with the Impressionists' adoption of a synthetic cobalt blue (rather than continued use of the priceless ultramarine developed from lapis lazuli), a new painting style (Abstract Expressionism) came into being.[76]

Representation, then, is often inextricably tied in with techno-material conventions. Because notes cannot be sustained on a harpsichord except by holding down the keys, a player has to increase the number of notes played in a particular time span to make the music sound 'loud.' It is this that separates the music of Bach, for example, from that of Mozart and Beethoven, who were able to compose for the pianoforte, with its technical ability to play both loud and soft notes.[77] At the same time, a composer selects one key rather than another for a melody, and then one note or phrase rather than another, because a particular aesthetics of music allows it and not the other.[78] S/he also writes for one instrument or group of instruments rather than another—because stringed, not brass, instruments are seen to be more 'suitable' for a romantic piece of music, for instance—and each of the musicians then makes choices about the phrasing or bowing of the final score.[79] Such conventions allow us to call that score (classical, pop, jazz, rock, and so on) 'music' rather than mere 'noise.'

So, materials afford techniques; techniques afford styles; and styles afford finished products, which are themselves afforded by time and place, as well as by other participants collaborating in creative work, and are exchanged for sums of money (or returns of favours, or objects in kind). The same holds true for them all in reverse. Sociological explanation should not privilege any one affordance (although those engaging with and negotiating them in a creative world may well do so for one reason or another). Because they interact with and play off one another like a musical quartet, we may see affordances as together forming a multifaceted circuit, or ensemblage particular to each creative context (Figure 1) where, although the structure of explanatory language itself does not so permit, it is possible to start at any given point (techno-material, social, representational, and so on) and arrive at the same distribution, circulation, and transformation of attributions and connections making up an "actor-network."[80] Each affordance is entangled in the others to such an extent that the only way out of their enmeshment would seem to be to refer to them all by an overarching (and, ultimately perhaps, meaningless) concept like 'creativity.' It is because affordances are continuously evaluated and re-evaluated that we can think of cultural products as creative processes based on a sequence of transformations. Different forms of cultural production, then, operate within an "economy of qualities."[81]

FIGURE 1: A Circuit of Affordances

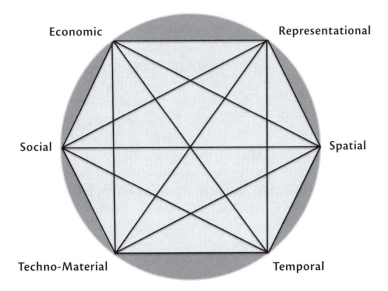

CHAPTER 2

Putting on a Show

Having outlined the circuit of affordances, I now want to provide an ethnographic case study of creativity so that we can begin to understand how "groups are made, agencies are explored, and objects play a role"[1]—in short, how affordances work in practice in the creative industries. At the same time, this case will help us understand how people engage with perceptions of creativity and the different values that they bring to bear on cultural products. These values often reflect their particular skills, knowledge, and professional roles and together form *ensemblages of worth*. This point I will discuss in detail in the following chapter.

Perhaps one of the better ways to initiate a discussion of creativity and the engagements that take place during the course of conceptualizing, designing, making, evaluating, promoting, and selling a cultural product is by describing an event in which I myself played an important part: my own pottery exhibition in Japan. Of course, there is always a danger in listening too uncritically to creative people telling us how they do their work, especially when—as is often the case—they are relating their successes (and never, ever their failures), but I think that in this case a fieldworker's own experiences might be a fruitful way to pursue the ramifications of creative encounters and the engagements that ensue.

Although, at first glance perhaps, this case may seem a bit esoteric (*pottery? Japan?*), it is in many ways typical of what goes on in creative industries. It describes in detail the following interrelated activities that accompany different forms of cultural production:

> **1.** *Framing*: In the creative industries, there is usually a need to *frame* creative production. Precisely because creativity seeks to bring together such unlikely associates as cabbages and kings, and because it is an integral part of a social world that comprises opposed ideals like aesthetics and commerce, creative processes need to be framed in such a way that everyone understands what they are required to do, with whom, and for what purpose, as well as believing in the product to which they have been asked to contribute their skills and knowledge.

2. *Event*: As part of the framing, those responsible for managing a creative product or performance try to make it into an 'event.' By their very nature, events jut out from the normal routines of everyday life and it is this 'jutting out' that is interpreted as the first step towards recognition of 'creativity.'

3. *Sponsorship*: All creative work needs financial support of some kind, either by way of salaries or other kinds of remuneration to creative personnel, or through contributions by outside parties who believe that, for one reason or another, a particular creative project needs to be carried out and is worth supporting. Sponsorship is not necessarily limited to financial support, although this is usually the case. A sponsor can contribute support in kind: a venue for a creative performance, for example, or free media promotion. The expectation, though, is that s/he will get something of value in return. In this respect, creativity is embedded in a system of both monetary and non-monetary exchange.

4. *Pricing*: Because all creative work involves the expenditure of money, costs incurred must be covered to avoid financial loss. Film and concert audiences, therefore, are charged admission to a cinema or concert arena; art lovers buy entrance tickets to a museum. CDs, DVDs, paintings, *manga* comics, fashion magazines, and so on do not come free. Each of them has a price. Prices are set by those managing creative outputs, and take into account economic, social, aesthetic, and other factors.

5. *Creative processes*: Any work (product or performance) deemed to be 'creative' consists of underlying creative processes that may or may not be immediately apparent. Generally speaking, such processes are first and foremost aesthetic: a creative product or performance is normally framed and developed in terms of its *genre* and a particular set of aesthetic ideals relating to techniques and materials, as well as to anticipated style. However, to be creative by breaking the bonds that constrain him, an advertising copywriter, fashion designer, or cartoonist may well make use of other processes that are more overtly social and/or cultural and that may include economic considerations. Different creative contexts give rise to different ensemblages of such processes (Chapter 3).

One-man Show

Some years ago now, as a post-doctoral researcher, I conducted anthropological fieldwork on the production, marketing, and aesthetic appraisal of contemporary ceramic art in Japan. The research question asked was simple enough: how was a potter selected to be the holder of an Important Intangible Cultural Property (*jūyō mukei bunkazai*), the highest honour awarded to a traditional artist-craftsman in Japan, and popularly referred to in the media as a "national treasure" (*ningen kokuhō*)? The answer was also simple, on the surface at least: by exhibiting his or her (mainly his) work in department stores.

I therefore spent a large proportion of my early fieldwork attending the one-man gallery shows and group exhibitions that were held on a regular basis in Japanese department stores located in various cities in the southern island of Kyushu, where I was plugged into a network of ceramic artists (some of whom were happy to call themselves simply 'potters'), as well as in the capital, Tokyo, where they all ultimately aspired to hold an exhibition. As I delved deeper into the working of the ceramic art world and into the different retail and media fields in which it operated, I learned a number of things. One was a classic "collective misrecognition" or "disavowal"[2] of the importance of commerce in art: critics denied that aesthetic value had anything to do with economic exchange, even though potters themselves used sales to judge 'success' and assert the 'quality' of their work. Another was that there was a mutual playing off of status—what Pierre Bourdieu refers to as social and cultural capital[3]—among potters, critics, department stores, and the occasional media organization publicizing a ceramic art exhibition. On the one hand, the ranking of potters to a large extent reflected the ranking of department stores, and vice versa; on the other, potters approached well-known critics to endorse their work and give it a 'provenance'; critics happily did so because they received from potters in return 'payment' examples of their work, whose value then increased because of the endorsement that they had given it: what some people like to call a 'win-win' situation. In general, as I soon learned, the ceramic art world was made up of a tight-knit network of critics, department store representatives, media journalists, and eminent named potters. The difficulty, so far as my fieldwork was concerned, lay in how best to break open the black box that constituted the art world of contemporary Japanese ceramics.

The—or one—resolution of my difficulty emerged in the form of Miyamoto Reisuke, a gallery owner in Fukuoka City, who was buying and

PUTTING ON A SHOW   63

selling contemporary ceramics from his gallery, as well as arranging shows of potters' work for various department stores located in Kyushu, but also further afield in Hiroshima and Kobe. For no other reason than that he was tired of the wheeling and dealing of those involved in the ceramic art world, he decided to take me under his wing as his unpaid assistant and tell me all he knew.[4] During the course of the next nine months, therefore, I accompanied Miyamoto around the potteries of northern Kyushu, collecting pots for exhibition; being introduced to potters to whom I could then talk at my leisure and follow up the various issues that came up during the course of my research; and going into department stores by the back entrance on their weekly holiday and meeting gallery managers who, in their shirt sleeves and jeans, happily told me all the 'backstage' stories that in their official 'front stage' capacity (replete with suit and tie) they never referred to when we met at other times during the week.[5]

During our travels, Miyamoto and I discussed pottery and the ceramic art world at considerable length, and he gave me his dealer's-eye view of what was going on, of who was taking advantage of whom and for what purpose, and of the obvious difficulty that young and talented potters had in making their way to the top of the ceramic art world. Unless they conformed to the demands and expectations of those whom these potters themselves (using a Japanized English word) called 'mafia', unless they tailored their work to suit the status quo of accepted standards of taste, they had little hope of introducing acceptable innovations. In this respect, their work seemed doomed to stylization. Moreover, if they really wished to advance their careers, they had to be prepared to 'play the game' and enter into a world characterized, it seemed, by bribery and corruption. By participating in the game played by others, they became "adversaries in collusion" upholding the "social alchemy" of the ceramic art world.[6]

The suggestion that I should hold my own pottery exhibition emerged during one of our lengthy talks as we drove around the kilns of northern Kyushu. After I had concluded that there was a lot that was unsatisfactory about the quality of contemporary ceramics, Miyamoto advised me to be more objective. Did I really appreciate the potters' problems?

It's easy to criticize from the outside, but what you really need to do as a researcher is experience what it's like being a potter yourself. I'm not saying you're wrong in your conclusions. But you need to understand things down here [he pointed to his solar plexus] and not up here [he tapped his head]. Why don't you hold your own exhibition? That way you'd really begin to appreciate some of the paradoxes potters find themselves caught up in.[7]

I was intrigued by the idea. After all, I had learned the rudiments of pottery when doing fieldwork in a folk art pottery community for my Ph.D.[8] and had continued to make pots during my current research fieldwork. In some respects, it would be fun to see whether I could sell my work. At the same time, as I realized from the apprehension that immediately gripped me, holding my own exhibition would be a challenge, and in all likelihood a nerve-wracking experience. In this respect, Miyamoto had given me good fieldwork advice. Learn through my body, not my head. Like Loïc Wacquant in his study of a boxing gym, I needed to practice observant participation, and not just participant observation, as an integral part of my fieldwork.[9]

Establishing a Frame

To get my exhibition off the ground, Miyamoto and I needed to establish a frame, for it was the frame that would afford the kind of creativity that would later emerge. Our first concern was access to materials and the means to make pots. I therefore approached a pottery household that I knew well in Koishiwara, two hours from the city of Fukuoka where Miyamoto had his gallery, and asked Kajiwara Jirō if he would provide me with access to clay, glazes, and a kiln in which to fire my stoneware 'craft pottery.' Permission was willingly given.[10] Our second concern was to frame the exhibition appropriately by persuading a department store to provide a venue, and a national newspaper the cultural backing and PR necessary for the show. This pairing was necessary because stores needed newspapers to 'consecrate'[11] them with a cultural aura and newspapers needed stores to legitimize their taken position as cultural consecrators. The aim, then, was to find out if either of these organizations thought that there might be some business mileage in my holding a one-man exhibition and, if so, whether they would commit themselves to getting involved.

Miyamoto decided to approach the Mainichi newspaper, because the enterprise and promotions manager there already knew me and would therefore be likely to be well-disposed towards the idea. This was sound judgement. Later, the manager concerned explained why.

For a start, we know Miyamoto. He's been doing business with us for several years now, putting on shows in our art gallery and acting as our agent in dealing with potters around Kyushu. We trust him. But there's something else. A department store spends most of its time and energy trying to find some means of making money, and only money. So when an idea like this comes along, we tend to jump at it. After all, it's nice to enjoy ourselves occasionally. As far as we're concerned, it doesn't really matter whether your pots sell or not. The important thing is that people will come along and enjoy themselves and that'll be good for the store's reputation.[12]

This initial discussion reinforced a point made in the Overture (to be returned to in Chapter 5): the importance of trust among people working in the creative industries (as well as in Japanese business more generally). It also neatly illustrated Howard Becker's point that an art world consists of "networks of people cooperating,"[13] as well as Bourdieu's emphasis on the disavowal of commerce that frequently takes place in art worlds. Here the newspaper-department store relationship was critical to the functioning of the ceramic art world. A newspaper provided its readers with 'cultural commentary,' which a department store needed in support of its commercial activities (thereby transforming economic capital into cultural capital). My own exhibition was from the start designed to make it *appear* as if a department store was putting on a fun show; it was to be used towards building a store's cultural capital. This would encourage people to visit the store and indirectly persuade them to spend their money there, either on pots or on other things for sale, both then and in the future, thereby contributing to the store's overall turnover and profit (its economic capital).

At this stage, Miyamoto himself played a double game with the Mainichi newspaper and Tamaya, the store that he approached about holding my show:

With all shows, you have to have a framework in which to work, and it is this frame that's the most difficult thing of all to establish. So when I visited the enterprise and promotions manager at Mainichi, I told him that Tamaya had agreed to hold the show in their Fukuoka store, even though that wasn't actually the case. And then, when I visited the publicity manager at Tamaya, I told him that the Mainichi newspaper was going to be the official sponsor of your show, even though that wasn't true either. The thing is that neither of the two men concerned knew this.

Of course, in your case, things are comparatively simple. Both men have known you for some months now and want to help you out. Even so, *officially*, things aren't fixed yet. We're still working at the level of informal contacts. It's this, of course, that is the vital aspect of Japanese business. Formalities come much, much later, once the frame has been securely established.

The relation between informal contacts and formal endorsement was, however, not *that* simple. When I met the enterprise and promotions manager the following week, he said:

I haven't officially committed the Mainichi newspaper to sponsoring your exhibition for two reasons. One is that I don't at the moment want personal connections to dictate a newspaper company project, without first checking up on one or two alternatives. More importantly, if the Mainichi newspaper were to decide officially to back your show, it would mean that we could rely on the RKB Broadcasting and TV station to help out, because they're part of the Mainichi media network. But then there would be a good chance that none of the other media organizations would pay any attention to your show. What I mean is, a combination of rivalry and jealousy would prevent the Nishi Nihon, Asahi, or Yomiuri newspapers from writing about your exhibition, and that would, of course, ultimately be detrimental to publicity both for Tamaya and for yourself.

As a result, I've another idea which I think would work very well, and which would allow us more freedom when it comes to media publicity. There's an organization known as the Anglo-Japanese Association (*Nichi-ei Kyōkai*), which is based in Kyushu University and whose members are primarily industrialists and intellectuals. What I'd like to do is get *it* to sponsor your show: in name only, of course. Then the Mainichi can take a back seat, while at the same time doing all the real promotion. In the meantime, Miyamoto can get in touch with his friends at the Nishi Nihon newspaper and ask them to write about your show, and they'll have no objections because the Mainichi won't be acting as front-running sponsor.

While illustrating the difficulty of determining who in fact "creates the creator,"[14] the enterprise and promotion manager's plan revealed a very delicate juggling act, in which a number of institutions were keen to get in on an exhibition, but not willing to accept responsibility for anything should the act misfire. If the show was a failure, the only people to blame would be the official sponsors: an amorphous body that hardly ever met. If, on the other hand, the show was a success, both Tamaya and the Mainichi newspaper would certainly claim the credit. In other words, the criteria to be used for evaluation of my work were not simply aesthetic, but extended to both financial and social considerations (see also Chapter 11).

Having realized this, I decided to obtain additional backing from another organization: the British Council. By chance, I knew the current director of this organization in Tokyo, since he had introduced me to an English-language teaching job when I first went to Japan in 1967. Making use of this tenuous connection, I quickly persuaded him to bestow the British Council's name on my show, with the proviso that "we don't have to finance you or anything like that, old boy." The Anglo-Japanese Association also agreed to act as official sponsor of the show, so gradually the framework began to come together. In this way, all those concerned—potter, gallery owner, store manager, newspaper journalist, and cultural sponsors— carefully evaluated various means by which a 'rub-off' effect would be generated among themselves, as well as on the show, and thus on the perceived quality of the ceramic 'art' on display.

Strategic Packaging

Venue and sponsorship were not the only elements in establishing a frame, however. The timing of the show and the product to be exhibited were also crucial aspects of the 'strategic packaging' essential to every creative endeavour. Somehow we had to make my show into an *event*. For this Miyamoto overtly sought to make the show 'jut out' by associating two hitherto separate planes of reference.

The first thing he had to consider was *timing*. One question that remained unresolved for some weeks was when to hold the exhibition. One-man shows in department stores usually lasted for six days and Tamaya, of course, had a schedule that had to be filled for its gallery. Some weeks were already reserved for shows, but a few others were open. Miyamoto, however, needed a reason to hold the show in one week rather than another: a 'big idea' that would entice the business side of the ceramic art world to support my exhibition wholeheartedly. This 'big idea' remained elusive until one evening when Miyamoto's wife, Fusa, suddenly suggested over dinner:

What we really ought to do is hold your show at the same time as the *Dentō Kōgeiten*, the annual Traditional Crafts Exhibition, which is put on at Iwataya, Tamaya's rival department store down the road. *Every*body goes to that: potters, patrons, collectors, critics, as well as the general public. Holding your show then would really appeal to the publicity manager if we had the proper media backing, because that's the one week in the year when *nobody* visits Tamaya. If your show were to be properly advertised, *all* the potters visiting the Traditional Crafts Exhibition would drop by to see your pots. Just for the fun of it.

I protested: I couldn't have experienced potters coming to see my own amateurish work. It was just too embarrassing. In spite of my protestations and embarrassment, however, Fusa had hit on the hitherto invisible and so 'blindingly obvious,' and Miyamoto quickly arranged with Tamaya for my show to be held in the second week in March. This temporal affordance was the bait that coaxed the octopus into its basket frame. By putting on my show during the same week as the national Traditional Crafts Exhibition, Tamaya was overtly declaring that it, too, was rising above commerce as it engaged with "spectacle" and the "carnivalesque"[15] aspect of the ceramic art market. It finally had a weapon with which to fight its rival down the road. As for myself, as a potter I now had a deadline to meet and a whole range of pots to be made. This exhibition of mine was now a reality.

This reality in itself led to a second aspect of strategic planning, this time connected with *the product*. As mentioned earlier, I had access to a household making stoneware pottery in Koishiwara, and it was stoneware that I had always made. However, much of my research had focused on potters who made porcelain wares, since the town of Arita in northern Kyushu was famous for its kaolin deposits, which had been discovered in 1616, and enabled porcelain to be made and fired to a much higher temperature than the more common stoneware. Generally speaking, potters specialized in either stoneware or porcelain, since each was evaluated according to different sets of aesthetic standards: stoneware was 'rough,' 'muddy' (*dorokusai*), and 'folksy,' while porcelain (which is perhaps technically more difficult to make, glaze, and fire satisfactorily) was 'fine,' 'clean looking,' and closer to the Japanese concept of 'art.' For the most part, therefore, ceramic 'artists' (*tōgei sakka*) like Tomimoto Kenkichi and Kondō Yūzō worked with porcelain clay, although it was also possible for stoneware potters who worked in particular areas of Japan noted for their traditional wares (Bizen, Mino, Tokoname, and so on), or who devoted themselves to making tea bowls and other pots for use in the Japanese tea ceremony, to be recognized as 'artists.' This latter group included such potters as Kawai Kanjirō, Arakawa Toyozō, Kitaoji Rosanjin, and Hamada Shōji.

The village of Koishiwara where I was working was not one of the famed six traditional kilns of Japan. As a result, there was little chance of my work being seen as 'art' (*bijutsuhin*), however proficient or skilled I might have been at making pots. The best I could hope for was that people recognized it as 'art-craft' (*bijutsu kōgeihin*); the real test was whether they would categorize what I exhibited as mere 'pottery' (*yakimono*) or as 'ceramic art' (*tōgei*).

To help people elevate my pots from mere 'pottery' to 'ceramic art,' as well as to differentiate my exhibition from the one-man shows held by other potters in Kyushu's department stores, Miyamoto came up with a second bisociative leap: I should make and exhibit *both* stoneware *and* porcelain:

> Nobody's done that before. Look at all the famous potters around today. People like Imaemon, Kakiemon and Inoue Manji [naming three nationally famous potters living in and around Arita]. All make porcelain. None of them ever makes stoneware. On the other hand, Miwa Kyūsetsu, Sakada Deika, and other tea ceremony potters make only stoneware. They never touch porcelain. So you'll be the only person in Japan essentially who dares to try his hand at both. That'll get people talking all right. And it's talk—word of mouth—that we need to set this show alight.

Here was 'thinking aside.' Miyamoto had cunningly brought a "blurred periphery" into focus,[16] showing once again how a blindingly obvious possibility (the making of two genres of pottery) had been overlooked because of its familiarity. He therefore arranged for me to make some porcelain pots with a potter working out of Ureshino, Tanaka Hajime, whom I had met several times and with whom I had got on well during the course of my research.

Although the combination of stoneware and porcelain in a one-man show was a good marketing strategy, it was not sufficient in itself to ensure success. After all, what if people decided that both the porcelain and stoneware pots that I showed were of poor quality, which was likely if they bothered to compare my work with that of professional Japanese potters?

One way out of this conundrum lay in the custom of 'recommendations' (*suisenbun*) that usually accompanied gallery exhibitions. One of the things that had to be prepared well in advance was the announcement of any show. In this, potters (and artists more generally) introduce themselves, or have themselves introduced, to the general public. The simplest way is for them to write up a kind of 'potted history' (*tōreki*) of their career, in which they cite where they studied pottery, to whom they were apprenticed, what exhibitions they have contributed to, and what prizes they have won. Alternatively, they can write up some sort of introductory note and talk about their work: about the traditions and history of their kiln, for example, or about the techniques they use and their origins.

A third way to establish this sort of social and cultural capital is by persuading someone to write a recommendation on their behalf: their teacher, for example, if famous, or a well-known critic, or (considerably lower down the symbolic capital scale) a member of the department store's art gallery staff. Miyamoto, however, decided to approach a *potter* to write a recommendation on my behalf. The potter he chose was Imaizumi Imaemon, thirteenth-generation Nabeshima overglaze enamelware artist, whose work we will encounter later on in this book (and several years later designated the holder of an Important Intangible Cultural Property; see Chapter 10). Miyamoto rationalized his decision this way:

> Imaemon is totally unusual in the world of contemporary Japanese ceramics. *Everybody* respects him. You never hear anybody criticizing him or telling tales behind his back. He's a one-off. With Imaemon's name signed at the bottom of the recommendation printed on the announcements of your show, I can send them off to every potter in Kyushu and *know* that a lot of them will come simply out of curiosity because Imaemon has chosen to endorse your work.

This decision coincided with Miyamoto's aim to sell my pots to potters, rather than simply to casual passers-by who might drop in to see my show.[17] This strategy was rational in that, like artists elsewhere,[18] Japanese potters did, and still do, tend to buy one another's work, partly out of personal acquaintanceship (known as *tsukiai* in Japanese), partly as a way of congratulating the potter holding a show. By so doing, potters know that the favour will be returned when it is their turn to hold a one-man show. In my own case, I happened to have translated a Japanese book about the history of overglaze enamel porcelain and Imaemon pottery into English, and had been introduced to the potter when he had visited England a few months before the start of my research. In Japan, this meant, crudely speaking, that

Imaemon 'owed me one.' Because he knew very well the rules of social interaction, he readily acceded to Miyamoto's request that he write a 'recommendation' on my behalf.

Making Pots

All this strategizing assumed one thing: that I could actually make pots that would pass muster for a department store exhibition. But assuming and doing some things are two rather different matters, as I soon found out when I settled down in Kajiwara Jirō's workshop and started to make my stoneware pots.

There were several concerns that hit me one after the other (and occasionally, on a bad day, simultaneously) as I thought about what to make for my exhibition. The first was the ever-present awareness that I was not a skilled potter who had been through an apprenticeship. As a result, I could hardly pretend that I knew what I was doing when it came to addressing different clay forms. I knew the rudiments of wheelwork, of course, but I was essentially an amateur with limited capabilities. How, then, could I dare to play the department store exhibition game engaged in by professional potters? What on earth would they have to say about my less-than-professional work?

The first lesson learned, then, involved what has been called "the anxiety of creation"[19] and the realization that I was terrified of being laughed at. And yet that was precisely what everyone in the ceramic art world was doing when they gossiped about other potters, critics, department stores, and so on. This led not just to a sense of discomfort, but also added to my lack of self-confidence: something that I now realised was characteristic of many of the potters I knew when they were preparing for a one-man show. Would I be able to make a sufficient variety of pots to be credible as a potter and attract people to my show? Would I be able to make enough pots to fill a gallery in the first place? How much help could I ask of my potter friends? How was I supposed to price those pots that I did make? Was there anybody, realistically, who would want to buy my pots when they were put on display? If so, what kind of people were they?[20]

The next thing I had to come to terms with was my lack of technical skill. I could draw designs for different pottery forms and decorations, and my notebooks gradually filled with promising sketches, but I had difficulty in converting these designs into actual pots. Part of this difficulty lay in the fact that I wasn't skilled enough to throw certain forms on the wheel; part was due to my inexperience in firing a kiln. Practice, of course, helped me overcome these deficiencies to some, though not great, degree. But another part of the difficulty was more a matter of 'aesthetics', in that I soon came to realise that matching a two-dimensional design to a particular three-dimensional form in fact required a trained hand, a good eye, and a proper sense of balance. And I hadn't had enough practice to acquire any of these.

As a result, I often found myself doing things that were totally unplanned. For example, unable to find a particular tool I needed one afternoon when preparing to decorate some slabware plates with a thick slip clay, I decided on the spur of the moment to brush them with an iron solution instead, before trailing them with a thinner slip and using a rubber comb to create a black-and-white effect on the surface of each plate. Since this seemed to work well, I proceeded to try the same technique with different decorations on some other plates. Then, when I had finished, there was still some iron solution left over, so I applied it to the surfaces of some small dishes, drawing unplanned triangles here, pine trees there, and finally a plate with a noughts and crosses pattern on it. This was very much an exercise in David Pye's "workmanship of risk" (as opposed to that of certainty),[21] as Kajiwara Jirō recognised when he came back to the workshop (he had been out all day). Surveying the results of my somewhat wild abandon, he exclaimed: "You know, I wouldn't *dare* to do anything like this. Perhaps I should. Your brushwork is so *alive*."

So improvisation of this kind was one way of my combatting a lack of technical skills. But it also made me realise that being an amateur was not just a weakness; it could be my strong point, too. Here I was lucky, for there is a tradition of 'play' in the history of Japanese ceramics that allows the recognition and positive appraisal of amateur work. My playful improvisations in fact became a strength (as Jirō hinted) since they did not conform to the general clichés of form and style found in ceramics exhibitions in Japan.

This in itself was linked to a third problem with which I had had to wrestle right from the start: the *genre* of pottery that I wished to exhibit. During the course of my research, I had seen an enormous number of 'exhibition pots' (*kaijō tōki*)—primarily very large plates, bowls, dishes, and vases—that Japanese potters made to show off their wheelwork and glazing skills. At the same time, I knew from my surveys that exhibition visitors liked pottery in general because it was *functional*, even though most of what they saw was decorative. Because of my own entry into pottery through Bernard Leach and the folk art tradition, I myself was firmly convinced that

I should make functional, and not decorative, wares. That was why I had been working in Koishiwara and Onta.

Here, however, lay the rub. Precisely because these communities were part of the *mingei* folk art movement, they tended to produce a particular genre of pottery that was readily recognizable as 'folk art,' just as celebrity gossip, bizarre human interest stories, and true-confession accounts of misfortune or abuse identify daytime talk shows on TV or different tabloid newspapers. In a way, the decorative techniques that Koishiwara and Onta potters used (for instance, the *hakeme* brushwork and *tobiganna* chattering) *branded* their work as a particular kind of stoneware, which was different from other kinds of stoneware found in Karatsu, Tokoname, or Bizen, for example, as well as from porcelain. Somehow, I had to avoid being branded in this way. I had to escape the rut of 'tradition' and produce something 'different.' Yet, because I was using Koishiwara clay and glazes, this 'difference' necessarily fell within the bounds of the *mingei* genre produced by other potters in the village. So, I could use the white slip clay and iron solution in the way that Jirō and two or three other Koishiwara potters did, but try out some rather different designs (like noughts and crosses!). My engagement with creativity, then, was both limited and enabled by the affordances of the genre. It was an engagement with *typicality*.

One way out of this difficulty was, as mentioned earlier, to make pots of two different styles: one in stoneware, and the other in porcelain, which tended to be less constricting as a genre (unless one happened to be working in a particular *sometsuke* or overglaze enamel style). This is not to say that the clay itself, with its mixture of kaolin, did not 'afford' certain methods of wheelwork and finished forms of the kind described in the previous chapter. I soon came to realize that it was totally different from the clay I had been using over the years in Koishiwara and permitted me to do some things, but not others, in ways that were totally new and (to myself, at least) refreshing. In a way, if the art of making stoneware could be said to be based on *throwing* on the wheel, that of porcelain was in the *trimming* of partially dried thrown forms. With porcelain clay, as I soon found out, I had to throw open forms with thick walls of clay that could then be paired down to extreme thinness once they had dried sufficiently. This was impossible with stoneware clay, which inevitably cracked if made and/or trimmed too thin.

Because I was a novice when it came to making porcelain wares in Ureshino, I tended *not* to trim my pots thin enough. As a result, they were on the heavy side, but had a 'roundedness' and 'softness' that my host, Tanaka Hajime, himself really appreciated, precisely because porcelain potters like himself had been socialised into imagining that porcelain could *only* be, and thus *had* to be, razor thin. Inexperience, then, permitted an acceptable break with precedent.

The other good thing about working in two different genres was that it allowed crossovers between the two. Thus, I was able to adapt some of the rather more traditional decorative techniques found in Koishiwara to the pots that I made in Ureshino. I thus found myself trying *tobiganna* chattering in a blue cobalt wash on porcelain clay, and *hakeme* brushwork in *yuri* lilac wash, instead of on white slip as I would have done in Koishiwara. I also took some ideas from Tanaka's decorative brush designs and applied them on Koishiwara clay, but in iron on slip, rather than—say—in cobalt on porcelain clay. These effects worked rather well as creative engagements with materials and genre.[22]

If there were some successes, my work was also subject to one disappointment after another, through carelessness, necessary sacrifice, and/or sheer incompetence. A lidded jar that I had made (and been rather proud of) cracked when it was left out in the sun by mistake; a promising vase came out of a firing totally bloated because, to get the temperature to sufficient height in the upper part of the kiln, I had been obliged to overfire it lower down (where the vase was placed). I managed to pierce holes in the bottoms of some bowls when I was overenthusiastic with my trimming tool, and to destroy others by slipping them when they were not dry enough. I struggled with the fact that I was working in both stoneware and porcelain clays, since what worked for the former did not do so for the latter, and vice versa. There were days when everything seemed to fall apart and I was in serious doubt about whether I would ever have enough pots to put on display; and there were other days (fewer in number) when I felt a little confident.

One such day was when I hesitantly opened up the kiln after my third firing and found that a circular tray, 60 centimetres in diameter, had not only come out unscathed from a difficult firing process, but looked really good. I had taken an idea from Ishiguro Munemaro (an extremely famous, deceased Japanese potter), and drawn a series of birds in cobalt facing opposite ways on alternate lines. As I looked at the design, with the cobalt slightly blurred, sometimes pale blue, at other times almost iron-like in colour, I judged this tray to be the best piece I had ever made, and decided there and then that I should keep my 'bird tray' for myself, and not include it in the exhibition.

Nevertheless, that evening I took it, along with some other pots, to Miyamoto's gallery where a well-known collector happened to be sitting, drinking tea and conversing with the gallery owner's wife. When he saw the bird tray, he immediately said that he wanted to buy it. I quickly responded that it was not for sale.

> What do you mean, 'not for sale'? If you make a good pot, you should be happy to sell it to someone who wants it. You know that it'll be in good hands, and that it'll make its owner happy. You can't not sell it. If you're going to be a potter, you've got to learn not to be attached to your work.

He was right, of course, although I didn't care to mention his own attachment to pots as a collector (he used to boast that he liked to hug some of his pots when he took a bath in the evening). I had never actually *sold* a pot of my own before, and had never needed to do so either. The pots that I made, I kept or gave away to friends. The ones I gave away were the ones to which I felt less attached; in other words, the ones with which I was less engaged at the time, although there was always the possibility that a 'disengagement' from the pots that I kept would come later, as I realized some deficiency or other through usage.

But now I was expected to sell my work, and sales were going to be *the* measure of my 'success.' And yet, when I stopped to consider what was about to happen, I knew that all I wanted was for people to *see* my work. I didn't need to sell it: I was, after all, employed at a university and had a regular salary. So here I was, stuck in the typical quandary of a cultural producer, torn between the so-called 'artistic' and potential 'commercial' aspects of my work:[23] a quandary that resulted from a desire to keep track of 'good work,' rather than from an inborn antagonism towards money-making as such.

This was the potter's catch-22. Miyamoto's client, like all collectors, wanted to buy a potter's *best* work (and I had, rather vainly, let slip the fact that I thought my bird tray to be pretty good). He wasn't going to be satisfied with second-grade stuff, and became indignant when he couldn't get what he wanted. And yet, like many other potters I knew, I wanted to keep my best work, because it would act as a 'standard' against which I could then

76 ▣ **CHAPTER 2**

judge my progress over the coming years. In this way, I was resisting market pressure. But this in itself led to another paradox faced by potters: by holding back their best work, they could delay the advance of their reputations.

So what should I do? Exhibit those pots in which chance had favoured me, build a reputation, and so tread the path towards 'art' pottery? Or remain the amateur scholar-potter (who was fast becoming unofficial critic as well) and keep 'chance' pots for myself? Not knowing the answer to this question, my immediate reaction was to go and make more bird trays and see if I could get the same results![24]

Pricing and Display

One more thing I had to do was have boxes made for my larger pots once they were ready for the exhibition. I was doubtful about this, but Miyamoto was adamant. As he explained, the Japanese have been boxing pots (and some other crafts) for centuries as a means of first initiating, and then safeguarding, the provenance of a work. Traditionally, each box has the name or type of pot inscribed in calligraphic handwriting by the potter who has made the pot concerned, or by someone recognized as having the power to 'consecrate' an art work in this way. Tea masters, for instance, regularly sign boxes for tea bowls (to which they give such poetic names as 'autumn moon' or 'spring breeze'). Depending on the status of the school of tea concerned,[25] as well as on his (or possibly her) own status within its hierarchical organization, a tea master's calligraphy on a box can raise the price of the pot by between five and twenty times. In my own case, Miyamoto felt that it was enough for me to inscribe my boxed pots myself, since my (left-handed) Japanese 'calligraphy' was unusual enough to give each pot an immediate, and obviously distinctive (!), 'provenance.'

Having done this, however, we next had to price the pots. This was extremely difficult because Miyamoto knew from experience that pricing was often an arbitrary act that had little, if anything, to do with 'intrinsic' aesthetic qualities. Usually it was potters themselves who set their own prices, on the basis of comparison with other potters' work, as well as of their own previous experiences of 'what the market would bear.' In such cases, all Miyamoto had to do was add on his commission and the retail price was set. This, however, was not the situation that we faced.

The trouble is, in your case your pots are 'priceless.' I mean, there's no standard against which we can measure them. And yet we have to take into account your production expenses; my commission, which, admittedly, I can always wave; the store's commission, which we can't; and the number of pots that we can realistically show in a gallery with a limited display area. Somehow we have to break even.

Given all these factors, the temptation is to price on the high side. But if you charge high prices for your stoneware, it'll almost certainly upset other potters working in the same village of Koishiwara. After all, your pots aren't that different from theirs. What I mean is, we need to price your work in such a way that people won't object to what we charge.

For Miyamoto, then, as for art dealers elsewhere in the world,[26] prices had to be 'justifiable', not just to clients, but to other potters exhibiting similar work. Genre thus affected pricing, and not just style. However, there was an underlying implication that the *artist*—as opposed to craftsman—potter was someone who ignored the tried and tested market value of work similar to his own and created an arbitrary pricing scale. Somehow, therefore, we had to arrive at a price level that signaled not just my anticipated reputation, but the status of Miyamoto as a dealer and of the intended purchasers of my work.[27]

There was another issue, though, that had to be dealt with when setting prices. In Miyamoto's words:

You've suggested that we're pricing pots by size, rather than by quality, and that in this respect we're not that different from painters who charge so much per square centimeter of canvas. You're right, of course. But at the same time, if you start suggesting that one pot is better than another, then you're setting a standard. A standard of quality. But, as I've said, in your case there's *no* objectively reliable standard to go by: only your own. So, if you start pricing one pot higher than another one similar in size, and possibly design, then you're going to have to do the same right down the line for *all* your pots, even the small tea and *sake* cups.

So what I suggest instead is that we stick to the idea of pricing by size. In other words, we decide what price is likely to attract a buyer for a particular size of pot and then leave the public to decide which pots they like at that particular price. That way, you'll learn which designs are popular and which aren't. Let the public set the standard for any future exhibition you may hold. We have to get it right, though. We mustn't price too high.

Miyamoto here invoked two anomalies in the pricing of art works: an activity that was clearly symbolic rather than simply economic. By pricing by size, Miyamoto ruled out an opportunity to set a price premium on pots that might sell more easily. By hinting at the taboo against decreasing prices in any future exhibition of mine, he chose to maximize price, rather than profit.[28] Having agreed on a maximum price of ¥100,000 (or US $400)[29] each for a set of dishes and a large wood-framed tray, we went about our work.[30] In the end, the 294 pots on sale (many of them forming sets of plates, dishes, cups, and saucers) yielded a total sales potential of a little over $10,000 (¥2.5 million). The aim was to sell 70 percent of this total to break even. Even if we achieved this sales figure, however, I would not have even climbed onto the lowest rung on the ceramic art ladder, which started at about ¥2 million for a one-week show.

A further issue surrounding the evaluation of the quality of a cultural product emerged the following morning when we went to Tamaya to arrange my pots in the gallery space. My initial reaction was that the space was too cluttered, and that the gallery looked more like a bargain sale counter than an 'artistic exhibition.' However, I quickly learned that there were two logics at work in the display.

One was a logic of separating genres. The department store's gallery personnel had arranged all my stoneware along one, and my porcelain along the other, side of the gallery. Surely, I said to Miyamoto, we should be mixing up the two sets of wares, matching similar forms and designs on stoneware and porcelain. The answer I got was straight to the point:

> The trouble with your idea is that it's typically 'artistic.' If you mix up pots too much, the porcelain will reflect back on the stoneware, and the stoneware will reflect back on the porcelain. People will no doubt enjoy *looking* at the subtle differences between the two, but they'd end up *buying* nothing at all because they'd be too confused. They wouldn't know what to look for where, nor which they liked better.

By arguing that prices should reflect size, rather than quality or artistic merit, Miyamoto was following standard pricing procedure in the art world, where all work by an artist has to be presented as if it were of equal merit. Different price levels along the lines I was suggesting therefore merely signalled that my work was not consistent (which, of course, it wasn't!).[31] During my research, I had in fact noted, though not fully appreciated, this difference in evaluative criteria between the creator and seller of a work. Miyamoto's attitude towards selling was precisely the opposite to that of potters when they took their work to be judged at a large exhibition. There I had noticed one famous ceramic artist carefully place his celadon vase between two pure white porcelain vases, precisely to make it stand out for selection by the judges. (I'll come back to exhibitions and prizes in Chapter 10.)

The second display logic was one of size (and thus of kinds of pots displayed). In arranging pottery exhibitions, Miyamoto followed a standard procedure that placed tea cups at the entrance to the gallery. Next to them were *sake* cups, then small dishes and bowls, with larger pots at the further end of the display area. The reason for this was part pragmatic, part psychological. First, people often stole *sake* cups, which were small but expensive, so they needed to be placed near the sales counter where store employees could keep an eye on them. Second, a good way to attract people to any exhibition (as well as into, for example, jewellery stores and fashion house retail outlets) was to show cheaper goods near the gallery entrance and lure them gradually further and further into the gallery towards the expensive artworks. The logic at work here was, first, seduction; then awe on the part of the visitor; leading, third, to a kind of aesthetic revelation that resulted, finally, in purchase of an artwork on display. In short, layout was designed to transform aficionados into collectors, people into consumers.

Mediating Representations

Eighteen hours later, I had appeared on a late night television programme, given two national and regional newspaper interviews, and sold just under $3,000 worth of pots. The gallery had been packed with people all day, including Imaemon himself and Tanaka Hajime, both of whom had been kind enough to take me round the display and tell me freely what they liked and disliked about my work. For the first time, I began to feel a bond of sympathy with a group of people whom I had hitherto tended to regard merely as objects of research.

As the exhibition went on, a number of things about how we evaluate artworks became clearer. First, there were my relations with the media. Each of the half-dozen journalists who came to interview me needed a 'story,' and it was my job to provide them (as well as two more television announcers) with such a story. In other words, the creator is expected to weave a tale around his or her cultural products.[32] I had recognized this earlier when I had negotiated sponsorship for my exhibition with the

Anglo-Japanese Association. Now, however, I had to create an integrated tale that would help those who had no way of assessing my work to evaluate it according to one of various art (or pottery) discourses current in the public domain. The way that I chose to do this was to locate my work within the aesthetic tenets of Japanese folk art, which espoused the benefits of hand-made as opposed to machine-made crafts; the beauty of imperfection and irregularity; use of natural rather than synthetic materials; and so on. During the course of such story-telling, I placed myself very firmly in a tradition that stretched back to William Morris and others living and working in nineteenth-century Britain,[33] and provided the media with an overarching discourse from which they could select parts that fitted their own agenda. This led to two newspapers describing me as "the second Leach" (!),[34] and, as a result, something like 1,000 people a day came to see my show, a phenomenon that had *all* the senior management of Tamaya department store (including its CEO) coming to congratulate me on the 'success' of my exhibition (even though pots were not *selling* that well), and inviting me to hold a new show there the following year.

Second, a lot of pots were sold on the first day of the exhibition, but was that the relevant factor to consider when evaluating purchases? Miyamoto was acutely aware that the prices that we had set reflected not just my pretensions as a 'ceramic artist', but his reputation as a dealer.

> So today was a success. But what made it so? A lot of small pots were sold. But then that's to be expected with a show like yours. What was important was that, fairly early on this morning, a plump middle-aged woman in a fur coat came into the gallery. She was a doctor's wife: the kind of person who has money to spend on art objects here in Japan.
>
> So once she started buying pots, I got interested. Not in *how much* she would spend, but in *which* pots on display she'd buy. If she'd stuck to those between $10 and $75, that would've been that. But she didn't. She went for one of the four pots in the top price range of $400, and another at $300 just below. As I see it, that doctor's wife was vital to the show because she helped create a mood among those visiting the gallery. Once people see somebody buying the more expensive works, they begin to want to do the same. It may sound ridiculous, but I can assure you from experience, it's true.
>
> I have to admit, for a time I was worried. I thought I'd overpriced your pots. But now I feel there's hope. It's funny, but every time I've had

a successful show, this 'mood creation' has come from a single stroke of chance. . . . It's all a matter of luck. But when it works, it really works.

Miyamoto's comment about the doctor's wife's selection of particular pots reinforced my earlier research findings that the 'herd instinct' tends to prevail in the purchase of artworks in department store exhibitions. The transformation of cryptic numbers (every department store has its own code) into red *Sold* tabs placed beside each work tends, at a certain point in their accumulation, to instigate impulse buying as collectors and other aficionados start to fear that they might be 'missing out' on something, although whether that something lies in the appreciation of a particular artwork, recognition of a new 'artist,' or a perceived opportunity to make a profit in the longer term usually remains unclear. At any rate, so far as I was concerned, I just hoped that the first day's pottery sales would act as red rags to a load of bulls in a china shop in the week to come!

Third, as is true of the art world in general, approximately 80 percent of my total sales (which came to ¥1.7 million, or almost $7,000, over five days and so just made Miyamoto's target) were made to people already known to Miyamoto, Tamaya, and myself. Some of these private clients ordered pots over the phone; others came and bought things in the gallery, while spending a lot of time chatting with Miyamoto who 'placed,' rather than 'sold,' my work.[35] In this respect, my show resembled more a social function than a purely sales venue (which is in part why the impulse buying referred to in the previous paragraph often takes place). As Miyamoto explained:

> People are what business is all about. It's the network of relations between people that really counts. There's a lot of give and take, you know. Precisely because I hold shows here in Tamaya, I'm expected to attend their special functions and buy myself a suit here, a fur coat or jewellery there for my wife. It's all part of the return for favours I've received from the store and it helps cement our business relationship. That's what connections (*tsukiai*) are all about.

It is to this uneasy alliance between aesthetics, money, and social relations that I shall now turn.

CHAPTER 3

Ensemblages of Worth

The interesting thing about creative industries is that they produce cultural goods and services that are 'one-offs,' or, in the words of Lucien Karpik, "singular" products.[1] No film or musical performance is ever *exactly* the same as the one that has gone before it, even when it comprises the same structure and the same personnel (Caves's "nobody knows" property). There are always slight differences in *production*. These differences stem from seemingly unrelated facts: a director has fallen in love with his supporting actress; a musician has had to borrow a clarinet for a concert because she forgot to bring a back-up reed for the one that broke during rehearsal; a technician forgets to angle a spotlight in a particular way because he drank too much the night before; and so on and so forth. These differences extend to audiences. Because their composition is never the same, the *reception* of a creative product or performance can never be the same. The same holds true of other forms of cultural production: computer games, animated cartoons, fashion shows, and magazines. It is this lack of standardization that separates creative from other, mass-produced commodities such as lipsticks, laptops, and loo paper.

As a result, we can say that creative products and performances are, unlike mass-produced goods and services in mass markets, multidimensional 'singularities' that, nevertheless, tend to be found in more or less "stable ranges of valuation."[2] In this respect, they constitute a "world of worth."[3] Take my own pottery exhibition, for example. The fact that each of the affordances outlined in Chapter 1 was inseparable from the significance of all the others in terms of the perception of my pots gave them a structure. Yet they were also characterized by a 'strategic' and 'quality' uncertainty. Miyamoto devoted his considerable knowledge of the ceramic art world in Japan to working out how best, and at what price level, to present to the public a foreigner's work which was unknowable beforehand and therefore its evaluation uncertain. The fact that I was, as a potter, an 'unknown quantity,' meant that my work was also incommensurable.[4] The challenge, then, was to achieve some kind of common agreement among the evaluative criteria applied by all those involved: potters, collectors, retailers, media organizations, consumers, and, of course, myself.

The circuit of affordances outlined in Chapter 1 goes only so far in explaining the creative engagements that took place during the course of arranging the exhibition and how agreement was in fact reached, at least in large part, if we are to judge from final sales. An affordance denotes the possibility of a *relationship* between, originally, an organism and its environment,[5] and specifies a range of possible activities, which are then acted upon by conventions, constraints, and other "matters of concern."[6] But to probe further into that relationship, we need additional theoretical tools. These in themselves will probably not be sufficient to tell us all we need to know in order to understand 'creativity,' but they should at least help us advance the argument.

The previous chapter described in some detail the different kinds of evaluating practices adopted by different participants engaging with an art world. A number of affordances came to the fore in this narrative. First, the fact that, on the one hand, I was studying department store exhibitions and, on the other, believed as an anthropologist in doing what my potter informants did (primarily make pots, but also drink and exchange gossip), led to the proposal that I hold my own pottery exhibition. This led automatically to a consideration of timing, which, once settled, afforded my target audience for sales (potters). Or was it that the existence of potential target audiences afforded the temporal selection? To strengthen this claim, Miyamoto approached a well-known and in character impeccable potter whose endorsement provided the social and symbolic capital necessary for the display of my work in a department store gallery.

At the same time, however, as part of his entrepreneurial search for market 'difference,' Miyamoto broke with established conventions by suggesting that I make both stoneware and porcelain. This possibility was afforded by the fact that I was a foreigner working 'on the edge' of the standard conditions experienced by Japanese potters. Their materials and associated techniques, combined with my own inexperience, brought out a spontaneity and playful improvisation that worked against the grain of established representational ideals (witness Kajiwara Jirō's remark about his not 'daring' to do what I had done). But they also led to a particular pricing strategy predicated on what other potters working with the same materials in the same places charged for their work. Prices were guided by an evaluation of my work, which was itself linked to the media stories or representations that I then provided. Eventual sales took place largely as a result of pre-established social connections.

84 ▣ CHAPTER 3

So the temporal afforded the representational, which afforded the social and techno-material. The latter then afforded the representational again, as well as the economic, which took into account the spatial, which itself afforded the economic (in terms of potential income from limited gallery space), while reflecting in consumer evaluation both the representational and the social. The ensemblage, then, is a veritable merry-go-round of affordances, which inevitably leads to a discussion of the values and worth of cultural products and so makes a contribution to what Michèle Lamont has referred to as the sociology of valuation and evaluation (SVE).[7]

My pottery exhibition may be said to have taken place in the context of what Luc Boltanski and Laurent Thévénot call an "inspired world," in which measures, rules, and laws—as well as, to a lesser extent, money—were absent; witness the privileged singularity at which the exhibition aimed and the uncertainty by which it was surrounded.[8] It was precisely the fact that its result could not be controlled, which ultimately made it a 'worthy' endeavour. Such worth was reinforced both by my own anxiety about my creative capabilities and by an accompanying spontaneity that accepted risk, rejected standard principles, and surrendered itself to unforeseen accidents. The "higher common principle" evoked was creativity itself (albeit imprecise in its content), which made it virtually impossible to separate the techniques that I used to make my pots and the finished pots themselves from my perceived 'uniqueness' as a potter.[9] This state of worthiness was ultimately guaranteed by Imaizumi Imaemon, who served as a reference point (nobody had a bad word to say about him) and contributed to the coordination of others in the ceramic art world. His was the 'unsullied' character of the 'true' artist-craftsman.[10]

To talk of 'worth,' however, invites a clarification of the terms used in the sociology of valuation and evaluation, since many of them—including valuation, evaluation, value, and worth—have often been used in a rather imprecise manner. This isn't all that surprising. Dictionary definitions of each of these words tend to overlap: thus, both *valuation* and *evaluation* can refer to appraising pecuniary *value*, which is itself equated with *worth* as the equivalent of a specified sum or amount.[11] However, since all of these words have secondary meanings that enable the confusion to be overcome, I'm going to use them in the following ways in this book: *valuate* will refer to the act of estimating or fixing the monetary value (or *Value*) of something (and *valuation* to the result of such estimation); *evaluate* to the act of estimating other properties of a cultural product that are not directly related to money or price (and *evaluation* to the result thereof); *Value* (with a capital V) to its monetary worth; and *worth* to the relative merits of such a product in respect of the overall estimation (that is, in terms of both evaluation and valuation) in which it is held.[12] I will use the word *values*, in the plural, to refer to the non-monetary constituents of worth arrived at through acts of evaluation. The question underpinning this chapter is: how might we establish equivalence between the values and Value of an Imaemon pot, Chanel dress, Academy Award, Stradivarius violin, Picasso etching, or other creative product, and so arrive at an estimation of its overall worth?

Values: Clearing the Ground

To say that business anthropology may be seen as a constituent part of the sociology of valuation and evaluation should not be interpreted as an attempt to relegate a subfield of anthropology to a subfield of sociology. On the contrary, my own position is that anthropology itself is, and from its inception has been, in very large part the study of evaluation, valuation, and values. The very fact that the discipline has always focused on cross-cultural comparison makes this abundantly clear. Anthropologists' interest in the *kula* ring, segmentary lineage systems, potlatch, pastoral nomads, irrigation systems, and so on, as well as in cultural concepts dominant in different societies, like honour, shame, patronage, obligation, reciprocity, and so forth, attests to their underlying concern with evaluating what they observe elsewhere and comparing it with what they have experienced in their own lives back home.

All forms of socioeconomic behaviour—as well as all statements, expressions, judgements, and justifications in language use—are motivated and underpinned by 'values' and accompanying evaluative dispositions of one kind or another. Likewise, all objects may be treated as "the trappings or mechanisms of worth."[13] The study of a culture—whether of its social organization, economic structure, religious beliefs, artistic forms, legal system, or other phenomena—is a study of the values that constitute that culture and the evaluations that are practiced by, and negotiated among, the people living therein. In their plural form, values constitute our sociocultural beliefs and moral principles: the criteria by which we judge or evaluate what is worthwhile in our everyday lives.[14] Anthropology, then, is in large part the study of values and their corresponding "tracing of associations" that amount to worth.[15]

In this it differs from, but also in part embraces, the discipline of economics, with which it has engaged in inconclusive arguments over many decades.[16] Most mainstream neoclassical economists regard the notion of Value (they use the singular, not plural, form of the term) as the origin of, and motivation for, all forms of economic behaviour and have built their theories of Value around the concept of a price system and "the technical means for analysing how prices are arrived at."[17] So far as they are concerned, Value relates to economic utility, price, and the worth that individuals and social groups assign to commodities in the market.[18] In its singular form, then, Value has been examined principally as a means towards equating the 'inherent' qualities of commodities with their quantitative worth.

The dichotomy between Value and values—between economists, on the one hand, and sociologists and anthropologists, on the other—has been attributed to "the Parsons' Pact." Many decades ago, when mapping out his ambitious sociological programme, Talcott Parsons more or less came to a tacit agreement with colleagues in the Harvard University economics department that economists would study Value (thereby claiming the economy for themselves), while he and other sociologists focused on values (thereby claiming the social relations in which economies are embedded).[19] As David Stark goes on to argue,[20] this treaty was broken, first by Harrison White when he developed a sociological theory of markets, and later by Luc Boltanski and Laurent Thévenot, who, in arguing that economies consist of multiple principles of evaluation and multiple orders of worth, have been engaged in constructing a sociological theory of value.[21]

In the meantime, proponents of one branch of economics, cultural economics, have also transgressed the Value/values pact by arguing that a distinction should be made between "economic and cultural value, and that it is the nature of these twin concepts of value, how they are formed and how they relate or do not relate to each other, that needs to be investigated."[22] In this, cultural economists have impinged upon the territory of economic sociologists and anthropologists who, for many decades now, have also seen culture and economy as inseparable: the one 'embedded' in the other.[23]

Ironically, while cultural economists have written about, and recognize the part played by, all kinds of values—including the aesthetic, spiritual, social, historical, symbolic, and authenticity values found in artworks,[24] as well as "non-user values" of option, existence, bequest, prestige, and innovative values[25]—they still cling to a theory of Value (in the singular).[26] This is also true of the anthropologist David Graeber, who, in spite of his wide-ranging discussion and analysis of values held by different peoples in different parts of the world, still titled his book *Towards an Anthropological Theory of Value*.[27]

There is, then, a "double discourse" of Value/values: one concerned with money, commerce, technology, industry, production, and consumption, together with the people engaged therein; the other with culture, art, genius, creation, and appreciation, and their proponents.

> In the first discourse, events are explained in terms of calculation, preferences, costs, benefits, profits, prices, and utility. In the second, events are explained—or, rather (and this distinction/opposition is as crucial as any of the others), 'justified'—in terms of inspiration, discrimination, taste (good taste, bad taste, no taste), the test of time, intrinsic value, and transcendent value.[28]

Not surprisingly, perhaps, there is little coherence among the different disciplinary approaches in their conceptualization and measurement of these different kinds of values.[29] This in itself suggests that Stark is justified in calling for an economic sociology (and, by implication, an economic anthropology) that dispenses with "the dualisms of value versus values and economy versus embedded social relations," and takes as its object of study "the sociology of worth": that is, "the ongoing processes of valuation."[30]

And yet, Stark also sees processes of *e*valuation as being "central to the problem of worth." This raises a Janus-faced issue, which has not been entirely resolved in the literature. The problem with assigning the term 'valuate' to the estimation of monetary value and 'evaluate' to other properties not related to money or price is that the very dualism between Value and values that Stark wishes to overcome is reintroduced. This, in my own opinion, is unavoidable. To arrive at any estimation of worth, we need to take into account the patterns of values held by different professional groups occupying different structural positions in different organizations; the ways in which such values are negotiated among them; and how, as a result, they motivate social behaviour. We also need to find out how qualitative values are converted into quantitative Value, on the one hand, and how, on the other, Value itself has an effect on the evaluation of quality (or values). For instance, just as a Picasso painting or unblemished diamond ring signifies a high price tag, so does a high price tag for a painting or piece of jewellery suggest that the artist who painted it *must* be well known (even though s/he may not be Picasso), or that the stones set in the ring are

88 ▣ **CHAPTER 3**

not made from glass. It is this balancing of values with Value that gives rise to an estimation of worth.

In that such processes of valuation and evaluation are always contingent on who is (e)valuating what for whom, when, where, how, why, to what ends, and in what context, we may go further and suggest that, together, they form interrelated 'assemblages,' or *ensemblages*, of worth. Such assemblages encompass, in varying emphases, materials and accompanying techniques; aesthetics and related moral ideologies; organizational and social values underpinning, and underpinned by, names and brands; and the uses to which the objects of valuation and evaluation are put. Ultimately, they afford cultural products themselves, and the (re)e/valuation— or "consecration"[31]—of artworks, books, fashions, films, music, and so on "is one of the central processes in the cultural industries."[32] It is such *ensemblages* of worth that business anthropology can usefully analyse.

The anthropology of worth needs to resolve two further problems beyond nomenclature. First, in some writings,[33] we find that objects are perceived to possess a value of their own, an 'intrinsic value.' This position is also found in the theory of *l'art pour l'art*, which sees an artwork as part of a closed system.[34] If art is an aim and a purpose in itself, as some artists and art historians claim, then sociologists of art cannot begin to explore the means whereby art achieves ends which lie beyond it.[35] Similarly, if absolute worth is claimed to be inherent in cultural objects in general, economists' theory of marginal utility based on the response to an object by an individual consumer becomes superfluous. An individual does not have to experience Value for it to come into being; it is already there.[36] Consequently, the differential in an individual's willingness to pay for one object rather than another cannot be measured as a difference in cultural value.

The position taken here, however, is that there are *no* intrinsic qualities of objects, other than those derived from the materials of which they are made (wood, plastic, alloy, fur, and so on) and the forms that they are afforded (round, square, rectangular, rough, smooth, and so forth). In other words, as an anthropologist, I cannot accept the idea that there is "absolute cultural worth."[37] But does such a position justify economists continuing with their current assumptions when valuating creative products? No, because various individuals in various social worlds assert that there *are* intrinsic qualities in particular cultural goods and, in spite of most economists' desire to the contrary, one cannot ignore what people say and do in their everyday lives.[38] In this way, the waters of the pond are nicely muddied by the leaping of an occasional frog.

A second problem concerns the very nature of economists' reliance on *individual* preferences. David Throsby suggests that the willingness-to-pay principle as an indicator of cultural value runs into difficulty when benefits accrue to individuals *only* as members of a social group.[39] Benefits, therefore, may exist in a collective, rather than in an individual, sense. Taking a leaf out of the theory of values propounded in structural linguistics, I would go further and assert that the 'individual' as such is a meaningless concept (as conceived by economists), except in so far as s/he exists in relation to other 'individuals' (just as the phoneme /i/ in the English language only takes on signification or value vis-à-vis other phonemes therein).[40]

Moreover, individuals experience and negotiate their way through a variety of social worlds, each of which allows them to take on, build, and sustain an 'identity'. It is in such social worlds (of family, for example, or education, work, leisure, and so on) that preferences are formed and acted upon. Preferences formed in one social world (a potter's preference for faience, a musician's for a Smallman guitar, or a golfer's for playing on the St. Andrews Old Course) may make little sense, if any, in another.

The argument that follows stems directly from what I learned during the course of putting on my own pottery exhibition. While the function of economic exchange may be to create Value, all sorts of other, different kinds of values—material, social, temporal, spatial, appreciative, and others—are introduced through the circuit of affordances and promoted as part of the negotiation of the Value of an artwork, fashion collection, book, film, television programme, or other creative product. From this it follows that Value is never an inherent property of objects, but arises from a series of judgments made about those objects by people whose whole lives consist in making such evaluations and valuations. It is these that constitute each *ensemblage* of worth.

In other words, the conceptual meaning of Value or valuation is not itself part of the world, but "the whole world viewed from a particular vantage point."[41] This book shows how particular professional worlds, bounded in space and time, are viewed from the vantage points of different participants for whom the values they hold form a comprehensive part of their world views and are thus a counterpart to their very being. It is those participating in the art, fashion, film, music, or publishing worlds who identify, name, and negotiate what is and what is not important when evaluating a particular cultural product. It is they who establish particular ensemblages of values constituting worth and, in so doing, maintain a boundary around their worlds of worth.

Ensemblages of Worth

Not surprisingly, perhaps, the values that I articulate here form an ensemblage that closely parallels the circuit of affordances outlined in Chapter 1, although I have chosen to represent it differently (Figure 2). During the course of my research, members of the contemporary ceramic art world in Japan regularly distinguished between three different, but complementary, kinds of value or merit, each of which affected the others. One of these they referred to as 'aesthetic value' (*biteki kachikan*) and related specifically to the formal properties of an artwork in the context of the genre in which it was situated. It was in the historical and cultural context of porcelain production, for example, that my pots were judged by ceramic artists such as Imaizumi Imaemon XIII and Tanaka Hajime. 'Aesthetic' values were in this sense historical and part of an evaluative ideology.

Although my informants used the term 'aesthetic,' I prefer the more encompassing term of *appreciative* values. These are primarily, but not exclusively, aesthetic (focusing on such concepts as taste, harmony, creativity, form, style, and so on) and emerge from the ways in which cultural

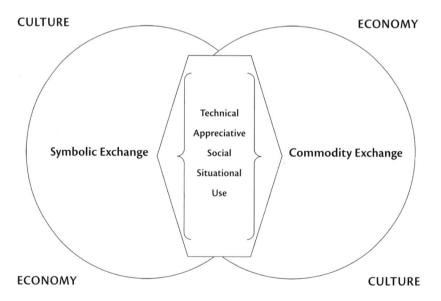

FIGURE 2: Ensemblages of Worth

products are praised or damned by critics in books and other forms of media review (as in "his style is superbly musical and allusive, but the content is vague"). Certain kinds of aesthetic language come to be used for certain kinds of cultural products (think fashion, food, film, or wine), and can even be used to make distinctions within categories. The language used in England and the United States to appraise traditional craft pottery, for instance ('pregnant beauty', 'rounded form'), differs radically from that used to describe less functional sculptural forms ('dynamic masculinity', 'vertical upward thrust'). At the same time, however, such language is not necessarily strictly aesthetic, since product advertising, for example, can make use of a different kind of appreciative language designed to attract consumers to buy the product in question and, ideally, convert it into a 'brand' (think "Guinness is good for you" or L'Oréal's "More beautiful by design"). Appreciative values also include moral judgments (about how to establish monetary equivalences, for example, "for such things as death, life, human organs, and generally ritualized items or behaviour considered sacred"[42]) and legal evaluations (affecting, for instance, copyright in some creative products), so that they are in many respects ideological values which affect the perceived economic (or commodity exchange) Value of a cultural product and its overall worth.

A second kind of value used by my informants in Japan was 'social value' (*shakai kachikan*). This occurred in a variety of forms, some institutional, others more interpersonal, yet others in the form of language use. For instance, the selection of one department store (Tamaya) rather than another (Iwataya) sent out a message to prospective visitors that my exhibition was more 'cultural' than 'sales' oriented. This message was reinforced by my choice of sponsors, who were *not* national newspapers, but appeared to be (and in fact were) cultural organizations far removed from commercial activities. This foregrounding of the cultural over the economic also permitted the main actors—Miyamoto, Tamaya, and the Mainichi newspaper—to adopt a 'carnivalesque' approach to my exhibition, as well as participate in a characteristic 'disavowal' of the importance of its financial outcome.

At the same time, social values were generated through interpersonal connections. One obvious example here was our success in securing the public 'recommendation' of my work by Imaemon, thereby smoothing the path towards its favourable reception by other potters living and working in northern Kyushu. In this respect, Miyamoto merely followed time-honoured practice in the literary (and academic) world:

92 □ CHAPTER 3

As regards getting published, one fact has been observable since at least the eighteenth century—the fortunate situation of anyone who is in personal touch with writers who are well known and have their public and a certain prestige with the publishers. Their recommendation may carry sufficient weight to smooth away the main difficulties for the newcomer. Thus it is almost a rule that the beginner's work does not pass direct from him to the appropriate authority, but takes the indirect and often difficult course past the desk of an artist of repute.[43]

Another example of the importance of social values stemmed from my own foray as a researcher into the ceramic art world. It was because of previously established personal connections that my show was accepted in principle by the institutions concerned (newspaper company, department store, and the British Council), which themselves then conferred social status on myself as an 'artist' by means of their public reputations; so, too, with my 'choice' of Miyamoto, rather than of another gallery owner, to use as go-between. Miyamoto, Tamaya, and the British Council guaranteed a kind of 'pedigree,' offering potential buyers a sense of security about the worth of my work that my name in itself could not afford.[44] It is probably fair to say that none of my most expensive pots would have been sold without this social guarantee. It was only because they did sell that I could in any way be referred to as an 'artist' potter (*tōgei sakka*).

Last, social values underpinned the gossip that pervaded the art world of contemporary Japanese ceramics where having the inside story on a particular person or event indicated weighty connections, and so reflected one's own position within that art world. That this situation was by no means unique may be seen in the following comment on the Western art world:

> The Art Establishment subsists on words—much more, in fact, than it does on pictures. Talk there has more power than elsewhere because decisions are less sure and the consequences of acting on them more uncertain. In this sense, everyone in the art world has power, at least the power to pass the word along, mention names, repeat stock judgments, all of which produce an effect. The first qualification for entering the Art Establishment is to be familiar with its jargon and the people and things most often referred to.[45]

Thus, on the one hand, those who gossip possess and exhibit their knowledge of certain conventions, which define the art world concerned.[46] On the other, by focusing on the personal affairs of participants in an art world, gossip hinders artworks from being evaluated independently of such personalities (a feature, as I have already noted, of an 'inspired' world of worth).[47] The artwork "becomes a success only if…one gets talked about."[48] As a general rule, one can say that the greater the 'buzz,' the higher the prices that can be charged.[49]

Third, members of the ceramic art world talked about 'commodity value' (shōhin kachikan), or, in my phrase, commodity exchange Value: the price attached to an artwork on the basis of the ensemblage of appreciative and social values, and at which it is then exchanged between seller and buyer. The difficulty in establishing a price for an unknown artist was made clear in the previous chapter. Between them, "aesthetic value, social value, and economic value all intertwine to make it difficult to arrive at a reasonable choice" when it comes to buying a pot or other artwork.[50]

Although, as I said, informants themselves clearly distinguished between these three sets of values, my study of evaluative practices associated with creative engagements and ensemblages of affordances brings to light three other values. These I will refer to as technical, situational, and functional.

Let me start with technical values.[51] These consist primarily of materials and associated techniques afforded by materials. As I pointed out in the previous chapter, I had never made porcelain before my exhibition. As a result, when I came to do so, I approached the clay as if it were stoneware and very quickly realized that porcelain clay was extremely dense in structure and totally different from the kind of clay that I had been used to throwing at the wheel. As a result, I had to learn how thick the walls of my pots should be (much, much thinner than in stoneware, but only through trimming), how wide it would be possible to make a foot rim at the base of a pot (much wider), what forms would or would not collapse on the wheel, and so on. As I learned from these affordances, I came to be able to judge their effects and to develop evaluations about which parts of my work were technically 'good' or 'bad,' as I also dealt with other questions relating to decoration, glaze materials, kiln firing, and so forth. In the time available to me, I could not hope to understand all such technical values, but it is their mastery that distinguishes the 'professional' from the 'amateur' potter.

Technical values or evaluations came into play at all stages of the production process: something that we will come across time and time again in this book. For example, I had to decide (sometimes experimenting on the spur of the moment) on which kind of design and which of several glazes to apply to which kind of pots. I had to be careful not to dry pots too fast in the sunshine, as well as to ensure that they dried evenly. Otherwise, they would get warped and cracked in firing. I also needed to ensure that they were fired to the right temperature at an even pace, and to judge when it was appropriate to allow a lot of smoke to generate inside the kiln (known as reduction firing), since this affected the final colouring of the glazes. My evaluation of the overall worth of my own work depended in large part on my evaluation of the success of the techniques and materials that I had used (as well, of course, as on the aesthetic conventions in which I had been socialized as part of my training as a potter).[52]

So, technical values are in part aesthetic (or appreciative), but they are not necessarily shared by nonprofessionals (although critics can make it their business to find out about and highlight them when making aesthetic evaluations of artistic work; see Chapter 11). They also came to light in a more general formulation when I found myself having to make up a story about my work for the benefit of the media. Here, I resorted to a number of technical explanations with regard to the advantages of handmade versus machine-made work, to the use of natural rather than synthetic materials, and so on. The fact that natural materials—a few grams of feldspar in a glaze recipe, for instance—tend to vary in quality, depending on their source and seasonality (as with wood ash, for example), means that it is virtually impossible to reproduce *exactly* the same pot from one firing to the next. It is with such technical unpredictability—occasionally picked up and made into an aesthetic ideal—that potters working with natural materials are always wrestling. Some make a virtue out of it; others try to conquer chance.

Second, there are *situational values.* These came to the fore at two points in preparations for my exhibition. The first of these was connected with timing. *When* my show was to be held was an important consideration for Miyamoto as he set about framing the exhibition. The fact that his wife came up with the suggestion that it be held concurrently with the national Traditional Crafts Exhibition provided the show with a *raison d'être* that had a knock-on effect upon the social evaluation of my work (potters, rather than the general public per se; and Tamaya's agreement to go ahead with the show), as well as on its appreciative values (that it should be seen as 'fun' rather than 'money-making').

Situational values also encompass place. The selection of one department store (Tamaya) over another (Iwataya) established an overall appreciative frame for my work, since the former was seen to be 'cultural' and the latter 'commercial.' The size and rectangular space of the gallery established in large part the overall layout of my work, in terms both of genre (porcelain and stoneware) and size (large versus small). Place also affected the pricing of my pots, since I could not 'afford' to charge more for my work than other potters working in either Koishiwara (stoneware) or Ureshino (porcelain).

Finally, there are *use values*. As part of my technical approach to pottery, like many other potters, I emphasized the uses to which my work might be put. A dish was made to serve food, a vase to hold flowers, a cup to drink tea from, and so on. However, there was no guarantee that my pots would in fact be functional in the manner that, as their creator, I had intended. A vase might end up being placed in its buyer's home as a purely decorative object without holding flowers; a tea cup might serve as a pen and pencil holder; a rice dish might be transformed into a tea ceremony bowl (and vice versa); a set of plates might be put away in their box in a storehouse and kept for the sole purpose of reselling at a profit.[53] Actual use values are almost entirely beyond the artist craftsman's control, since they depend on the purchaser of a work. In this respect, evaluating practices can slip beyond the negotiated conventions of the art world. The engagements that take place are between user and singular product, and not just between singularity and its maker, distributor, or seller.

Together, these different values or evaluations constitute different criteria for valuation. They form a field that influences our selection of various cultural products. Sometimes we are influenced by the beauty of an object, at other times by its utility, craftsmanship, or brand association. We weigh up the different aspects of technical/material, social, situational, appreciative, and use values in every cultural product, and try to calculate their combined *symbolic-exchange value*, which we then test against an economic criterion: money or price. Does this porcelain vase that we like have one too many zeros on its price tag? Does that dress that first attracted us on the clothes rack in a store turn out to be 'cheap and nasty'? If the price established for a product meets our symbolic exchange evaluation, and we decide to purchase a little black dress by Chanel, a photographic print by Helmut Newton, or a dish by Lucie Rie, then we have engaged in what might be termed *commodity-exchange Value*. Although some values may be given more emphasis than others (a fashion model's social recommendations rather than her appreciated beauty per se, or the technical skills achieved by an artist or potter rather than the finished work that each produces), it is here that quality meets quantity, culture meets economy, and values are converted into Value.

As I said earlier, the ensemblage of worth outlined here in large part parallels the circuit of affordances proposed in Chapter 1. Where they build on the concept of affordance, however, is in their ability to provide a coordinating framework for the virtually *simultaneous* interpretation, evaluation, judgement, and calculation of singularities.[54] What do I mean? When making, criticizing, selling, or buying an artwork, different participants in an art world interpret, evaluate, judge, and calculate its technical, appreciative, social, situational, and use values, which they then calculate and convert into the artwork's overall 'symbolic' value.

At the same time, precisely because they are dealing with a market of singularities, they interpret, evaluate, judge, and calculate, on the basis of this symbolic value, the price at which it *should* be bought or sold. This is the potential commodity exchange (or economic) Value of the product in question. It is the moment when evaluation judgement becomes a calculative decision.[55] The question is: will the symbolic value—transformed into a price—as estimated by the seller, be accepted by the buyer? If so, a transaction (or exchange) ensues. If not, the buyer may either resort to bargaining, as a means towards establishing parity between the seller's and her own symbolic/commodity exchange values until they both concur and money is exchanged for the artwork, or she will simply walk away from the deal.[56]

The interaction between symbolic and commodity exchange values is mutual and coordinating. On the one hand, the commodity exchange Value of an artwork almost certainly increases or decreases in proportion to the density of the other values found therein.[57] At the same time, economic Value (in terms of price) can itself quickly generate symbolic and associated values (an artwork *that* expensive must be 'good'). In other words, the various processes of (e)valuation described here enable the mutual, ongoing transformations of 'culture' and the 'economy' in which we all engage. It is with these transformations and with how people juggle the different values as they engage with creative works of one kind or another that many of the remaining chapters in this book are concerned.

Theoretical Extensions

One advantage of the approach to the study of values of cultural products outlined here is that it accounts for their ongoing social construction and negotiation as people go about their everyday lives. Another is that it links the evaluation of commodities with more general evaluative practices in social worlds, or fields, and thereby complements previous theorizing of values in terms of *social relations*. For instance, Pierre Bourdieu has argued that all kinds of different interests are at stake in every field, and that participants invest in these and often compete for control of the resources of the field in which they operate.[58] Such resources are sometimes material, sometimes social, sometimes ideological or symbolic, and the way that they are distributed defines each field.

Bourdieu developed the concept of "capital" to describe these resources, and analyzed the various forms of economic, educational, cultural, social, and symbolic capital that *people* try to build up, before converting it into another form that they lack, as part of their struggle for power in a particular field: something to which we will return below. Thus a designer who has graduated from a prestigious fashion school can use her educational capital to obtain a job with a well-known fashion house and thereby convert her educational into social and cultural, and thence economic, capital. A fashion model who appears on the cover of *Vogue* (for little more than US $200) can use the symbolic capital accrued to increase her rates for other magazine fashion shoots or an advertising campaign. Similarly, a traditional potter who is designated the holder of an Important Intangible Cultural Property by Japan's Ministry of Culture can convert this newly acquired symbolic capital into economic capital by raising his prices three- or four-fold overnight. In other words, people are trying to capitalize on a particular situation and turn it to their advantage, depending on their position in a particular field of cultural production. The conversion of different forms of capital is made possible by the different values that different people bring to bear on their activities depending on their positions within a particular field or social world.

The approach to the study of values proposed here examines the *things* produced by people making use of different forms of capital. It suggests that a designer dress, fashion model,[59] or stoneware pot is 'beautiful' not in itself, but because of the different technical, social, situational, appreciative, utility or use, symbolic, and commodity exchange values that are associated with its aesthetic and commercial judgement. Such an approach stresses their ongoing social construction and negotiation of things as we go about our everyday lives.[60] Different people in a social world will tend to stress different kinds of values: a seamstress is likely to be more focused on technical/material values, and a fashion designer on aesthetic values, than a fashion model for whom social networks are more important, while for the consumer the wearability (utility) of a garment is probably a decisive factor in the symbolic-commodity exchange equation. Similar considerations come into play in the art, film, music, and other creative worlds, and they tend to take centre stage in events like art fairs and exhibitions, film festivals, and so on, where cultural products are on display and transformations of symbolic values regularly take place.[61]

Now that a theory of worth has been proposed, we need to ask how we can best put it into effect. In particular, we might ask how and how much each of the technical, social, situational, appreciative, and use values contributes to the equation between symbolic- and commodity-exchange values. In other words, how are qualitative values to be measured in quantitative terms? Is it possible to convert values into Value? How are we to (e)valuate ensemblages of worth?

The short answer is that we do not yet know. We can, however, make a stab at finding out answers to these questions. For example, given that fashion houses regularly supply film stars with the latest fashionable dresses to be worn in the full media glare accompanying the Oscar awards, and given that these same fashion houses are in possession of week-by-week sales of each item made, one should be able to correlate media reportage of the Oscars with sales reports. This would indicate the extent to which both the situational (Academy Awards) and social (star) values of a particular dress take on a symbolic connotation that is transformed into commodity-exchange Value. Over time, by tracking other media appearances of the same star in the same dress (or of the same star wearing a different dress produced by the same fashion house; or of a different star wearing the same, or a different, dress, and so on), it should also be possible to isolate a film star's social value from the particular context of the Oscar awards, as well as the quantitative differences in social value brought to fashion items by a hierarchy of film stars. This hierarchy of social values could then be set against the actual sums of money earned by each actress for every film in which she appears, together with its box office success (or lack thereof), to see if there is a further correlation between symbolic and commodity exchange values.

A similar experiment could be conducted with pottery exhibitions in Japan. We have already noted that department stores are ranked according to a social value based on prestige, with metropolitan stores ranking higher than provincial ones, and Tokyo stores placed at the pinnacle of the hierarchy, with Mitsukoshi and Takashimaya department stores battling it out for top spot among traditional artist craftsmen. At the same time, while there is some, but by no means exact, correlation between department store rankings and overall sales generated, potters themselves are ranked according to the sales that they generate from their one-man exhibitions. However, this ranking is blurred in a number of ways. First, the prices potters give to each of their works depends not only on prices charged and sales made at their previous shows; some potters are able to charge more for their work because of direct lineage, in the form of master-apprentice relations, with famous forebears (social value). Second, their pricing mechanism is also affected by reviews of their work by critics and museum curators (appreciative value). Third, as a general rule, porcelain is priced higher than stoneware, although exceptions exist, especially with regard to stoneware pots made according to the Japanese tea ceremony tradition (technical [material] and appreciative values).

Given this information, it should once more be possible to measure through exhibition sales the social value of department stores and master-apprentice relations.[62] Similarly, by taking critical appraisal into account, we can measure the effects of appreciative value on a potter's pricing practice. Moreover, given that potters frequently contribute to national and regional ceramics exhibitions, there should be little difficulty in gauging further the economic effects of success in having work accepted for one or more exhibitions, as well as for prizes awarded therein (with accompanying media exposure, something we will come back to in Chapter 10). It should also be possible to establish a rough correspondence between exhibition prizes and overall appreciative value, in the manner calculated for film awards.[63]

But, it may be asked, what of technical and use values? How, if at all, do they come into play in the calculation of Value? Clearly, they occupy less-central positions in the overall schema of worth, since, as a general rule, technical values are held by producers and use values by consumers of cultural goods. However, there are circumstances in which each interacts with other values. For example, one of the marked features of pottery appreciation in Japan (and often of art appreciation worldwide) has been an elision of the appreciative value of the *product* with that of the *producer*. This is demonstrated by master-apprentice relations (facilitating the transmission of knowledge and experience) and social value.[64] At the same time, though, a critic will often relate details of an individual potter's working environment and incorporate the technical values held by her in his overall aesthetic appreciation of her work. In this way, technical values are transformed into appreciative values, which may then be quantitatively evaluated in one of the ways suggested here.

Use values provide a sterner test of ingenuity. If we continue with the example of pottery, we can see that in part, use values constitute a form of

100 ▣ CHAPTER 3

consumer feedback. Thus, one form of slip decoration known as 'chattering' (or *tobiganna* in Japanese) leaves the surface of a dish or bowl uneven. Although this is acceptable to consumers who use wooden chopsticks, to those preferring metal or silver cutlery the surface of the dish emits an unpleasant, grating noise while eating. Pottery aficionados, therefore, have been known to ask a potter to reserve this form of decoration for the outer surface of a dish and to leave the inner surface smooth. This in itself *may* have an effect on critical appreciation if the new style conflicts with experts' opinions about what constitutes the 'tradition' of the pottery style in question.

A second example of the effect of use value may be seen in the conversion of traditional folk pottery functional jars into decorative forms. In the community of Sarayama (Onta), on the southern island of Kyushu, Japan, potters were known for the functional wares that they made for rural homes. These consisted, among other forms, of large storage jars for pickled vegetables, soy sauce, and water. These were all priced more or less the same according to volume, since they used more or less the same amount of materials (clay and glazes) and took up the same amount of space in the kiln in which they were fired.

During the post–World War II boom in folk art, however, urban consumers began to demand smaller versions of these pots for use as tableware. At the same time, they continued to buy the large storage jars, but they did not use them for soy sauce and pickled vegetables. Instead, they used them as decorative works and placed them in the *tokonoma*, a 'sacred' space in the main room of a Japanese home. As a result, the prices for such jars charged by potters and gallery intermediaries were increased by as much as ten times. Water jars, however, which consumers now bought to be used as umbrella stands, only sold for twice their previous price because they were placed in the *genkan* or ground-level entrance to a raised Japanese-style house, where shoes are taken off and put on by those going in and coming out of the home. The *genkan* is both physically and symbolically 'below' the interior space and thus does not merit the same appreciative value.[65] Here, functional, social, and appreciative values coalesce nicely as symbolic- and commodity-exchange values. With the notable exception of affective values, the apparently immeasurable becomes measurable. This is the aim of ensemblages of worth.

CHAPTER 4

Shooting an Ad Campaign

Creative engagements, then, bring six different sets of value into play to form ensemblages of worth. Sometimes, it is the situation that is first and foremost in people's minds as they dream up a new advertising campaign or go about preparing the next issue of a fashion magazine. At other times, it is who they have to work with, or for, that concerns them most. At some stages of the work process, materials and aesthetic ideals take precedence; at others, what it is the client really wants; at yet others, what one can realistically achieve within the limitations of a budget and time scale for completion. For the most part, creative people engage with all—or at least most—of these values simultaneously; sometimes, one or two of them dominate as others recede into the background. But they are always there all of the time, ready to be picked up and juggled in the creative process, although, as often as not, the only thing that ends up in the air are the despairing hands of the potter, copywriter, fashion editor, and so on. That is what comes of engaging in the game of values and affordances.

I suggested at the beginning of the last chapter that my pottery exhibition took place in the context of what Luc Boltanski and Laurent Thévenot have called an "inspired world."[1] But, given that I was working in a somewhat different cultural context, my readers may well wonder if a set of theoretical propositions developed by two French academics can be applied *in specie* to a similar phenomenon in Japan. Before going further, therefore, I should perhaps add that when considering 'creativity' in Japanese ceramics, the higher common principle for both potters and critics is 'detachment' (*mushin*; literally "no heart") rather than inspiration per se. Detaching oneself (*mu ni naru*) involves surrendering oneself to nature (*shizen ni makaseru*), and it is this that gives rise to that state of worthiness known as "humanity" (*ningensei*). Without humanity a craftsman cannot create "beauty" (*bi, utsukushisa*), and his or her pots will be judged negatively, if s/he is perceived not to have properly developed as a human being (*ningen wa dekite inai*) and tries to assert his or her "self" to be noticed (*jibun o medatataseru*). Such development depends in large part on a person's "spirit" (*kokoro*; literally, "heart"), which has to be put into creative work (*kokoro no komotta shigoto; kokoro ga haitte inai to ikenai*) for it to display charm

102 ▣ **CHAPTER 4**

(*miryoku*), serenity (*yasuragi*), generosity (*yutakasa*), familiarity (*hita-shimi*), intimacy (*najimi*), playfulness (*asobi*), and joy (*tanoshimi*).

There are two paradoxes at work here. First, the Japanese word for detachment is literally "no heart" (*shin* being a variant reading of the Chinese character used to write *kokoro*). And yet, to be 'detached,' one must somehow instil one's heart in what is being made. In this respect, creativity for Japanese appears to lie in the animation of a *thing*, rather than in the *person* making that thing. And second, detachment leads to an involvement between maker and user (*hito to hito to no kakari ai*), so that creativity lies more in a social relationship *between people,* rather than in a singular individual.

In this respect, as Boltanski and Thévenot observe for the inspired world, "the objects and arrangements that equip worth are not detached from persons."[2] Thus we find that hands and body are as important as the head in learning (*tada atama de oboeru no janakute, te de oboe, karada de oboeteiru*), while in appreciation a pot becomes "familiar to the skin" (*hada ni hitashimu*), allowing a "taste to float up to the surface" (*aji ga ukande kuru*). A pot should also have a "scent" (*kaori*). Uniqueness, the relation of worth in the inspired world, is expressed in the detached world through difference (*chigau aji; kawatta katachi*), novelty (*atarashisa*), rarity (*mezurashisa*), and accompanying *divertissement* (*omoshirosa*), rather than through such ideas as 'genius' and 'originality,' although "individual character" (*kosei*) and "freedom" (*jiyu*) are highly valued.

Although this is by no means a complete rendering of the detached world of worth in Japan's ceramic art world, it is sufficiently complete, I think, to suggest that perceptions of 'creativity' in Japan operate according to slightly different premises from those found in Europe and America. This point will become clearer as we turn to a different form of cultural production: advertising. In the following ethnographic case study and in the chapter that ensues, I'm going to focus in particular on what I perceive to be embedded structural tensions in the organization of creativity in Japanese advertising production because these will help us understand when, why, and how what is generally recognized as 'creativity' comes about. Such structural tensions arise from the fact that an advertising campaign, like many other creative products (including my own pottery exhibition), is conceived and produced by 'motley crews' of personnel from both within an agency contracted to dream up and prepare the campaign (an account team) and external freelance professionals hired to assist in the creative work required to put it into effect (a production team). As we shall see, the formation of such motley crews is often founded upon what participants themselves call 'encounters,' and it is these encounters and ensuing engagements that 'afford' creativity.

A Day in the Life of an Ad Campaign

The Meiji Seimei Life Insurance (MLI) advertising campaign is being filmed over three days in the last week in July, when the temperature is hovering in the high nineties and more or less the last place anybody wants to be is outside in the streets of Tokyo. One way to avoid the heat is to film early in the morning, and a five o'clock start was first proposed by the agency's creative director, but the campaign celebrity, a rock singer called Watanabe Misato, retorted that there was no way she was ever going to get up at that unearthly hour of the morning. So I find myself accompanying Honma, a young woman assistant in the advertising agency Asatsū's Creative Division, to the Yanagibashi Bridge round about noon. Two or three people from the production company are sitting on the corner of the junction beyond the bridge over one of Tokyo's many canals leading into the Sumida River, and up a small driveway to a large building called Cosmetics Hall is parked a minibus, where we help ourselves to *onigiri* rice balls and *mugicha* barley tea. The bus engine is running to keep the inside air-conditioned, and several people sit or lie inside, taking the occasional call on the bus's portable phone (this in those halcyon days before mobile phones became *de rigeur*). Otherwise, nothing much is happening.

Ten minutes later, five young models turn up with a chaperone who greets two agency personnel like old friends. The girls stand around in very tight, very short skirts, and compare their suntanned arms to see whose is darkest. They are soon led off to get changed in the 'makeup' building, where—I am told—a room has been rented for the day, and a few minutes later a taxi draws up and the hair stylist arrives with his assistant. At first glance it's hard to tell whether it's a 'he' or 'she' who has joined us, for s/he wears shoulder-length hair, a white blouse, skirt-like shorts, short white socks with sandals, and a blue floppy jacket. I am assured that while Saburō (that's his name) may be bisexual, he's the best hair stylist in the business.

Next, a large Hino motorhome, with "Midship Engine and Suspension" printed on the back window, rolls up. At least half a dozen people are sitting inside. This is the 'location bus,' where Misato will have her hair and makeup done, and it is backed slowly into the driveway. In the meantime, the models come out and walk off together down the road, giggling in the clichéd way that young women are supposed to behave when together in small groups. A small covered van with "Nitten Shuchō Party" written on its side draws up, advertising "Bentō packed lunches with the taste of Japan." One of the girls working for the production company runs across the road to get the order, but needs help to carry the two large boxes back across to the shadow of the driveway, where all sorts of things are being unpacked from the location bus, including half a dozen walkie-talkies and the clothes that Misato is to wear for filming. By now, two dozen people are standing or milling around. Basically, the agency people (who include the creative director's three-person TV commercial team, plus two from the magazine ad creative department, and two more from the Account Services Division who are accompanying the client, MLI's product development manager) are standing around; the production company people are doing the milling, with the girl in jeans running everywhere, as she does for the rest of the day.

Misato arrives in a silver BMW driven by her manager and goes straight into the location bus to have her hair and face done. The models come back with packed lunches and cans of juice bought locally as we tuck into our luxurious repasts. It transpires that they have nothing to do with our filming, but are doing some work in the Cosmetics Hall.

At 1:15 p.m., some of us go off purposefully with Ishii, the creative director, and Mori the cameraman in search of camera angles. The former thought it might be good to film from the concrete parapet running along the edge of the Sumida River at just above water level, but we soon find that it is impossible to get down there. Two barges loaded with garbage are towed out from under the Yanagi Bridge into the main river. It is very hot. Mori eventually decides on a position to one side of the bridge, after he has climbed over some barbed wire to get to it. He sits perched on the edge of a concrete parapet high above the river with camera between his knees and— at 1:40 p.m.—a stand-in is brought on to pose on the bridge. A young girl who more or less resembles Misato in size and shape, she wears the same clothes that the singer is to wear: white T-shirt, black slacks, white sneakers, and golden brown jacket. She is instructed to stand here and there, and once the position is fixed, an assistant sticks two strips of brown tape in a T shape on the pavement by the railing of the bridge. Another—sweating profusely—checks the light on the stand-in's face before climbing back over the wire barricade and adjusting the camera shutter opening. Yet another assistant brings up some silver reflection panels to direct light onto the stand-in's face. A young woman passes by in a purple dress that shows off her rather large breasts. A couple of the agency men comment on them in low voices, before one breaks out into a loud peal of laughter.

In the meantime, Mori has taken two shots of the stand-in—one in black and white, the other in colour—and is having the Polaroid prints developed. He and Ishii check them, agree that everything is okay, and wait for Misato. The production company girl runs off to the minibus and comes back with a cushion for the cameraman. Another young man from the same company starts chatting up the stand-in, telling her how beautiful she is and what a waste that she is only a stand-in, and not a model in her own right. It transpires that she is a junior college student earning pocket money (¥30,000 a day), and that this is her very first job of this kind. She finds it all very exciting.

Pedestrians pass by curiously. Drivers—sensing that something is happening although they cannot tell what—slow down and peer sideways through the bridge's heavy green iron girders. Misato's manager sits in the front seat of his BMW and puts in his contact lenses. The MLI publicity manager arrives. He is almost the only person on the bridge wearing a suit and tie, and he fans himself from time to time with an expensive-looking collapsible fan. It is hot, but at least there is a slight breeze blowing off the Sumida River, the lifeblood of the city.

There is a lot of hanging around while the hair and makeup people finish their jobs, but at last—at 2:28 p.m.—Misato appears, walking under a white parasol held for her by an assistant as the androgyn, Saburō, fusses around her, applying finishing touches to her frizzled curls, and the stylist dabs off one or two specks from her soft suede jacket. Ishii explains to her where she is to stand and what needs to be done (the still shots first) before Misato smiles into the camera, leaning against the bridge's railing and gazing wistfully out across the river. Mori starts shooting and, whenever he pauses to change film, the androgyn darts forward to touch up her hair here and there. The breeze is just strong enough on the bridge to dislocate the curls over her forehead.

A couple of these test shots are shown to Misato, who seems to be very conscious of her neck and ears. She points to the print and says something, while the androgyn polishes her fingernails. We get ready to shoot once more and Saburō manages to get one snap taken with himself and Misato between rolls (when an assistant stands beside her with a parasol over her head to protect her from the sun). For the most part, though, Mori carries on pressing the shutter of his Hasselblad as Misato, without prompting, adopts various poses as already agreed upon with Ishii during one of their late-night meetings.

At 2:44 p.m., enough shots for one of the print ads have been taken, and Misato is ushered back to the location bus for a few minutes of touching up while the camera team moves its equipment and the stand-in stands in. Within a few minutes Misato is back and the whole process starts once more, with the usual brief stoppages for film changes, pedestrians, and hair adjustments. I count 35 people standing around, most of them doing very little. Mori keeps shooting, while his assistants start setting up the movie camera in his original position on the parapet above the river.

The second scene is finished at exactly three o'clock, when the sun goes behind a cloud. Now Ishii takes over properly and arranges for the television monitor to be set up so that he can watch each take. The head of the production company finds himself making apologies to a couple of shop owners who have complained about all the equipment left lying around in front of their establishments, and he gets one of his assistants to take them boxes of rice crackers to atone for the inconvenience caused. In the meantime, all eyes are turned towards the sky, which is ominously grey. It looks as if we are going to get a summer shower, and that is worrying. A studio light is brought onto the bridge and wired up to a portable generator, which is started up for the Morse transmitter Misato is to hold. It works excellently and is taped to the iron railing of the bridge, on the other side of which a group of women has gathered and gazes curiously across the road. Fingers are pointed, mouths bared to reveal toothy, knowing grins, or brows knitted in puzzled frowns. Even the young petrol station attendants with their dyed ginger hair come halfway across the road to see what's going on, after they have ushered out a couple of cars from the station forecourt and bowed to their departing back mirrors.

At 3:28 p.m., Misato is called; seven minutes later, after the usual adjustments to hair and clothes and a last minute addition of tape to the Morse transmitter, we are ready to go. Ishii goes up to Misato and briefs her briefly. The first take is shot and more instructions are given after Ishii has gazed into the monitor. Pedestrians are restrained from crossing the bridge and the production company assistants are very busy with their walkie-talkies, trying to work out when they can release their temporary—and often confused—hostages.

Both Ishii and Mori are satisfied with the second take, but decide to do one more for safety's sake. Misato suddenly wants to see it herself, but Ishii has forgotten to tape it on video, so we do it again. More pins are placed in Misato's hair by the androgyn as we wait for the traffic to clear a bit. It's all over by 3:42 p.m., although the videotaping hasn't worked properly and Misato looks a bit peeved. Ishii is apologizing profusely and promises to show her rushes of the takes that evening if she wishes.

Now there's a lot of movement. The camera team packs up all its equipment, puts it away in the van, and drives off to the other side of the Sumida River for a long-distance shot of Misato with her Morse transmitter blinking across the city's heartbeat. "I love you," goes the message tapped out on a button by one of the production company's temporary employees. Ishii goes with them and Misato returns with Saburō—the loving, friendly, chatty, girlish androgyn—to the location bus. Some of the production company people wait at either side of the bridge. Two or three of us stand in the centre keeping the stand-in from getting too lonely and bored. There's a long wait as nothing happens and even the walkie-talkies grow quiet. The clouds gather even more ominously. The sun has gone. But it's sultry and still very hot.

At 4:30 p.m., Ishii suddenly appears in a sweat from the other side of the Sumida River to say that the shot has been postponed. The light's all wrong. We'll do it the day after tomorrow once the studio session has finished. In the meantime, we can go off to Toyomi to film the third of the commercial's seven cuts with Misato standing by the sea. The delay will also allow her to see today's takes and permit a retake if she doesn't like them.

There's a lot of packing up: of generator, chairs, boxes, lights. The Morse transmitter's wires are removed from the bridge's railing and the tape peeled off. The odds and ends of our sojourn are also collected—from the cameraman's cushion to discarded cigarette ends—and the production company girl in her jeans does even more running around, her face as calm and unperturbed as ever. Finally, we move off from the shade of the Cosmetics Hall, and most of us fall asleep during the twenty-minute ride. At 5:03 p.m., we're unpacking all the essentials—generator, lights, reflector panels—while the stand-in sits on a quayside bollard with her back to Tokyo Bay and the city beyond, where a ferry boat comes into dock and a fireboat sprays its hoses spectacularly in the late afternoon light.

Ishii explains to Mori what he wants. Everyone else is standing around in groups of four or five: the camera crew, the lighting assistants, MLI representatives with the agency account executives. Some of them practice their almost inevitable golf swings, something which Honma reckons brings out the very worst and most boring in Japanese men. One assistant threads the wire to the Morse transmitter through the sleeve of Misato's suede jacket. A hydrofoil approaches close to the quayside. Is it really going to moor at the very bollard that we want to film? At the last minute, the captain moves the vessel away into the mouth of the river. Like others, he was merely curious. The camera equipment is being unloaded from the van now, while a couple of production company assistants are sweeping the quayside clean of cigarette ends, empty bottles of vitamin juice, used fireworks: the usual litter that accumulates at deserted places where people, for one reason or another, like to gather on odd occasions.

It's 5:50 p.m. and, after a lot of camera angle shifts and lens changes, we are ready to go. Misato is walkie-talked out of her location bus and Ishii points out the jellyfish in the water before talking her through the scene they are about to shoot. The stand-in is still in position so Misato can get an idea of what he means. Then she takes over. More pins in her hair, as Ishii decides to make her stand rather than sit. An assistant cameraman measures the distance between her face and the camera lens with a tape measure, and away we go. Mori seems quite satisfied; Ishii, too. Fine, but let's do one more for good measure.

Next to a sitting position. More instructions and two takes, but Saburō looks *very* worried about how her hair looks on film and brings out a whole army of pins to attach here and there in an attempt to curb the singer's curls as they are blown awry by the sea breeze. By 6:06 p.m., however, the final take is shot and all is over. Misato is ushered back to the location bus, where she cleans off most of the makeup before being driven away by her manager in the silver BMW. The rest of us pack up our equipment and leave separately: camera crew in their van, agency men in the luxury of the location bus. This, they all agree, is the only way to travel in Tokyo!

Putting the Creative Brief into Practice

Over the years, MLI, which is a prominent member of the Mitsubishi Industrial Group, had steadfastly refused to use a 'talent' (the Japanese-English word for generally short-lived celebrities) in its commercials and was the only one of the major life insurance companies not to do so. As a result, when it came to the recruitment of new employees, MLI found that it was the lowest ranked company among its rivals, being seen to be "stiff" (*katai*), "gloomy" (*kurai*), and "stuck up" (*ebatteru*). So it decided to celebrate the appointment of a new company president and the company's 110th anniversary by asking Asatsū to produce a new campaign using a celebrity. The agency responded by saying that what its client needed was not just a television commercial, but a whole 'movement' to attract attention, and the creative director, Ishii, decided to make use of a rock artist called Watanabe Misato. Although she didn't appear on TV very often, she had an enormous following among high school and university students who—I was told as part of my briefing—regarded her as rather like the goddess of some new religious movement and felt 'reborn' when they heard her songs.

Ishii decided not to bother with making a visual mock-up of his campaign idea for MLI since the executives he had to deal with were all too old to understand Watanabe Misato. Instead, he just showed them a close-up of the singer's face, and somehow managed to get the idea accepted. The first commercial, shown from April that year, was an enormous success, its impact gauged by the fact that, in the space of just two and a half months, MLI had jumped in the recruitment ranks from 88th in the previous year to 41st in the current one. People were writing in, saying that if the company gave them a poster or telephone card of Misato they would take out life insurance at once. The publicity department employee in charge of the campaign was promoted to department head as a result!

The basic objective behind the first commercial, in what was now an ongoing campaign, was to link MLI and Misato and anchor that link in people's minds. The singer wasn't required to do any dancing, singing, or acting. The commercial merely showed a close-up of her face for most of its fifteen-second duration. However, the new commercial had to delve deeper in search of the 'real' Misato and show how she had 'meaning' for MLI. After all, it wasn't just her popularity that had created the first commercial's success. She was seen to be different from the usual singing 'talent' in that she had her own lifestyle, her own individuality; it was this 'presence' that now had to be dug out to show her 'life' in the context of Meiji Life Insurance. The idea was to film her as she was, 'life-size,' rather than place her in some kind of false dramatic situation suggesting she was something else.

This was where bisociations began to be found in the creative brief. The concept of 'life' was then linked to Misato's 'way of life,' which was itself connected with 'information.' This she got from her audiences and returned to them in song. So the theme of the new commercial was to be 'signal,' where Misato would stand in some crowded street or crossing sending out Morse signals with a torch or transmitter, while everyone passed by without paying any attention. At the same time, the creative director, Ishii, wanted to give the commercial special 'tension' by inserting one monochrome cut in the colour video and by using 8 mm rather than 35 mm film (to make it very coarse and so give it 'reality').

The signal itself wasn't fixed. It could be something like "I love you," "Thank you," or something like that. What Ishii hoped was that the media would take it up and discuss the message. In other words, he wanted to create word of mouth communication (*kuchikomi*), or 'buzz'. The exact message he would decide with Misato, with whom he had been working closely because she liked to be involved in the making of the commercials and had her own 'creative' ideas. Indeed, when he briefed me, he'd been talking to her until two o'clock that morning. He vowed that he'd never met such a serious 'talent' and, as a result, now found himself involved in the actual story line and the production of the film: jobs he'd normally have passed over to a production company after the client presentation stage. Misato had asked him personally to stay on, since she didn't want others to be brought in. However serious and cooperative she might seem, though, Misato was like almost everyone else in the world of entertainment, and one of Ishii's main tasks was to make sure that her feathers weren't ruffled and that all went smoothly.

In a meeting prior to shooting the commercial, Ishii as creative director was very much in charge as he briefed five colleagues from his own agency, and six from a subcontracted production company (producer, assistant producer, cameraman, production manager, assistant manager, location, and creative). His aim, he explained, was to show Misato mainly in close-up: not in the 'bright' manner of the previous commercial, but this time in such a way as to bring out her 'inner' self, hence the transmitter to be used as a signal.

This apparently simple objective raised a number of technical and other issues. For example, the first cut of three to four seconds should consist of a close-up of the upper half of Misato's body, with the Morse transmitter held just below her breasts. She should be neither smiling, nor crying. The cameraman should also make use of a zoom-back technique while circling Misato from front to side. How far back? To about the knees.

A number of questions were then raised about the nature of the transmitter. Was it to be a sharp beam—something like sunlight—or a softer ray? "Just signal-ish," replied Ishii, which meant that filming would have to take place in the very late afternoon, at that 'magic time' when it was neither light nor dark, unless they filmed at dawn. But wouldn't filming at dusk be too 'sad' for the mood the creative director was aiming for? Perhaps it would be better to film in daylight and doctor the video with filter work to bring in 'tone.' That was fine, provided that tone wasn't interpreted as purple or even pinkish blue. They needed to aim for a whitish purple.

And what about the transmitter itself? Ishii didn't want anything trendy or new, like the machine in a magazine photo shown him by the assistant producer, but instead something old-fashioned, like the square lamps one used to find on the front of bicycles in the old days. Probably the best thing would be for the production company to make its own signaling machine, rather than go around trying to find one in the shops. But should Misato herself work it? Or should it be done by technicians? The latter option would save Misato a lot of worry.

Another discussion concerned location. At some point, Misato needed to be filmed standing in the middle of a big pedestrian intersection, in which case a crane would be necessary. The question was: where? The Ginza atmosphere was too "expensive"; Shinjuku too "scruffy"; Harajuku too "impish." Only Shibuya offered the right range of people passing to and fro in the background. But videos of pedestrian crossings in each of these areas revealed that it was going to be impossible to film Misato there live. There was in some cases only a 40-second interval between red and green traffic light signals, and once people recognized Misato they would start crowding round her asking for her autograph. Even without this, there was the question of how long one could film a full cut of her without people getting in the way on a crossing.

This realization led to the suggestion that they make use of the old railway yards at Shiodome, where there were several hectares of open space and the production team could create its own intersection by bringing in extras. The summer vacation would have started by filming time, so there should be plenty of students available.

Then there was the bridge scene. The production company had prepared colour photographs on white boards, showing various bridges that could be used for one of the cuts. One problem here concerned surrounding buildings and hoardings. They would all have to be checked beforehand, since MLI would object if any of the buildings filmed in its commercial belonged to a direct competitor or firm from a rival industrial group. The problems seemed to be insuperable. One bridge had Casio, Visa, and JCB hoardings conspicuously topping distant buildings behind it; another had a giant crane looming over a construction site nearby; yet another had an overhead expressway which blunted the bridge's arched form; all the bridges across the Sumida River itself were too wide. The production company had also taken video of other possible locations: a rival industrial group's railway train passed behind one bridge, and its beer company head-quarters stood beside another!

Another problem pointed out by the cameraman was that most of these bridges shook because of passing traffic. As a result, it would be impossible to get good shots of Misato except in the early morning when traffic was light, unless we could find a bridge that was comparatively quiet during working hours. There was one such bridge, in fact, but the scene was ruined by a jumble of moored *yakatabune* entertainment barges where salary men wined and dined at nights. Moreover, the nearest bridge to it was only just within reach of a 300 mm zoom lens and, since Misato had to be filmed from another bridge, the barges couldn't be framed out of the cut.

Having got most details of the commercial settled (for the time being, at least), the production team turned its attention to the accompanying still photographs for the magazine advertising part of the campaign. Here the idea was to use the bridge scene, but photographing Misato not from the front, as before, but from the side to show her profile and hence her "inner self" (*sic*). The main concern here was that the rock singer wouldn't be able to jump from commercial filming to still photography just like that, since she wasn't a professional model and didn't know how to pose at will. This meant that the agency would have to draw up a fairly strict schedule for each part of the campaign, so that she knew precisely what was to come when. Everyone agreed that it would be better to use natural locations for the posters, but the art director would also book a studio for the three days, just in case. Finally, there were stylists and makeup artists to decide on and hire, but Misato's manager was in Osaka and couldn't be contacted, so that would have to be left for now.

Summer Winter Clothes

The second day of filming dawns bright and hot. Today we have arranged to film in the wide space of Shiodome, the old railway goods yard in the centre of Tokyo near Shinbashi, and now used for the occasional summer beer tent, disco, or cultural event. The two buses are parked under the roof of the old station, separated by two white cloth–covered reception tables, a dozen rows of chairs, and more trellis tables on which are placed iceboxes filled with cans of juice and tea. As usual, the minibus engines—and those of a nearby car—have been left running to allow internal air conditioning systems to work. Inside one young man is sound asleep on the back seat.

Today's the day when extras are to be used. Honma and I have already wandered round most departments in Asatsū, trying to recruit people here and there for this part of the commercial, and a dozen or so of this year's new recruits have turned up, glad, it seems, to escape the boredom of their company training. Others have been recruited through a couple of model agencies, and each is obliged to check in at the reception desk, where s/he is issued with a badge on which has been written the simple letter *A, B, C,* or *D.* Each of these indicates a point on the mock intersection that is to be filmed with Misato blinking her Morse message of "I love you," while everyone crosses this way and that, seemingly oblivious to her presence.

Although filming is not due to begin until mid-afternoon, the production company people get in early—at 8:00 a.m.—followed by the agency's creative division two hours later. There is a mobile crane set up for a moving shot, and Mori is sitting in its seat in a bright mauve shirt, baggy shorts, and very dirty track shoes without socks. His assistants are sheltering under a reflector panel, while others seek refuge from the heat that rebounds viciously off the concrete and asphalt by sheltering in the back of the camera equipment van nearby.

In the middle of the space marked out as the 'intersection,' the stand-in stands, wearing the same outfit as yesterday and carrying the Morse transmitter in her hands. The first full-scale practice—with models, students, and agency employees all intermixed—starts at 12:58 p.m., just as her mustachioed manager drives Misato up in the inevitable BMW 735. Each group is controlled by a production company assistant who communicates through a walkie-talkie, while another assistant oversees the whole show with a bullhorn, acting on instructions from Ishii, who watches everything on his monitor.

The first two or three walks from one side of the intersection to the other are pretty haphazard, and instructions are given, getting some people to go in one direction rather than another, separating out a few to pass in front of the stand-in, rather than behind her, splitting others into subgroups of half a dozen so that they don't all collide in one mass in the centre of the intersection. They range across all types, from an elderly man with briefcase, who marches purposefully ahead of everyone else whenever the signal is given to cross, to excessively thin models in very tight black dresses who seem more concerned with the swing of their hips and overall effect of their bodies as they walk than with the task at hand.

After a dozen or so practice crossings in the blazing sunshine, Ishii is beginning to be satisfied with the scene that he's watching on the heavily shielded monitor screen. The stand-in is given the Morse transmitter to hold and the next take is so good that everyone is dismissed to the shade of the goods station, told to eat and drink and make sure that they are ready to start *in winter clothes* at 2:45 p.m. Apparently, the commercial is due to be aired during the winter months and has to look immediately seasonal.

So there's a long lull as all eat, drink, talk, laugh, examine their faces in hand mirrors, and adjust clothing, hair, and the occasional ornament. At the appointed time, they put on coats and jackets—although one model still reveals her belly button in an attempt to stand out from the crowd—and go back to their allotted points at the intersection. The cameraman climbs aboard his mobile perch. An assistant calls for Misato over the walkie-talkie, and out of the location bus she comes, escorted by the androgyn once more and a parasol-bearing assistant. Ishii tells her what the scene is about, using the video monitor to explain details, and at 3:25 p.m. we embark upon the first take. This is followed by the usual hair adjustments before what the cameraman and director call the "real thing" (*honban*).

Just then the sun disappears. We wait a few minutes for it to come out and start shooting once more. But the extras all seem to want to converge on Misato, who gets quite lost in the sea of bodies, and more instructions are given to separate people out a little more. The next take, however, is deemed to be fine and all the extras—who get ¥30,000 a day and two MLI telephone cards for their services—are allowed back into the shade, while the crane is moved for the next scene. By four o'clock, they are all back out on the asphalt for the first of several rehearsals, this time with the crane circling above their heads as they walk past Misato's stand-in. A quarter of an hour later, in spite of the overcast sky, Misato is called. Her T-shirt reads "It has come to my ears that . . . I want to go another way." So, it seems, do two small children, who detach themselves from their mothers and walk onto the set without anyone noticing in time to stop them. Slight confusion as the production company girl in her jeans redirects them round the back of the camera, crane, van, and equipment. Misato is wired up with the Morse transmitter, whose wires are taped to the ground and across the 'intersection,' and off we go once more. The take is very successful, so that all that's left to do after a few minutes is dismiss the 101 extras and take one final shot of Misato with an 8-mm camera.

We're only just in time, though, for as we finish, the first drops of rain begin to fall.

Wind-up Cop Chronicle

On the third day, Misato spends the morning in the studio for still shots. She's an 'artist', she's 'sensitive'. The vast array of extras who've littered the commercial filming scene over the past two days are forbidden to put in an appearance. I take the morning off and cycle down to the 'willow' Yanagi Bridge after lunch, since I've decided to follow the example set by Saburō and the cameraman and turn up in T-shirt and shorts for a change.

The location buses are back in position in the driveway of the Cosmetics Hall when I arrive, engines running endlessly as usual. (I had thought it was illegal to keep a vehicle engine running when parked, but nobody seems to care.) Production company assistants are lying around like corpses, snatching sleep in the way that the Japanese always seem to do during odd moments of relaxation from long hours of work that extend (like Ishii's visit to Watanabe in the early hours of the morning) well into the night. There's a new stand-in girl sitting forlornly in the bus. Misato's studio session is taking longer than anticipated.

At half past two, Ishii and Honma arrive, before going off almost immediately to eat a belated lunch. Hearing that filming is unlikely to begin before 4:00 p.m., I pedal off for a tour of Asakusa and the Sumida River precincts. Halfway back, it starts to rain quite seriously. Thunder peals in the distance; clouds blacken the sky. Ishii and three or four others are lolling in the location bus, and decide to watch a video of *1941*. After half an hour or so, there is a phone call to say that the studio session has finished and that Misato is on her way. Reluctantly, we get out of the bus to prepare the camera equipment, generator, Morse transmitter, and so on. It has stopped raining and the sky has cleared considerably, although Ishii is worried and occasionally mutters "What are we going to do?" between his very white teeth.

There's a mass of food and drink in the minibus—cream sponge cake, *sembei* rice crackers, popcorn, potato chips, *onigiri* rice balls—to which people occasionally help themselves between bouts of work. The first *yakatabune* pleasure boats are untied from their moorings on the other side of the bridge and, loaded with tense-looking revellers, guided out into the broad reaches of the river by men in white overalls and *hachimaki* headbands twisted round their suntanned foreheads. The MLI section chief arrives and joins us as we peer over the bridge. Like spies, we have little to do but wait before the action can begin.

At 4:45 p.m., Misato arrives and the stand-in, who has sat forlornly in the minibus wearing the same clothes as her predecessor the days before, is called to the bridge. The Morse transmitter is taped to the railing. The camera crew is already setting up everything on the far side of the river. The MLI publicity manager arrives, with folding fan in hand. An assistant wipes the bridge railing clean of rainwater in front of the stand-in's feet. The sun comes out, slightly watery. Ishii starts praying that the androgyn will not take hours over Misato's hair. More and more pleasure boats go out under the bridge and some of the more cheerful occupants wave and shout at us. The Morse transmitter is switched on and I can see its light flickering on and off, reflected in the camera lens on the other side of the river.

Saburō, the androgyn, strolls up from nowhere and suddenly starts to talk to me about his work. Hair styling's no longer creative, he says in a matter-of-fact voice. When he first started twenty years ago, there was much more scope for the imagination, but nowadays corporations sponsoring commercials don't want anything spectacular, just something that's "normal, but slightly different." Saburō works in films and commercials, and for fashion designers, getting through 60 models' heads in an hour and a half during the course of a show. Not that he can do all the work himself, of course, which means that he has to have others imitate his creations, and that limits his creativity immediately. As he talks on, telling me about his boyfriend who lives opposite Mick Jagger's flat in London, Saburō comes across as much less the androgyn that s/he makes himself out to be in his movements and clothes, and becomes a perfectly normal human being with his loves and concerns, ambitions and disappointments. So much for prejudice.

In the meantime, Misato has come out onto the bridge. She is shown where to stand and how to hold the Morse transmitter, which flickers its message to the pleasure cruisers passing down the river to Tokyo Bay. Assistants from the production company stand at each end of the bridge and on either side of it, holding back pedestrians and cyclists during the takes. The walkie-talkie system is really useful here, with the camera crew separated from us by half a kilometre or so, and a crackly voice informs us when the camera has started or stopped rolling. The sun is just about out, and we go through three takes before pausing while Ishii (who has come across to be with Misato and make sure that her 'artistic' temperament is not upset in any way) goes back to check everything on the video monitor. Misato leaves the bridge with her entourage, a mustachioed manager and two casually dressed young men with long hair who, for all we know, are members of her band, but whom we dub Sukesan and Kakusan, after the two retainers accompanying the feudal lord in the television series *Mito Kōmon*.

Police sirens wail on the overhead freeway that passes along the far side of the Sumida River above the camera crew. It is rush hour and the traffic seems to be at a total halt. The sirens wail for a very long time, but somehow seem to thread their way through the cars and trucks and get lost in the distance. The ginger-haired petrol station attendants are still—or again—ushering cars in and out of their garage forecourt on the corner opposite where we're standing, although today there are no models traipsing in and out of the Cosmetics Hall. A man comes up the slope with a poodle on a lead, and a plastic bag in hand with which to clean up the animal's feces. Not that the pink ribbons tied to its ears and tail would make one suspect that the small dog was capable of such offensive acts as 'fouling a footpath.' But I realize that I saw the same man, with the same dog, two days previously, and that I am already beginning to witness the regularity of a neighbourhood's daily life.

The sun goes in: this time for good? The sky is really overcast, and there are no signs of blue to relieve the grey monotony of the steamy city. Somehow, though, the sun creeps through thin wisps of cloud. The light has changed considerably, but Ishii's voice comes crackling over the walkie-talkie that he wants another take, and we prepare to bar pedestrians and persuade cyclists to stop a while as the cameras, which of course cannot readily be seen, start rolling. Clearly, passersby find the whole effect somewhat mysterious. It seems as if a film's being made, but there's no evidence of the necessary technology to substantiate the supposition. Have they unwittingly stepped into the eerie otherworld of a Murakami novel?

Two more takes, and at 5:35 p.m. it's all over bar the shouting. Or is it? Apparently a close-up shot has to be taken of the Morse transmitter, and since the cameras are on the other side of the river, this means that we all have to usher Mohammed to the mountain. Not that Misato comes *with* us, of course. The BMW sees to that. The production company people walk over the long bridge across the Sumida River; the girl in jeans does her usual trot; I take my bike, much to the startled amusement of everyone from Ishii to the MLI publicity manager, and even of Misato herself when we are introduced (in an effort to while away the time as the cameraman shifts his equipment and prepares for the necessary shot) and go through a desultory conversation in which such exciting topics as my nationality, height, and ability at Japanese are 'discussed.'

CHAPTER 4

It is at this point that I notice the MLI publicity manager being accosted by a policeman who has emerged from his police box on the northeast end of the bridge and is demanding to know what's going on. An assistant from the production company hurriedly interposes and leads the policeman away towards his box, thereby relieving the sponsoring company's representative of embarrassment. It seems that we're "obstructing traffic" on a small patch of deserted road by a dead-end junction and that we should have obtained permission to film there. The assistant disappears from view into the wound-up policeman's box and we do the necessary filming. This takes hardly more than a minute, but—as we go back across the bridge—we see the assistant seated in the police box, with the policeman hunched over a printed form that he's filling in in accordance with the answers provided by the assistant to his, or Bureaucracy's, questions. At the end of every sentence the policeman checks his watch and writes down the time in his chronicle of boredom, in his busy-ness failing to notice that we have in fact finished filming. This time it *is* all over.

CHAPTER 5

The Organization of Creativity

While I have followed Arthur Koestler in arguing that creativity involves a fusion between two normally incompatible matrices, thereby nudging fixed codes in a new direction,[1] it may well be asked, on the basis of the previous chapter's account, where the creativity lies in the shooting of an ad campaign. Yes, improvisations may and almost certainly do take place. For the production team's preparations, the cameraman still had to climb below a bridge's parapet in search of the optimal spot from which to film Misato. He also had to deal with unstable light conditions, entailing an unanticipated change in the filming schedule, while the androgyn hair stylist spent the best part of two days competing with the wind that insisted on blowing the celebrity's hair out of place. But these, surely, needed little more than the skills for which they had both been employed in the first place?

The answer to this concern lies, I think, not so much in seeing creativity only in the *execution* of creative work, but also in its *conception*. It is on how different forms of cultural production are conceived and planned, therefore, that we need to focus our attention, while not ignoring, of course, their execution. After all, two bisociative strategies were devised by Miyamoto Reisuke in the preparations for my exhibition. It was on the basis of one of them, the combination of both porcelain and stoneware as a material affordance for the exhibition, that I then spontaneously performed my own aesthetic 'cross-dressing' of decorative styles. In my account of a couple of days in the life of an advertising campaign, the bisociation took place primarily in the formulation of the creative brief as the creative director, Ishii, made (to the uninitiated, perhaps somewhat tenuous) links between the celebrity's personality and 'lifestyle' which she would then 'signal' in such a way that viewers would naturally perceive her as personifying a 'life' insurance company. The fact that the campaign worked (in the sense that it clearly raised MLI's public profile and increased its sales of policies, especially to young people) meant that Ishii somehow had intuitively been able to fuse two separate entities—one a charismatic rock artist, the other a 'stuck-up' and boring Japanese company—to create a new trendy image for his agency's client.

120 ▣ CHAPTER 5

This is the way that advertising works. Critics and discontents may regard such 'creative' leaps as vacuous and mind-numbingly unoriginal, and perhaps this was so of the campaign I've described. But there *are* images, songs, and plays-on-words in advertising that even the most cynical can all recall for their startling vivacity and effect. What is interesting about them, perhaps, is the fact that every new successful image, tagline, or jingle involves a *dis*sociation from previous images, taglines, and jingles. Advertising, therefore, like most other forms of cultural production, involves a double-take which separates a product, brand, or firm from its past and propels it forward into the future, until it is once again separated from that future into a past as a new image, tagline, or jingle is introduced to transform it yet again. While perhaps making itself more explicit, this process is no different in principle from that affecting fashion collections, television drama series, various kinds of musical concerts, and pottery or other art exhibitions.

Perhaps what was most interesting about the three steamingly hot days I spent with the production team out in the streets of Tokyo was precisely the *dis*sociations that were needed to enable bisociation of the creative brief to take place. Potential filming sites were rejected because of a hoarding and railway line that advertised the names of one of MLI's competitors. Extras employed for the 'intersection scene' at the old Shiodome railway goods yard had to wear winter clothes in mid-summer because the commercial in which they were appearaing was to be aired during the winter months. In other words, bisociations can be *dangerous* in certain contexts (rather like a risqué joke), and affordances need to be carefully controlled, a fact which inhibits creative freedom.

Although I have earlier outlined the different values that different players bring to bear, depending on their roles in a creative encounter, in this chapter I am going to make use of two other theoretical approaches to analyse some of the descriptive detail in the previous chapter, as well as what goes on in a studio setting where ad campaign concepts created by an account team are realized as visual images by a production team. One picks up on Miyamoto's framing of my own exhibition by making use of Erving Goffman's concept of frame analysis to look at the symbolic space of the studio and the transformations that occur there. The other relies on Howard Becker's analysis of art worlds and examines the production team as a network of people whose cooperative activity, organized by means of their joint knowledge of conventional ways of doing things, produces the kind of ad campaign that an advertising world is noted for.[2]

It is in such forms of cooperation that we see how both circuits of affordances and ensemblages of worth are acted out in everyday practices. They also show how different actors—in particular, art director, photographer/cameraman, and client—take up and challenge the positions of other players and creative products in the "space of possibles" characterising the field of advertising. In the process, this chapter reveals deeper structural issues connected with occupational roles, the distribution of advertising budgets, and, in a studio setting, the relationship between magazine and advertising production.

Advertising Worlds

Advertising enables a client to deliver a message to many people through an impersonal medium for which the client pays, and advertising campaigns—like that by Asatsū for MLI—are usually conceptualised and realised by advertising agencies working on behalf of corporate clients. Most advertising is designed to market goods and services as part of a sales campaign to launch a new product or reposition an unsuccessful brand vis-à-vis competing brands. But it may also be used to show support for an advertiser's sales force, or—as was the case with the Watanabe Misato campaign for MLI—change consumer attitudes and improve a client's corporate image.[3] The main aim of every advertising campaign is differentiation. As in totemic practices found in certain 'primitive' societies, it is the creation of differences per se between products, brands, advertisers, and so on, rather than the content of such differences, that is of crucial importance in the production and consumption of advertising.[4] The same might be said of *all* creative industries. Crudely put, creativity is about finding ways to avoid sameness.

For a long time, with one notable exception,[5] detailed descriptions of the work and organization of advertising agencies came from within the trade rather than from academic research.[6] Scholars interested in creative practices were obliged to take at face value insiders' interpretations of what did and did not constitute 'creativity' and of how best to manage it.[7] They were assisted in their endeavours by the occasional informative journalistic account, albeit painted with a broad brush for effect.[8] From the early 1990s, however, a handful of anthropologists began to explore the world of advertising practices in places as far apart as Norway, Trinidad, Japan, and South Asia.[9] Their research, in turn, has encouraged others originally trained as anthropologists, but thereafter working in the advertising industry, to reflect on their hands-on experiences and to publish detailed case study analyses of some of the creative strategies in which agency personnel engage during the course of their everyday work.[10]

As a result, we are beginning to get a clearer picture of the kinds of social, cultural, economic, and political constraints affecting the production of advertising campaigns. This picture reveals an advertising agency's internal organization and dynamics, as well as external agency-client relations, and focuses on the fact that advertising campaigns are conceived by account teams, comprised primarily of accounts, marketing, creative, and media-buying personnel, each tending to pay heed to one particular set of affordances over another. Thus, while an account planner is concerned primarily with meeting client expectations (social and economic affordances), copywriter and art (or creative) director focus on target audience appeal, while taking into account the means to achieve selected images (representational and techno-material affordances). This organizational landscape reveals that, like other creative industries, advertising suffers from a number of tensions arising from what Richard Caves has so felicitously described as "the motley crew."[11]

Such tensions arise from the different tasks and sets of expertise that different members of an account team bring to the conception of an ad campaign. They may be internal to the team, as when marketing and creative personnel disagree with one another,[12] or externally generated, as when the account manager who represents both agency to client and vice versa,[13] fails to satisfy the differing expectations held by the agency's client and his account team.

The account team, therefore, is mired in an organizational paradox in that, to meet all its client's needs and do its job properly, an agency has no alternative but to bring together potentially incompatible personnel with different world views.[14] Among devices put into place to limit rivalry and promote mutual tolerance and understanding are project deadlines[15] (which is where temporal affordances come into play) and, in Europe and the United States, the establishment of a relatively stable set of core relationships among team members, especially between copywriter and art director, working on a single account. The downside of such devices is that, by working with a stable set of colleagues, members of an account team develop team, rather than agency, loyalty.[16] Moreover, the very limitation on collaboration enforced by a project deadline prevents a permanent resolution *within* an agency to the competing logics of 'art' and 'science' held

THE ORGANIZATION OF CREATIVITY 123

by different sub-teams (creative and marketing, respectively), although *between* an agency and its clients creativity is the magic by which the latter are dazzled.

In Japan, the former problem is resolved by teaming different personnel to work together on multiple accounts. This is made possible by the fact that Japanese, unlike American or European, advertisers do not allocate the whole of their account to a single agency, but tend to split them by product or media, or some combination of the two, and to allocate accounts among a number of different agencies.[17] This distribution of work enables every member of an account team to learn about and appreciate the variety of numerous others' worldviews of advertising and its practices, as well as get a broad range of experience in different kinds of advertising problems brought to an agency by its clients. Thus, in contrast to the European and American emphasis on specialization (brought about by the fact that no single agency is allowed to handle the competing accounts of—say—two different automobile or soft drinks manufacturers), Japanese agencies seek to make generalists out of their staff whose allegiance is to the agency as a whole and not just to an account team. The competing logics of 'art' (aspired to by the creative team) and 'science' (espoused by the marketing team) are not resolved as such, but they are given a little less weight, perhaps, because of the sheer number of accounts handled and of account teams formed with multiple personnel. Individual egos have neither the time nor occasion to become inflated.

So, although attention has been paid to advertising practices within an agency, what happens when the latter contracts a production company, studio, cameraman, photographer, model, hairdresser, and other personnel to carry out the actual production of the visual images to be used in one of its ad campaigns has received rather less attention. Here we find a second-level motley crew (the 'production team') assigned to carry out the task of transforming a creative team's concepts into visual representations. How is this done? And what tensions arise—and why—from the interaction among these professionals with different sets of expertise and tacit knowledge, as well as between them and the advertising agency's art director who has employed them for the task at hand? Questions like these should enable us to understand better the organization of creativity in advertising production, both in Japan and elsewhere, as well as help us reflect on what we learned in Chapter 2.

The Production Team

The job of the account team is to come up with an acceptable idea for an advertising campaign that meets its client's requirements and brief. However, once the client has given its OK to an account team's creative proposal, those concerned have to initiate actual production of the campaign in question. This was what brought Ishii and his account team together with members of the subcontracted production company, in order to discuss how best to achieve the—in many ways somewhat vague—campaign ideas accepted by MLI. It is at this point, then, that an agency's creative team brings together a second-level motley crew, or production team, led by the creative director,[18] who selects and employs a photographer, model or celebrity, stylist, hairdresser (or hair stylist), makeup artist, studio, and, in the case of a television commercial, production company.[19] This "performance team"[20] cooperates in staging the single routine of shooting an ad campaign, to which each member brings a specific expertise. Some are accompanied by their own personnel: a photographer, makeup artist, and hairdresser by their assistants; a model by her booking agent; a celebrity by her manager (and BMW); and a production company or studio by its own staff. Almost all of them work freelance and are hired by the agency, for which they work very intensively for two to three days on the project at hand.[21]

How does the production team go about its job, and how do participants come to terms with one another's different spheres of competence? An uninitiated visitor's—indeed, my own—first impression of a location shoot or studio set is one of total chaos. Some people appear to be sitting around doing nothing but drinking tea and chatting in a minibus or at a studio table, while others are running to and fro frantically, or busy arranging lighting, moving furniture, papering one part of the studio floor, and so on. Meanwhile, there is a 'location bus' (or small cubbyhole adjacent to the studio) in which a celebrity (or model) is being tended to by a trio of makeup, hair, and fashion stylists.

This initial sense of confusion reveals with time a reasonably defined demarcation of participants and their duties. For example, on location for the MLI campaign shoot, Asatsū used two buses for its personnel: one, a minibus, was filled with food and drink, and used by agency and production company, as well as client, personnel; the other, an extremely smart 'location bus,' was used by the celebrity, Watanabe Misato, and her attendant hair stylist, fashion stylist, and makeup artist. Agency personnel had to attend to two aspects of the campaign shoot: overall management of the creative work (by Ishii and his creative team), and liaison with two MLI managers (by two Asatsū account executives). Production company personnel were broadly divided into camera (Mori and his assistants) and general coordination teams, overseen by a producer and *his* assistants (who, nevertheless, had titles like assistant producer and production manager). While the creative director and cameraman focused their attention on the technical side of the location shoot (positioning of camera, instructions to celebrity, and so on), the production company's coordination team dealt with extraneous matters (such as pacifying disgruntled local shop owners, holding back pedestrians and cyclists to keep the bridge clear while filming, and assuaging a wound-up policeman). The 'location bus' team of celebrity, androgynous hair stylist, fashion stylist, and makeup artist worked entirely independently and separately from the others. This spatial and functional demarcation of personnel on the location shoot is mirrored particularly clearly in the spatial organization of a studio during an ad campaign shoot.

Using frame analysis to examine social behaviour is one useful way to come to grips with what goes on in advertising production, since frames organize who does what, where, and when before, during, and after a studio shoot. There are more and less important frames in every field of creative activity, but one that renders what would otherwise be meaningless into something that is meaningful we may call, following Goffman,[22] a "primary framework." A department store exhibition is a good example of a primary framework in the Japanese art world, and an auction or gallery show in the Western art world. In the advertising world, primary frameworks include competitive presentations, where different agencies are invited to compete for an advertiser's account by presenting creative ideas based on a client's marketing brief;[23] client workshops, where agency personnel interact with a new client's team in an attempt to overcome marketing uncertainties, assess interpersonal dynamics, and direct and control as much interaction with their client as possible;[24] and studio (and location) shoots. Each allows participants "to locate, perceive, identify, and label a seemingly infinite number of concrete occurrences defined in its own terms."[25] Although they may not be consciously aware of such organized features and would be unable to describe them coherently when asked, they can easily and fully apply the framework in their everyday activities.

Like other primary frameworks, both location and studio shoots are regarded as relevant and important to the tasks undertaken by members of an advertising world. What we find in them are the "guided doings"[26] of individuals: guided because they are subject to certain standards, norms, expectations, and social appraisal. Certain kinds of behaviour are expected (at certain stages) during the course of a shoot (total stillness when the photographer starts shooting a scene; shifts between concentration and casual playfulness among personnel; the kind of music played in a studio and how loud; and so on). Those present behave according to such norms and expectations because they know that to do otherwise would invite criticism and possibly social sanctions of one sort or another. Location and studio act as both spatial and temporal affordance.

Frame analysis helps clarify the "guided doings"—or characters' roles[27]—of a production team at work. But it is more than the analysis of a spatial framework per se, since the aim is to be able to point to and explain the transformations that take place in a setting like the studio, rather than the setting itself.[28] The frame analysis which follows, therefore, serves to reveal in later sections of this chapter the tensions underpinning the organization of the production team's creativity.

As intimated in this chapter, every production team tends to be organized into four distinct spheres of work practice and related personnel, and these we will now look at in the context of a studio shoot. First, whenever a model, actress, or celebrity is being used in a campaign, s/he will be tended to by the fashion stylist, hair, and makeup teams in what may be called a "beauty room," leading off the main studio.[29] Their activity is carried on more or less independently of what is going on in the studio itself, until the model is called for a session, when she will be ushered onto the set and given final administrations by her attendants before the photographer takes over. This is no different from what we noticed in the previous chapter's description of Watanabe Misato's role in the MLI shoot.

Second, and again this was made clear in the ethnographic account, there are the photographer and his two assistants—one of whom is an assistant to the other—whose job it is to set up the *camera* in a particular spot, arrange the lighting, and prepare the film, making sure that each spool is properly numbered and packed after use. They will also develop the film (if not working digitally) and make the final prints required for the advertising campaign.

Third, there is the art director (or, on location, creative director), who usually instructs the studio stagehands in how to set up the *set* and who works closely with the photographer to ensure that, together, they get the image effect that both of them think is right for the job in hand. In this respect, there is some crossover of responsibilities, as the photographer ensures that the set, camera, and lighting are in accord. The art director, however, does not interfere with the photographer and his assistants.[30]

Although the art director moves about the studio, giving instructions or consulting staff as appropriate, his "home base"—or fixed point of return[31]—is a table set up in one unused part of the studio (but almost invariably near the studio entrance). It is here that client personnel and random visitors (of whom there tend to be many, including the occasional anthropologist) are invited to sit, and to which other personnel will gravitate during a slack moment during the day's work. This is the *client base*, which serves as a general liaison point between client, agency art director, and subcontracted freelance personnel.

There is one other point of reference in the studio. This is a special stand or table to which photographer and art director repair after every session to examine the Polaroid photos (or computer images) just taken. All staff members, including the model, usually gather silently around this *photo stand* between takes, as photographer and art director examine and discuss the images before them. It is from here that further instructions are issued for the next session.

The location of these points of reference reflects the importance of each of the tasks being carried out, as well as of their personnel and the relationships among them. Thus the "outsider," the client, is located at the point nearest to the studio entrance and thus the "outside" (or *omote*), while the camera and set are located in the "interior" (commonly referred to as *oku* in Japanese) of the studio. It is in this highly charged symbolic space that the two pivotal actors, the art director and photographer, take up their positions, although the art director is obliged, as an 'employee' of the client, to move back and forth between interior and exterior locations. The liminal point linking client to camera and set, and attracting all members of the production team at particular points during the course of the day's action, is the photo stand[32] (see Figure 3).

The primary relationship guiding the production team in its work is that of art director and photographer. Although it is the former who, together with other members of his account team, has come up with an idea for an advertising campaign, it is the latter who has to transform that idea into a series of visual images. It is important, therefore, that the art director explain carefully his concept (often with the aid of illustrations or photographs) and that the photographer understand it, before adding his or her particular take on the creative idea in question.

FIGURE 3: Symbolic Space of the Studio

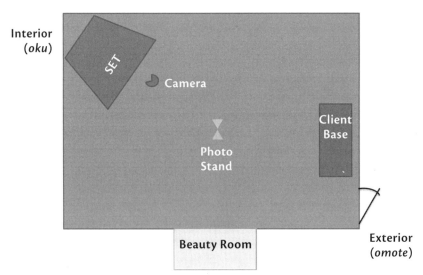

Other members of the team take on greater or lesser importance according to the product being advertised. In a hair products campaign, for example, the hairdresser will be brought into the art director–photographer discussions, and may—as we shall soon see—even take over the role of the art director entirely. In a cosmetics campaign, the makeup artist will take precedence; in fashion, the stylist. But all members of the beauty team can, and will, make unanticipated interventions, as they feel appropriate, during the day's shooting. In a contact lens campaign, for example, while the photographer was in the process of posing an actress for the second print ad photo, the hairdresser suddenly stepped forward with a pair of chopsticks, twisted the actress's hair upwards behind her head, and fastened it with his impromptu 'hair pin' before stepping back theatrically to admire the effect. The photographer checked the image in his viewfinder before inviting the art director to take a look. All agreed that this was an excellent way to pose the model, even though the effect was somewhat different from the art director's initial intention. It is in such improvisations that creativity is recognized.[33] But we might also note that each member of the production team acts to support the others. In so doing, it becomes very unclear who is *the* creative person and who are the support people in the production of an ad campaign.[34] Creativity is almost invariably a collaborative venture.

A Revealing Encounter

What does frame analysis of the symbolic space of the studio reveal in terms of the organization and "guided doings" of the performers? Maybe we should start by noting that every production team acts as an informal training ground for the acquisition of both technical and social competences. Assistants to the photographer, hairdresser, and makeup artist are all involved in on-the-job training, and learn to master a variety of technical solutions to problems arising during the shooting of different advertising campaigns. At the same time, the learning process takes place across professions as photographers learn from the accumulated experiences of art directors, hairdressers from those of makeup artists, models from those of fashion stylists, and so on. Such technical competence is in this way transformed into social competence, as different personnel reveal their knowledge in each of the encounters and engagements that the formation of a production team creates. We thus find a synthesis between concrete know-how and abstract knowledge as members of the team act in concert with one another in what Keith Negus and Michael Pickering term "a mutually enhancing absorption and understanding."[35] This is what I mean by "ensembling" or "group flow": highly attuned and synchronized interaction among participants who have a particular shared aim in mind and who act in a state of more-or-less unconscious awareness, open and fully attentive to what others around them are doing, while carrying out their own part in the collaborative task at hand.[36]

It is during this long-term process of multiple memberships in production teams that a photographer, fashion stylist, or makeup artist, for example, comes to be recognized as an 'insider.' While at their periphery motley crews provide a site for training, therefore, at their core they establish an organizational context in which reputation—that is, social and cultural capital—is established.[37] Such reputations develop through a process of consensus-building in advertising's creative world. The reputations of art directors, photographers, stylists, makeup artists, hairdressers, and models result from their collective creative activities, which in turn produce the ad campaigns on which their reputations depend.[38]

"Encounters" are the social form by which members of production teams in Japan describe this social process:

> Everything starts with the people you choose for a job. Encounters (*deai*) are crucial here. Like my choice of Nicky, for example. I saw his

130　□　CHAPTER 5

work in a magazine and liked it, so I got in touch with the staff there and asked how I could contact him. Then I met him and really liked him. His work was the start, but it wasn't everything. He's also got love, and a philosophy that I like. He's easy to communicate with, and this makes him much better, so far as I'm concerned, than some incompetent Japanese. So, it's a spiritual (*seishinteki na*) way of thinking, rather than just what's trendy, that influences me in deciding who to choose for a job, as well as what kind of work to do in the first place.[39]

Just how such encounters enable freelance photographers and others in a production team to move from 'outsider' to 'insider'—that is, to someone with her own recognized symbolic capital—depends on a number of factors. One is the technical and social skills that each brings to a situation and the ability to work within social conventions. A second is explicit knowledge of the "portfolio of connections"[40]—of who's who—in the advertising and fashion worlds. A third factor involves the longer-term building up and maintenance of trust as an integral part of social networks.[41] Encounters ultimately create mutual confidence in "this is how we do things here": the taken-for-granted, tacit knowledge unknown to outsiders (including the advertiser), which is based on impression management and pervades each production team's activities. The organizational result is what Pierre Bourdieu has felicitously referred to as "social alchemy."[42]

In this respect, it is in the recognition granted by one set of producers (freelance personnel) producing for another producer (advertising agency)[43] that advertising is legitimated as a creative process. In other words, their performance serves to express characteristics of the task performed, rather than of the performers themselves.[44] It is *how* something is done, rather than *who* does it, that matters. Here, two factors are important to the relationship among individual members of the production team. First, each relies on the proper conduct and behaviour of other members of the team. In other words, there is reciprocal dependence among them. Second, precisely because they are accomplices in maintaining an appearance of how things should be done, teammates who are "in the know" are bound by reciprocal familiarity.[45]

The contradictory nature of reciprocal dependence and reciprocal familiarity can lead to a breakdown of dramaturgical cooperation in the production team: a breakdown that embarrasses the spontaneous appearance of creativity and teamwork staged in the studio and based on fragile compromise in the service of a common good.[46] For example, at the end

THE ORGANIZATION OF CREATIVITY 131

of one particular hair product's print ad shoot, an unexpected difference of opinion arose between photographer and hairdresser, who had assumed the role of art director for the day. The two of them had worked closely together, picking out images that the hairdresser liked best, then rearranging the model's hair, before taking and selecting more photos, until, in the end, just one was isolated for the poster that the Japanese client wished to send out to hairdresser salons all over the country for the New Year. All this was done on the photographer's computer which, placed between set and client base, served as a symbolic 'photo stand' during the day.

The photographer checked with the hairdresser that she was happy with the chosen image, made sure that the client had no objection, and then gave the order to his assistants and studio staff to dismantle the set. A few minutes after they had begun to go about their work, however, the hairdresser suddenly came back into the main studio from the beauty room where she was tending the model with two assistants and asked the photographer to take another set of photos. She felt that she could get an even better effect than the one they already had.

The entire production team froze in its tracks. Faced with this unexpected request, the photographer quietly asked why and was told by the hairdresser that she had thought of a new way to style the model's hair. He pointed out that the set was already being dismantled, that the camera had been put away, and that it would take an immense amount of time to re-establish everything exactly as it had been. He noted the extra costs that the client would incur both in terms of labour and studio rental. The hairdresser was adamant. She could do a better job.

By this time, even the music to whose rhythm everyone had been working all day had been turned off. Then, the art director, who had sat all afternoon at the client table without interfering in the work being done by photographer and hairdresser, suddenly spoke up. He reminded the hairdresser rather sharply of the sequence of events that had taken place that day, and of her responsibilities to the photographer, client, and the production team as a whole. He emphasized the different sets of professional expertise that each had brought to the set, but insisted that each should know where to draw the line in terms of perfection. Should the client be obliged to pay for extra studio rental and labour time for little more than a 'marginal improvement'? Was the hairdresser really going to insist?

Standing in the midst of the assembled crew around the photographer's computer, and in an icy silence, the hairdresser pondered the situation. Caught in the classic predicament of "negative experience" described by

Goffman,[47] she floundered over the formulation of a viable response in a frame that she had herself broken. After a long 30 seconds, she bowed her head quickly, in acknowledgement that the art director was in the right, and apologized before going back to the beauty room. The studio staff and photographer's assistants immediately unfroze and carried on dismantling the set. The loud, rhythmical music was turned back on. The photo stand—that liminal point in the studio designed to bring together and harmonize the production team's different sets of expertise—had served its symbolic purpose. The "false note"[48] of open disagreement in front of the combined audience of client and other team members quickly receded into dramaturgical cooperation once more.

The reason for this sharp, but potentially explosive, exchange between photographer, hairdresser, and art director had to do precisely with the kind of knowledge "in the air"[49] that surrounds all production teams (and, by extension, motley crews in general). By suddenly demanding that the photographer reshoot a scene, the hairdresser was questioning the taken-for-granted knowledge that all those concerned had known precisely what they were doing all day, and thus the trust that they had performed properly.[50] She not only placed her own professionalism in doubt; she opened up an avenue of disagreement that could easily have torn apart the carefully wrought harmony between advertiser and ad agency, on the one hand, and the ad agency's art director and his production team, on the other.

What this event shows us is that, while creative work in the production of this ad campaign "was characterized by a shared form of authorship, responsibility and control were not shared equally. The social organization of production distributed authorial agency along a hierarchy of responsibility and power," exercised by the art director who himself was subject to the control of his client.[51]

Advertising's Space of Possibles

One question arising from this description and analysis of a production team at work concerns who controls whom, and at what points, during the production of an ad campaign. My particular focus here is on the broader field of advertising and the "space of possibles"[52] that orients the lines of demarcation between art director, photographer, and client, as the symbolic space of the studio is transformed into a "stake of struggles"[53] in which performers discover whether their vision of how things should be done prevails and, if not, *whose* vision does prevail.[54] In other words, collabora-

THE ORGANIZATION OF CREATIVITY   133

tion in creative work of all kinds is conducted in a competitive arena, so that working *with* simultaneously becomes working *against*.

An advertising campaign is "the deposit of a social relationship" between advertiser and advertising agency, in much the same way that a fifteenth-century painting reflects a relationship between painter and the client who commissioned and paid for it.[55] In advertising, as in early Renaissance art, the client is often an active, determining, and not necessarily benevolent agent, who is mindful of the positions being taken by his competitors as they stake out an "ensemble of relations" in the field.[56] The funds allocated by a client affect the finished ad campaign in terms of content, function, size, and quality of materials and skills applied, in much the same way as they did a fifteenth-century painting, but—however great or small an advertiser's budget—he expects, indeed demands, that his campaign be 'creative,' for it is creativity that enables him to (re)position his product. Creativity, then, dominates the space of possibles in the field of advertising.

It is the pairing of copywriter and art director that has to respond to the client's demand for creativity. Although their established roles often collapse in the process, the copywriter's job is to spin words around a sales pitch,[57] while the art director is responsible for accompanying graphic images and composes the visuals and layout of the print (and occasionally video) ads accepted by the client. However, while the copywriter is active during the conceptual stage of an advertising campaign, the art director's role extends into its production, where he has to mediate between client, photographer, model/celebrity, and other members of the production team, and "to resolve tensions arising from uncertain identities and frustrated experiences."[58] It is when he brings together a production team to transform his creative ideas into actual images that the art director needs an astute use of administrative, rather than just creative, skills. The production team—consisting of photographer, fashion stylist, makeup artist, and hairdresser—then dons the mantle of creativity.

Here lies the rub. Art (and creative) directors sometimes confuse these different responsibilities and interfere with a production team's work in the misguided belief that success depends upon their maintaining absolute artistic control.[59] Such a belief may have something to do with the fact that the art director is usually (though not necessarily) a regular employee of an advertising agency. His (or occasionally her) past and potential career in the organization decides which particular jobs he is allocated and he tends to orient what he does to the needs of his agency, as well as to those of individual clients. He thus develops motives and positions that are rather

134 ▣ **CHAPTER 5**

different from those of the contracted production team with which he works. The photographer, for example, like the other specialists employed in a production team, is one of a pool of similarly qualified freelance professionals and is contracted separately for each ad campaign. Freelance assignments are always contingent upon a photographer's background experience, creative style, reputation, geographical location, client, and budget.[60] However, there are other photographers (as there are other stylists, models, and so on) who are equally competent and who could equally well have been asked to do the same job. This means that the photographer needs a network of connections who will contact him and nobody else when the occasion arises.[61]

The result of the different occupational structures underpinning the work of art director and photographer is that the latter is necessarily constrained in his work by the fact that s/he has to please two clients simultaneously: his client, the advertising agency which employs him; and his client's client, the advertiser who employs the agency.[62] As a result, "the photographer must supply visual expertise, must possess a cheerful and easygoing manner, must take orders in an accommodating way and must communicate a special quality called 'faith in the outcome' to people whose business is fraught with uncertainty."[63] Here, disposition (or habitus) confronts the taking up of a particular position in the available space of possibles.[64]

Although both Rosenblum and Bogart have noted the potentially explosive relationship that exists between art director, photographer, and client in the American advertising industry, my research in Japan reveals a more harmonious distribution of and respect for responsibilities. For a start, the advertising client almost invariably takes a back seat when it comes to the actual shooting of a campaign. Although the advertiser will inevitably engage in long and detailed (and on occasion tediously repetitive) negotiations with the advertising agency's account team over the exact contents of a campaign prior to its production, when it comes to production itself the client does *not* interfere with the professionals whom the art (or creative) director has hired—even when, as we saw earlier, a disagreement breaks out between the photographer and hairdresser. He does not, therefore, tell the photographer to make sure s/he photographs his product in its best light,[65] but leaves him to get on with his work in the conviction that s/he— and not the advertiser—is the one who knows best at this point. Similarly, he will leave it to the art director to adjudicate in the case of disagreement among members of the production team and not himself intervene, even when appealed to. In other words, positions available to and occupied by

THE ORGANIZATION OF CREATIVITY 135

actors in the field of Japanese advertising appear to be more clearly defined and respected than they are in American advertising.

A second point worth noting in support of this hypothesis is that in Japan it is the art director—and not the photographer as in the United States (and Scandinavia[66])—who makes separate contractual arrangements with a studio, photographer, and other employees (hairdresser, stylist, model, and so on) necessary for a particular campaign shoot. Although he may make recommendations about personnel, or help choose the model, the fact that he does not himself directly hire anyone other than his assistants relieves the photographer of a lot of tension during the course of his work, as well as of responsibility when things go wrong.

Both these points underline the fact that in Japan an advertising campaign shoot is, on the surface at least, an extremely egalitarian gathering of professionals who work together in a climate of mutual respect for one another's expertise.[67] The main actors in the production team—the art director and photographer—cooperate closely, while working for the most part independently, and so mirror working relations in the account team where planning, research, media buying, and creative activities tend to be carried out in semi-independent parallel. Decisions are made on the basis of discussion and mutual agreement, rather than by means of some form of hierarchical control structure. Control is, of course, exercised, but by different actors at different points in the shoot.

This is, perhaps, surprising in a society well known for its overall hierarchical structure, but in Japan we do *not* find that "the social organization of advertising has the net effect of chiselling away at the broad range of knowledge and expertise that the photographer brings with him."[68] Nor do we find that "the photographer's contribution is virtually reduced to technical labor"; nor that s/he "is often given direct orders by the art director and is told to photograph the models or objects the art director's way and not his way."[69] The Japanese photographer (or Western photographer working in Japan) does *not* have an unsolicited comment "overruled by the coalition formed by the advertiser and art director."[70] Rather, he is expected to use technical expertise to resolve an art director's conceptual difficulties and to add his own inimitable style to the images that he conjures up for the advertising campaign on which he is working, while taking into account the constraints afforded by the client's brand. Although a photographer's work is evaluated according to his ability to find "the solution to a technical problem for which there are no standardized solutions"[71]—as in when he uses Vaseline on a sheet of plate glass to simulate rain blobs—his creativity is also judged by his stylistic inputs. In this way, his work is extremely competitive since it is being judged against that of other participants, as well as of all the photographers who might have been employed instead of him, but in this case weren't.

Such stylistic inputs may be found in a broad array of activities, for photographers do not confine themselves to working in just advertising, news journalism, or art photography, but rather cover as many different spheres as they can. These include, in particular, fashion magazines (a subject to which I will soon return), but also music videos and other kinds of work, all of which are used to fill a photographer's portfolio or 'book': the photographic record of his work that is used to solicit more jobs.[72] The preferred form of work in Japan is advertising, since the amount of money lavished on a campaign permits a photographer freedom to work in different, interesting, and 'creative' ways. Even though an account is split, thereby leading to some form of economic constraint, an advertising budget is still far greater than that available for a magazine fashion shoot, which is marked by what might be termed "an overload of social constraints." As a Swiss photographer working in Japan put it:

> One reason why I don't like to work for magazines very much is because there're too many vested and political interests in the shooting of fashion stories or covers. Which means I can never really achieve the kind of effect I'd like. So, when I *do* get involved in this kind of work, it's because I know a freelance fashion editor who's been contracted to put something together for a magazine and I want to help a friend out. I know that then I'll probably get some really good work through the same friend when it comes along. It's a matter of give and take, isn't it?[73]

The kind of assignments that photographers working in Japan dislike, then, is magazine work. This is understandable, given Patrik Aspers's comment that a magazine editor's task is to hire photographers who, she thinks, will mirror and reproduce her magazine's style.[74] But there is another reason for this dislike. In the words of a young Japanese photographer:

> As far as I'm concerned, foreign magazines place their main emphasis on *image*. But here in Japan it is always the *clothes*—their flow and the materials they're made of—that are the focus of the camera's attention. In this respect, even magazines like *Vogue* have to adapt to their Japanese readers a bit. As a result, of course, photographers in Japan are

more restrained in their work. They can't indulge in the kinds of experiments that European and American photographers, and their employing magazines, take for granted. This makes them seem less creative.[75]

Why should advertising work in the United States, but magazine work in Japan, be seen as constrained? Why does magazine work in the United States, but advertising in Japan, afford a photographer the chance to show off his creativity? Why the difference in focus, on images or clothes? Here we need to consider the subfield of fashion magazine publishing. As we shall soon see, in Japan editors need to pay a lot of attention to their *readers* because their titles are not sold by subscription, but have to be sold and resold to readers with every monthly issue. This is not the case in Europe or the United States, where the subscription system ensures a stable readership for fashion magazines, whose 'vital statistics' are then sold to *advertisers* who themselves then become more important than readers, a point made clear by the way in which fashion magazine text and advertisements are structured. As a result, photographers can ignore readers' expectations and perform all sorts of technical and aesthetic tricks to attract advertiser attention in European and American magazines, but are rather more constrained in Japan until contracted to shoot an advertising campaign. This supports Barbara Rosenblum's argument that creative style is partially determined by socioeconomic arrangements relating to work organization and working roles.[76]

The Organization of Creativity

In this chapter, I have analysed how a number of tensions inherent in the conceptualization and production of advertising by two different motley crews are in fact embedded in larger structural issues related to the field of advertising as a whole: the dual creative-administrative roles of key personnel; a double client system; the distribution of advertising budgets; the relation between advertising and fashion magazine publishing; and the overall need for differentiation. To conclude, I want to add a few more words about the organization of creativity.

First, although the idea of creativity tends to be associated with individual agency and freedom of action, it is clear that creativity itself is shaped by—and itself comes to shape—numerous constraints and conventions that together 'afford' the work of the motley crew. This was the argument put forward in the first chapter of this book. Participants in a

138   ▢   **CHAPTER 5**

production team, for example, do not decide things afresh every time they produce an advertising campaign. Rather, they rely on earlier customary agreements that have since become the conventional way of doing things. Such conventions make possible an easy and efficient coordination of activity among team personnel:[77] something that is encouraged further by their careful selection in terms of personality and stylistic tendencies.[78] They also enable particular forms of advertising (print and broadcast, for example) to be recognized as such and differentiated from each other, as well as from other media forms that make use of photographic images (for instance, news journalism). At the same time, team members' involvement with and dependence on mutual cooperation constrain the amount and form of creativity that they can contribute to an ad campaign. This demands compromises that can themselves lead to both agreements and disputes—not just in advertising, but in many other forms of cultural production, including, notably, theatre and film—among the various actors in a motley crew, who explicitly formulate and rely upon these 'rules of the game' to judge success or resolve problems.[79] In this respect, creativity involves a negotiation of differing interpretations and authorial power.[80]

Creativity is enabled, outlined and constrained, then, as I argued earlier, by various techno-material, temporal, spatial, representational (or aesthetic), social, and economic affordances, together with their accompanying values, none of which is entirely independent of the others. The product itself—beer or bargain sale—for example, to some extent contextualizes and determines how much creativity takes place because of the symbolic properties that can be attached to it. This is why advertisers devote considerable time, energy, and money to converting 'information' into 'experience' goods, since by so doing they increase potential opportunities for creative advertising and marketing. Also, the size of the budget set aside by a client for an advertising campaign often influences choice of personnel ("A List" for high-budget work, "B List" for low-budget work), accompanying aesthetic styles, location (Tokyo studio or beach in the Bahamas), and media coverage (television commercial or print advertising). The time frame, too, for completion of a campaign impinges on the availability and selection of personnel, which in itself has knock-on effects. For instance, the decision of whether to go for traditional film or contemporary computerized images in the selection of two available photographers influences the finished campaign style, since the 'modernist' can manipulate images in a way that the 'traditionalist' finds impossible (and often distasteful).

THE ORGANIZATION OF CREATIVITY   139

Second, creativity is not the only requirement of creative personnel, since almost all concerned need also to be able to *manage* those who come under their command. This means that 'creative' becomes a sliding category that depends very much on context. An art director is 'creative' when trying to come up with a creative platform for his account team's client, but takes on an administrative role once he enters the studio and is required to transform his creative concept into a tangible product by giving instructions to photographer, studio staff, and other members of the production team. Similarly, a cinematographer may well become an on-site director as she decides what to focus on and how much to shoot for a particular scene, while conferring with the producer or director between takes.[81] Although photographers or hairdressers are employed for the creative contribution they can make to a particular task, they, too, have to manage their assistants and ensure that they do their part of the job in a professional manner. This combination of creative and managerial roles is to be found in creative positions in other fields of cultural production—fashion designer, magazine editor, film director, and so on—as well as among humdrum personnel who see their work as, in part at least, creative, and so brings into question the absolute distinction made by Richard Caves between creative and humdrum personnel.[82]

Third, we have seen that the production of advertising is based on a double-client system. An agency is employed by an advertiser, but at the same time employs a photographer, hairdresser, stylist, model, and others in a production team, which ultimately owes its employment to the advertiser. However, this double-client system, in which power relations are established by the flow of money, is carefully controlled by overt recourse to trust and reciprocity in social interaction, and by a classic denial of the importance of 'commerce' in creative work. This can be seen in the art director's comments quoted earlier, where his selection of a photographer depended on such abstract and non-commercial criteria as "'love,' 'philosophy,' and 'a spiritual way of thinking'" (the 'dignity' of the detached world).[83] The hairdresser's intervention at the end of the shoot in the 'revealing encounter' laid bare, and threatened to upset, this hidden structure. Both photographer and art director were obliged to justify their positions not to accede to her request in terms of the financial implications for the client.

So, in spite of appearances to the contrary, the denial of power relations in the everyday work processes of a production team is not based on a sense of social egalitarianism. Rather, it is designed to enable creativity to take place in a commercial vacuum.[84] In other words, acutely aware of the potential constraints imposed by power relations, people in Japan's advertising world do their best to minimize them in the actual production of advertisements. In this way, they hope, participants will feel free to improvise as they go along, for it is such cultural improvisation that affords numerous, and minute, touches of interactive creativity.[85]

In a sense, then, the concept of creativity itself involves a double process. On the one hand, it is used to deny the obvious power relations, based on money, that drive advertiser-agency and art director–studio personnel relationships. On the other, it creates new spaces that instead permit the establishment of new forms of power among art director, photographer, makeup artist, stylist, and hairdresser, as each competes with the others to reveal his or her creativity within the field's space of possibles.

At the same time, an ad campaign also creates new spaces for an advertiser by repositioning its product vis-à-vis competing products, which themselves are forced to release old, and seek new, selling (pro)positions in a constant juggle for consumer attention. Creativity thus exerts power over the consumer as it enables the advertising industry to continue its activities ad infinitum. This, then, is the function of the organization of creativity and the motley crew in advertising: to enable a space of possibles in which different actors use the tool of creativity to continuously reposition their collective endeavour.

CHAPTER 6

Editing Fashion Magazines

There's something seductive about fashion magazines. When I was doing my fieldwork in Asatsū many years ago, I soon discovered that employees would throw out dozens of magazines on the landings of the back stairs of the old building in Shinbashi where the agency was then housed. On my way home in the evenings, I used to go through them in search of what seemed to me to be interesting examples of contemporary Japanese ads, and quickly realised that for print and paper quality there was nothing better than a fashion magazine. That's how I started reading—or, at least, looking at—them.

I have to admit that at first I found everything in these fashion magazines alluring, from the way models were (very often, revealingly) dressed, made up, and posed, to the range of fashion, beauty, and other consumer goods on display. Advertisements in particular dissected women's bodies: sheer, smooth legs for stockings and shoes; eyes, lips, and nails for glittering and colourful makeup products; suntanned hands, necks, and navels for jewellery; breasts and bums for lingerie; and always luxuriant hair on models' heads (although never, never anywhere else visible, like in a woman's armpit, or on her legs, or arms, or upper lip) for shampoos, dyes, and all the other paraphernalia put out by that sector of the beauty industry. The images of the women presented in fashion magazines were equally fragmented, both in how they were portrayed as ideal types (mother, lover, virgin, and vamp), and in their potential aspirations (celebrity, socialite, and CEO). Magazines told readers that by dressing fashionably, looking beautiful, and mingling with the 'right' people, they could become anyone they wished.

When I moved to Hong Kong a few years later, I soon discovered that Japanese, French, and American fashion magazines often had their Chinese cover versions, so I started comparing their style and contents. As I delved into what other scholars had written about women's magazines, I realised that, like me, most of them had focused on the magazines' contents to frame their (predominantly feminist) critiques. What they hadn't done was talk to those who produced the magazines and found out what they were trying to do, how, and why.[1]

This led me to do just that (people in cultural studies at that time seemed overly concerned with reception studies at the expense of production),[2] and I spent the next three or four years off and on talking to as many magazine editors and other staff (fashion editors, photographers, art directors, advertising managers, and so on) as I could get hold of in different parts of the world. These conversations raised a number of questions. What were the purposes of a fashion magazine? To inform readers of the latest fashions, of who was wearing what in the entertainment world, and where they might find the clothes shown in its pages every month? To provide a venue for advertisers to reach a readership potentially interested in their—primarily fashion and beauty—products, and generally to provide a supportive editorial environment that encouraged firms like Chanel, Gucci, Dior, and LVMH to place advertising regularly so that the magazine's publisher could stay in business and make a profit? To appeal to and reassure—the possibly fragile egos of—fashion designers, photographers, models, makeup artists, hair stylists, and everyone else working in the fashion world by displaying and praising their work? Such questions pointed to the fact that fashion magazines were produced for, and their contents aimed at, multiple audiences. It is this basic 'insight' that forms the focus of this chapter.

Creativity's Audiences

The thing about creativity is that you're always being creative for somebody else, in spite of whatever protestations you may make (or delusion you may have) about the work of art speaking for itself in some kind of universalistic, contextual-less vacuum, and all that. Just who that someone is, however, isn't always that easy to work out.

I guess this issue of creativity's audiences first struck me when I set out to make pots for my own exhibition in a Japanese department store. Then, for the first time, I found myself obliged to put aside my amateur aesthetics and think about who, precisely, my work might appeal to. Were they Miyamoto's collectors? The store's own special clients? Ordinary run-of-the-mill shoppers? Or other potters? I never did think through the answers to these questions and perhaps in the end it didn't matter too much, given that this was a one-off event, where both Miyamoto and Tamaya Department Store persuaded some of their established clienteles to buy my work. But I would have had to do so if I'd been making pottery for a living. As the previous chapters have made clear, most people working in different forms of cultural production need to consider their audiences very carefully when coming up with creative ideas. This is one aspect of social affordances.

The fact that there is rarely a single audience at whom cultural producers direct their work affects the contents of that work in a variety of ways. Fashion magazines are a case in point. Magazine staff members have to negotiate continuously a series of intricate relationships with at least three different audiences for their work: the advertisers upon whose budgets they rely; the fashion world of which they form a part and with which they interact on a regular basis; and their readers. Each of these constituents needs to be represented in, and has an effect on, the contents and layout of a magazine's pages.

Although the previous two case studies of creativity at work reflect the fact that I was able to carry out long-term fieldwork in the ceramic art world and at an advertising agency in Japan, the research underpinning this particular chapter was a little different, for it consisted of more than 40 open-ended interviews with fashion magazine publishers (feature, fashion, beauty), editors, and art directors working in Paris, London, New York, Tokyo, and Hong Kong. It covered four international fashion magazines— *Vogue, Elle, Harper's Bazaar,* and *Marie Claire*—published over a decade between 1995 and 2005 in the five countries concerned, and positioned vis-à-vis competing titles (both local and international) within their different magazine industries. One of my main aims was to find out how women— and issues relating to women—were, or were not, represented differently by these four titles (two American, two French) in various parts of Europe, Asia, and the United States.

As a social anthropologist accustomed to carrying out long-term participant observation among a selected group of people (the *locus classicus* of anthropological fieldwork), I would have preferred to supplement this kind of "'multi-sited' or 'network-based' fieldwork,"[3] in which I was passed along a chain of contacts from one editor or art director to another around the world, with a more standard ethnographic study of at least one cycle of magazine production (or "frame-based fieldwork"). There are at least two reasons for this. First, I have always felt that it is only through actually working on a project oneself that one comes to experience and understand its underlying social processes and unstated assumptions physically (as opposed to intellectually). In other words, I believe that an important aim of fieldwork should be the acquisition of knowledge through embodied experience,[4] which was why I agreed to hold my own pottery show, in spite of numerous reasons for refraining from such exhibitionism. Second,

144 ▣ **CHAPTER 6**

previous frame-based fieldwork (in a pottery community and advertising agency) had made me realise that there is invariably some disparity between what people say they do and what they actually do (however well-meaning they may be in their explanations and answers to questions). The job of the fieldworker is to prise apart informants' own theory and situated action.

During the course of this particular research, alas, I was unable to gain permission to witness a magazine production cycle.[5] Although, as we saw in the previous chapter, I was able to participate in and observe studio fashion shoots in Tokyo (and in Hong Kong), I have in very large part had to rely on what I have been told during interviews, and make my own subjective interpretations (on the basis of what I have read and heard elsewhere) of the extent to which my informants were telling the truth, the whole truth, and nothing but the truth as they perceived it, or were unconsciously, subconsciously, or consciously presenting a rather more glowing picture of that unattainable truth.[6] As part of this subjective interpretation, I should add that, overall, I was very impressed by the apparent openness and self-irony with which those concerned—for the most part women—spoke to me about the hectic world in which they worked and struggled every month to create a product that was meaningful to their readers, to the fashion world of which they were a part, to their advertisers, and to themselves. In general, they seemed less guarded about what they told me than male potters, department store managers, advertising executives, and creative personnel among whom I had previously conducted fieldwork.

Because of these difficulties, but also because of the very nature of fashion magazines, which act as pivotal intermediaries in the value chain between upstream suppliers and downstream customers in the fashion industry, I found myself paying considerable attention to the magazines themselves as written texts and image banks. I used this focus on content analysis both to endorse and to question what my informants told me during interviews. The encounters and engagement here, then, are with creative products, as much as with their producers and consumers.

Structural Issues

There are two aspects about the production of fashion magazines that make them sociologically interesting. First, they are both cultural products and commodities. In this, as I mentioned in the Overture, they do not differ from other mass media productions such as advertisements, pots, art, film, newspapers, and radio and television programmes, as well as fashion itself.

As *cultural products*, magazines may be said to circulate in a cultural economy of collective meanings. They provide how-to recipes, illustrated stories, narratives, and experiential and behavioural models—particularly in the realms of fashion and beauty—in which the reader's ideal self is reflected and on which she can herself reflect and act. As *commodities*, magazines are products of the publishing and print industries and important sites for the advertising and sale of commodities (especially those related to fashion, cosmetics, fragrances, and personal care). Like women's magazines in general, fashion magazines are thus deeply involved in capitalist production and consumption at national, regional, and global levels.[7]

The second aspect I have already mentioned. Magazine production—like that of a number of other so-called 'creative' industries—is characterized by what I have called a 'multiple audience' property. Precisely because they address both readers and advertisers, magazine editors—like newspaper editors, television film directors, and classical concert orchestra conductors, among others—find themselves having to satisfy two main audiences.[8] This leads to a schizophrenic structure of magazine contents, in which the 'purely' cultural can only with difficulty be disengaged from the surrounding sales pitch for fashion, cosmetics, and related commodities. It also gives rise to two anomalies on the financial side. On the one hand, editors publicly talk of reader circulations as an indication of success, thereby suggesting that it is the cultural content of their magazines that sells them. Yet it is primarily advertising income, and not cover price or subscription sales, that enables a publisher to stay in business and make a profit.[9] On the other hand, a title's circulation figure is boosted by various means (such as the practice of cut-price annual subscriptions) to persuade an advertiser to spend his money therein. In other words, magazine publishers sell their readerships to (potential) advertisers,[10] while editors sell advertised products to their readers.

The fact that magazines are simultaneously both cultural products and commodities addressed to two main, and several minor, audiences underpins what follows, as well as the following chapter's discussion of symbolic and commodity exchange markets as they relate to the distinction between culture and economy.

Fashion Magazines and Fashion

The driving force behind the publication of fashion magazines is, of course, fashion itself, an industry characterised by most, if not all, of the economic

properties ("nobody knows," "motley crew," "A list/B list," and so on) outlined by Richard Caves in his comprehensive (and pioneering) study of
creative industries.[11] Like the magazines that derive from its existence, fashion is also both cultural product and commodity, and thus addresses multiple audiences, some of whom are there to show off clothes, others to buy
them, and yet others to create a buzz around them. These audiences include
what Fred Davis has called the "fashion leadership,"[12] consisting most notably these days of celebrities from the film, music, and entertainment worlds,
but also, of course, leading fashion houses and their designers, photographers, models, stylists, and so on; fashion buyers, chiefly from large department store chains; and the international press, including fashion magazines, which reviews and comments on each season's collections, and brings
new trends to general public attention. To understand fashion, we need to
understand the interconnections between its production and consumption,
between the ideals of fashion and how clothes are actually worn, between
what Joanne Entwistle has referred to as "discursive, textual and lived bodies."[13] It is each country's fashion magazines that help us in this quest. They
make styles of dress meaningful, often by means of a system of oppositions
established by comparing this with last season's fashion. In this way, they

> ... offer the reader a map for making sense of the choices of clothes
> available at any one time. In setting out choices in this way, fashion
> magazines not only play a role in promoting certain looks, but in mak-
> ing sense of fashion for potential consumers. The fashion magazines
> is therefore one example of the way in which 'fashion'—as an abstract
> idea and aesthetic discourse—and 'fashion'—as the actual clothing
> made available for purchase each season—connects with everyday
> dress. The advice offered by fashion journalists and editors plays a part
> in framing the choices of consumers in their everyday dress.[14]

Magazines, then, like the pottery critics I will discuss in Chapters 10 and 11,
are important cultural intermediaries in the production-consumption
chain.[15]

Because of the inseparability of fashion magazines from the fashion
industry, monthly editions closely follow the latter's seasonal calendar.
Given this temporal affordance, it is normal for an editor-in-chief to make
use of the seasonal discourses of fashion to prepare a general outline of her
magazine six months in advance. The March and September issues of most
magazines (there is some seasonal adjustment in Japan because of a title's

early publication date each month) are devoted to the latest spring/summer and autumn/winter collections shown in London, New York, Paris, and Milan. Usually, one or two trends in particular are picked out for focus in a following issue. Each season's shows are then generally followed by one special issue devoted to beauty, as seen in runway models' makeup and hair styling, and by another focusing on fashion accessories (in particular, handbags and shoes, which themselves may simultaneously be run as a video during the showing of a collection).

The remaining four issues tend to follow pre-established patterns, some of them related to other aspects of fashion: for example, love, romance, and Valentine's Day in February, often leading to lingerie specials; swimwear specials or what to wear on holiday in July/August; and gift-giving (accessories, jewellery, fragrances) in December. These make use of seasonal trends to put across the chosen theme, and have given rise to the presentation of related commodities as themselves constituting 'collections': from lingerie and swimsuits to watches and jewellery, by way of mobile phones and chocolates as fashion trends. The commodities featured on its pages— either as text or as advertising—themselves become 'fashion' items, subject to constant and regular cycles of change.[16]

Although there have been indications in recent years that the traditional two-season fashion system is giving way to more fluid, continuous production schedules attuned to consumer demands and the technological ability to supply them (the *raison d'être* of stores like Zara), the spring-summer and autumn-winter seasonal distribution of clothing remains very important for fashion magazines on a number of related accounts, both cultural and economic. First, it imposes order on a potentially chaotic mass of clothing that needs to be shown and described to magazine audiences. At present, readers are more or less reassured by the fixed seasonal boundaries within which trend changes take place, so that magazines' creativity *depends* upon temporal and accompanying affordances. Many fashion (and other glossy) magazines now have computerised templates which set story length and picture size in advance; standardise typefaces, headline sizes, picture credits, and other aspects of design that make up what is known as the "furniture" of a page;[17] and contribute to what, in the context of travel guidebook publishing, has been called "spreadsheet culture."[18]

Second, that very order is an essential part of magazines' production processes since, without it, publishers and editors would be obliged to forego their current fixed annual structure of issues and devote far more time and energy to the planning of more content-varied monthly editions.

CHAPTER 6

This would make it difficult for a magazine title to maintain a regular monthly publication schedule on the basis of its existing personnel and financial resources. In other words, creativity as such is *limited* by temporal affordances.

Third, it conveniently structures the solicitation of advertising material, which itself forms the financial base influencing a publisher's decision to launch, maintain, or cease publication of a particular title. In that it depends upon money, creativity is thus *made possible* by temporal affordances. Since magazines are very important to the fashion world, it would seem, in the long run, to be counterproductive for the traditional seasonal structure of the fashion industry to be completely put aside, unless those concerned decide that they want a very different kind of medium in which to publicise their outputs. (This is where the Internet has begun to make inroads on the traditional magazine publication structure.)

Textually, fashion magazines' creative *raison d'être* lies in the monthly 'fashion well'—somewhere between 40 and 52 full-page colour photographs of the latest designer clothes, uninterrupted by advertisements, and featuring well-known designers, photographers, and models (as well as makeup artists, hair stylists, and so on, whose renown is more or less circumscribed by the fashion world). Ideally, a fashion well's photographs should be edited in such a way that the clothes shown fill between 60 and 70 percent of the page, with background amounting to 30, at most 40, percent. The fabric, too, should be clearly shown, although this is by no means always the case.[19]

The clothes themselves are lent by fashion houses, which are more or less cooperative and/or fussy, depending on the status of the magazine asking to use them in a photo shoot (and, of course, on the self-perceived status of the fashion house itself). Magazines use preferred fashion house names, based on advertising placed in their pages, and they ring the changes as best they can to ensure that all are represented over a season, or—failing that—a year. But what is included in a story and what not also depends to some extent on what is popular among readers and sells well in the country in question.[20] In editors' words, magazines *propose* ways in which fashion may be transformed into the kinds of clothes worn in readers' everyday lives. Without the clothes, without the images with which fashion is portrayed, and thus without the magazines themselves, there would be no 'fashion system' as such. It is the fashion magazines that bring together producer and consumer, supply and demand, by means of a host of intermediary figures.

The fashion well is usually made up of around half a dozen 'stories,' each ranging from four to as many as 18 pages in length, and using visual images to illustrate some new fashion trend (for example, "Paint the Town" to illustrate "the power of colour").[21] In international editions of the same magazine title, a 'story' can change quite radically in translation.

For example, "A Fashion without Frontiers" (*Une Mode sans Frontiers*) in the French edition of *Marie Claire* (March 1997) was given the title "In Search of Real Value" (*Honmono no kachi o motomete*) in the Japanese edition, and "From the Village" (in English) in the Hong Kong edition (both April 1997). This means that—as with a model's "look"[22]—a fashion story should not be too sharply defined, but malleable to reinterpretations when creatively encountered by other stylists, directors, makeup artists, and so on.[23]

Lack of space, or the need to include local stories in local editions, may also bring about changes affecting the narrative structure of a fashion story as first conceived and shot. Quite often, a series of photos originating in New York or Paris will be cut from twelve to six or eight pages in Tokyo or Hong Kong. At the same time, pictures may be placed in a different order from the original, and reversals take place when, as in Japan, the magazine opens from right to left, rather than from left to right as in Western-language magazines. This is not always the case, especially when magazines are using the work of well-known photographers who insist on retaining the original form of their story worldwide, in spite of an art director's well-reasoned objections.[24] Nevertheless, it *does* happen, as one deputy editor laughingly explained:

> *Elle Japon's* fashion well consists of six or seven themes and is always 42 pages long—shorter than in the U.S. edition which is about 50 to 52 pages. This means that we have to cut down on some of the stories that we get from there. About half of what we use comes from *Elle International* and half we shoot here. Of course, because we have fewer pages than the American edition, we have to cut their fashion stories. So where Gilles Bensimon will publish a 12-page story, we will only put in six or eight pages. We never tell him, and he doesn't seem to notice—at least, not so far! What's more, we also start changing the 'story' itself quite a lot after it's been edited by the AD over there, and we put the photographs in a different order. Sometimes you begin to wonder whatever happened to the 'story' as it was originally conceived![25]

Ideally, each issue's fashion well should mix up colour and black-and-white photos to create its own rhythmical beat.[26] Each story should link with the others to fit into an overarching theme and create a "flow" that runs through each month's issue of a magazine.[27] Accompanying text (or "bylines") includes anything from a bare description of the clothing shown to details of price and retail outlets at which items are available for purchase. Ideally, bylines reinforce the fashion 'story' told by the visual images.

The stories published in each month's issue of titles like *Vogue* and *Elle* stem from the biannual collections in New York, London, Milan, and Paris (thereby reinforcing the point I made earlier about the industry's need to maintain the two-season system).[28] Fashion editors and stylists from all over the world attend as many as 100 collections each season. There they pick up on certain 'moods' and proceed to imagine the clothes they have seen as 'themes' which are then expressed as fashion 'stories.'

What, precisely, is meant by the word 'story'? Tsukamoto Kaori, at the time fashion director of *Vogue Nippon*, gave me the most complete account.

> The idea of a fashion story is a very difficult concept to explain. In the first place, there are all the clothes I see in all the shows during the different fashion weeks. Together they create inside me a certain seasonal mood, I suppose. Most designers have a message that they want to put across in their shows. This they may have got from everyday events. Or from reading books of one sort or another. Or, most often, from travelling somewhere exotic like North Africa or Japan. Somehow they manage to transform things they've seen into clothing. Of course, there are all sorts of different themes as a result. This means no season is ever totally monotonous in mood, even though to some extent the textile industry may control what's put on display in terms of colours and materials.
>
> Anyway, from the clothes I see on the runways I get some ideas and come up with themes like "a new way to dress up," or "monotone dress-up style," or "elegant but rough"—things like that. I may have in mind something John Galliano did in his show for Christian Dior. Or I may say I want something more specific—like "Grace Kelly–like fashion," or the pictures Irving Penn took of so-and-so in a particular magazine in a particular year. Or I might just hint that I want a "Burberry look," of the kind you find in their current ad campaign. . . .
>
> These ideas are then taken over by a stylist[29] who carries out the shoot and who usually has her own ideas about which clothes, models, photographer, makeup artist, hair stylist, and so on to use. I may agree or disagree with her choices and make counter-suggestions, so

it's really a matter of discussion and negotiation between us before we arrive at a finished idea.

All this is then given a further twist by the photographer. I think photographers tend to start from a different standpoint from ours. They often have a visual image they want to work on and then look for particular clothes to illustrate it. I mean, a photographer may want to capture a mood depicted in a Gauguin painting, for example. Or he may feel like returning to David Bailey's late-60s camera style. Or he may want to recreate the image of Jane Fonda in *Barbarella*. All that sort of thing. This means a story can change again before it finally gets shot in the studio or on location. For me, though, as fashion editor, I start with the clothes, move to a story idea, and then come back to the clothes to illustrate that idea. Probably every editor and stylist in the business keeps in mind all the clothes they see in every collection and are able to match them to different stories that come up. That, really, is what their job is as professionals.[30]

This matching of designer clothes seen on the runways to fashion stories looked at by a magazine's women readers usually takes place immediately after each season's collections. Magazine staff engage in intensive discussions over the course of two or three days, before fixing on certain keywords ('romantic,' 'sexy,' 'power,' and so on) as overarching themes based on the different kinds of materials, colours, and clothing styles presented at the shows.[31] These may figure as appetizers in the opening fashion pages of an issue: for instance, "Sparkling Diva," "Blue Symphony," "Retro Graphics," and "Bohemian Rhapsody."[32] They are then incorporated as the guiding principle of an issue—"Myth and Magic,"[33] "The New Volume,"[34] and "Bold Moves"[35]—and magazine editors set about informing their readers of the "latest fashion trends," praising their qualities and what makes them 'different' from preceding trends, showing how they are actually worn by celebrities, and hinting at how best readers might incorporate them in their own everyday lives.

Although particular keywords are repeated globally in different fashion stories ('volume,' for instance, or 'power' in the Spring-Summer 2005 collections), different emphases (or ensemblages of worth) are brought to bear, so that there is no necessary thematic consistency in fashion wells, either between different editions of the same title, or between different magazines published in the same country.[36] There are two main reasons for this. First, individual personnel compete among themselves as producers

152　▣　CHAPTER 6

to come up with the most successful image formulae, since such success enables them to maintain their current positions while perhaps seeking better positions in other (generally higher-status) magazines. Second, every magazine title competes for readers and advertisers with other titles in a magazine market. It needs to differentiate itself as a product from its nearest competitors to achieve this aim. A worst-case scenario is for it to publish an issue whose thematic contents and/or images are in places identical to those of a competing title. Matsuzawa Shōko laid out the full implications of this concern as she explained how she and her co-editors put together each monthly issue of *Elle Japon:*

> To be frank, probably the thing that worries us most is what our rivals are up to. You see, our nearest rival, *Vogue,* appears on exactly the same day as *Elle. Marie Claire* comes out a few days earlier, and *Spur* a day later. It's absolutely crucial that none of our material nor our magazine cover "doubles" with what's in the other magazines.
>
> How do we ensure this? We have to keep our ears to the ground all the time. This means making use of all our personal connections. We learn a lot from photographers, hair stylists, makeup artists, and even the press, who always let us know when they find out that something we're planning is being done—either exactly or in a similar manner—by a rival magazine. This is what enables us to produce a unique issue every time, but we're always worried about duplication and it is this worry that underlies our monthly editorial meeting.
>
> Fear of duplication also means that, once we've decided on the contents of an issue, we do the photographic work as early on as possible, so that others will be obliged to change their plans if—or rather, more likely when—they find their plans duplicate ours. Then we don't write the text part of the magazine issue until the very end, so that we can be sure that what we say is different.
>
> I have the impression that abroad magazine editors don't have to worry so much about the competition and, as a result, are much freer to do what they want. But you can't do that in Japan. It's a really tough market and you ignore the competition at your peril. So you keep your eyes and ears wide open all the time. That's mostly what editing a magazine is all about.[37]

This extended quotation shows the multifaceted nature of both social and temporal affordances in fashion magazine publishing, and provides an additional take on the role of interpersonal connections in creative work. The net result of this double process of differentiation (which is reinforced by the differentiation inherent in the products of the fashion system itself as presented in the magazines) is that, as Arnold Hauser remarked of art, fashion comes to be defined as what is now consumed as fashion.[38] It is the fashion magazines that in large part contribute to this definition.

Multiple Readerships

The description given here of how editors go about putting together a magazine issue has quietly raised the issue of competing forces, both within the fashion world itself (fashion editor, stylist, art director, and photographer) and between the interests of readers on the one hand, and those of a magazine's advertisers on the other. The omnipresence of advertising of one sort or another in a fashion magazine has led to considerable academic criticism of the relationship between advertising and editorial matter.[39] Such criticism, however, tends not to take account of the delicate balancing act required of magazine editors who cannot afford to take an 'either-or' attitude towards their two main audience constituents:

> When it comes to fashion and beauty, we have to cooperate with advertisers subtly. We borrow different clothes for our fashion pages and have to choose our brands very carefully. We try to balance the interests of both readers and advertisers by representing *everything*. We can't publish whole product ranges, so we take turns among different products put out by different fashion and beauty companies.[40]

Although a lot of academic writing has focused on the role of advertising in the construction of women's and fashion magazines,[41] the point that I wish to make here is that fashion magazine editors are not just torn between the interests of their readers and those of their advertisers. Rather, they have to address several different constituencies within the fashion world as well.

> What you should realise about an international fashion magazine is that there's a secret ranking of its contents among those working in the fashion industry. An "A Class" magazine is one whose fashion stories appeal to and are readily understood by the international fashion village. A "B Class" magazine allows some local content, while "C Class" magazines are more or less entirely local.

This means that a fashion magazine's fashion pages are crucially important. They have to be made abroad for us to get international recognition.... But making fashion stories abroad in the way that we do is extremely expensive. I mean, it costs us something like two and a half to three million dollars a year to produce 60 stories, ranging from 6 to 12 pages each. This is an enormous—and in some respects meaningless—sum of money. But what it does do is get international recognition for *Vogue Nippon* in the fashion village—that is, among photographers, models, makeup artists, PR people, and so on. It'd be easy to lift pages from the American and British editions of *Vogue* and pay very little for the stories, but then there would be no creation. So far as the fashion village is concerned, it is a magazine's ability to be creative that counts. And it is the fact that we produce such high-quality pages that also attracts advertisers.

So my aim has been to make *Vogue Nippon* part of the fashion village. And that means being treated as an insider, not an outsider—which in itself enables us to get quick and immediate access to information and news, because we are seen as an integral part (nakama) of the fashion village.[42]

There are two lessons to be learned from this account. On the one hand, creativity is associated with the *interior* of a social formation (with what Boltanski and Thévenot would call a "domestic world")[43]. This parallels what we learned in the previous chapter: that creativity resides within an individual's 'spirituality,' which itself affords detachment, while creative work itself is framed by, and conducted in, the innermost part of the studio. Creativity, then, is recognized as something that is transferred from an individual's inner self to a cultural product, but also as taking place within a bounded social group: an 'innerness' that is then marked spatially by where creative activities take place.

On the other hand, the tripartite, multiple audience property of fashion magazine publishing referred to by the editor-in-chief of *Vogue Nippon* becomes very clear once we focus our attention on the contents of a title.[44] Page after page is devoted to the activities and public appearances of fashion designers (either as individuals or as a group of professionals), fashion houses, models, celebrities, photographers, hair stylists, makeup artists, and magazine staff themselves. In this way, magazines present not just the clothing that they designate as fashion, but the people and institutions that constitute the fashion world, at both local and global levels.

There are important underlying objectives in this structuring of contents. First, since the fashion industry is marked by continuous change, those involved necessarily seek to impose stability on the instability wrought by the incessant quest for new trends. Magazines assist in this task by commenting on, highlighting, and publicising fashion designers and their collections to create an overall image of 'fashion' itself, its history and development. In particular, they serve to link new trends back to previous seasons in order to create a reasonably harmonic continuity and logic of progression.

Second, as part of this process of stabilization, magazines seek to establish connections among the various different constituents of the fashion industry. They thus print regular features on such topics as "Le Who's Who de la Mode,"[45] and "Who's Bagged Who: Fashion Houses Go on a Shopping Spree,"[46] in which they show—usually through 'genealogical' lines joining a series of portrait photographs—connections between a master and apprentice designer; a film star who is 'muse' of the former and recently selected 'face' of a fashion house, headed by a man who 'discovered' the model, who herself is the apprentice designer's girlfriend, but who previously dated a musician, whose own daughter is fashion editor in a well-known magazine, and so on and so forth. In this respect, magazines not only make known (at a superficial level) the organization of the fashion world; they also situate that world within neighbouring social worlds of the film, music, publishing, art, and entertainment industries. In other words, they make the suppliers of fashion socially relevant to readers who are the industry's consumers.

At the same time, magazines also feature their own roles as intermediaries in the fashion industry's value chain, bringing in fashion editors, stylists, photographers, models, makeup artists, hair stylists, and so on, as well as the activities that they carry out as part of their everyday work... and play. A fashion story, for example, will depict backstage scenes from a fashion show, a fashion shoot, or a model at work as a guest fashion editor: arriving at the magazine's offices, meeting a designer, watching a catwalk collection, and casting a model for an upcoming shoot.[47] In this way, magazines provide an 'inside' view of the fashion world as a means of reinforcing its members' subconscious belief that creativity comes from 'within' the individual and her social world, while at the same time building intimacy with their readers: an intimacy that sustains this belief at the level of consumption.

Third, as part of this production of social relevance, and precisely because the fashion system has become, like so many other creative industries, a system of names, magazines function to make those names familiar, and the work of those names known, to readers. This often involves blatant name-dropping (as well as inventive interpretations of logical causality). For example:

> Toscan du Plantier's scrupulously arranged closets at the legendary Art Deco Mamounia hotel are testament to her organizational skills, brimful of Vuitton, Lacroix, and Dior shoes. There is also a saleful of sparkling gewgaws by Cartier (for whom she is an ambassador). In short, Toscan du Plantier is the essence of faultlessly groomed Parisian chic.[48]

Fourth, through strategies of structural stabilization, social relevance creation, and naming, magazines also provide readers with an entry into the consumption of the products supplied by the fashion industry. This they do in two main ways. In the first place, they juxtapose products in such a way that consumers learn how to move from low- to high-ticket items (from perfume to dresses, by way of shoes and accessories), as their economic well-being permits. In the second, they endow fashion items—a Chanel dress, a Prada bag, Jimmy Choo shoes, Cartier jewellery—with a symbolic value (or capital) that a consumer may then exchange in an economic transaction. For instance:

> Pukka Party Cartier International Polo at Windsor Great Park was one of the most glamorous events of the year. Not only did Cartier command a star-studded guest list, they somehow arranged for the sun to make a brief appearance, too.[49]

As part of this process of linking (and creating?) supply and demand, fashion magazines make full use of both models and celebrities who perform a triple function. First, they sell the clothes, accessories, and makeup that they are shown wearing in fashion photographs ("Rebecca Romijn-Stamos in an Yves Saint Laurent top and Gucci pants").[50] Second, they sell fashion magazines themselves, by appearing on the cover of each title's every issue.[51] Third, by locating themselves, or being located in, a fashion context, they sell the fashion and entertainment world itself ("Nicole Kidman in Christian Dior at the Academy Awards").[52]

Models and celebrities function at both top (supply) and bottom (demand) ends of fashion production. On the one hand, they are photographed on designer collection catwalks and at 'red carpet' events where they are portrayed as virtually unattainable beauty and glamour role models, living in dream homes, with ideal partners, and so on. On the other, they are portrayed as ordinary people, who wear ordinary clothes in their everyday lives (e.g., "Angela Lindvall in her own style"),[53] and who are subject to the customary pangs of broken love affairs, and despair brought on by drug or alcohol addiction (e.g., "Purr! Naomi's feline fine").[54]

The importance of the interaction between these different reader constituencies should not be underestimated. As intimated in the extract from my interview with the editor-in-chief of *Vogue Nippon* cited at the beginning of this analysis, fashion magazines address other fashion magazine and industry personnel as part of a strategy of legitimization and incorporation in the 'fashion village' that they so busily advertise to their general readers. In particular, a title on the periphery can in this way build a cachet that enables its editor to gain privileged access as an insider, rather than outsider, to the latest technical developments, business information, and social gossip taking place at the very core of the fashion world. It is this combination of information and gossip that can then be relayed, ideally ahead of other magazines, to the general public. In this respect, fashion magazines—like many other forms of cultural production—contribute to and sustain a system of names which itself comes to dominate their discourse. Because, as we have seen, production personnel are themselves hired on the basis of their reputations (Richard Caves's "A List/B List"), we may perhaps refer to creative industries as forming an integral part of what is now a *name economy.* This is a theme that I will take up again at the end of this book.

Anchorage and Flow

The fact that every magazine has at least two primary audiences—one of readers, the other of advertisers, each of which is indispensable to enable it to remain in print—means a magazine publisher needs to employ two different kinds of staff. Each of these is concerned with satisfying one audience's needs: the publisher and related personnel in advertising, PR, sales, and marketing, who deal with advertisers; and the editor-in-chief and related feature, fashion, beauty, and artistic personnel, whose job is to put together a magazine's pages in an attractive enough manner to appeal to targeted readers.

Not surprisingly, given their different primary tasks, editorial and publishing staff may find themselves at loggerheads over how the products of their work—editorial and advertising pages—might best be put together in

158 ▣ **CHAPTER 6**

each issue of a magazine title. One of an editor's major concerns is about how the advertisements in her magazine will be distributed throughout each issue, as well as about which particular ads are likely to be found opposite particular editorial pages. Her editorial 'integrity' pushes her to counter the 'commercialism' of her publication's advertising department. There is also a general point of publication policy about whether full-page ads are to be placed on the left or right pages of an issue since, depending on how a magazine is opened, the reader's eye is more likely to alight on one page rather than the other.

What is of note here is that the structure of text and ads in Japanese fashion magazines (like *Vogue Nippon,* for example) is very different from that found in European and American publications (for instance, the French, British, and U.S. editions of *Vogue*). What we find is that in Japan the reader is given precedence over advertisers, whereas in the United States, in particular, the reverse is true. This can be seen in various ways. First, the sheer proportion of ads in American *Vogue* is overwhelming (60 percent of all pages). Moreover, the ratio of editorial to advertising pages in the first half of the magazine is close to 1:15 (compared with 2:3 in V*ogue Nippon*). Second, there is a marked tendency for ads rather than editorial text to be placed on the right-hand (or recto) pages of each issue since it is on this 'static' page (in a Western magazine) that the reader's eye rests.[55] Even important textual material like the "Contents" pages is placed on the verso (left-hand) page and is not run consecutively, but separated by advertising matter (a characteristic of all feature material in the magazine).

A Japanese magazine like *Vogue Nippon,* by comparison, can be a model of reader friendliness. For a start, it keeps strict pagination—unlike its American counterpart, whose actual page numbers run ahead or behind pages as numbered. Then it makes sure to keep its recto (which, in Japan, because of the way in which a magazine is opened is the left) page for editorial, not advertising, matter. In the 2002 fashion issue, for example, only three out of 213 left-hand pages were used for full-page ads, while 151 were used for textual material (the rest were for two-page advertising spreads). Ads are structured differently, too. Instead of placing one ad after another for hundreds of pages on end, as does American *Vogue,* the Japanese title places its ads in blocks between uninterrupted features and thus enables a more equal distribution of advertising and editorial matter. For example, in August 2002, after an initial 20-page block of double-page ads, the "Contents" are presented on three consecutive left-hand pages, before being followed by the "Editor's Letter," which itself leads directly into the regular "In

Vogue" feature of four pages, followed by "Nostalgia," four more pages of "In Vogue", and then "Blythe Style Child" and "Contributors" pages, all on the left-hand page, all with ads facing on the right page. The first substantial textual matter, an uninterrupted six-page feature on the actor Sean Penn, follows. Its end is marked by three two-page ad spreads before the start of a new 17-page uninterrupted fashion feature, "City Girl Goes Tyrolean." This is then followed by a single (left-page) ad before the next feature begins. And so on. This is a typical issue structure and is designed to maintain reader interest.

We may well ask why it is that Japanese and American magazines are so different in their overall structure. It took me a long time to work it out, but the answer was finally provided me by a Japanese magazine advertising manager: in the United States and United Kingdom, magazines like *Vogue* are sold for the most part by subscription, whereas this is not the case in Japan. Many American and British readers take advantage of cover price discounts to pay in advance for their favourite magazines to be delivered through their mailboxes at home. As a result, magazine publishers not only sell their readerships to advertisers, they can afford to pay attention to those advertisers' preferences about where their ads should be placed, as well as to what advertisers would like to see in the editorial pages of each issue. In Japan, on the other hand, there is virtually no subscription system. As a result, publishers have to make each and every issue appeal to potential readers as they browse through dozens of competing magazines in book and convenience stores every month. This they do by keeping editorial matter intact, and by placing advertisements together in blocks, as well as on the right (verso) pages of each issue.

One paradox that emerges in the structuring of magazines that rely on advertising as well as cover prices is that of anchorage versus flow. As will have already become apparent, perhaps, magazine editors believe that it is crucially important to lead their readers from one topic to another, so that the latter actually read through the whole of each monthly issue of their favourite magazine. This they talk about in terms of "flow" (*nagare*), a word that has been used by scholars to describe creativity itself.[56] Advertisers, on the other hand, try their best to make readers stop at the page on which their advertisement is placed, so that they will notice the goods advertised, the name of the advertiser, and so on. This technique, following Roland Barthes's discussion of an advertising image, I will call anchorage.[57] Anchorage and flow (or, in Barthes's terms, "relay") form a fundamental structuring principle of most forms of commercial media.

160　▣　**CHAPTER 6**

One method of anchoring an ad is to have it placed opposite a page of text which in some way reflects the ad itself, usually in terms of product, but also of design (colour, grid structure), image, model's gaze, and so on. As we have already seen, women's magazines in general encourage covert advertising of one sort or another by including textual references to a facing-page ad. Another method of anchorage (though also of flow) is the magazine cover. Since fashion magazines in general are so closely involved in, and act as the mouthpiece for, the fashion world, it is not surprising to find headlines in which names of designers and/or fashion houses (as well as celebrities, models, and so on) are mentioned.

The magazine cover is, of course, a means by which an editor 'anchors' the contents of an issue to make casual newsagent, book, and convenience store browsers stop to look through and, hopefully, buy her magazine. This quickly became apparent during the course of my interviews when *all* those I talked to alluded to anchorage and flow in one way or another. For example, editors said that they would construct each issue around one or more basic 'concepts', based on a particular fashion personality, or on the different materials, colours, and clothing styles people had seen in the collections, "to take the reader from front to back cover in an effortless flow."

In this context, however, the editor-in-chief of *Vogue Nippon* (who was also the title's publisher) made a rather startling admission:

How do I reconcile my search for flow with advertisers' desire to make readers stop at a particular page? That's a tricky one, isn't it? In fact, I believe that my readers actually enjoy looking at ads. This means that I want to know in advance—and the sooner the better—which ads are coming where in the magazine. Some editors abroad like to pin up the whole of an issue on the wall of their offices, with text stories and fashion features filled in, and ad pages left blank. If I had the space to do this here, I'd do the same. But I'd put in pictures of all the ads first, before the text and fashion pages were produced, because knowing what ad is going where helps me construct the text page. You can't really separate the two. It's the two-page spread as a whole that really counts. Each page should play off the other. That's why you can find all sorts of little links between ads and textual matter in terms of layout, content, colour, and so on. [He pauses to show some examples from the latest issue.] It definitely doesn't work all the time, of course, but the simplest way to create a link between pages is through colour matching. This goes on a lot.[58]

This comment contrasted rather markedly with the attitude of the creative director, who said that he hardly ever knew which advertiser's ad was going to be placed where, and therefore that it was virtually impossible to create the kind of flow between pages that the editor-in-chief aspired to. It also was at odds with almost every other interview I had conducted all over the world with fashion magazine publishing and editorial staff, who insisted that the kind of anchorage between advertising and text that I have talked about here—and which by my database reckoning constituted about 10 percent of all magazine pages among titles studied—was for the most part fortuitous since the left hand, so to speak, was generally unaware of what the right hand was doing, and vice versa. Still, it was clearly an ideal to be aimed at. The fact that it was only sometimes overtly practised suggests that the juxtaposition of textual and commercial matter brought up in practitioners' minds the old distinction between 'art' and 'money.' This in itself then raised doubts about how much, if any, 'creativity' editorial staff could display.

CHAPTER 7

Symbolic Markets

The previous chapter's description of how fashion magazines are edited raises a number of issues that are characteristic of creative industries in general: issues that reflect upon the very nature of creativity and a market in which it occurs and is valued. Three issues in particular are of general importance.

First of all, the fact that creative goods are both cultural products and commodities means that cultural producers always have to balance those two sides of the equation between symbolic and commodity exchange values that I outlined in the earlier chapter on ensemblages of worth. Thus, even though a film studio may wish to create a 'blockbuster,' that potential blockbuster must have some sort of cultural content with mass appeal (glamorous spies, UFOs, vampires, pirates, and so on). Such cultural appeal is, however, unpredictable. Nobody knows beforehand if a product will be successful; nor is it understood why it should have become so. Films that are designed to appeal to a smaller, culturally elite audience of some kind tend to be shown in 'art theatres' and to use much smaller budgets for their production. Occasionally, a small-budget 'cultural' film like *The Best Exotic Marigold Hotel* will become a commercial success, with cinema takings far exceeding the income anticipated of its initial budget, but for the most part Hortense Powdermaker's finding of more than 60 years ago is still valid: people in the film industry believe that the more money they put into a film, the more likely it is to be successful.[1] This was an attitude that prevailed, too, in the world of Japanese advertising at the time of my research, and account executives would often complain to me about how a client's 'stinginess' with regard to the budget of an account prevented him and his creative colleagues from doing a 'proper' job. To overcome the fact that "all hits are flukes," people and organizations in different forms of cultural production aim for the blockbuster, even though the latter may be more "a belief than a reality."[2] In other words, a "market world" is not populated exclusively by business relations between buyers and sellers, but also by objects.[3]

Second, this balancing act between culture and commerce was most obvious in my discussion of the relations between textual and advertising

SYMBOLIC MARKETS ▣ 163

matter in fashion (and indeed, in many other kinds of) magazines. Not only do magazines (like ad agencies and film studios) employ two different kinds of personnel—one 'creative' (editor), the other 'commercial' (publisher)[4]—these personnel engage in two kinds of opposing activity: *flow*, which is intended by editors to help readers move seamlessly from one end of a magazine issue to the other; and *anchorage*, which is used by advertisers and a magazine's advertising personnel to stop those same readers in their tracks.

This is by no means a feature of magazines alone. In his study of the making of the *Childhood* documentary series, for example, Barry Dornfeld discusses how producers and editors structured film footage into two distinct types of sequences. One of these he terms "extended"; the other, "juxtapositional." The former, which I see as equivalent to flow, refers to "edited segments featuring a single culture, following recognizable subjects through a series of events." The latter, a form of anchorage, refers to:

> . . . sequences juxtaposing corresponding practices or events across cultures, constructed intercutting analogous material from more than one cultural setting. These structures represent two different documentary modalities between which *Childhood moves.*[5]

Extended and juxtapositional sequences, as Dornfeld notes, may not be entirely discrete categories since the former are "sometimes juxtaposed in longer comparative structures,"[6] but it is clear that flow and anchorage are two fundamental mechanisms for structuring cultural products and performances, whether we are talking of classical music composition, a theatre play, catwalk show, or art exhibition. In other words, the combined usage of flow and anchorage (by whatever name) is found in *all* forms of cultural production, both *within* and *between* products. Consider, for example, the structure of a television police drama, with its primary anchorages of crime scene, car chase, and apprehension of the suspected criminal, and flows of dialogue between paired detectives (Starsky and Hutch, or Inspector Morse and Sergeant Lewis, or Inspector Lewis and *his* sergeant, James Hathaway, in a more recent series), between them and other members of the police force, and between them and a number of witnesses and potential suspects.

At the same time, the television network showing the police drama carefully inserts it into its overall evening programme, which consists of a more or less routinized schedule that might go along the following lines each evening of the week:

- 6:00 p.m. news (national and/or local), followed by the weather;
- 6:30 p.m. quiz show/nature programme;
- 7:00 p.m. comedy/soap;
- 7:30 p.m. reality/variety;
- 8:00 p.m. drama (crime, horror, romance, etc.);
- 10:00 p.m. news and weather;
- 10:30 p.m. sports/documentary; and
- 11:15 p.m. late-night talk show.

In this manner, programming is designed to create a flow that keeps a network's viewers from switching channels during the evening. In other words, the flow is designed to anchor audiences. This is something to which I will return in Chapter 9 when I discuss craftsmanship and creativity.

Third, the fact that many creative goods are directed at more than a single audience has an enormous effect upon their cultural content, and therefore on the kinds of creative inputs (and thus on final products) permitted by those involved in their production. In the previous chapters describing a pottery exhibition, an advertising campaign, and fashion magazine production, we have, time and time again, seen the nature of these effects upon creative processes, as well as upon the coordination of different actors in a market.

The fact that my own pottery exhibition was staged to appeal to potters, as well as to a general public, meant primarily that I had to do something that was different and 'jutted out' from the everyday work of potters. This 'something' consisted of my making *both* stoneware *and* porcelain. Since I had been 'trained' to make stoneware and had never made porcelain before, the work that I created was closer to accepted norms of what stoneware as a genre should consist of, rather than to those of porcelain. This allowed my porcelain ware to be seen as 'soft' compared with the Japanese norm. The decision to work in both types of clay also allowed a crossover in decorative techniques, two or three of which were then adopted by the potters at whose kilns I had made my pots. At the same time, the multiple audience property affected pricing decisions and the establishment of an acceptable level that would not antagonise my potter audience.

The same sort of thing goes on with advertising campaigns, which are always directed at both clients *and* consumers. In a contact lens campaign, for example, the creative team had to struggle with how best to resolve two conflicting demands. The client insisted on advertising its advanced *technology* (product benefit) used to make the new lens being advertised.

The agency's marketing team, however, knew from research that consumers were not interested in technology, but in *comfort* when wearing lenses (user benefit). There ensued a conflict between client and agency stemming from this difference in emphasis on product or user benefit. In the end, since the advertiser was financing the campaign, the copywriter and art director had no choice but to include the client's insistence on mention of its technology, together with its comfort-based appeal to consumers.[7] Compromises like this lie at the heart of most so-called 'creative' collaborations.

Fashion magazines also face this dilemma of having to meet the requirements of at least two audiences: one concerned with advertising commodities; the other with providing textual material that will attract readers of every month's issue. In the case of fashion magazines, the commercial would seem to take precedence over the cultural. Titles have been discontinued because of a lack of advertisers, even though sales were comparatively healthy at the time. This emphasises the fact that magazines sell their readers as much as they sell copies. This confusion of commerce and culture in the markets for cultural products extends to models and celebrities depicted in the magazines. Although readers take a cultural interest in the likes of Kate Moss, Gisele Bundschen, and other 'supermodels,' magazines and fashion designers actually select them for their 'look.' Models are little more than "display objects," with "commodified bodies for sale."[8]

Fashion Magazines and Fashion

So, where does all this take us? In the previous chapter, I applied, once again, Becker's analysis of art worlds as "networks of people cooperating"— this time to the fashion world—and showed how sensibility, public taste, and aesthetic or stylistic discernment in fashion are, as in art, influenced by a long series of intermediaries—designers, fashion editors, stylists, photographers, models, makeup artists, celebrities, connoisseurs, critics, and others—who, through mutual encounters, develop some sort of taste standards and criteria of aesthetic value in relation to the collections offered every season in the fashion capitals of the world (see Figure 4).

The argument I developed went as follows. If, as I think Bourdieu is right in arguing about cultural production in general, the sociology of fashion "takes as its object the field of cultural production and, inseparably from this, the relationship between the field of production and the field of consumers," then we need to consider carefully how that relationship is created and sustained.[9] Reception cannot take place without a special

FIGURE 4: Fashion World Value Chain

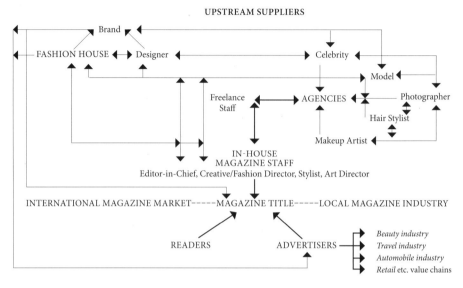

institution which serves that reception and which thus brings about a fruitful dialectic (or creative engagement) between producer and consumer. In fashion, this institution is the fashion magazine.

As intermediaries between producer and consuming public, fashion magazines exist to teach the lay public why fashion should be important in their lives, what the latest trends may be, who are the names that drive them, and where the clothes themselves may be purchased. In other words, they provide the necessary critical authority to legitimise fashion and the fashion world in cultural terms.[10] They make meaningful connections between things that seem to be essentially independent; they give them social lives by creating an imaginary world about them; they create awareness in participants of the field of fashion in which they work; and they provide historical and aesthetic order in a world whose products, by their very seasonality and potentially chaotic quantity, are likely to go unnoticed.[11] In this way, a fashion magazine helps form a collective concept of what fashion is, although—during the course of its administrations—aesthetically irrelevant forces such as snobbery, elitism, trendiness, and a fear of lagging behind the arbiters of prevailing taste are obvious all along the production-consumption continuum.[12]

The production and reception of fashion are thus interdependent, both in terms of communication and of the organization of production and consumption. The 'creative act' of designing fashion is in a state of constant flux because it is influenced by the habitualized expectations of the buying public and intermediary fashion world. These more or less determine what innovations can and cannot be made, how 'creative' such engagements can and cannot be. "Too sharp and radical a break with what is already in vogue may end up as a massive flop in the marketplace."[13] Designers thus need mediators and interpreters of one sort or another to ensure that their work is properly understood and that this appreciation then translates into sales. In other words, like politics, art, or academia, fashion is marked by a struggle to enlist followers, and one task of fashion magazines is to convert the agnostic. In this way, the reception of fashion is a product of social cooperation among those who form "a community of faith" based on a collective belief—or misrecognition[14]—in the power of *haute couture* and *prêt-à-porter*. It is this faith that drives the fashion system.

The apostles who spread the word, who portray and interpret designers' collections each season—giving them a meaning which readers can cling to, removing all the strangeness that accompanies novelty, and reconciling what at first glance may be confusing with the already familiar and thereby creating continuity between previous, present, and future trends— are those working for the fashion magazines. Their job is not simply to appreciate new stylistic trends (often by setting up a series of oppositions between these and the previous season's styles),[15] but to recognize new discoveries, re-evaluations, and reinterpretations of styles that have been misunderstood and/or belong to the past. If designers create the form of fashion items, then fashion magazines create their legend.[16] In this process, they fabricate mythical personages out of designers and the fashion houses for which they work, as well as of other members of the fashion world. This leads to a situation where collections may be judged not by their appreciative or aesthetic value, but by the names with which they are labelled.[17]

At the same time, the public needs fashion magazines since they help their readers distinguish what is 'good' from what is 'inferior' in the apparent chaos of each season's collections in New York, London, Milan, and Pàris. In this way, magazines help transform fashion as an abstract idea and aesthetic discourse into everyday dress.[18] This does not mean, though, that they address a single, unified public. Rather, there is a plurality of publics, each of which brings to bear its own predilections on what magazine editors

168   ▣   **CHAPTER 7**

select as part of their process of legend-making based on culture, lifestyle, age, and prevailing gender norms. Editorial creativity lies in large part in being able to satisfy the diverse tastes of these different publics.

Coordinating Creative Markets

It has become clear that most creative work in the creative industries is carried out by freelance personnel who come together in different combinations of expertise to carry out specific projects: an advertising campaign studio shoot, a pottery exhibition, development of a computer game, and so on. From this the question arises: how are such personnel selected, and what effect does their selection have on the market for creative goods and services?

Creative industries operate in a number of different kinds of markets simultaneously. Some markets, like that for fine wines or Japanese porcelain, are comparatively small; others are very large. But markets are not limited to goods and services per se. They extend to the personnel and organizations providing them, as Bourdieu noted in his distinction between fields of large-scale and restricted production.[19] Large markets include the producers of megabrands: luxury conglomerates like Louis Vuitton and Gucci, for example, and umbrella brands like Walt Disney, Virgin, and Nike. Small markets embrace professional groups of architects, as well as trendsetters, critics and other 'experts,' and all sorts of freelance creative workers (designers, art directors, photographers, stylists, models, makeup artists, copywriters, IT analysts, and so on). Each of these markets operates according to different regimes of economic coordination, in which relative qualities, quantities, and prices are expressed in mutually independent dimensions.[20] Together they coexist as two antagonistic economic logics.[21]

What Lucien Karpik calls a "market of singularities" is marked by the multidimensionality, quality uncertainty, and incommensurability of its cultural products and professional services. It therefore requires coordination devices of one sort or another to help consumers judge and decide what is and what is not 'good.' Such devices include different kinds of networks, appellations, cicerones (critics or guides, like fashion magazines), rankings, and confluences. Together, he argues, these create trust in a situation of uncertainty and lead consumers to judge products and services in terms of qualities, rather than of price, when making purchasing decisions.[22] I am not convinced, however, by Karpik's suggested hierarchy that emphasizes evaluation over valuation since, as I explained in Chapter 3, an equation between symbolic and commodity exchange values has to be calculated if a purchase or sale is to be followed through. These I have discussed as ensemblages of worth where evaluation and valuation coincide in an establishment of "market worth."[23]

To account for the relations between particular cultural products (fashionable clothing, pots, and ads), particular judgement devices (fashion magazines, pottery kilns or terroirs, and "blue chip" accounts), and particular forms of consumer commitment (fashion world and high-street consumers, collectors, and advertising clients), Karpik develops a typology of markets which he calls "regimes of economic coordination," each of which (there are seven in all) is distinguishable from the others by "a particular working logic." It is this logic that separates art and fine wine from films and luxury goods, for example, or literary prizes from popular music.[24]

To take a concrete example, the market for ceramics in Japan functions in what Karpik calls the "authenticity regime" (*honmono shikō*, or "pursuit of authenticity," in Japanese), whose characteristics include large numbers of products carrying a rich symbolism (from tea ceremony wares to folk art [*mingei*], by way of the "six old kilns"); numerous judgment devices (in particular, gossip and word-of-mouth; personal, trade, and practitioner networks; potter names and terroirs of production; critics; magazines and art books; and rankings of both potters and the department stores in which they exhibit their work); primacy of quality competition over price competition (although this is muddied somewhat by one-man exhibition and department store rankings based in part on sales); relatively balanced competitive forces, where potters, collectors, gallery owners, department stores, and media organizations are able to balance one another through short- and longer-term alliances; critical pluralism, in the sense that critics tend to specialise—as we will later see—in different kinds of ceramic art (contemporary, traditional, tea ware, craft, and so on); and a reliance on two types of antithetical consumer: the connoisseur and the layman, with the former "driven by a sufficiently strong aesthetic passion to invest thought, time, and money to arrive at the desired choices," while the latter tends to be thrown back on trial and error.[25] Nevertheless, customer competence, activity, and autonomy are promoted by means of exhibitions and media publications, which reinforce fairly strong consumer commitment. Like the authenticity regime of fine wines, there are few barriers to entry in the ceramics market. It is composed in large part of small producers who can, and do, become extremely successful, although there are also larger concerns. The market for Japanese ceramics functions according to names;

its logic is primarily 'aesthetic' and based on the notion of 'originality' (generally phrased, as I mentioned earlier, in terms of 'difference').

Fashion magazines, on the other hand, operate in the so-called 'mega-regime,' together with the fashion houses whose products they promote and advertise. Fashion magazines provide that dense fabric of texts, images, representations, discourses, and social celebration with which the fashion world clothes itself. It combines luxury goods (accessories) with fashion (clothes) to propose 'good taste,' whose worth is associated with social superiority (so that no purchase can be a 'mistake'), and whose appeal is to continuity of the 'timeless classic' (in spite of the six-monthly spiral of seasonal 'changes'). Social status and timelessness coalesce in the brand—that "name that designates other names" (Chanel, Versace, Dior, YSL, Prada, Ralph Lauren, Armani, Louis Vuitton, Burberry, and so on)—each guaranteeing reliability (a promise) and pointing to a symbolic universe (a sign). Competition is waged between these names, and not their products as such, and it is the belief that products can become signs that makes the fashion industry.[26] In this fashion magazines are virtually indispensable, as they "help decide among social and aesthetic codes, judge works, celebrate creators, fuel the People columns, accompany certain evolutions and refuse others, castigate denials or betrayals, spark genuine and false controversies, and play on images."[27] In many ways, fashion magazines are not so different from the authenticity regimes of ceramics and fine wines. They make use of similar judgement devices (gossip, names, networks, and so on); they also appeal to two kinds of consumer (fashion-conscious celebrity and social elites on the one hand, and middle-class consumers on the other). But they are influenced by and represent commercial (advertising) rather than critical (text) devices, as well as being driven by a clear profit motive (seen in a publisher's decision to close down a title because of its lack of advertisers, even though it may have a large and regular readership). Titles like *Elle* and *Vogue,* each with local variants in more than 20 countries worldwide, propose "a global logic of aesthetics"[28] that brings together would-be consumers in places as different and as far apart as the United States, Colombia, the Czech Republic, China, and South Africa. It also proposes "a global logic of names."

While the authenticity and mega regimes discussed here make use of impersonal devices (as does the expert-opinion regime to which I will come back in Chapter 11), there is also what Karpik calls a "network-market" underpinned by personal devices. In general, network-markets don't have any specific activity that you can readily name: they are not like a "stock market," for example, or a "commodities market" or "energy market," or anything tangible like that. They don't advertise their goods or services, either, which means that practitioners' fees and particular expertise tend to be secret. In fact, network-markets exhibit very few public signs of their existence since they "exclude the spontaneous encounter of supply and demand."[29] They operate regularly, however, because they are embedded in social relations and personal 'devices' of one sort or another: this is very important when it comes to producing singularities.

Karpik distinguishes between personal, trade, and practitioner networks, and it is the last that interests me here because it is the least understood by scholars. When it comes to the operation of network-markets in cultural production, features of one kind of network are to be found in the others. This is primarily because, in the creative industries in particular perhaps, practitioner networks are simultaneously personal and trade networks. Thus, as we saw in the previous chapter, word of mouth is the crucial means by which knowledge is communicated. Stories, gossip, personal experiences, names, judgements, and evaluations all provide information and knowledge that enable decision-making based on comparison. These personal devices are an efficient way of organizing creative work in a job market where impersonal devices, such as a degree or other form of certification, provide no more than basic information about a person's capabilities.

Each practitioner of creative work needs to engage with other practitioners. These 'encounters' may be with people doing the same work—photographers associate with other photographers, musicians with other musicians, and so on—but more often they are with other kinds of practitioners, without whom they cannot do their work. Thus photographers create relationships with models, bookers, stylists, hairdressers, art directors, fashion designers, magazine editors, and so forth. Musicians, on the other hand, tend to build connections with other musicians, though primarily with those who play different instruments from themselves, since by so doing they can form new and different groups playing new and different sounds.

In creating more or less diverse, and more or less dense, networks, creative practitioners rely in large part on trust. And it is trust that builds reputations and allows some people to be employed, and not others. It was on the basis of trust that the agency art director delegated the day's work in the studio to the photographer and hairdresser. It was this trust that the hairdresser threatened to break when she insisted on one more shoot of the model's hair. Trust, then, is a device for ordering a practitioner's network-market, because it removes, lessens, and/or suspends the uncertainty surrounding a market founded on personal relations, with all its accompanying rumours, criticism, gossip, anecdotes, and so on. The only reason it is able to do this is because "trust is rooted in a symbolic system that combines knowledge and belief."[30] Precisely because network-markets are not characterised by objective information, calculation, and/or contracts, participants have no alternative but to resort to trust. Creativity, then, is ultimately founded on belief. It affords a system of magic.

Symbolic Markets

It is clear that fashion magazines, like fashion itself, simultaneously embrace and operate according to two distinct types of market: one, in the words of Patrik Aspers, "aesthetic," the other commercial or economic.[31] This broadly parallels the general distinction made between 'culture' and 'economy,' as well as that between magazine-as-cultural product and magazine-as-commodity, although it brings the market as an institution into sharper economic focus. If we accept that markets are where calculative agents live from goods and services which organize, mediate, and maintain their social worlds,[32] and that they are constituted by the different values these agents bring to bear to such occasions,[33] we need to explore such worlds in the context of creative goods and services. It is in markets that evaluations relating to their perception, knowledge, representation, and use are brought to bear and played out among competing agents.

A neat example of how a field of cultural production is so divided can be seen in Ashley Mears's discussion of prestige (editorial) and mass market (commercial) "distinct yet overlapping spheres" in the world of fashion modelling:

> We can think of editorial and commercial fashion as "circuits of value" because players in each share different measures of success and value. Editorial and commercial producers have distinctive understandings of what counts as good taste, good work, and fair payment. In fact, a large sum of money from catalog clients, when looked at from the editorial circuit, is worthless compared to the few hundred dollars to be earned from a magazine shoot. Editorial and commercial producers share different ideas about what counts as the 'look' at all. Within this field, models, bookers, and clients all grapple for better footing in what amounts to a prestige hierarchy. The fashion field, from a sociological point of view, looks at times like a battlefield.[34]

SYMBOLIC MARKETS   173

This "look" divides between "edgy" for catwalk and magazine models and "soft" or "classic" for those who are photographed for catalogues, with the former produced for other *producers* in the fashion world and the latter for mass market *consumers*.[35] In exchange for low payments for their work, "edgy" models gain considerable symbolic capital, whereas "classic" models are symbolically worthless, even though they bring in steady above-average earnings that keep model agencies in business.[36] So why bother to model on the catwalk or for magazines in the first place? Because:

> Agencies and models are betting against the odds that symbolic capital will eventually pay off in the long run should the model score a luxury-brand campaign. This is the occupational jackpot, which can pay millions of dollars, renewable for several years.[37]

Mears, like Patrik Aspers and Joanne Entwistle,[38] refers to this kind of economy (rather than market as such) as "aesthetic": a word that makes me somewhat uneasy, as my earlier discussion of affordances and values should have made clear. There are two reasons for this. First, "aesthetic" tends to suggest an appreciative unity that rarely—if ever—exists in any creative world. As I have already suggested, different participants bring to bear different sets of aesthetic, or appreciative, values at different points in the commodity's path from production to consumption, primarily because they have different ambitions in mind with regard to the final disposal of that commodity. These competing sets may well exist side by side (as when a fashion photographer thinks carefully about the equipment he is using while simultaneously composing a picture in such a way that it is aesthetically pleasing), but they may also be partially incorporated in the other(s) as required (as when a photographer using digital equipment convinces a client that an offending wisp of hair can be removed from the model's face at the click of a computer mouse, and thereby perfect the image in the client's eyes). Every aesthetic economy or market, however, is marked by a plurality of competing aesthetics, which needs to be accounted for.

Secondly, when applying aesthetic criteria, people almost invariably invoke factors other than the purely aesthetic in their judgements. A respected designer, for instance, will receive rave reviews for his work, simply because he is a respected designer and not because of the clothes he shows (and woe betide the magazine that dares to be lukewarm in its review).[39] Of this Aspers is himself clearly aware. He notes how photographers build up social capital through skills, conventions, and trust, making their work as much to do with people in the photography and related markets as with their technical knowledge. The fact that they use agents also enables them to avoid talking about money, and to focus instead on technical and aesthetic issues in their interaction with fashion stylists, hair stylists, makeup artists, and so on.[40]

This suggests that the overarching concept of "aesthetic" needs to be broken down into constituent parts before being reassembled (which is why I introduced the notion of ensemblage in Chapter 3). For instance, a fashion designer views an item of clothing somewhat differently from a photographic opportunity–conscious film star, on the one hand, and from a sales-conscious buyer, on the other. Whereas the first brings a professional's *technical* eye to bear on an item's aesthetic elements (its material, weave, cut, and so on), the second considers the *uses* to which she can put her dress, the *appreciative* impact it will have on her admirers, and her enhanced *social* image as a celebrity when her name is linked with that of a famous designer, ideally in a particular *situational* context (like the Grammy Awards, for instance). Together, as I suggested earlier, these five sets of values constitute a *symbolic exchange* value. The buyer, on the other hand, looks hard at how best to convert this symbolic exchange into *commodity exchange* value leading to sales, turnover, and profit. In other words, all contribute to an ensemblage of worth, although each comes to it from a different perspective.

So, as in the ceramic art world, we find that different people in the fashion world bring multiple values to bear on an item of clothing. Some pride themselves on the unusual uses to which they put things: a tie brought into service as a belt around the waist, or a pair of chopsticks pinning loose hair behind the head. Others are concerned primarily with technical aspects of their work as professionals: lens aperture, film, and shutter speed for the old-fashioned photographer; language and typeface for an art director when asked about his magazine's visual style.

We've developed a special typeface from Futura, which I call Elle Nova. It has ten different weights, from ultra-light—which you can hardly see—to ultra-black, which is really dark. But we hardly ever use the full range of weights and end up using three to four of them for headline display, and two weights in Futura Light for what we call "the deck": that's the subheading below the headlines. [Guillaume indicates the mock-up of a cover on his computer screen.] We prefer to use all capitals here, rather than large and small letters, because the latter leave a lot of spaces when the script goes up and down with each letter. But capitals are very hard to read, so we have to compromise here and there, and adapt to particular circumstances.

We have a lot of readers who've been taking the magazine since it started, you know, and they sometimes write in to complain about the size of typeface we use. So we have a minimum size of 8 for captions and usually use 11 or 12 point Garamond for the body copy. Garamond is very easy to read. I've experimented, you know, with about 20 different scripts and printed out a whole page in each of them to see how they come out differently. Garamond is to my mind easily the best for reading. I really like it. I find it gives the text a depth, a vertical depth that you don't see at the first reading.[41]

This detailed technical account is not meant to suggest that art directors are *only* caught up in techno-material affordances. They also pride themselves on their aesthetic vision (model's pose, background lighting, set colour coordination, and so on), and prefer to work with people whom they know and like, as we saw in Chapter 5 in an art director's reasoning behind his selection of a particular photographer.

Yet others think almost entirely about the social world in which they find themselves, and couldn't care less how a particular dress is made, or even how much it costs, provided it is made by the 'right' designer and looks 'right' for them on the 'right' occasion. Still others might value the name of a particular designer or fashion house, because it adds kudos to their store, but they view the fashion items coming from that designer as a commodity that must be sold. Thus their appreciation of a dress or suit takes on a rather different nuance from that of the disinterested 'creative' professional, since it is closer to an ideal consumer's taste (which itself, is influenced by all kinds of social, cultural, and symbolic factors).

This suggests that a market is aesthetic, therefore, only in so far as, compared with an economic market, it bears more obvious signs of appreciative values in its makeup. It is still influenced, however, by techno-material, temporal, spatial, social, and economic factors, all of which contribute to its traded objects' worth. Likewise, when a market is defined as economic, the aesthetic is not absent as such, but merely played down. This raises the question of what to call them, since each market is constituted of separate combinations and weightings of the different affordances outlined in Chapter 1, leaning now towards the aesthetic, now the economic. The issue is further complicated by the fact that in the market world, consumers are *att*ached to objects through desire, but *de*tached from one another "in such a way that they lend themselves willingly to every opportunity to engage in a transaction."[42] And yet, as we have seen, creativity in production in Japan rests upon *de*tachment of maker from object, which itself affords *at*tachment in the form of collaboration between different people involved in the creative process.

So where does this leave us in the game of classification? If we are going to stick with a dualism, and clearly it is easier to do so than adopt an unwieldy hexagonal structure of the kind portrayed in Figure 1, my suggestion is that we follow Pierre Bourdieu's example (even though it may be unfashionable to do so) and drop the term "aesthetic" in favour of "symbolic"[43] and that we keep in mind the potential fuzziness of "symbolic" (not to mention "cultural") by focusing on the five values that I suggested constitute symbolic exchange: technical, appreciative, social, situational, and use values. These, too, are brought to bear in different combinations and with different emphases by different members of the fashion world, depending on their internal location along the value chain between supply and demand, and on their habitus formed externally in the society in which they live and work. This is what I mean by ensemblages of worth.

CHAPTER 8

Designing Ceramics

The encounter that takes place in creative industries between 'artistic' endeavour and 'commercial' imperative is the subject of this chapter, in which I will focus on the often conflicting ideals of 'good work' and the 'need to sell': in other words, at appreciative versus economic values. In so doing, I am going to go back to pottery for my subject matter, but this time turn not to Japan but to Denmark, where I recently looked at the conceptualization, design, and manufacture of a faience dinnerware series by the Danish Royal Porcelain Factory, now known as Royal Copenhagen.

Royal Copenhagen was founded in 1775 and has been producing porcelain dinnerware for more than two hundred years. It is particularly well-known for its so-called "Flora Danica," a blue fluted dinner service with gilded edges and cobalt floral designs (known as *musselmalet* in Danish). In 1993, Royal Copenhagen broke with its porcelain tradition and launched a new faience dinnerware series, which it called "Ursula" after the potter who designed it, Ursula Munch-Petersen (b. 1937).[1] The fourth generation of potters living and working on the island of Bornholm in the Baltic Sea, east of Denmark and south of Skåne in Sweden, Ursula Munch-Petersen worked as "artist in residence" at the Royal Copenhagen factory in Frederiksberg from the late 1980s into the early 1990s.[2] It was then that she designed the Ursula series and, together with a number of colleagues at the factory, nursed it into production.

I came across Ursula pots fairly early on after moving to Copenhagen from Hong Kong in the late 1990s, mainly because our daughter has the same name and my wife and I used to buy the occasional small pitcher or dish when giving presents to friends or other members of the family. I have to admit I wasn't that impressed by these pots. Having been brought up to appreciate folksy "Dartington brown" wares made by English and Japanese craft potters, I wasn't particularly keen on the slightly flamboyant colours of the Ursula range. I also thought it grossly overpriced, although I did appreciate the functionality of the different dishes, bowls, jugs, and so on. It was this, in the end, that won me over and led me later to embark on the study that forms the subject matter of this chapter.

178 ▣ **CHAPTER 8**

The story that I am about to tell is, unlike my long-term participant-observation in Japan, based on interviews rather than on fieldwork (although I twice visited the Royal Copenhagen factory in Glostrup and was shown all the production processes taking place there). As a result, there is less immersion in the nitty-gritty of everyday activity (such as we witnessed in Chapter 4, for example), or in struggles with creative processes, but I have done my best to explore the various evaluative practices, or 'editorial moments,' that took place during the conception, design, manufacture, distribution, and sale of the Ursula series, as told to me by the potter herself, the (now retired) product development manager at Royal Copenhagen, the chemical engineer who worked with her on the glazes used in the series, and a designer who was also "artist in residence" at Royal Copenhagen at the same time as Ursula Munch-Petersen.[3] Their recollections together reveal their perceptions of Ursula as a potter and craftswoman, as well as of Royal Copenhagen as a company, and the resultant clash between two different forms of engagement: one with design aesthetics, and the other with a marketing image and brand.

A Tale of Two Factories

Ursula Munch-Petersen's training in ceramics was broad and closely linked to mass production practices. After childhood exposure to her mother's pottery, she worked for a couple of years in a well-known Danish pottery turning out "functional art" wares (*brugskunst*) before starting at the School of Arts and Crafts in Copenhagen in 1956. After graduation, she spent a year working in her grandfather's terracotta factory on Bornholm, before finding employment in an experimental workshop located in the Bing & Grøndahl ceramics factory (where her aunt Gertrude had worked from 1949–1959). This gave her an opportunity to show her work in a number of exhibitions both in Denmark and abroad. From 1970 to 1975, Ursula worked at home on a series of salt-glazed wares for home use. During this period, she was employed at the School for Arts and Crafts (*Skolen for brugskunst*), where she held a position until 1990. In 1982, she published a book titled *Clay Forming* (*Lerforming*).

We can see immediately that I am talking about a very different kind of potter from the ones we met (including myself) earlier. Here we have an 'intellectual' craftswoman who both teaches and writes about pottery, and in so doing acts as the standard-bearer of a particular set of aesthetic values. Her work has been strongly influenced by folk craft utensils, as well as by her long-standing interest in botany, whose methods of taxonomy, she claimed during one interview, often influences the form typologies that she develops. Following the initial success of her Ursula dinnerware, which was first manufactured in 1993 and which won the Design Plus Prize in Germany that same year, Ursula Munch-Petersen has striven to combine precise, functional internal forms with 'accidental' and natural external forms and decoration. In this respect, her work is conceptually not *that* far apart from the folk art *mingei* ideals espoused by Yanagi Sōetsu and his colleagues in Japan, and later taken by Bernard Leach back to England, from where they spread to other parts of Europe, including the Scandinavian countries.

In 1985, after spending the best part of a decade working in Bing & Grøndahl, another pottery factory located in Copenhagen, Ursula was invited to make a dinnerware series by Erik Magnussen, a fellow student during her years at the School of Arts and Crafts, who was then artistic consultant to the company. As she explained:

> This was when the Ursula idea all started, although the year before I'd made a serving set (*serveringsdele*) for a show at the Industrial Arts Museum in Copenhagen. The well-known cookbook writer, Camilla Plum, used it in the museum café to serve food to visitors one weekend. I decided to develop this idea and design a simple set of serving dishes: a large oval dish, three or four smaller dishes, and a raised cake plate of the kind Camilla Plum had used.

As she set to work on her designs for the Ursula series, however, Bing & Grøndahl was taken over by the Royal Porcelain Factory, as it was then called, and in 1987 the new company of Royal Copenhagen was formed. After a period of uncertainty, Ursula suggested that Royal Copenhagen produce the simple series of pots that she had in mind for serving food. The new management, however, was unable to come to a decision: at times it said yes; at other times, no. In 1988, just as she was beginning to despair, Ursula was awarded a three-year bursary by the Danish Arts Council. This obliged Royal Copenhagen to provide her with a workshop, and with what she called a "symbolic salary" as she gave up teaching and devoted herself full-time to designing the Ursula series.

Things did not go at all smoothly, however, in large part because of the new company's management style, something that Ursula herself said she never really came to understand. Finn Næss, product development manager at the time, explained things to me as follows:

CHAPTER 8

One of my jobs was to oversee all the young artists who were taken on by the Royal Porcelain Factory at that time. So when Ursula Munch-Petersen arrived, she naturally came under my care. I had to deal with all sorts of so-called 'artists' and a lot of them were extremely egocentric and overly self-confident. But not Ursula. Ursula immediately came across as different. She was really humble, right from the start. She was someone who wanted to *learn*. I liked that. We all did.

When she came to the factory, Ursula brought with her a limited range of utensils that she'd made in her studio at home. But they were still pretty primitive so far as their development as *products* was concerned. The forms weren't properly finished, and the glazes weren't at all even, or anything like that. All in all, you could say that they were very much based on a concept of something that was *hand* made. So we had a lot of work to do to develop that concept into something that could be sold as a Royal Copenhagen product, which, of course, is very far from being hand-made.

What Ursula was unwittingly up against was the new company's management style, which somehow had to reconcile the different corporate cultures that had existed in Bing & Grøndahl, on the one hand, and the Royal Porcelain Factory, on the other. Finn Næss continued:

Compared with the Royal Porcelain Factory, Bing & Grøndahl always treated its artists extremely well and the company developed a milieu that enabled both close contact with management and fine artistic work. The trouble was that a lot of this artistic work didn't *sell* very well. And because there was a lot of it coming off the production line, Bing & Grøndahl found itself with a large stone hanging round its neck, dragging it down. That's why it was taken over by the Royal Porcelain Factory and the two of them merged into Royal Copenhagen.

Unlike Bing & Grøndahl, the Royal Porcelain Factory didn't place all its artists together in one big workshop. Rather they distributed them around according to their particular speciality. So a sculptor would be placed in the modelling room, and a painter in the painting room, and so on and so forth. This meant that, after Bing & Grøndahl was taken over, it was difficult to separate their artists physically because they were used to working all together.

There was also a totally different chemistry between artists and management. At the Royal Porcelain Factory, senior management didn't come and see what their artists were up to every day or even two or three times a week, in the way they used to do at Bing & Grøndahl. Instead, they told their artists to display all their work in one room once every three months and the new Royal Copenhagen leadership would turn up in their fine suits and ties, look around at what was on display, and say things like, "that's OK," "that's no good," and so on and so forth. This was the way they selected work for further development or rejected it for the dustbin.

During this process, the artists weren't allowed to be present. So it was my job to find out what was right or wrong about each of the products and let the artists concerned know. They never got a chance to hear anything directly from senior managers. Nor were they able to question their decisions or explain to the leadership why they were doing things the ways they were.

Of course, two or three of Bing & Grøndahl's former managers were there, too, because they'd also become part of Royal Copenhagen after the merger. So there were two totally different worlds at work in the same room. On the one hand, there were the old Royal Porcelain Factory lot, in their fine suits and colourful ties. And, on the other, there were these really down-to-earth production-oriented people from Bing & Grøndahl. And, of course, they had totally different opinions about what was 'good' and what was 'bad,' about what was worth developing further and what wasn't.

And Ursula's work was something they *really* disagreed on. The Royal Porcelain Factory managers thought her work was "a little primitive" and asked what the point was in having it included in the Royal Copenhagen production line. The Bing & Grøndahl people, with whom Ursula had developed very strong connections during her time there, thought it really exciting and imaginative.

As you can imagine, this was a dilemma for both sides. What were they going to say to Ursula, who—let's face it—had a big vision? The Royal Porcelain Factory managers just didn't like this kind of work, while the Bing & Grøndahl managers obviously did. In the end, the Royal Porcelain Factory lot *pretended* to like what Ursula Munch-Petersen was doing. Privately, though, they said her work would never sell. It was all a matter of internal management politics. The two groups had to keep face.

What we can see in this account are four interlocking creative encounters and attempted appropriations of what they found there. One was Ursula Munch-Petersen's own engagement with faience materials and design aesthetics. It was these that drove her to experiment with one shape rather than another, and to test some glazes rather than others, as she tried to create form and colour combinations that, to her way of thinking, matched perfectly the faience clay with which she had chosen to work. Two sets of people—managers of Bing & Grøndahl, on the one hand, and of the Royal Porcelain Factory, on the other—then struggled with each other as each encountered Ursula's work in the light of their previous experience in faience or porcelain production. Bing & Grøndahl managers praised her work in *aesthetic* (and accompanying *technical/material*) terms because they were used to faience and appreciated its subtleties, but also because they prized the *social* relations they had developed with the potter when she was working in their factory. The Royal Porcelain Factory managers, on the other hand, took Ursula's aesthetic ideals at face value, but then applied them to the already tried and tested designs that had made Royal Copenhagen porcelain so famous. In other words, they applied *different* technical/material values (vis-à-vis porcelain, rather than faience) and were concerned with the image of the Royal Copenhagen brand. This is a point to which I will return later on in this chapter.

Clay and Glazes

I have already shown in my account of my own exhibition how materials and production processes afford certain kinds of pottery. What differs in this account is that, in addition to production practices, corporate structure and management practices also had an effect upon the final outcome of the form taken by the Ursula tableware range. Let me start, though, with technical issues because these also came into play, particularly with regard to form and decoration (glazing).

There was sound reasoning behind Ursula Munch-Petersen's decision to work with faience clay, rather than with porcelain. As she put it:

I personally like faience, what people call "the poor man's porcelain," but most artists or craftsmen at that time preferred the real thing: porcelain. In fact, even though the production of faience is said to be 'cheap,' it's just as expensive as, perhaps a bit more so than, porcelain. Anyway, so far as I was concerned, faience was what was interesting because you could get such fantastic colours with it. Royal Copenhagen had bought up a faience factory called Aluminia quite a long time previously. As a result they had a treasure archive of glazes that nobody ever used. It was these that I wanted to try out on my Ursula line. . . .

Faience ware is fired twice. First, pots are fired to a comparatively high temperature of 1160 degrees Fahrenheit.[4] Then they are spray-glazed and refired to a lower temperature of about 1065 degrees. The two firings prevent the pots from being porous. Both the clay and the transparent glaze materials—feldspar and quartz—are natural and purchased from Cornwall in England. But Royal Copenhagen also uses synthetic pigments for the different coloured glazes. Although not herself trained in chemistry, Ursula Munch-Petersen, like all potters, used to make glaze tests in her kiln at home and wrote down all her recipes and results meticulously to ensure repeat results. However, working with faience at Royal Copenhagen proved to be a challenge, not only because faience is very different from earthenware or stoneware, which Ursula was used to, but also because of the different kilns and firing methods used.

> I soon learned that firing glazes at home and firing them at the factory were rather different things. In my own kiln, I could make adaptations as I went along, by increasing the temperature, adding more air to the fire, and so on. But Royal Copenhagen used a tunnel kiln. Pots went in one end and came out the other. There was nothing you could do in-between. . . .

The man she worked with closely on developing glazes for the Ursula series was Peter Poulsen:

> Ursula's samples had been glazed at home and were for earthenware basically. Not for faience. This meant that they had to be adapted, and that we had to find glazes that would fit the faience clay body used by Royal Copenhagen. That was my job, and Ursula and I worked quite closely together, making adaptations to test results as we went along. We'd agree that one glaze was a bit too transparent, for example, and needed more yellow in it. Things like that.

Although they clearly got on very well together, they soon found themselves in difficulty, as Ursula herself explained:

There were two problems. Firstly, we couldn't use a lot of the old glazes because of new working environment improvements that came in during the 1950s and 1960s. A number of restrictions were introduced on materials like cadmium and chrome, for example, because they poisoned the atmosphere in the workshops. This meant that a lot of old glaze tests that were really nice just couldn't be used any more.

So we had to develop new glazes, or adaptations of old ones. At first, I wanted 10 different glazes: yellow, blue, reddish-brown, light green, green, dark green, grey, lavender blue, black, translucent white, and transparent. I planned to use as many as I could, within reason, on each form, so that a medium-sized dish, for example, would be made in all 10 colours.

This led to a second problem. In pottery factories in Germany, for example, a minimum number of forms are manufactured in a large number of different colours. Royal Copenhagen, on the other hand, was exactly the opposite. It produced a large number of forms in just one or two colours. I wanted them to change to the German style, because it made financial sense, and the pots would look better. I mean, you can change production colours from one day to the next, but not forms. They take ages to get right. But Royal Copenhagen refused. They're still working in the same way today. Multiple forms and few colours.

Exactly why the company refused to change its stance and cooperate remains unclear, but it would seem that the potter's approach also created its own difficulties. Peter Poulsen later commented:

I think Ursula was too ambitious in one respect. She wanted to have every single one of the pots in the Ursula dinnerware range in *all* of the colours that we developed. Her ideas were all right in principle, but they were too difficult to carry out in actual production.

After starting out with 10 different glazes, therefore, potter and chemist found themselves initially having to drop grey, black, and transparent for commercial reasons. They wouldn't sell.

But then [Ursula continued], the dark green became a problem because of the tiny amount of lead in the recipe, and we had to drop it. I wanted black instead, but the Royal Copenhagen marketing people wanted nothing of it and eventually we settled on the grey. They also wanted much more yellow than I did. I myself would have preferred to have had much more white than there currently is. . . .

During our talks, potter and chemist disagreed about the effect of lead in a glaze. According to Ursula:

Lead doesn't actually do any harm for the most part, even though people make a lot of fuss about it. You see, the fact that a glaze is vitrified prevents harmful substances from coming to the surface of a pot—except if you put some sour liquid in it and leave it there for a considerable length of time.

Peter Poulsen was less sanguine:

The dark green glaze that we started with had to go, unfortunately, because it contained copper, and copper can seep through a clay body and make it porous. And that won't do with dinnerware that you have to eat off and wash up all the time. I don't care what Ursula herself says. This is the fact. You can't have lead in a dinnerware glaze. So that was the end of the dark green glaze, even though it was really beautiful. Still, we did keep it on the handles of the Ursula cups, because nobody's going to lick them or anything like that. But we couldn't put it on the dishes, or bowls, or jugs, or any of her other dinnerware pots.

Lead wasn't the only problem the two of them faced during their many glaze tests. One dark green glaze that they succeeded in developing (without lead as an ingredient) was rejected because it affected another part of Royal Copenhagen's standardized production process. As we stood in her kitchen admiring a large dark green jug, Ursula explained:

That glaze isn't so bad either, is it? It's a thinner version of the other . . . . The trouble is Royal Copenhagen said it made their *sorting* too difficult. You see, the glaze varies in thickness and colour as it melts down the jug's outer form, and in places it's a bit speckled. Royal Copenhagen has always been very particular about sorting firsts from seconds. Look!

She picked up a very large, blue-rimmed white oval dish and showed it to me.

This is a second because it's got flaws on it here [she pointed to a red crayon mark on the surface of the pot near the rim, and then to another in the centre]. And here. Not those red marks. They wash off. They're there just to indicate where the flaw is. On the rim, it's this tiny spot here. See? In the middle, I don't actually know where it is. And frankly, as a potter, I don't think it matters at all. Anyway, a slight imperfection can add to a pot.

Still, you can see that, if they're going to be so picky about tiny little spots like these, the sorters at Royal Copenhagen would *never* be able to work out what was right and what was wrong in a glaze that was *designed* to vary in colour on different parts of a pot. So that was the end of that glaze experiment!

There were endless small problems like this all the time I was working with Royal Copenhagen. Take my jugs, for example [Ursula stood up and went to the far end of the table at which we were sitting to demonstrate]. Ideally, you should lightly wipe the rim of each jug after it's been glazed. Like this [she brushed the lip of a jug with a rectangular sponge]. That way, the glaze won't become too thick at the tip of the spout so the jug will pour better. But Royal Copenhagen refused to do this. I don't know why. It's a little thing perhaps, but it could have made the design just that little bit better and more practical.

Design and Form

Initially, Ursula Munch-Petersen designed the Ursula series in the same way that she designs a lot of her work, starting with two-dimensional sketches which she then converts into three-dimensional forms at home (like some of my own preparations for my one-man exhibition). After making a number of different shapes and sizes, she selected those that she thought were best and took them along to the factory to get samples made, glazed, and fired.

I prefer *not* to keep details exactly the same when I design things. So, while the handle here [she pointed to a middle-sized jug] is straight, on the large jug I have indented it slightly. It's the same with these plates. Royal Copenhagen said they should be oval like the dishes, but I said no. So we kept them round.

Sometimes there's no system in making a design, so you just can*not* draw what you're thinking of. Like this bowl here [she showed me a faceted white bowl that was lying on its side just in front of me]. I did this in an afternoon, working with plaster of Paris, cutting off each side as I went along, until I ended up with this nine-sided bowl. There are a lot of things like this that you can do, but just can't talk about coherently.

Ole Jensen, a designer who worked in the room next door to her in the old Royal Copenhagen factory in Porcelænshaven and who clearly shared with Ursula a craft attitude towards design principles, had this to say about her design process:

Ursula used to make a lot of clay models. A lot of them went into the waste bin, but some went on to the next stage when they were made in plaster, and from these a few moved on to the model makers and were cast in moulds. It's really hard work because a lot of things needed to be changed all the time. Remember, she wasn't working in a digital age then. There was no digital equipment at the factory, so everything was based on manpower in those days. It was really, really close to being… old-fashioned. For sure, it's a good way to learn.

Finn Næss explained what happened then:

Once we got the go-ahead to develop Ursula's ideas, I took her off to the Modelling Room and introduced her to the people there, in the same way that I did for other artists whose work we decided to develop. Ursula was very energetic and demanding—in the good sense of the word. She was very particular, for example, about the exact angle at which a handle should be fixed to the body of a cup, or how *precisely* a spout should be formed at its tip. This contrasted with the rather primitive look of the work that she'd made at home in her studio and then brought in to the factory. . . .

Ursula herself had more to say about teapots and spouts:

I've made at least 10 different teapot designs over the years. Some of them have had squarer handles; others lids over the top, rather than fitting inside; some spouts that are tapered, other that are cut off, and so on [she lifted the lid of one of the two teapots standing on the table between us]. It's difficult to get a really good fit when the lid is placed over the top of the teapot, and that's why I prefer this other style where the lid fits into the top. Ideally, too, a spout should be tapered like this teapot here, because that allows the tea to pour much better without dripping. This means I can make the spout itself a slightly different shape and angle to the body of the teapot. But, precisely because the tip of the spout is tapered like this, it is fragile and can get chipped easily. Hence this cut-off style, which Royal Copenhagen wanted.

Another example of a problem with form concerned the spherical lids that were designed to act as both jug lids and small dishes in themselves.

I designed these to be both lids and dishes in their own right. This is how I like to work—making multifunctional wares. There weren't any problems with these dishes as lids for as long as Royal Copenhagen made everything here in Denmark. But some years ago, they started to have some of the pots made abroad. This jug, for example, was made in Portugal, I think, before later being made by Nikko, a well-known porcelain factory in Japan. But the lid continued to be made in Denmark. But because there was more shrinkage in the Danish clay, the lids ended up being too small for the jugs, so they'd be too loose and sometimes fall into the jug itself. It was such an elementary mistake to make. But they made it!

Both Finn Næss and Peter Poulsen agreed with Ursula about this, although their perspective was somewhat different. Finn explained:

There were a couple of things that happened that should never have happened with the Ursula series. One concerned production, the other stock.

The first problem stemmed from the fact that Royal Copenhagen management began to get more conscious of production costs and started outsourcing. They decided to have the *whole* of the Ursula production done in Japan by Nikko. This meant we had to start production all over again, right from scratch. In other words, we found the original models, made copies of them, and sent the copies out to Japan, together with test moulds. Nikko then had to use these moulds with *their* clay, make adaptations, and send them back to us for inspection and approval. Ursula and I would examine them closely, make comments about how we wanted forms improved—pinching a lip here, softening a line there. I'd write everything down longhand in Danish and then give it to a secretary who'd translate it into English. Then we'd send the English instructions back to Nikko, who then made more tests, which they sent back to us for further examination. And so on. It was a *lot* of extra work, but, to their credit, Nikko did a really excellent job and their quality has always been really good.

The second problem concerned stock. There was a time when a lot of stock was kept over in a warehouse in Malmö in Sweden . . . and orders were being taken here before being sent over there. This caused everyone a headache because the Ursula series consisted of *so* many different items. I mean, you had all the dishes, jugs, cups, and so on in the first place: a couple of dozen or more different forms. And then you had each of them glazed in all sorts of colours: dark blue, light blue, russet brown, and grey for the big bowls, for instance, and all seven colours for the little ones. That made for an awful lot of stock items, because each one had to be labelled differently: 1189 571 for a small bowl with a dark blue glaze; 1189 575 for a middle-sized bowl; and 1189 576 for a large bowl, both with the same blue glaze. Keep the same pot but change the glaze and you had a different stock label: 1188 576 for yellow, for example, or 1187 576 for dark green. You can see how easily pots could get mixed up. And they did. Either we got our customers' orders wrong, or we just couldn't deliver the right orders in time. As a result we lost a lot of customers: big ones, too. In this respect, you could say Ursula's concept was too complex. . . .

Well, maybe. But it neatly supports Ursula's own argument, mentioned earlier, that Royal Copenhagen would have done better to emulate German factories and limit the number of forms that it manufactured, or else stick to its own strategy of one or two colours only. Peter Poulsen continued:

You see, one tends to simplify things once production gets started. With the Ursula series, for example, we started with a transparent white glaze on the underside of each dish, within the foot rim, and glazed the rest of the dish in green, yellow, grey, or whatever-coloured glaze. But once we started production, it became simpler to glaze the whole of each pot in the same colour, top and bottom. This is the sort of thing that goes on with every production line. It's normal procedure to change things as you go along during the first one or two years. But *stock* was something we should've thought about and worked out beforehand. Whether that was marketing's or Ursula's fault isn't clear in my mind. But one thing I *do* know. If she'd been told about the potential problem, she would have *listened* to advice. . . .

What, then, was the role of the marketing department in development of the Ursula series? After all, this was where a potter's aesthetic values would normally come up against commodity exchange or economic values. Did the marketing people talk to Ursula about consumer tastes or advise her to change her designs at all? At this she laughed sadly:

Designers weren't *allowed* to participate in meetings with marketing people. I know it sounds crazy, but that's how it was. I don't know why. Maybe it had something to do with the fact that we designers are immersed in design history and are influenced by one aesthetic movement or another, while the young girls in fashionable clothes and high heels who were in marketing knew absolutely nothing about Bauhaus and design schools like that. It struck me that marketing people were more concerned with copyright than with design.

So I wasn't ever involved in a discussion of forms with marketing people. At the very beginning, they insisted on my making round serving dishes because they said that the oval ones wouldn't sell. In fact, they were quite wrong. It was the oval dishes that sold, not the round ones, which were then discontinued! They also wanted me to develop the series beyond just serving dishes. That's why cups were added, for example.

In concurring with Ursula, Ole Jensen hinted once again at the importance of the Royal Copenhagen brand in many people's minds:

The marketing department in Royal Copenhagen was much more focussed on luxury products than on selling everyday common pieces. It was more trained to tell stories about luxury life in contrast to daily life. This is one of the reasons, I think, that the Ursula series didn't work commercially.

It was, therefore, the product development rather than marketing department that gave advice on designs, forms and glazes, as Ursula explained:

Finn Næss acted as intermediary and was really helpful during my time at Royal Copenhagen. He was involved in all kinds of meetings and told me what to do, saying things like: "Now you should write a letter to the director of the company," or "You'll just have to accept this glaze, or the whole things ends right here." It was Finn who told me that my idea of having a kitchen series of 10 bowls nestling inside one another had to be modified to five, so I agreed, even though I really wanted 10.

The factory's mould-makers had a favourite word they used all the time when talking about making forms. What was it now? Ah yes! *Compensate.* You had to *compensate* for this or that when making forms. It's sad, isn't it? Words like this are part of a lost language, now that production's been shifted abroad and pots are no longer made in Denmark. Anyway, they would talk about how to *compensate* for what happened to the clay during drying and firing and so on. You know, the clay would sag a bit, so they had to *compensate* by making the forms more vertical. Things like that. And I had to go along with these adaptations, although I think that perhaps in some cases I shouldn't have.

Corporate Practice

One of the sticking points through the entire development of the Ursula series was the fact that Royal Copenhagen's management did not seem to want it to go into production. Ursula clearly enjoyed telling the story of what happened to change things:

> At the end of three years, the company said it wasn't interested in my designs. I wasn't prepared, though, to take no for an answer. I countered that I had to show something for the Arts Council bursary I'd held while at the factory designing the Ursula series, and told them I wanted to hold an exhibition of my work. Very reluctantly, the company agreed to let me show 50 pieces of each design for a month in its city centre store. That was at the end of May 1991.
>
> The show turned out to be a great success and everything sold out very quickly. Then the fun started. A well-known journalist, Henrik Steen Møller, wrote a fantastic review of my exhibition in the newspaper *Politiken.* A few weeks later, he wrote a scathing critique of a Royal Copenhagen product in the same newspaper. This led to an

exchange between the CEO of Royal Copenhagen and the editor-in-chief of *Politiken* when the two men were sitting together on some board or other. The former complained about the newspaper publishing a critical article like that about a Royal Copenhagen product, so the latter asked to visit the factory to see things for himself. And, since he liked Steen Møller, the editor-in-chief took him along when he went. As they were going around, looking at all the work there, Henrik kept asking: "Why don't you produce Ursula Munch-Petersen's work? Is it too difficult? Are there technical problems, or what?"

And the Royal Copenhagen people couldn't answer these questions, so the CEO eventually said: "Of course, it will come." And once he'd said that, Royal Copenhagen had to do something about the design, especially after Steen Møller wrote about it in Politiken. They couldn't back out of things after that. Still, it took them some time to find the models and glaze tests we'd made while I'd been there, because they'd all been put away somewhere hard to find. As a result, things didn't get going for another two years or so.

Perhaps, though, she was not an entirely innocent bystander in this process, for she was clearly aware of the importance of *social* values in getting her work accepted. Finn Næss had this to add:

In a way, Ursula has always been her own marketing machine. She's been good at networking with people who matter: Erik Magnusson, for example, who was artistic consultant at Bing & Grøndahl; Camilla Plum, the well-known cook; and, of course, Ebbe Simonsen, boss of Bing & Grøndahl, who was Jewish and had his own connections with fellow Jews like the editor-in-chief of the *Politiken* newspaper, and—I think I'm right in saying, though I may be wrong—Henrik Steen Møller, the journalist.

But connections or not, things didn't proceed smoothly, primarily because of a difference in emphasis: one on *material,* the other on *brand* (or *appreciative*) values, which itself reflected a worker-management divide.

Ursula could see that the Board of Directors wasn't really interested in her work, but it didn't take account of her personality: of the fact that she was really engaged and believed in what she was doing. She'd move around the factory at will, pursuing her objectives with the Modelling

Room, Glazing Room, and so on, and everyone liked working with her. And as a result, *everyone* wanted to see the Ursula dinnerware project succeed.

What was missing in all this was that management didn't have any confidence in Ursula Munch-Petersen's decisions, even though all the factory floor workers did. As a result, everyone working with Ursula owed their loyalty to *her,* rather than to the company that employed them. We all wanted her to succeed.

Ursula herself clearly appreciated this, in spite of her reservations about the factory's management style.

> There were a lot of really good people working on the factory floor and I really learned a lot from them. They were all very different from one another, too, because in those days each "room" (*stue)* had a very different cultural environment from the others. So the Modelling Room (*modelstue*) was totally different from the Decorating Room (*maler-stue*), which was again different from the Glazing Room (*glasurstue*).
>
> But the factory as a whole had a special culture of its own. You always learned to look behind you and hold the door open for people carrying heavy loads of pots, for example. At the same time, some of the workers had almost been born in the factory so, as you can imagine, there were always plenty of intrigues going on. But I made really close friends with some of them. . . .

What emerged during the course of discussions was that Royal Copenhagen's management had trouble envisioning how the Ursula series should be positioned vis-à-vis the company's other products. Ole Jensen expressed this most clearly:

> Royal Copenhagen met with enormous success with its "Mega" floral design in the 1990s. This changed the company's international ambition and shifted its focus from artistic wares to its traditional designs. The Mega design was *extremely* important because it enabled the factory to survive and thrive. Perhaps it could have survived on the Ursula series and on my own designs, I don't know, but neither of these was *typical* of Royal Copenhagen ware, unlike the Mega design, which had a close link to the factory's classical tradition of Flora Danica. . . .

194   ▣   CHAPTER 8

If a company like Royal Copenhagen is to compete internationally, either it needs to be big and rich, or it has to focus on new pieces.
Royal Copenhagen chose to focus on its tradition, and this is one of
the reasons the Ursula series hasn't been a big commercial success. The
marketing people didn't feel comfortable with this kind of work. . . .

This observation led to Ole elaborating on Ursula Munch-Petersen's overall
approach to pottery design vis-à-vis Royal Copenhagen's, and thus on the
different appreciative values brought to bear:

When you buy Royal Copenhagen, you're buying luxury. Within this
concept, the Ursula series is a kind of *simple* luxury, but in fact it represents much more a kind of . . . *un*luxury. It's a sort of schism, a paradox.
When Ursula makes an unluxury product in the context of a luxury
brand, then something's wrong. . . .

He expanded on this observation in the following manner:

If you spend a lot of time in a porcelain factory, you begin to get
interested beyond unique pieces in making daily kitchen ware or
dinnerware for common use. . . . You get interested, too, not in mass
production as such, but in the production and reproduction of artistic
qualities. So, from that point of view, Bing & Grøndahl offered a really
good chance to a young ceramicist like Ursula.

At the same time, you find all sorts of different skills and different
specialists in a factory, so you need to harmonize with them in order
to be able to do your work. . . . I think the Ursula series represents the
very *best* of a craftsman's qualities, the best of Ursula Munch-Petersen
herself, and the best of the art industry itself: I mean, of the engineers,
painters, formers, and so on. . . . For this reason, I think it's a pity
they've stopped making it this year.

The quality of the Ursula design, the details, the sensitivity, the
glazes, and shapes are first class. Still, sometimes when you're working with factories and so on, even if you've done a good piece, you're
never sure if it'll be a commercial success or not. This is because a lot
of parameters have to be met beforehand. Artists often have no control
over this part of . . . the game.

So perhaps Ursula collaborated with the wrong company. Perhaps
she could have had more success elsewhere. I don't know. How can I

put it? As an artist, she had some eggs to lay, but perhaps she laid her eggs in the wrong nest. Sometimes, as an artist, you just can't control things. I think this is what happened with Ursula. . . .

Nevertheless, and in spite of discontinuing the Ursula series in 2011, Royal Copenhagen has occasionally taken advantage of its acclaim to boost its image, according to Peter Poulsen:

> We *worship* Ursula Munch-Petersen. And we worship the Ursula series. A year ago, to commemorate 50 years of something or other, the company used Ursula as a logo or icon to tell the world what it made. Ursula has become its flagship design. But they never said it was Ursula Munch-Petersen who designed it. Instead, they just took the credit themselves. That was *scandalous*. I wrote and complained to management.

Ole Jensen added:

> From the very, very beginning I'm sure Royal Copenhagen thought Ursula was going to be one of the big ceramicists in Denmark, and for sure, one of its cleverest and most important. But, at the same time, the company thought she was in opposition to what they liked and what they wanted to make and do. And it's true. She has been a little bit in opposition to the brand. . . .
>
> In a way, Ursula is looking for opposition. In her line of thinking, to be an artist is not simply a matter of making the right form, or of being a craftsman. It's a way of searching for the opposition role, in a positive sense. As a designer, you have to be in opposition, and a company like Royal Copenhagen needs designers whose way of thinking is in contrast to everything that's accepted, both in the market and within the company itself.
>
> Sometimes, being in opposition means you can change something in the factory's mindset. But, in the case of Ursula, although she's produced important artistic work that is respected, what she did *not* manage to change was the mindset inside the company: the management's mindset, that is. I'm sure Ursula spent a lot of time discussing things. She's a rebel in the best sense of the word and you need to be a rebel when you collaborate with the business part of design. I don't mean that you need to enter into a big discussion all the time about the ideal way of doing things. You can be a rebel without being one in *everything*

CHAPTER 8

you do. In the beginning, Ursula was in opposition to how to do business, but—as I said—this creates a kind of schism: you're against being a part of the business because you're a part of it. I think Ursula could have learned a *little* bit about how to be more dynamic in the situation in which she found herself.

An Aesthetics of Production

Unlike many potters or other craftsmen of the kind I have talked about in Japan, Ursula Munch-Petersen is known for being articulate about her work and about what makes a pot 'good' or 'bad'. Ole Jensen commented on her ability to see the potential in a design very early on in its process. "She has a good 'eye' and uses her thoughts to formulate and explain why something is interesting, or not." He continued:

> She is also one of the few ceramicists with the intellectual power to write down her thoughts. She's written and talked a lot about handmade craftwork. You could call her, perhaps, a little too intellectual. But she's much better than a lot of artists, craftsmen, ceramicists, textile weavers, and so on who aren't any good at talking. Their power is based only on the expression found in their work. Ursula likes to discuss her work in an intellectual way and she's always been very, very articulate . . . .
>
> I've learned a lot from Ursula, both in terms of technical ways of doing things, of course, but mainly through her ideas about why one should make a new product. Ursula finds it difficult to make something new just because the market is looking for it. It's not that she's a romantic or anything like that; rather that it's important for her to find the right reason for making a new piece. For Ursula, it's extremely important to be critical—not in a negative, but in a positive way—to enable her to communicate human, rather than just commercial, values. Of course, working in a company can be very stressful, because it consists of many different parts, and you have to take part in the game. But the whole thing about [the] Ursula [series] was not to make a new collection as such, but to produce something that consisted of human and functional values. . . .

These comments express an aesthetics of production, as seen by a designer. But Ole Jensen's ideas were clearly shared by others working at the Royal

DESIGNING CERAMICS 197

Copenhagen factory. Peter Poulsen, for example, who is a chemical engineer by training, gave a succinct summary of his attitude to work:

In our kind of work, we have to know what's 'good' and what's 'bad.' And that isn't something you can talk about or explain. It's not up for discussion at all. That's the way it is. Ursula knows what's good, and I like to think I do, too. To be able to make this distinction between 'good' and 'bad,' you have, first of all, to know your *materials*. You have your transparent glazes and your matte glazes. You have to know which materials dissolve, and with what effects, and which don't: things like that.

And then you have to *communicate*. You have to enter into dialogue with other people, learn to speak the same language as they do, in order to be able to make the necessary adjustments to the thing you're working on. Ursula was really good at this sort of dialogue.

Thirdly, you have to *work*. It's as simple as that. For me, I have my basic glazes that I then have to develop to create this effect or that. And that is simply a matter of work. Nothing else.

And the driving force behind materials, communication, and work is the idea. Without an idea, you've got nothing at all.

At the same time, though, you've got to understand other people's work. Otherwise you can't communicate. That's why the Royal Porcelain Factory used to give us a training in *every*thing. I mean, I first trained as a painter. That means I can paint Flora Danica: not well enough for production line purposes, maybe, but well enough to understand decorators when they talk to me about a problem they face.

I also learned how to make moulds and press clay, and how to fire, of course. I had to, in order to be able to communicate and understand different people's problems. In the old Royal Porcelain Factory, all of us were trained as generalists before we became specialists. That's all gone now, of course.

The fact that the Ursula series has now been discontinued was cause for reflection by those to whom I talked. Both Ole and Peter, in their different ways, felt that the Ursula series represented a craft tradition that was now lost. First, let us hear Ole:

There are still a lot of buyers—you may prefer to call them consumers—who can tell the difference between high and low quality. But when you no longer have the opportunity to make something in absolutely the best quality, then the public's ability to distinguish between good and bad quality disappears, in a way. This isn't to say that Royal Copenhagen now produces bad-quality products. It's just that it's not possible any more for designers to be close to other craftsmen, like the model makers, painters, and so on. The Ursula service really represents the kind of quality you get in your hands when a designer works closely with the craftsmen and people who produce it. In a way, this is what the art industry has lost during the past 25 years, but it was probably unavoidable. . . .

It's a pity Ursula isn't in production any longer. I wonder why it's not possible to make money out of making and selling her dinnerware, although I'm sure it will be a very important part of Danish design and ceramic history for a long time to come, because of its sensitivity and uniqueness. . . . But one of the reasons why production has had to be stopped is because it's too expensive. For a commercial success, you need a good balance between production costs and retail pricing. The Ursula series has been a little bit *too* expensive in its production because of its high quality.

This has always been the craftsman's dilemma, right through history. It was a dilemma for William Morris, a dilemma for the Bauhaus. What happens is that work based on an idealistic tradition of producing the best and highest-quality pieces for everyday users ends up consisting of luxury items. Their prices are always a little too high.

Here we find the classic opposition between art and money, between appreciative and economic values. To this Peter Poulsen added situational, social, and material values, as he talked about this sense of history and loss from his viewpoint within the company:

If there's one thing that stops me from walking out of this job, it's history. I mean, I've *inherited* other people's hard work. The transparent glaze that we still use was first made by the founder of the Royal Porcelain Factory more than two centuries ago. It's basically still the same recipe. Of course, over the years, we've added to it, and we're still doing so, but I don't want all that accumulated knowledge to disappear just because I retire and there's nobody left at the factory who knows what I know and who can continue my work.

DESIGNING CERAMICS   199

So that's what keeps me going. That and the fact that the people I work with here are fantastic. They're so committed, you know. Committed to the work they do and to what they produce. In spite of everything.

And it seems to me that it's all going to be lost. In the same way that we've almost lost the skill of how to decorate porcelain. In the old days, the Royal Porcelain Factory in Frederiksberg used to employ two thousand people. Now, we've got just *fifty* women working in the Decorating Room here in Glostrup, *eighty* of us overall . . . .

I learned the basics of chemical engineering from my teacher at Technical University, of course, but since then everything I've learned has been through *experience.* You learn through your *fingertips* in my job [Peter rubbed two of his fingers on his thumb]. This isn't knowledge that you can see or read about, even though some people believe all you have to do is make a video of something for other people to be able to do what's wanted. But learning with your fingertips isn't knowledge you can see or pass on just like that. A lot of people just don't understand that.

CHAPTER 9

Craftsmanship

In the previous chapter, I situated creativity in a tale about design and craftsmanship: about conceiving, making, modelling, glazing, and firing clay in such a way that the finished product—an oval platter, lidded jug, or cake plate—is appealing in itself, while contributing to a class of other products, in this case a line of tableware manufactured by Royal Copenhagen. Such appeal arose from a series of ongoing evaluations, of qualifications and requalifications, by potter, glaze engineer, product design manager, modellers, sales and marketing personnel, and Royal Copenhagen's Board of Directors about how to *transform* an original concept into a finished product. In this way Ursula tableware has had a career[1]—seemingly coming to an end when production was discontinued by in 2011, but later reborn when a well-known Danish restauranteur, Klaus Meyer, initiated negotiations for its renewed production in China for his restaurant chain, and given further life in my own account of its development. Thus do cultural objects pass through continuous "modalities of valuation"[2] and evaluation.

Embodying Skills

One of the themes underlying many chapters in this book has been that of craftsmanship. Craftsmanship of all kinds is founded on highly developed skills: in the previous chapter, a potter's or modeller's bodily understanding of the plasticity of clay and the accompanying possibilities and limitations of form afforded by it; and a chemical engineer's hands-on experience with certain ingredients—quartz, feldspar, and a variety of pigments—that, mixed in the right proportions, produce attractive colours appropriate to the forms. Their relentless pursuit of excellence allowed Ursula Munch-Petersen, Peter Poulsen, and their coworkers to take pride in their work, while anchoring them in tangible reality.[3]

Theirs is not an exceptional story, although it might be seen as such when compared to my own fumblings with pottery-making for exhibition in Japan. Cultural producers tend to know what they are doing, whether they are hairdressers who believe that they can, with one more take, execute the perfect style for a model's tresses, or photographers who know exactly what they can and cannot do with modern digital cameras and computerized images. Makeup artists can reproduce *exactly* an actor's bruised and battered face, including remade 'cuts' and the right shade of 'blood', from one day to another, when shooting takes longer than anticipated and makeup is removed at the end of a long day, so that the film's audience never realises that a particular scene has been shot over more than the time it takes to show in a cinema. An experienced silversmith knows how to hammer and roll a sheet of metal, thick enough not to break during subsequent stages of production (chasing, engraving, burnishing, polishing, gilding, even inlay inscription), but not so thick as to be unworkable (and waste precious material). S/he knows, too, how to estimate the size of a two-dimensional sheet that needs to be applied to three-dimensional objects (a chalice or lamp, for example).[4]

Craftsmanship, then, is skill based on "situated learning"[5] and trained practice. Just how long such practice is, or is thought should be, however, depends. In Japan, a pottery apprenticeship used to last for 10 years, calligraphy 21 to 23. Richard Sennett notes that, in a medieval guild, an apprenticeship was for seven years, and that these days "about ten thousand hours of experience are required to produce a master carpenter or musician."[6] What seems relevant, though, in assessing the amount of trained practice needed to become skilled is the market and accompanying economic affordance. The fact that there is little daily mass consumer demand for examples of Japanese calligraphy affords an extremely long apprenticeship. The greater the demand, the less time people seem prepared to undergo training. In medieval times, uncertainties brought on by an open market encouraged ambitious apprentices "to buy out or beg off the last years of their contracts."[7] In contemporary times, Sennett's ten thousand hours works out to be about five years of 40-hour weeks. Most Japanese pottery apprentices nowadays spend less than three years learning their trade because there has been great demand for pottery during the postwar period: enough to encourage young potters to believe that they can make an adequate living if they set up on their own. The fact that that demand has now fallen off may lead to lengthening periods of apprenticeship.

Craftsmanship depends upon—indeed, is born from—an ability to imitate. Copying exactly the master's work, therefore, is a critical part of the training of an apprentice who starts out by trying to reproduce a landscape painting, Chinese character, or teacup, day after day, week after week, month after month. This requires discipline and mental concentration (*seishin tōitsu*), but what is most important in such copying is not so much what is being copied, as how the copying is done. In particular, it is correct bodily movement that allows energy (*ki*) to flow into the brush, clay, or sword.[8] Eventually, the student is allowed to move on: to another landscape painting, another example of calligraphy, another ceramic form. It is mastery of form that instruction in Japan seeks to inculcate.[9] In Japanese Noh theatre, copying (or *monomane*) was raised to a fine art form by Zeami Motokiyo (1364–1444), for whom imitation finally ended in "non-imitation." It was when imitation became united with the imitated that the barrier between the inner mind and the outside world disappeared as the actor's concept of self evaporated. In this way, imitation was ultimately transformed into "the beauty of gentle gracefulness" (*yūgen*).[10] In other words, physical activity came to be closely associated with inner spirituality, and ultimately transcendence: something that has pervaded the work of John Ruskin, William Morris, Yanagi Sōetsu, and a host of others writing about arts and crafts in the nineteenth and early twentieth centuries as they sought to come to terms with industrial capitalism and mechanization:

> The hope of pleasure in the work itself: how strange that hope must seem to some of my readers—to most of them! Yet I think that to all living things there is a pleasure in the exercise of their energies, and that even beasts rejoice in being lithe and swift and strong. But a man at work, making something which he feels will exist because he is working at it and wills it, is exercising the energies of his mind and soul as well as of his body.[11]

This perceived link between the physical and the spiritual, then, is by no means peculiar to Japan. In the days before the invention of the printing press, manuscripts were copied laboriously by hand. A monk or nun who wrote six hours a day six days a week over a year would have copied out the entire Bible. By so doing, "a monk would hear and hold to matters eternal; through copying a nun would come to know by heart as by hand the slow turn of the Word."[12] This echoes the previous chapter's story of the interactions between head and hand, as Ursula Munch-Petersen and her colleagues sought, through many trials and occasional errors, to 'grasp' at solutions to the creative problems they encountered. As Peter Poulsen succinctly summarized a lifetime of working with glazes (coincidentally echoing the thoughts of Richard Sennett): "You learn through your *fingertips* in my job."[13] Touch is the arbiter of both form and colour when working with clay.

It is the "touchstone," too, of quality, as Len Greenham, former morocco-grainer, mentions while recounting his life in the shoemaking industry:

> When you retire, you are naturally drawn to leather shops; and when you feel this leather, it's like a blind man feeling his way on something you've offered him, and because your fingers tell you more than your eyes tell, it's degrading to feel these things after the quality stuff over the years.[14]

Touch is an inherent part of the sheer physicality of learning (what Miyamoto described to me as learning with my solar plexus rather than in my head), which allows that merging of actor and acted-upon, that breaking down of the boundary between inner and outer worlds. Len Greenham put it this way:

> I hated standing on the end of a machine, after I'd spent my life in a rhythm which I had had to learn, and which was the rhythm of the body: you went one shank, two shank, across the belly of the skin, from the neck to the butt, and from the butt to the neck. Then you hooked these things up, and after you'd done it, you looked at it and you thought, "Well, isn't that lovely."

Because work has been learned by the body, it is often possible to leave it for a period of months or years and go back to it. When I went back to Kajiwara Jirō's workshop a dozen years after my exhibition, for instance, and sat down to work at the wheel, Jirō watched me a while before exclaiming: "You can still do it, can't you. I mean, make pots. You learned it with your body. Once you've done that, you can never forget how to do something." In a smiliar manner, a former miner described going back to a mine as "like riding a bike, you go back to it as though you'd done it only yesterday."[15] Touch, then, like the magician's wand or healer's hands, engenders the magic of transformation.[16]

But if learning is physical, then we need to ask what the relationship is between craftsmanship and technology, especially in these years immediately following the digital revolution. Remember the golf course planner who told me how computer programmes had more or less deprived him of his old job of walking around a particular terrain, envisaging a golfer's shots, and planning holes accordingly? Again, Richard Sennett has things to say about computer-assisted design (or CAD) that echo the craft of the golf course planner, scrivener, or scribe. He quotes a young architect at MIT, who says:

> When you draw a site, when you put in the counter lines and trees, it becomes ingrained in your mind. You come to know the site in a way that is not possible with the computer. . . . You get to know a terrain by tracing and retracing it, not by letting the computer "regenerate" it for you.[17]

In a similar manner, one can imagine many a monastery abbot in the latter half of the fifteenth century bewailing the loss of his monks' spiritual ingraining as a result of the invention of the printing press. Indeed, one way of interpreting the clash between hairdresser and photographer, which I related as "a revealing encounter" in Chapter 5, would be to see the two protagonists as belonging to different technological eras. The hairdresser lived in a 'fingertips' world where hands were the be-all and end-all of her work with hair. Her fingers could weave magical effects which, on that particular afternoon as she experimented on the terrain of the model's hair, had in her estimation failed to materialise, hence her request for one final take. The photographer, on the other hand, relied on using Photoshop to resolve his problems. If something wasn't 'right,' his computer programme would make it so. So far as he was concerned, the only purpose of his hands was to type commands on his computer keyboard. It didn't really matter if the hairdresser did one, three, or a dozen heads of hair. Ultimately, they could be reduced to more or less the same image effect. So, why the need for a further take?

There is clearly a danger here of falling into the trap of nostalgia, the kind of trap that ensnared Ruskin and others as they looked back to medieval times and Gothic cathedrals as an exemplification of beauty and art in their attempt to overcome their aversion to mechanized forms of factory mass production. What we need to realise, though, is that it is not just a development in technology itself—whether it be the printing press, camera, or computer—that advances or hinders the acquisition and passing down of skills, but the *social forms* that develop around such advances. CAD programmes may indeed lead to a failure to engage with materials, scale, and proportions,[18] but it is how people interact with one another through such programmes that matters. As Trevor Blackwell and Jeremy Seabrook point out in their analysis of how Britain's working class, carpenters, blacksmiths, coopers, shipbuilders, and so on displayed ambiguous attitudes towards the machinery with which they increasingly interacted during the twentieth century:

> There was hatred for the implacable taskmaster which drove them and their labour, but at the same time affection often grew for the instruments with which they made such useful and serviceable necessities. There was no absolute break with those working more immediately upon natural resources—after all, they, too, knew where leather, wool and wood came from. But new rhythms came to dominate their lives, disarticulated from the more familiar tempo of the seasons. A new knowledge came to them of their growing loss of control over both the conditions of their work and the instrument of their labour. Their lives were circumscribed more and more by the world of the manufactory.[19]

Craftsmanship, then, is as much social as it is technical. The skills required are social (in terms of authority, control, collaboration, training, and ethics) as well as specifically job-related. At the same time, the skilled craftsman treats her tools and technologies as if they were extensions of her person; she assimilates them as part of her body.[20]

In the absence of formal apprenticeships, we might ask how skills are displayed and passed on to others in a trade. There are schools, of course, of one sort or another, but these are no match for *experience*. As Gisli Pålsson says of Icelandic fishing fleets, "Enskilment in fishing is not a matter of formal schooling and the internalization of a stock of knowledge; rather, it is achieved through active engagement with the environment, in the broadest sense of the term."[21]

Or, in the words of a Workington steel worker describing his "apprenticeship" as a blower:

> So for ten weeks I was on different shifts, watching the blower. A blower will not tell you what you're looking for. He can't tell you, you've got to learn it yourself. You've got to look at that flame, know what you're looking for and find it. Once you start finding it, it's a piece of cake. But you've got to know what you're looking for.[22]

Learning, then, is situated in communities of practice where you have to learn how to learn.[23] It is this which is of such importance in cultural production, where short-term *projects* (a pottery exhibition, advertising campaign, fashion collection, film, concert performance, and so on) are the primary means by which assistants learn from their 'masters' (makeup artists, photographers, cameramen, and so on) and imbibe techniques and modes of expression, while also having the opportunity to observe other forms at expertise at work in the studio, on the film set, or behind the catwalk scenes. Projects, then, act as a kind of substitute for the old craft workshops. They build and maintain a "quality of practice" in work which is "stretched out," rather than "immediate."[24] In short, in the creative industries, there is no substitute for the Nike approach: *just do it*.

Good to Think

Clay, like food, is both good to eat (*bonne à manger*) and good to think (*bonne à penser*). In one formulation, "earth must no longer be what men eat but must instead be cooked, like food, in order to enable men to cook what they eat."[25] A shapeless mass is first prepared and then given form before being dried, decorated, and cooked in a kiln. No wonder, then, that there are parallels in the myths explaining the origin of cooking fire and those that of clay.[26]

The pots that emerge are used primarily for food and drink. That was the purpose of Ursula dinnerware: to be *usable, practical, multipurpose*, and *sturdy*. But, in addition to this functional discourse, people talked about Ursula Munch-Petersen's (and other) pots in a different way. Cups, jugs and dishes formed a *family*,[27] which had "grown up" over many years of hard work.[28] According to a Royal Copenhagen pamphlet, individual pieces "mingle on the table in appetizing *harmony*" with their "*rich* forms and *generous* sizes." Words like *care, fresh, friendliness, gentleness, joy, mild, natural,* and *warmth* are used to express the potter's, as well as users', relations to the Ursula range.[29] Here we find ourselves immersed in a discourse of functional beauty, which, in the tradition of nineteenth and early twentieth century craft movements in both England and Japan, imbues inanimate objects with human characteristics, and sets the artificial apart from the natural. Thus, with such animistic practices, is the metamorphosis of clay transformed into the anthropomorphosis of material culture.[30]

Clay is good to reflect upon in another way. The fact that she decided to use faience, a medium that she hadn't experienced before, forced Ursula Munch-Petersen to think of a different way to conceptualise her tableware. Yes, it should be functional. Teapot spouts had to pour properly; their handles should enable a balanced grip. But it should also be multifunctional where possible. Oval plates could serve as lids to similarly shaped bowls; differently sized bowls could nestle inside one another to save space when not in use. In the potter's words: "the shapes of our utensils are like pictures of our actions."

But faience is not porcelain, like the other products made at Royal Copenhagen; and it is not stoneware, of the kind that she had been accustomed to working with. Faience might make use of decorative motifs, but it is remarkable first and foremost for the clear colours with which the clay can be glazed. Glazes, then, are also good to think. Not only did Ursula envisage a tableware series glazed in more than a dozen colours; she realised the economic advantages of such an approach. It was clay forms that required the most labour; the more forms, the more labour was required to press or mould them; and the more labour required, the more expensive was production. By designing fewer forms, fired in multiple colours, Ursula Munch-Petersen provided the opportunity for a radical innovation in Royal Copenhagen's production line. She fulfilled the craftsman's role of being, as the designer Ole Jensen said, "in opposition—in a positive sense." Her thinking had that "sharp social edge" required of thinking like a craftsman.[31]

That such a radical line of thought about clay did not materialize (or, in Ole Jensen's words, "change the mindset inside the company") reflects another aspect of craftsmanship. There is a difference between how something *should* be done and then getting that something to work in the way that it should.[32] Both Peter Poulsen and Ursula Munch-Petersen concentrated on what they perceived as 'objective' standards: on the function, form, and colour of the pot itself. But their discipline and commitment were thwarted by the corporate structure in which they found themselves. Their desire to do a thing well for its own sake came up against other standards, other evaluations of their work.[33] They faced the truism that "every new experience, every new impulse to communicate meets with obstacles in the process of expression, and at least a part of its originality, its immediacy, and its liveliness is sacrificed to these obstacles."[34] It may be the *idea* that is the driving force behind an understanding of materials, the ability to communicate, and sheer hard work, as Peter Poulsen so succinctly said, but the evidence suggests that Royal Copenhagen's managers wanted to whittle the 'big idea' into something as little as politically possible, without throwing it out altogether.

Or does it? At this point in time, it is hard to tell fact from fiction, and memory is often a false ally when it comes to relating the past. But *what if* Ursula had been given free rein—full artistic license—to do what she wanted? Would she have been successful in realizing her vision? I am inclined to think not. Perhaps, then, every creative vision needs an 'enemy', which is why the 'artistic' is so often opposed to the 'commercial'. It is the enemy (in this case, management: the worker's classic opponent) who spurs the craftsman on to realise something greater than he or she at first imagined possible. Could it be that Royal Copenhagen's managers *purposely* adopted a negative attitude to ensure the necessary quality?

That Ursula Munch-Petersen had a creative vision is not in doubt; nor was her ability to work hard and learn about materials. Was it, then, an inability to communicate that let her down? Not exactly. She was well connected with people outside the factory, and communicated well with enough people who "mattered" to be her own "marketing machine." Moreover, time and time again, people commented on how well she interacted with those working in the modelling and glazing rooms at the factory, on how much people were prepared to do for her, and to work for her rather than the factory as such, because they wanted her to succeed. The only apparent failure to communicate on her part, therefore, lay with her dealings with the factory's management.

As Richard Sennett has noted, the craftsman's workshop is "a productive space in which people deal face-to-face with issues of authority."[35] It can glue people together through shared practices and procedures stemming from highly specialized skills, as Ursula herself remarks about Royal Copenhagen's "factory culture." But it also reveals who commands and who obeys. Informally, the potter's obvious skills and willingness to learn from others created a charisma that encouraged those on the shop floor to see her as some sort of 'leader'. Formally, however, as "artist in residence," she was more or less outside the corporate structure of Royal Copenhagen and had no direct access to managerial staff and thus no opportunity to communicate her ideas in person.

Being an outsider, and perhaps something of a rebel, may have blinkered Ursula Munch-Petersen from realizing fully that what was relayed as a difference in managerial outlooks (Royal Copenhagen versus Bing & Grøndahl) was in fact a difference in *genres*, and that the problem she faced was not social, but in a sense aesthetic and material. Generally speaking, every newly created work owes more to previous work of that genre than to the inventiveness and originality of its creator.[36] While working for Royal Copenhagen, therefore, Ursula Munch-Petersen needed to subject her idea about multicoloured faience tableware to the company's "rules of grammar" (that is, the Royal Copenhagen brand) and its stylistic principles (hand-painted flowers in cobalt on a porcelain body), if she was to achieve fully her purpose.[37]

The fact that she opted for faience and disregarded hand-painted motifs in cobalt in some way, surely, singled the potter out as a maverick in the eyes of Royal Copenhagen's management. Although trained in conventional ways, Ursula Munch-Petersen worked unconventionally. How then was she to solve the riddle of Kant's pigeon, whose flight is made possible by the very atmospheric pressure that seems to hinder it? By developing two lines of social relations to circumvent, as best she could, management resistance. First, she cooperated closely with factory floor workers; second, she activated external networks with the power to voice public criticism. She was not able to get rid of the constraints that went with her—in many ways—advantageous position in Royal Copenhagen[38] because, however rebellious, she could only achieve production of the Ursula tableware series by remaining a part of the company. So, she was also a professional who changed some decorative conventions, introduced varieties of multifunctional forms, and had to accept, more or less, everything else thrown at her. In this respect, as Howard Becker points out, it is sometimes hard to "draw a firm line between the innovating integrated professional and the maverick."[39] But, in the end, her designs did take off and 'fly,' though not with quite the success, perhaps, of your everyday pigeon.

Because the actual connection between inner impulse and objectification is unclear and in some ways puzzling, those to whom I talked resorted to stories as a way of talking about—at times, perhaps, idealizing and dramatizing—the genesis and development of the Ursula dinnerware series. These stories were not quite as bold as Beethoven's attribution of his Eroica Symphony to the fate of Napoleon, or as surprising as Schubert's hearing the theme for his String Quartet in D Minor in the workings of a rusty coffee mill. But the linking, for instance, of an early version of Ursula to the decision by the well-known cook, Camilla Plum, to use it over a weekend when serving food in the Museum of Industrial Arts in Copenhagen provided as important an anchoring device as the biblical tale of Adam and Eve in the Garden of Eden: not that either "explanation," of course, explains the genesis of anything.

In a sense, "everything is a story, a narrative, a sequence of events with characters communicating an emotional content. We only accept as true what can be narrated."[40] People tell stories for two reasons: first, to transform private into public meanings (and sometimes vice versa); and second, to provide a sense of agency in the face of disempowering events.[41] Both strategies involve evaluation.

Stories change our experiences of events. In talking to me about things that happened more than 20 years ago, my informants began to reflect and go over the ground of their lives, retracing their steps to rework reality and render it comprehensible, both to myself, an outsider, and to themselves as participants. Finn Næss, Ole Jensen, Peter Poulsen, and Ursula Munch-Petersen all remarked at some point about how long ago the events that they were relating had taken place, about how much they had forgotten, but also about how much came back to them once they stopped to think about the people and the sequence of activities in which they were all involved. None of this would have happened without the intervention of the anthropologist who lives off the tales he is told by those he meets and, in turn, writes stories based on the stories he hears. In this respect, the anthropologist begins to draw near to the potter. He shapes his stories from a jumbled mass of data, just as a potter at the wheel shapes his vessels from a lump of wet clay. Each leaves his handprints on the material being worked.[42] Thus does each try to "grasp" and "give shape" to reality.

Creativity and Flow

A discerning reader may be wondering what this discussion of craftsmanship has to do with creativity. After all, to be skilful is not necessarily to be creative, although we should recognize, I think, that mastery of materials, tools, and techniques permits improvisation and, following the physical-spiritual equation alluded to earlier, 'transcendence' and detachment. The link, as I see it, is in the concept of flow, which I touched upon in Chapters 6 and 7. We have noted earlier that the apprentice needs to learn first and foremost body movement to enable the brush or sword to be filled with energy (*ki*) and "flow." Outside Japan, too, enskillment is seen seen as emphasizing "immersion in the practical world, being caught up in the incessant flow of everyday life,"[43] while, for Tim Ingold, things are animated by "flows and transformations of materials." He continues, "The cook, the alchemist and the painter are in the business not so much of imposing form on matter as of bringing together diverse materials and combining and redirecting their flow in the anticipation of what might emerge."[44] So, too, with the perfumer and incense blender, for whom smell is the purest form of flow: witness the trail of incense burned for the deities, or the *sillage* of a woman's perfume as

CRAFTSMANSHIP

she walks through a room or down the street. Three things are important to an incense blender as he goes about his work, and they contribute to the various fragrances that different incenses may have. One is the overall strength or weakness of a particular smell as it wafts unseen through the air: this affects how it is appraised. A second concerns the quantity of particular materials used, since a minute fraction of one material may give off an extremely strong fragrance, while a large quantity of another may give off only a faint smell. The third factor is heat. There is a considerable difference between raw and heated materials, since their molecular particles fragment when burned. This means that it is difficult—if not impossible—to judge a material's smell until it is burned. Moreover, because that smell changes during the course of burning, incense blenders have to develop an extremely detailed knowledge of the materials that they use.

An incense blender, then, has to imagine and work out how an incense will burn: what fragrances will be emitted when a stick is first lit, for example, and how a room will smell once the stick has finished burning, since different ingredients burn at different rates. The problem here is trying to ensure that the original smell that arises during the mixing of an incense's ingredients will be the same as the smell given off by that incense when burned. The flow here is from making to using, from production to consumption. In this respect, incense is seen to be very different from perfumes and eau de toilettes, which come across directly and for this reason demand great precision when blending their ingredients.

Incense is made in a more or less standardised manner that, to a fairly large extent, resembles flow processes found in other crafts like pottery. First, raw materials have to be purchased; then they have to be blended, kneaded, formed, dried, and packaged. It is the blending process which determines both the smell and the colour of a particular incense. Kneading involves a thorough mixing of an incense's aromatic ingredients with water and a fixative agent (*tabu* bark). In the forming process, the shape (stick, spiral, or cone) and size (and therefore the burning time) of an incense are fixed. The drying process is so designed to prevent formed incense sticks from becoming misshapen. Packaging is used both to protect fragile incense sticks from breaking and to provide some sort of linguistic and colour-coded guide to the scent of a box's contents.

Most independent manufacturers try to come up with new incense recipes, while also making use of tried and tested incense recipes that have been handed down over the decades. Incense production, however, is somewhat akin to preparing a dish according to a cookbook: things rarely work out exactly as a recipe suggests, and results tend to vary.

Three sets of factors prevent any recipe from being set in stone. The first is the variation in natural raw materials that inevitably accompanies each bulk purchase.[45] The actual quality of sandalwood, aloes wood, or *tabu* fixing wood being used, for example, determines whether an incense will contain a little more, a little less, or the same amount as originally written down in a recipe. Such quality differences are primarily regional: Vietnamese aloes wood, for example, is generally quite "sweet" (*amaime*), while that from Indonesia is more "spicy" (*karaime*). The second is the quality of water used in making incense sticks. Minute variations in quality can affect the hardness, colour, and shape of an incense. Third, related to this, are the workers who blend incense materials and form incense sticks, and the machinery they use for these purposes. Different workers have different ways of working and, because of the differences that result from such physical movements (think of the morocco-grainer), adjustments to how much water is included in a recipe have to be made accordingly.

Blending ingredients to make new incenses is a specialist job that is also extremely important. In Japan, most incense firms are family owned, and it is the current CEO who holds recipes handed down through—in certain cases, numerous—generations (a temporal flow) and who has been taught to blend incenses by his father, primarily by trial and error. A few of the larger and more established companies employ specialist incense blenders, who generally claim that they do *not* have a special gift in distinguishing smells other than the expertise they have developed over the years through hard work and experience. It is practice that enables them to distinguish all kinds of different smells, as well as which materials (not) to blend with which at what stage in the blending process.[46]

At the same time, the creation of a new incense is imbued with a sense of mystery and is very much a matter of trial and error, based on previous experience. One incense blender told me that he had once conducted 120 experiments with a particular incense, but that once he had got to that point it would have been better to start again at the beginning. In his opinion, 12 experiments should normally be sufficient to achieve a particular result. Another claimed that, after trying—and failing—to get the smell of a particular incense right for months on end, he had finally dreamed a recipe which, when he tried it out the following morning, turned out to be exactly right. In putting together minute quantities of different ingredients, an incense blender ideally needs to be able to concentrate for hours on end and to be in an appropriate physical and—yes—mental condition, since the latter—along with seasonal weather changes—is thought to affect the final result. One final complication is that blenders may perceive the same smell differently from one day to the next. It is, then, flows of materials and working methods, as well as of physical and mental conditions, that influence a blender's 'creativity.'

Flow, however, has another association in the context of creativity research. Cognitive psychologists have used the concept of "flow" to describe an optimal experience, or state of focused concentration involving a merging of action and awareness,[47] for an individual absolutely absorbed in creative work. This has been extended to collaborative work, where "group flow" is seen to be a property of an entire collaborative unit (such as a theatre troupe, orchestra, or ad campaign production team).[48] The idea of group flow seems to have emerged from accounts by jazz musicians of what they are aiming at when they play in clubs every night. Jazz is in many ways an extremely appropriate musical genre with which to discuss creativity in cultural production since it involves, ideally, a felicitous harmony of structure and spontaneity that is often also found in a recording studio, location shoot, or on a film set. To play jazz, a musician has to learn and master a particular instrument, of course, and then gain a fundamental understanding of the rules that govern musical progressions. These he then transforms during playing by altering the chord in which a song is usually played, by mixing together different harmonies, and/or by extending intervals between notes. This requires well-honed craftsmanship that can hear another player's phrasing, respond to it, and follow a musical idea together. Collaborative improvisation of this nature has been described as "chasing a piece of paper that's been blown in the wind."[49]

There are several features of jazz improvisation that can be extended to improvisation and creativity in other forms of cultural production such as those described in this book.[50] First of all, every studio recording, location shoot, or film set operates in a context of uncertainty. A celebrity may be late and delay production sufficiently to extend it into another day; it may rain when sunshine is required; a bored policeman might question a film crew's right to hold up traffic. In other words, the "nobody knows" property applied by Richard Caves to the sales success of finished creative products (records, ad campaign, or film) also characterizes its *production*. To overcome such uncertainty, cultural production needs to be structured, but not so structured as to prevent improvisation and creative responses on the part of participants. Minimal structures, therefore, are put in place around particular activities—there is this song to be sung, that scene to be shot—but, ideally, room is left in such coordination for participants to balance their own autonomy with interdependence. As a result, as we saw in Chapters 4 and 5, everyone knows where everyone else is supposed to be, and what parts they need to play. But beyond that there are few, if any, structural constraints and participants (creative director, cameraman, hair stylist, makeup artist, even celebrity) are free to express their opinions and contribute their diverse skills to the transformation of a script or brief into visual and/or auditory images, which never exactly reproduce what was initially imagined and conceived.

Second, as I have been at pains to point out, cultural production and its products are *social* accomplishments. What characterizes creativity is the give and take between participants who, in their search for elusive, vital, and emergent qualities evaluated as 'creative' by a particular advertising, fashion, film, or other world, engage in flows of activity marked by "empathic competence, a mutual orientation to one another's unfolding."[51] It was clear during my fieldwork that my Japanese "informants" (as we anthropologists like to refer to people who help us understand their different worlds) continuously adapted their behaviour and activities to others' expectations, trying to anticipate what their colleagues would do before they did it, and thereby preclude mistakes, while also contributing positively to the task at hand.[52]

When this mutual orientation to one another worked in such a way that people went about their distributed tasks without needing to question or check that what they were doing was 'right' or 'wrong,' creative work resulted in a seamless flow: an "ensembling" involving a simultaneous "sensing" and "acting" on the part of all participants,[53] akin to jazz musicians "achieving a groove":

> Groove refers to the dynamic interplay within an established beat. It occurs when the rhythm section "locks in" together, when members have a common sense of the beat and meter. Establishing a groove, however, is more than simply playing the correct notes. It involves a shared "feel" for the rhythmic thrust. Once a group shares this common rhythm, it begins to assume a momentum, as if having a life of its own separate from the individual members. There is a sense that the groove acts as . . . a "holding environment," a reliable nesting that provides a sense of ontological security, a sense of trust that allows people to take risks and initiate actions.[54]

While it may be obvious to participants when they have reached this ideal state of what my Japanese informants liked to call "no mind" or "detachment" (*mushin*), it is not necessarily obvious to audiences or observers (whatever cultural producers themselves say in this regard). Indeed, my own conscious recognition of the group flow in advertising production only came about because of an incident that brought everything to an abrupt halt, or "anchorage," when a hairdresser decided to ask for an extra take even though she and the photographer had already agreed on which image was best for the advertising campaign in question and the set was being dismantled. Suddenly, the focused concentration—the merging of action and awareness among studio participants, each of whom had been charged with a particular task (studio lighting, makeup, posing, photographing, and so on)—was broken. The hairdresser's intervention made them conscious of the fact that they were not, after all, in control of what was going on. Even the music, it will be recalled, was turned off during the ensuing discussion that went entirely against the groove, threatening participants' "ontological security" and a sense of trust that each knew what s/he was doing.

Group flow, then, affords improvisation and creativity, but the latter do not have to take place in a group context. I have described my own flow in making pottery one afternoon in Koishiwara where unconscious immersion in the task at hand led to unanticipated results (like iron-brushed triangles on square dishes and a plate design of Snoopy in a bathtub). A more technical and detailed account is provided by David Sudnow in his search for jazz piano improvisation:

> What happened, suddenly appearing and disappearing in this way, was dramatically different from what my former practices had achieved. For a brief course of time while I played rapidly along, a line of melody *interweavingly* flowed over the duration of several chords, fluently winding about in ways I'd never seen my hands move before, a line of melody whose melodicity wasn't being expressly done, as in my reiterative attempts to sustain continuity. Somehow, a sequence of notes flowing from one chord's jazz-related ways to the next's, singing this jazz, was achieved.[55]

We see here that strange experience noted by a number of artists and musicians of being simultaneously in a state of "no self," while also going outside the self and observing it: the kind of transcendence and detachment that I have mentioned earlier in the context of craftsmanship and creativity. But the question that has to be asked is: does (group) flow necessarily give rise to creativity, improvisation, and 'good' work? My own experience, based on a fairly lengthy immersion in the worlds of pottery and advertising, suggests not. We need to distinguish between the flow of creativity and the anchorage of judgement that follows. Yes, flow leads to the production of satisfying work (this is what all cultural producers aim at ideally). I have become so engrossed in making a tray of teacups or bowls (as well as in writing this book) that I become totally unaware of what is going on around me until, suddenly, I have used up all the clay or finished a chapter. But I may be sometimes satisfied, at other times dissatisfied, with the results of this work. And while I may perceive some work as 'good,' there is no guarantee that it will be so perceived, let alone recognized as stemming from 'flow,' by others who may, instead, choose to praise work that I myself have rejected. This is because of the ensemblage of values that they bring to bear on my work: its craftsmanship, form, design, price, and so on, as well as when and where they view it. In other words, both creativity and quality evaluations are subject to ongoing negotiations, not only during processes of production, but also in those of consumption. It is to the critical appraisal of creative products that I will now turn in the last two chapters of this book.

CHAPTER 10

Judging Artworks

On a hot, wet, and humid afternoon in the middle of June, the elevators in the Daimaru Department Store, located above Tokyo Station, are packed full of people, most of them trying to get to the twelfth floor where that month's attraction, the Japan Ceramic Art Exhibition (JCAE), has just opened. As the elevator in which I am riding disgorges another dozen and a half visitors, I hand over my complimentary ticket and find myself—one of 2,000 visitors every day—moving down an aisle with an imitation Zen temple–like rock garden on the one side and, on the other, a row of display boards on which are printed comments by those called in to jury this year's exhibition and to award its five prizes.

It is only after this liminal space between the main retail space of the department store and the exhibition itself, which Daimaru is putting on in conjunction with the Mainichi newspaper, that visitors get to see the pot that has graced advertising hoardings in the stations and on the trains of Japan's capital city during the past week: a charcoal-grey porcelain bowl with an enamel overglaze spray of pink flowers and green leaves, made by a thirteenth-generation potter living and working in Arita, a pottery town in northern Kyushu, some 2,000 kilometres from the capital.

This first room of the exhibition is carpeted in grey. On the left side are lined the JCAE's five prize-winning pots, each with its own grey-papered stand lined with white pebbles at the base and accompanied by a placard giving a brief description of the potter who made the work and a discrete set of numbers (lacking the final three zeros) indicating the price for which it may be purchased. On the right side are the works of a very select, invited group of potters who represent all that is deemed to be excellent about modern Japanese ceramics: Arakawa Toyozō, Kusube Yaichi, Kondō Yūzō, Fujiwara Kei, Yamamoto Tōshū, and the recently deceased Kiyomizu Roku-bei. Three of these are holders of Important Intangible Cultural Properties, popularly known as "National Treasures." Their work, too, like all the other pots in the exhibition, is for sale. This is clearly a "prestige market": even, perhaps, an "economy of prestige."[1]

218 ▣ **CHAPTER 10**

There is a slight bustle behind me, and Princess Chichibu walks into the room, accompanied by a couple of suited bodyguards and a lady-in-waiting. Like many members of royalty around the world, she seems to favour pink. She starts by examining the works of the specially invited potters on her right, as there is already a crowd of people looking at the prize-winning pots, and seems particularly interested in a vase by Kondō Yūzō. After a minute or two, a space opens up around the prize-winning pots and she immediately moves across the room to look at the enamel overglaze porcelain bowl which has been awarded the prize that bears her name: the Princess Chichibu Cup (*Chichibu no Miya-hai*).[2]

As she does so, a middle-aged man with longish hair swept back from his forehead, wearing gold-rimmed glasses to go with his dark brown suede jacket and loosely dangling leather bow at his neck (of the kind worn by sheriffs in Hollywood westerns), pushes his way forward towards Her Imperial Highness. As he hesitates at the front of the exhibition's visitors, who by now are nudging one another and whispering behind their hands as they jerk their heads discretely in the direction of Princess Chichibu, he is noticed by one of the dignitaries beside her and permitted to bow himself into her presence. He is the thirteenth-generation potter, Imaizumi Imaemon, who has won the Princess Chichibu Cup at this year's JCAE (and who wrote a recommendation for my own exhibition described in Chapter 2).

At this point, a distinguished-looking old man in his mid-80s with a goatee beard, and wearing a more conventional suit and tie, makes his way forward accompanied by his kimono-clad wife. He is immediately ushered into the presence of Her Imperial Highness, whom he proceeds to accompany through the exhibition, acting as critical interpreter of the more than 200 pots on display. He is joined by two other men—one slender and in his late 70s, the other more portly and in his mid-60s—each of whom has comments to add from time to time as they move from one pot to the next. These men are members of the JCAE's Executive Committee and are all panellists on the jury that awarded the Princess Chichibu Cup and other prizes at this year's exhibition.

The entourage surrounding Her Imperial Highness contains other dignitaries: the Chairman of the Daimaru Group, the President of the Mainichi newspaper, the Minister of Culture, and a senior official from the Ministry of Foreign Affairs (the Minister himself was unable to attend and in fact resigned his post two days later). In the background hover more than a dozen potters who have travelled to Tokyo from all over Japan especially to see their work displayed in the exhibition. On this first afternoon of the Japan Ceramics Exhibition, when the prize-winning ceremony takes place before a select audience of potters, critics, and journalists, the field of Japanese ceramics is well and truly "configured."[3]

Japan's Ceramic Art World

I suppose one issue reinforced by the previous chapters is that there is rarely, if ever, such a thing as a purely aesthetic encounter (or "purely" anything, for that matter). We have seen that cultural producers—whether they are potters, members of an advertising production team, or fashion magazine editors of one sort or another—all struggle with a number of conflicting demands and constraints on the creative ideals that they hold most dear. As a result, aesthetics gets mixed up with money, money with use, use with people, people with situations, situations with aesthetics, and so on in a never-ending circuit of affordances and ensemblages of worth. Perhaps, then, we should be examining those cultural intermediaries who adopt a rather stricter and purer attitude (at least, in theory) towards creative products. Although we've seen that, as one such kind of intermediary, fashion magazine editors find themselves facing all sorts of difficulties in their work, perhaps art critics are free of such concerns. Could it be that *they* are able to act in a kind of aesthetic vacuum, where social, commercial, and other such considerations do not affect their judgement? To answer this question, I'm going to describe how a prize was awarded by a group of critics at a major ceramic art exhibition in Japan some years ago.

If protagonists in the tale told in the previous two chapters remarked on how long ago events now seemed, this chapter delves even further back in time to when I conducted fieldwork on ceramic art marketing in Japan. But, whereas I first wrote about my pottery exhibition reasonably soon after returning from the field,[4] what I am about to recount here has remained under wraps for the past 30 years. This is primarily because, as anthropologist, I found myself embroiled in an art world characterised by exchanges of favours that at best made many of my informants uncomfortable, and at worst extremely angry at what they described as blatant bribery and corruption. Until now, therefore, I have held my peace: a peace encouraged by an involvement with other research topics, as well as with the humdrum, and often exasperating, detail of university life. But three decades seem sufficiently long for the black box of secrets now to be opened up for scrutiny.

After all, many of the protagonists have retired or died, while the ceramic art world itself has, hopefully at least, moved on. So, as a Japanese pilot once advised his passengers: "Sit back, relax, and enjoy the fright!"

I have already given some background detail about the art world of Japanese ceramics in Chapter 2, but perhaps some further explanation is necessary, to situate this account of how a group of jurors decided to award the most important prize at a major biennial ceramics exhibition. To recap: when I conducted fieldwork among those constituting the art world of contemporary Japanese ceramics, my aim was to learn how a potter (and by implication, other Japanese craftsmen) might be awarded one or other of the highest accolades available to craftsmen in Japan: holder of an Important Intangible Cultural Property (*jūyō mukei bunkazai*) on the one hand, or the Award of Cultural Merit (*bunka kunshō*) on the other. What I learned was, on the surface at least, simply put: it was through exhibiting his or her work that a potter (*yakimon'zukuri*) came to be accepted as "ceramic artist" (*tōgei sakka*), and by selling that work and winning prizes at exhibitions that s/he might eventually receive one of the accolades in question.

One of the peculiarities of the art-craft world in Japan in the postwar period has been that department stores, rather than museums of art, have been the sites of exhibition, and thus of the consecration, of (ceramic) art.[5] This had much to do with stores' strategies of using cultural events to attract customers and with the fact that pottery *sold* (which, remember, was what my own one-man show was all about). Another feature, as we saw in Chapter 2, was the presence of media organizations, but in particular of national newspaper companies, as cultural sponsors of major exhibitions;[6] again, in a bid to attract readers and increase sales. Precisely because the legitimacy of such cultural activities could only be assured if they called upon the services of experts in the field of ceramics, newspaper companies and department stores established (at times somewhat less than holy) alliances with museum curators and academics (scholars in the fields of ceramics, art, craft, and the histories thereof). These "critics" (*hyōronka*) thus came to constitute a third and powerful force in the public delineation of what constitutes ceramic art in contemporary Japanese society. It was within this tripartite structure of critics, newspaper companies, and department stores that potters who wished to become ceramic artists had to position themselves and manoeuvre to work their way to the top. In other words, to receive public recognition, a potter needed to be master not only of ceramic techniques and "creative flair," but also of the kind of social skills[7] that Ursula Munch-Petersen possessed (discussed in the previous chapter).

Ceramics exhibitions can be neatly divided into one-man and, less frequently, group shows, on the one hand and, on the other, competitive exhibitions which are juried and have prizes attached. It is to the latter that I shall now turn, since they evince a slightly different kind of creative encounter to those described and analysed so far. Those participating in the ceramic and, indeed other, art worlds have ranked Japanese department stores in an informal hierarchy, based on location (Tokyo vis-à-vis other cities in Japan), sales potential, clienteles, and prestige (based on an amalgam of sales and other cultural factors, such as history and past cultural activities): in other words, on an ensemblage of stores' worth. This ranking has had a major influence on potters' strategies regarding where and when to hold their one-man shows.

Like medieval and contemporary trade fairs,[8] competitive exhibitions have formed a mutually dependent 'network' or 'circuit' in terms of their geographical location, content, and timing. In this sense, they constitute a national "geography of prestige," in which there is a careful structuring of both national and regional ceramics exhibitions. For example, the Western Crafts Exhibition (*Seibu Kōgeiten*; the Asahi newspaper), for craftsmen and women working in Kyushu, is held at Tamaya Department Store in Fukuoka in early June, in anticipation of the national-level Traditional Crafts Exhibition (*Dentō Kōgeiten*) held at Mitsukoshi Department Store in Tokyo in late September. At the same time, it positions itself vis-à-vis other regional ceramics exhibitions held at other department stores in northern Kyushu in the spring and summer months. It also positions itself vis-à-vis other national exhibitions sponsored by other newspapers in different parts of the country for other regional groups of potters (for example, the National Ceramics Exhibition held in a Nagoya department store). Among the latter group is the JCAE (*Nihon Tōgeiten*; the Mainichi newspaper) held at Daimaru Department Store in Tokyo every other June.[9] It is to this that I shall now turn as I focus on how engagements with creativity take place in the realm of appreciation and consumption.

The Japan Ceramic Art Exhibition

The JCAE is a juried exhibition sponsored by the Mainichi newspaper and, at the time of my research, held every other year in June at the Tokyo branch of the Daimaru Department Store. It was then taken to other Daimaru store branches (in Osaka and, later in the year, Kobe), as well as to other department stores such as Tamaya in Kokura, Kyushu, and Meitetsu in Nagoya. The exhibition was first held in 1971 when, to celebrate the centenary of its foundation, the Mainichi newspaper 'upgraded' a local exhibition that it had sponsored in the western part of Japan to a national exhibition of ceramics. In its early years the exhibition was taken abroad, but since 1977 it has remained in Japan as a primarily 'Japanese' ceramics exhibition, although foreign potters resident in Japan are allowed to send in their contributions.[10]

The JCAE has an Executive Committee, chaired ex officio by the Chairman of the Japan Arts Association (*Nihon Geijutsu-in Inchō*) and consisting of five other members, of whom four served as jury members in 1981. Other judges included curators of well-known Japanese art and/or craft museums, as well as university professors (who had also often been museum curators in the past). Together they constituted three panels of jurors, each of which was assigned to judge submissions to one of the exhibition's three sections. One of these was the Traditional Section (*Dentō bumon*) for "individual traditional and creative works" (*dentō oyobi sōsaku ni yoru ippin sakuhin*); another was the Abstract Section (*zen'ei bumon*) for "free-form *objets*" (*jiyu na zōkei ni yoru obuje*); and the last was the Functional Pottery Section (*jitsuyō tōki bumon*) for "folk art, craft, and mass-produced pottery" (*mingei, kurafuto, ryōsan tōki*).[11]

In addition, to ensure that the exhibition appealed to the general public, and reached what the Exhibition Administrator referred to as "a certain minimum standard of quality," up to a dozen potters, who had already attained the highest level of recognition, were formally "invited" (*shōtai*) to submit their work for exhibition, while 50 to 60 more were "recommended" (*suisen*). The pots of both groups automatically qualified for exhibition and were eligible for its prizes.

In the 10 years prior to my research, submissions had increased from 740 pots in 1971 to just under 1,200 pots 10 years later. By far the greatest number of submissions (810 in 1979) was to the Tradition Section, of which only 130 were selected for exhibition. In both 1979 and 1981, the JCAE consisted of a total of 238 pots (including the 62–64 invited and recommended submissions), meaning that a potter submitting his work had a one in seven chance of having it accepted for exhibition in the JCAE.

Five prizes were awarded at the JCAE that year. Of these, the Princess Chichibu Cup (*Chichibu no miya-hai*) was the most prestigious, both because of the size of the award (¥1 million) and its association with a member of the Imperial Household.[12] The other four prizes were worth ¥500,000 each. In order of perceived status ranking at the time, these were the Foreign Minister's Prize (*Gaimu Daijin-shō*), the Minister of Education's Prize (*Monbu Daijin-shō*), the Mainichi Newspaper Company Prize (*Mainichi Shinbunsha-shō*), and the Japan Ceramic Art Exhibition Prize (*Nihon Tōgeiten-shō*).[13]

In 1981, as in previous years, submissions were solicited in the third week of April[14] and jurying took place at the very end of the same month on the ninth floor of the Mainichi Newspaper Company headquarters over-looking the Imperial Palace grounds in Takebashi, Tokyo. Although large ceramics exhibitions often included practising potters, as well as critics, academics, and museum curators in their juries, Mainichi selected its judges from the latter group only, on the grounds that artist potters tended to form cliques and to vote only for their own (former) apprentices and students. In other words, the exhibition's organizers were clearly aware that social encounters among *people* could easily masquerade as aesthetic encounters with *pots*.

Critics, on the other hand, were considered generally less biased. Although the full jury consisted mostly of the same members over time, with one or two changes every other year, they were revolved biennially from one section to the next to create new combinations of personnel. The reasoning behind this was to ensure that critics, who tended to be special-ists in one of the three styles of ceramics exhibited, did not form cabals and vote for their personal favourites, while also introducing some variety among the panellists. What this reasoning overlooked, as we will come to see in this chapter, was the fact that critics themselves operated in a social network that depended in large part on relations of patronage not dissimilar to those found among potters. During the first decade of the exhibition, five judges were assigned to each of the three sections, but in 1981 this number was increased to six for the very large Tradition Section. However, owing to withdrawals and absences, each section ended up with four judges for the final awards that year, thereby breaking the golden rule that a jury panel should always consist of an odd number of panellists.[15]

The Selection Process

Jurying involves an engagement with creative products, and an evaluation of their appreciative or aesthetic value, but also—as we shall see—of their overall worth. As such, it is just one of a number of creative encounters that take place after a product has left its maker's hands. Jurying, however, has repercussions that an ordinary consumer evaluation does not, for the decision to award a particular pot or other 'artwork' (including film costumes, book cover designs, and music competitions,[16] as well as beauty queens[17] and livestock animals) a prize of some kind usually reflects back upon and inflects the prize-winner's future output in one way or another, if only because of a tendency towards "cumulative recognition." Once you are awarded one prize, you're likely to get another. And once you get another, you're even more likely to get a third. And so it goes on in a "winner takes all" spiral of success known as the "Matthew effect."[18]

Jurying of the JCAE took place over two days, and consisted of two primary activities: selection and prize awarding. The selection process took the whole of one long day and involved a three-stage winnowing of the approximately 1,200 submissions. First, individual jury members selected pots that they liked (168 out of more than 800 submissions for the Tradition Section, which I was observing). These were then brought five at a time to a table to be viewed by the section jury as a whole. Just under two-thirds of the first-stage selections passed this second stage. However, since 130 pots were needed from the Tradition Section to make up the exhibition's final numbers,[19] the judges were then asked to reconsider those pots that they had failed. During this third stage a few submissions that had been totally overlooked in both the first and second stages of selection were picked out and passed by jury members.

The selection process involved two other sets of people apart from the judges (and the ethnographer): half a dozen employees of the art transport company which managed submissions and logistics at selected cities around Japan, and the Exhibition Administrator, a full-time employee of the Mainichi Newspaper Company, who—together with a team of three female employees—arranged and oversaw all activities connected with the JCAE, including submissions, jurying, exhibition set-up, catalogue preparation and printing, prize-giving ceremony, press relations, and so on and so forth. The Exhibition Administrator did not interfere in the actual selection of submissions, but since he represented his organization's interest in displaying as 'good' and 'broad-based' an exhibition as possible for the general public, he did twice advise panellists on their selections along these lines.[20]

One incident during this lengthy selection process deserves mention, since it had a bearing on the prize-awarding process on the following day. Because they had few submissions to judge in the first place, and because they had selected even fewer for exhibition, the Chairman of the Functional Pottery Section panel (Imai)[21] requested that one of the submissions selected by the Tradition Section panel (a set of small bowls) be transferred to his section. Although the potter himself, when consulted on the telephone, initially objected to this arrangement (he thought his work was being categorized as folk art), one of the judges who knew him (Murata) intervened personally to persuade him to accept the two jury panels' arrangement, and the submission was duly transferred from the Tradition to Functional Pottery Section.

The Prize-awarding Process

Once all three sections' submissions had been juried and the required number of pots selected, the Exhibition Administrator asked the Tradition Section's judges to select six pots that they considered of prize-winning quality. After briefly conferring with one another, jury members agreed that each should pick out as many pots as he wished from among the 122 that they had selected, and that they would then vote on them all together. In this way, their engagement with particular pots would move from individual to collective assessment.

Jury members then picked out 21 pots in all. They were then each handed five voting slips, which they placed on, in, or beside those pots that they liked. In this first round of collective voting, six of the 21 pots received no votes at all, one got three votes, three got two, and the rest (11 pots) got one vote each. The pots were next rearranged according to the number of votes received, and the Exhibition Administrator handed each of the judges four slips of paper. This time, five pots got two votes, one three votes, and the rest one vote or none at all. This enabled the Exhibition Administrator (who, remember, required six pots in all) to suggest that the six pots with two or more votes be put forward from the Tradition Section as candidates for the Princess Chichibu Cup to be chosen the following day. These six would be joined by three from the Abstract section and four from the Functional Pottery section, as well as by six more pots to be selected from the Invited and Recommended Sections. This was quickly accepted by all four judges.

On the following afternoon, 11 jurors assembled to select the pots that they judged to be the 'best' in that year's JCAE. They were first addressed by the Exhibition Administrator, who laid out the procedure for deciding the award of the Princess Chichibu Cup. They were first to select potential prize-winning pots from the invited and recommended submissions. Would they prefer two votes each for this, or three?

226 ▣ **CHAPTER 10**

The jury members decided that were in favour of three to start with. They then looked at the invited submissions, touching some and picking up others to examine them more closely. Some of the judges (from the same section) went around in pairs and chatted to each other as they looked at what was on display; most worked independently. Two were extremely quick in making up their minds about which pots to vote for and finished within two and three minutes, respectively (making use, perhaps, of Yanagi Sōetsu's concept of *chokkan*, or direct perception, and even practicing Csikszentmihalyi's idea of "flow"); others took a good quarter of an hour to cast their votes.

Once the Exhibition Administrator had received all the voting slips, he handed them to one of his female colleagues, who read out their numbers one by one. Four pots ended up with three votes; six with two; nine with one; and 41 with none at all. The Exhibition Administrator again addressed the judges and asked them whether they wished to limit themselves to those pots with three votes in the next round of voting, or to include all those that had been voted for at least once. At the suggestion of the Chairman of the Abstract Section panel (Kitano, in his mid-60s), the single-vote pots were reviewed to ensure that all jury members were satisfied that they be discarded. Since there was no dissent as each was held up by one of the art transport company employees, all nine single-voted pots were removed from further voting and placed under the tables.

The judges were then asked to vote again with three voting slips. The process was much quicker this time, but, just as the Exhibition Administrator had more or less finished reading out which numbered pot had garnered how many votes, the hitherto absent Chairman of the Jury (Tanabe) entered the room with a mumbled apology and was asked to vote. This he did. In this second round, two pots garnered six votes apiece; one five; and two four, with the remaining receiving three votes or fewer.

This pattern made it comparatively simple for Tanabe, as Chairman of the Jury, to suggest that the five pots with four votes or more be selected to compete with the pots from the other sections for the Princess Chichibu Cup. This was agreed without further ado, and the art transport employees proceeded to place all the sections' preselected prize-candidate pots on the tables together with those just selected. New numbers were placed beside each pot, and these were recorded, as diligently as ever, by the three female Mainichi employees.

Round 1 of voting proper then got under way, with each jury member given three voting slips and the results read out as previously (see Table 1).

Together, the Exhibition Administrator and the judges fairly promptly agreed that those pots with three votes or more should remain in the running. The rest were removed as the judges proceeded to Round 2, this time with only two votes apiece (a number determined by the Exhibition Administrator). The results led to some discussion. Tanabe asked his colleagues whether they should make the cut at three or four votes. Imai suggested that they might perhaps give the prize to the outright winner, Number 6 from the Invited Section, which had five votes. Kitano and one or two other jury members thought not, since there was only a single vote difference between

TABLE 1: Voting Patterns for the Princess Chichibu Cup at the JCAE

Section	Potter	Pre 1	Pre 2	Main 1	Main 2	Main 3	Main 4	Main 5
Invited	1	2	6	3	2			
	2	3	2					
	3	2	1					
	4	2	3					
	5	2	3					
	6	3	5	4	5	4	4	6
	7	2	4	1				
	8	2	2					
	9	3	6	1				
	10	3	4	4	3			
Tradition	11			2				
	12			4	4	2		
	13			1				
	14			2				
	15			1				
	16			1				
Functional	17			3	4	3	4 +1	
	18			0				
	19			0				
	20			2				
Abstract	21			1				
	22			3	4	3	4	6
	23			3	2			
Voting slips		3	3	3	2	1	1	1

228   ▣   **CHAPTER 10**

Number 6 and three other pots (which, conveniently, belonged to each of the other three sections). It was therefore agreed that they should make the cut at four votes.

In Round 3, the Exhibition Administrator allowed each jury member just one vote. As a result, Number 6 again came out as the 'winner' with four votes, but two other submissions had three votes each. Tanabe once again addressed his colleagues.

> This is not very satisfactory. There isn't very much difference in our votes for the four remaining pots. What should we do? It is really rather uncomfortable (*guai ga warui*) not getting a proper majority for one pot. But maybe, at this point, we should remove Number 12 since it got only two votes, and vote on the remaining three?

This suggestion was agreed to without dissent, and the jury members moved to Round 4 with a single vote apiece for the remaining three pots. As the Exhibition Administrator read out the results and worriedly proclaimed a dead heat, there was a lot of laughter among the panellists. One of them, Hayashi (in his late 50s), suggested lightly that they settle the issue with a *janken* (scissors-paper-stone) solution.

At this point, the Exhibition Administrator suddenly remembered that one of the jury members from the Functional Section, who was unable to be present that day, had left a sealed envelope with his written vote for the Princess Chichibu Cup before going home the previous evening. He asked permission to open the envelope, and the jury members' expectant silence permitted him to proceed.

Now, it was clear that the odds on the absent jury member having voted for one of the three pots still in contention at the end of Round 4 were rather slim. After all, the judges had had to select half a dozen pots from among the invited submissions, and then to choose once more from among the 23 pots put forward in total. The Exhibition Administrator tore open the envelope, took out a slip of paper, and read aloud: "Number 1634."

This caused some confusion since the absent judge had written down the original submission number. This was checked against the records fastidiously kept by the Mainichi employees, one of whom informed those present that Number 1634 was now Number 17. The absent judge's vote appeared to have broken the deadlock.

Or had it? Imai immediately stood up to address his colleagues:

I have been in charge of the third section, which this year has had its title changed from *Mingei* Folk Art to Functional Pottery or Craft. In this respect, it can be said to be a new section in the Japan Ceramic Art Exhibition, and it would, perhaps, not be appropriate *this* year to award the overall prize to a pot from this section. A second point that needs to be made is that Number 17 was not originally submitted to the Functional Pottery, but to the Tradition section. It was transferred at the request of the judges of the Functional Pottery panel, of which I am Chairman, on the grounds that the section lacked good-quality submissions. The potter himself, however, initially objected to this, although this objection was overcome, thanks to the intervention earlier this afternoon of Murata *sensei* [he indicated a member of the Tradition Section panel]. The question arises, however: would these dishes have been picked out as prize-worthy if they had remained in the Tradition Section? I myself, as Chairman of the Functional Pottery Section, would have no objection if it were decided *not* to give the Princess Chichibu Cup to Number 17. I should add in this respect, perhaps, that I myself have been voting for Number 6.

Murata (Tradition Section): Does this mean that we are to forget Number 17 entirely?

Imai: No. No, not at all. It is just an issue of whether we should award the main prize to a new section in the exhibition.

Tanabe and Kitano got up to examine the remaining three pots more closely while the discussion continued, with different judges stressing different values that they thought relevant to the issue at hand:

Hayashi (Tradition Section): We have to ask ourselves, though, whether Number 17 is really the very best pot submitted to the exhibition this year: one that reveals the uniqueness of Japanese ceramics (*Nihon tōgei no yunīku-sa*). Yes, it is quite charming (this word in English), but what about its merits *technically* speaking?

Judge A (Functional Pottery Section): Number 17 can always get another prize, so we don't *have* to give it the best prize of all now.

Judge B (Functional Pottery Section): Number 17 is a bit on the expensive side for everyday functional craftwork, isn't it? These dishes seem a bit borderline in terms of their price.

230 ▣ **CHAPTER 10**

Hayashi: Frankly, I think the pot is a bit weak (*yowai*) for an absolute overall prize (*zettaishō*). It probably wouldn't have been selected if it had remained in the Tradition Section.

Imai: I suggest, then, that Number 17 be put aside.

Judge A: I agree.

Tanabe (Tradition Section—now returned from the table where the three pots were standing): I've now had a good look at those dishes. And I must say that they are full of defects and have too many weak points. I suggest that we agree to Imai *sensei*'s proposal.

So Number 17 was removed from the table. The judges were then asked once again to cast one vote for one of the two remaining pots. This they did, only for there to be another dead heat. If only the thirteenth judge had been present!

This time the laughter among the panellists was tinged with embarrassment. Tanabe asked that the names of the potters who had made the two remaining submissions be formally identified (although it was clear that they all knew one of them, at least). Number 6 was by Imaizumi Imaemon, a thirteenth-generation potter living and working in Arita, Japan's oldest porcelain manufacturing centre in Kyushu, and the man who was to endorse my own work a year or so later. Number 22 was by an unknown potter.

Hayashi suggested that Tanabe, as Chairman of the Jury, make a decision. So the old man stood to address his colleagues once again.

We have here two pots: one by an invited artist and the other by a potter virtually unknown to us. Personally, I have to say that I don't actually think very much of the Imaemon pot submitted to this exhibition and standing on the table in front of you. And I'm sure that there are several among you who will agree with me on this point. Imaemon has certainly produced better work [Tanabe turned towards the Exhibition Administrator]. But who is Number 22 exactly?

One of the Mainichi employees handed her boss a file, pointing to a particular page.

Exhibition Administrator: Born 1945, in the Tōhoku region. Currently employed as a schoolteacher. No previous submissions to the Japan Ceramic Art Exhibition. In fact, no record at all of participation in any exhibition that we know of.

Tanabe: Well, his work is certainly very good. But then I suppose one might argue that this type of three-layered clay abstract design is not in itself a particularly *original* (*dokutoku*) idea. Certainly, a number of people have tried it before . . . . So, if one is to take the notion of *tradition* into account, one has no option but to go back to Imaemon's submission. We're talking about a thirteenth-generation potter specialising in enamel overglaze porcelain ware. Still, I think it necessary that we have a good discussion at this point, if only because Imaemon *can* produce better work. On the other hand, in Number 22, we have the work of a completely unknown potter. If we choose the latter for the Princess Chichibu Cup, we'll be attaching a lot of *meaning* (ōki na imi) to it and giving the potter quite a reputation.

Imai: Actually, *I* think that Imaemon's vase is rather good. It is in a new style, as you can see.

At this point, Tanabe asked that the vase be brought over for closer examination.

Hayashi: We should, perhaps, not forget that Imaemon nearly got the Princess Chichibu Cup four years ago.

Imai: And he made *this* vase, unlike many artist potters who get their apprentices to do the work for them.

Tanabe (with a laugh): Well, one has to consider whether Her Imperial Highness would like to have her name associated with an abstract lump of clay made by an unknown schoolteacher, or with a nice porcelain vase by a very famous artist potter. We all know which she'd prefer! So what I suggest is that we wait to see how Number 22 progresses in the future and then award him a major prize when a suitable occasion occurs.

This was met with general murmurs of assent and handclaps on the part of the assembled judges. The overglaze enamel porcelain bowl by Imaizumi Imaemon XIII had won the Princess Chichibu Cup!

CHAPTER 11

The Politics of Evaluation

Now, what are we to make of what was more, in Victor Turner's phrase, a "social drama" than a mere "creative encounter"? And what does the previous chapter tell us about evaluation in the light of my earlier discussion of values and ensemblages of worth? Do prizes, and those who decide on such awards, affect public estimation of different forms of cultural production? Do they have some bearing on people's judgements of 'creativity'? Or are they some kind of ruse to delude people into believing that someone or something is 'better' (and therefore can be valuated higher) than they might otherwise have thought? This suspicion is neatly encapsulated by James English in the opening paragraph of his book on what he calls "an economy of prestige":

> The custom of awarding prizes, medals, or trophies to artists—selecting outstanding individuals from various fields of cultural endeavour and presenting them with special tokens of esteem—is both an utterly familiar and unexceptional practice and a profoundly strange and alienating one.[1]

This uneasy alliance of familiarity and strangeness (the anthropologist's credo) makes itself known in the extraordinary range of activities for which prizes are awarded: adult videos, airlines, architecture, arts, B2B marketing, beauty, composition, computational physics, design, education, food technology, hair styling, hotels, human rights, journalism, law, literacy, magic, manga, meteorology, a nuclear-free future, peace, politics, research, retail, scouting, toys, trade finance, wine, and so on and so forth. Whatever activity you name, it almost certainly has some sort of award attached to it, for the 'best' this, or the 'most something' that (and you will note that I haven't even mentioned your standard film, book, music, advertising, fashion, television, and other creative industries' awards). It doesn't matter who you are; there are always some prizes that will seem to be misplaced and deserving of an occasional chuckle or sneer, which probably explains the institution of the Ig-Nobel Prize, the Razzies, and the Darwin Awards for not-so-meaningful contributions to the advancement of civilization. Not that these spoof prizes are markedly different in aim from the real McCoys. From the giddy heights of Nobeldom to a retail chain's Employee of the Month, people are rewarded for things that they've achieved (or for things that others think, or for one reason or another wish to assert, they've achieved), so much so that you might be excused for thinking that at times there seem to be more prizes than there are potential prize-winners.

Because prizes do pick out winners and place them, however briefly, in a public's eye, they also by default create losers. This is where unexceptional practice can be transformed into alienation, and it is alienation, I suspect, that underpins the scandals that tend to coalesce around a prize's 'sphere of legitimacy.' Scandal and accompanying gossip suggest that people in a particular social world (of publishing, film, fashion, and so on)—in particular, perhaps, those who feel that they should have been a prize's recipient—resent prestige accorded to others and resort to "strategies of condescension" that cast a shadow over a prize's recipient or a prize itself.[2] On such behaviour do art and creative worlds thrive, if only because, in the long run, it helps reinforce their collective belief in the disinterested judgement of taste and worth.[3] Still, detractors have to be careful about how far they go. If their criticisms are too obvious and damning, they are more than likely to be themselves damned when, or if, they receive the accolade that they feel they deserved all along. There are rules, as well as strategies, by which the game should be played and prestige produced: something that we witnessed in the manoeuvrings of jury members as they narrowed down a vast array of more than 1,200 pots to just the one that they could select as worthy recipient of the Princess Chichibu Cup.

Prizes and awards are interesting sociologically for a number of different reasons. For a start, they represent the outcome of an engagement with creative products on the part of people who, as jury members, are deemed to be aesthetic specialists. They are also economic instruments well suited to achieving cultural objectives along social, institutional, and ideological axes.[4] As a result, scholars in a number of different disciplines, building on comparatively early work by William Goode,[5] have begun to consider the sociological and economic effects of prizes and awards.[6] This is in part due to reflection upon the observed proliferation of prizes in many different sectors of contemporary society.[7] But it is also in part due to an interest in observing how exactly culture and economy, together with their respective forms of capital,[8] interact with each other in symbolic markets in which different constraints and values are brought to bear in different ensemblages of worth. Indeed, Bourdieu's distinction between "restricted" and "large

234 ▣ **CHAPTER 11**

scale" forms of cultural production has formed the theoretical basis for a number of studies of prizes, especially in the fields of literature[9] and film.[10]

Critics

What can we learn from this? Prizes in the world of Japanese ceramics ally the authenticity regime of economic coordination discussed in Chapter 7 with what Lucien Karpik calls an "expert-opinion regime."[11] A prize like the Princess Chichibu Cup rests on the authority of specialists in different genres of Japanese ceramics—museum curators, university professors, and men of letters—whose social position is equated with a recognized appreciative competence that qualifies them to make public pronouncements on the quality of potters' work and to make periodical selections of what they pronounce as a 'good' or 'the best' pot. Ceramics exhibitions, then, "offer a simple, almost routine, solution to radical quality uncertainty" inherent in singular products manufactured by the creative industries.[12] The prizes attached to different exhibitions also act as a powerful device to gain an audience and "serve as a collective reference point," if only "because a symbolic value is attributed to the jury and through it to the institution it represents" (although I myself would see this single movement as multiple movements among the four main players in the ceramic art world; see below).[13] Although they cannot construct a market in themselves, prizes function first to help consumers buy 'good' pots without having to go through the trouble of obtaining the necessary information, or acquiring the appropriate knowledge, to enable them to make their own decisions. Japanese consumers rely on newspapers and other media for their information, and on department stores to provide a site at which to observe firsthand and purchase works of ceramic 'art.' And second, exhibition prizes become linked to the authenticity regime in that they allow buyers to move into the more hallowed ground of collecting prestige objects.[14]

These two functions of exhibition prizes impinge upon the role of the "critics" (*hyōronka*) who form the juries that make the awards. The self-appointed task of Japanese pottery critics is to educate the general public—as well as collectors and potters themselves—in matters of taste and discrimination.[15] In this they act as professional representatives of mediation between cultural producers, products, and their publics,[16] who are themselves composed of friends, collectors, buyers, and exhibition appreciators, as well as critics themselves.[17] How do they do this?[18]

THE POLITICS OF EVALUATION   235

Because contemporary Japanese ceramics is a comparatively new field (marked by the word 'contemporary'), the first task for its critics has been to *develop an aesthetic vocabulary* that is acceptable to their publics.[19] This they have done by making use, in part, of evaluative words and phrases that have relied on both material-technical (clays, decorative techniques, glazes) and appreciative values ("a weak footrim" [*kōdai ga yowai*], "a strong line" [*sen ga tsuyoi*], "touch" [*tezawari*], "taste" [*aji no aru*], "detached" [*mushin*], "artless beauty" [*soboku*], and so on), used in the appreciation of tea ceremony and other traditional Japanese pottery genres. But they have also 'modernised' their appreciative vocabulary to incorporate and appeal to changing and expanding middle class consumer tastes. They thus talk of a pot's having a "modern feeling" (*gendai kankaku*), or of being "out of kilter with the times" (*jidai hazure no mono*), with contemporaneity being marked by English nouns like 'vitality' and 'originality', as well as by such adjectives as 'sharp' (also Japanese, *tsurudoi*), 'pure' (also Japanese, *seiketsu*), 'simple,' 'clear,' 'rhythmical,' and 'individual' (*koseiteki*, contrasting with *mushin* above).

Given this concerted effort by critics over time to develop an acceptable language of evaluation, what to my mind was remarkable about the Japan Ceramic Art Exhibition (JCAE) was how little it featured in jury members' comments during the course of arriving at their decision about which pot should receive the Princess Chichibu Cup. In this respect, unlike most jurying processes described by other scholars, the JCAE prize awarding process was remarkably *a-linguistic*. In academic peer reviewing, as in film and book jurying, panellists use language to assess and evaluate proposals, films, and books, which themselves use language as a, or the, primary form of expression and communication. Panellists may argue points, listen to counterarguments, persuade and be persuaded, and agree or disagree with fellow panellists on the basis of opinions expressed about the products before them.[20] Pots, however, like all other kinds of artwork, use form, colour, and pattern/design—not language—as their primary means of communication. Panellists, therefore, must first evaluate them in terms other than by means of language, which is then used to interpret sensations and emotions induced by the physical form of the pot or artwork in question. Such sensations are independent of, and cannot be tied down by, language. As a result, like wines, they are resistant both to consistent and universalistic standards (of beauty or taste), and thus to mutual understanding and agreement in their own terms, and so allow other criteria—such as interpersonal relations—to sway deliberations among panellists.

236 ▣ **CHAPTER 11**

What stands out from the previous chapter's account is the fact that judges rarely gave voice to what may broadly be termed 'aesthetic' criteria when arguing for or against a submission. This does not mean that they did not adhere to the kind of "universalistic terms" discussed by Michelle Lamont. On other occasions, for example, they were more than prepared to outline before their different publics (as well as explain to an inquiring anthropologist) their conceptualizations of "modern beauty" (*gendai no bi*) in relation to ceramics. However, the criteria then used (and described above) were not openly brought into play in the prize-awarding process, although during the *selection* process judges *did* comment both positively and negatively in aesthetic terms on a particular submission's form, glaze, technical execution, or design, as they debated whether to pass or fail it.

During the prize-awarding process, on the other hand, jury members rarely engaged with pots in this way. When aesthetic judgements were overtly made, they tended to be expressed in negative, rather than in positive, terms, thereby stating clearly what jury members saw as a lack of the quality of worthiness.[21] This was to be seen in Hayashi's use of the English word "charming," and judges' general aversion to pots that were "weak" (*yowai*). Even when Imai asserted that Imaemon's pot (Number 6) was "in a new style," he did not explain, nor did his fellow jury members ask, in what this style consisted.[22] Rather, extra-aesthetic factors were again brought into play to make an argument. Thus Imai put forward extended procedural reasons for not awarding the Princess Chichibu Cup to Number 17 at the end of Round 4. For his part, Tanabe advocated the prestige associated with a thirteenth-generation potter, traditional Japanese porcelain, and a member of the Imperial Household (thereby equating the quality of a worthy object with that of a worthy subject, and manifesting the higher common principle of 'tradition'),[23] when delivering his coup de grâce on Number 22 at the end of Round 5. In these respects, the 'creative' aspect of jury members' encounters with different pots took on a rather different nuance from that of the potters who made them.

The second task of critics has been to act as guides, presenting their advice to both potters and the general public. Murata, for example, spent several days in Kyushu twice a year where he was driven around from one pottery village or town to another to comment on pots brought to him by potters anxious to know how best to get their work accepted in the JCAE or some other exhibition. Over the course of a couple of hours, he would suggest that a form needed to be "sharper" here, or a glaze "lighter" or more "lucid" (*meikai*) there; he would say fairly directly what he liked and disliked about a particular decoration or a bowl, vase, or tea caddy as a whole. He would hint at what, in his opinion, was likely to pass and what not to be successful (while being sure to make it clear that a jury worked as a group, hence absolving him of individual responsibility for failure, but allowing him, nonetheless, potential credit for success). As he spoke to the potters, he would from time to time bring in examples of work by other famous contemporary potters such as Kitaoji Rosanjin (clearly his own favourite), Ishiguro Munemaro, Tomimoto Kenkichi, and others. In this way he established the credibility of his taste against the backdrop of the history of twentieth-century ceramics in Japan.

He also gave lectures from time to time in a department store or museum of art or craft that was putting on an exhibition of ceramics. There, before an audience of several dozen people (mainly women, and sometimes including a group of potters for whom he had 'prejudged' submissions), he would pick out the virtues of individual works on display: virtues that almost invariably merged into stories and histories of the potters who had made those works. In this way, he seamlessly merged appreciative with social values, while simultaneously expounding upon what he referred to as "the pleasure of ceramics" (*tōgei no tanoshisa*). This actually consisted of four interrelated activities: the pleasure of looking at pots (*miru tanoshisa*), of using them (*tsukau tanoshisa*), of decorating them with food (*ryōri o moru tanoshisa*), and of pleasing others through them (*hito o yorokobasu tanoshisa*). In this way, Murata cleverly argued for a potential transformation of 'untouchable' exhibition pieces into pots for everyday use, thereby encouraging his listeners to enter into the authenticity regime that his expert opinion supported and validated.

Critics' third task has been to act as *teachers*. This they did directly by giving courses on Japanese ceramics and related topics at the universities where many of them were employed, as well as by contributing essays to the numerous series of illustrated Japanese art books that were published in the 1970s and 1980s in particular. But they also acted as teachers indirectly by curating exhibitions and selecting for them those works that they themselves particularly liked. Indeed, Murata was said to have instigated the very first JCAE when he proposed to the Mainichi Newspaper Company that it sponsor an exhibition of pots that he would select from among the considerable number of potters in Kyushu.

Finally, building on their abilities to use aesthetic language persuasively, as well as to be guides and teachers, critics have acted as *high priests* celebrating Japanese people's long-held belief in great pots as works of art. In this respect, we should perhaps note that:

> The feeling for quality and the ability to judge works of art according to their aesthetic quality can never be absent in a critic, but they are not among the most indispensable prerequisites for the fulfilment of his task. Of greater importance is the correct interpretation of the meaning content of an artistic creation.[24]

Now, we may wish to question what Arnold Hauser means by "correct" since the "appropriate interpretation" of an artwork's meaning is seemingly based on intelligence, maturity, experience, and "the proper assessment of problems of existence, social points of view and humanitarian problems," together with the sensibility deriving therefrom (although all of these characteristics are assumed and remain undefined by Hauser). However, what we should realise is that "correctness" lies in the overall *reception*, and not pronouncement, of a critic's aesthetic explanation, judgement, and interpretation. For so long as people (believers) accept that contemporary Japanese ceramics should be *rhythmical*, *sharp*, *clear*, and *simple*, imbued with *vitality* and *originality*, and so on and so forth, then critics will continue to administer a communion in which pots are both the life blood and body of Japanese culture.

Those who pose the greatest threat to critics' sanctity are the potters themselves, who, like artists in the Western world, "are involved in a serious tug-of-war with critics—a hip-and-thigh struggle which reflects the desire of each to be the ultimate arbiter of 'good art.'"[25]

Critics wield great power, first because of their role as judges of competitive exhibitions, to which potters felt that they *must* contribute to gain and sustain a reputation. Many potters—especially those living in remoter parts of the country[26]—resented this power, but simultaneously felt a need for critics' recognition, approval, and support. They thus displayed a deeply ambivalent attitude towards them, now claiming that critics' judgements were irrelevant to contemporary Japanese ceramics (mere "pen pushers" [*bunpitsuka*] whose 'eye' was quite different from that of potters), now taking strategic steps to secure the confirmation of their work that they so avidly sought. One such step was for a potter to ask a critic to write a "recommendation" (*suisenbun*) for his one-man exhibition (of the kind written for me by Imaemon XIII). Another, often as part of what became a series of exchanges, was to give a particular critic examples of his or her work, not just in the hope that the latter would then mention it in one of his numerous forms of communication, but because critics also gathered around them a 'stable' of collectors who, at a well-placed word, would then purchase a bowl, or vase, or large dish by the potter concerned. Although critics would proudly take credit for such exchanges, what they seemed not to realise (or care about) was the fact that by, albeit indirectly, introducing money into what ideally was an aesthetic equation, they had weakened their position as untainted high priests of ceramic art.

If the raising up of particular potters to the status of "ceramic artists" (*tōgei sakka* or *tōgeika*) led to the lowering of critics in potters' eyes from the heights of Parnassus, critics were able to remain high priests by not acting in concert and by masking actual power relations among them (of the kind we witnessed during jurying of the JCAE). Potters knew that there was a power hierarchy, but were unable to arrive at consistent evaluation of who was more powerful than whom. For potters working in stoneware in Kyushu, for example, Murata was the man to please. He was, after all, the man who knew all about *contemporary* Japanese ceramics. For those in Hagi, across the water separating Kyushu from the main island of Honshu, it was Hayashi who was deemed to be *the* expert in aesthetic appreciation; in particular, of tea wares for which Hagi potters were famous. Neither of these two men, however, had managed to build a power base in other parts of Japan, particularly in Kyoto, where Imai ruled the roost for porcelain, while also reaching out to potters like Imaemon XIII in Kyushu, even though his specialization was oil painting and sculpture. Abstract clay art he left to Fujiwara, professor at the Kyoto University of Art and fellow panellist at the JCAE. This distribution of expertise and the consequent scattered nature of critics' individual power led, paradoxically, to an assertion and acceptance of their authority overall.

Jurying Exhibitions

So what did we learn about how jury members went about the task demanded of them?

First, the section panels and the jury as a whole tended to adhere to the opinions expressed by their chairmen, who themselves were appointed on the basis of seniority in the ceramic art world. Thus Tanabe, although retired, was a member of the prestigious Japan Academy of Arts (*Nihon Geijutsu-in kai'in*), while Imai was former curator of a well-known Kyoto art museum, of which Kitano was the current director. As a result, we find Judges A and B of the Functional Section agreeing with their panel chairman Imai's arguments for the removal of Number 17 (their own section's submission) at the end of the fourth round of voting.

But the relative seniority of each section's chairman also influenced the selection process. For example, the chairman of the Abstract Section panel, Kitano, remained silent and did not openly argue for the merits of Number 22 (an abstract work) when his predecessor, Imai, openly supported Number 6. This was, without doubt, a tactical move by the latter, who used his social position to stifle open disagreement with his opinion.

There was, then, an informal pecking order among jury members, based in large part upon pre-existing networks and reputations, which were determined—as one would expect in Japanese society—by age and seniority. As Michelle Lamont has pointed out with regard to peer-review research panels:

> It is impossible to eliminate the effect of interpersonal relationships, including clientelism, on the evaluation process. Nevertheless, panellists proceed as if they were free of these influences. Their individual preferences are usually construed in universalistic terms, despite the particularistic aspects introduced by real-world considerations.[27]

In the case of the JCAE, the "universalistic terms" adopted by jury members were in large part framed as regional expertise in different styles of Japanese ceramics (noted above in my discussion of the relations between potters and critics). Such regional expertise led to two kinds of particularism. On the one hand, it became clear during the selection process that jurors made a point of seeking out the work of certain potters to whom, for one reason or another, they felt 'indebted.' Murata, for example, at one point during the first afternoon expressed considerable concern over the fact that he couldn't find the submission by the leader of a potters' association whose members he had been advising over the past year. Eventually, we found it—a small tea caddy almost totally obscured by the arching form of a very large vase—and it was passed by the panel.

On the other hand, judges would make use of a potter's 'name' to justify their selection of a particular pot. When there was some collective doubt, for example, about a large plate, Hayashi volunteered the information that it was in fact made by a German potter, Gert Knapper, living in Mashiko. "Oh, *Knapper!*" said all the other judges immediately. "Pass!" Also, a judge

THE POLITICS OF EVALUATION 241

would occasionally check the name of the maker of a particular pot (which was stuck to its underside) by pretending to examine its foot rim closely as part of his 'aesthetic' appraisal. Alternatively, when a panel's jurors were collectively uncertain, its chairman would ask the women employees who had made, for example, Number 1294. The answer came without hesitation: "So-and-so in Shigaraki." "Well," exclaimed Tanabe, "We'd never have guessed. That *is* unusual work for him. Pass!" Clearly, such strategies tended to reproduce jury members' tastes, and in so doing amplify their authority, as well as affect indirectly the overall development of contemporary Japanese ceramics.[28]

Second, to impose a sense of order on what they perhaps saw as evaluative randomness, jurors said that in large part they voted for pots in their own sections throughout the voting process. If this were so, they would be conforming to standard sociological analysis that the primary allegiance of Japanese is to the 'in group' to which they belong.[29] Certainly, this seems to have been the case with the absentee judge who voted for one of the pots in his own section. However, voting in the early rounds shows quite a broad distribution of votes outside the sections to which jury members were assigned. It was only later that a division of votes along section lines might have taken place, although anomalies prevailed. An obvious crossover was Imai, who admitted his support for Number 6, rather than Number 17, in Round 3. Also, Murata (who, it will be recalled, had volunteered to telephone the potter concerned when his work was transferred to the Functional Pottery Section) almost certainly voted for Number 17, rather than Number 12 in his own Tradition Section, until it was withdrawn. Moreover, given that Number 6 would have been classified as a 'traditional' pot if it had been an ordinary instead of a recommended submission, one would have expected all four judges in the Tradition Section to vote for it in the final round. The fact that they did not do so suggests that jury members exercised a measure of independent aesthetic judgement throughout the jurying process, but that such judgement was also tempered by interpersonal relations that led to bloc voting based on alliances and schisms.

Third, while awards and prizes are overtly bestowed by jurors—critics, in the case of the JCAE, but also potters in other exhibitions—those who receive awards, as well as those who observe them, can also play a part in legitimizing these events.[30] We have seen that, in the JCAE, prizes are awarded by a jury selected from among, and thus representing the interests of, Japan's art and educational institutions. This jury is deemed to have the expertise that the organizers of the exhibition—the Mainichi newspaper

242 ▣ **CHAPTER 11**

and Daimaru Department Store—themselves lack. A jury, then, is absolutely essential on two counts: first, its members select and then reward contributions to an exhibition; second, by so doing, they directly influence the exhibition's credibility in the eyes of its public.[31] In these respects, jurors link production to consumption and thus perform a crucial structural role in the manufacture and reception of 'taste' and discrimination.[32] The honour of being asked to serve on a jury, even though dismissed by judges themselves (whether critics or potters) as burdensome, reproduces the power of the jury and reminds readers of its members' importance and centrality in the field of Japanese ceramics.[33]

At the same time, the judges serve the organization, which 'owns' the prizes that they allocate. In this respect, their role is symbolic, rather than structural, so that judges are not unlike those who initiate a *kula* exchange path in the islands of the western Pacific.[34] They have the power to *circulate* awards, the ownership of which, however, remains elsewhere.[35] Who, then, *owns* the prizes? Ostensibly, it is the bestowing organization, the Mainichi Newspaper Company. But the latter does not own all of the prizes that *it* allocates, since only one of the prizes bestowed bears the company's name, and another that of the exhibition itself. The other prizes bear the names of *other* persons—Princess Chichibu, the Minister of Foreign Affairs, and the Minister of Culture—who have lent their names, and the names of their organizations, to the exhibition and the bestowing organization. That all those concerned were very aware of this was made clear when the panel of judges, finding itself at an impasse after the final round of voting, discussed which of the two extant pots her Imperial Highness might like to have her name associated with. So, Mainichi acts as custodian and holds some of its prizes in trust. In this respect, its symbolic position is no different from that of the panel of judges that it employs. By linking symbolically the national production of ceramics to the Imperial household and Japanese government (as well as to itself, a media organization), it reinforces the cultural institutions of art and education represented by the panel of judges. As its title implies, the JCAE 'consecrates' *Japan*, Japanese *ceramics*, and an *exhibition* culture.

A fourth point to note is that the ceramics art world in Japan is constituted of a quadripartite structure consisting of potters, critics, media (newspapers), and department stores, all of whom interact with one another as "adversaries in collusion." Potters exhibit and sell their work in department stores, which in lieu of cash payment will often oblige potters to buy other works of art that they have on sale. Critics will praise the work of a particular potter because he has received some examples of it and wishes to raise their market price.[36] They will do this through newspapers that promote and take the credit for ceramic (and other) art exhibitions, claiming 'sponsorship' when in fact it is department stores (or gallerist intermediaries) that usually front expenses. Department stores claim that they make no money from exhibitions, but are 'returning culture' to their customers, who have enabled them to make a profit over the years by loyally purchasing the goods that they put on sale. Exhibitions, especially juried exhibitions, are the focal point of such collusion.

What emerges from these considerations is that, in both the selection and prize-awarding processes, judges did not consider pots on their own merits, but invariably *in relation to* other pots, a trait that we also came across in Chapter 6 when we heard the Deputy Editor-in-Chief of *Elle Japon* explain how she put together each issue of her magazine. This was obvious in the selection process, when pots were brought before judges in groups of five, leading to a strong tendency for them to opt for 'similarity' and 'difference' as basic criteria for selection. They would thus make comments like "we don't really have any forms like this, so we could pass it" (*kō iu katachi wa ichiyō nai kara, tōte mo ii*); or "we have few examples of *sometsuke* underglazing, so . . ." (*sometsuke wa sukunai kara . . .*). Occasionally, a submission would be compared with the standard expected in another exhibition and passed accordingly if it met the criterion of stylistic difference: "this is a different taste from traditional crafts" (*dentō kōgei to wa chigau aji*). And yet, if a submission was the 'same' as one accepted in a previous exhibition, it was also deemed to have met the required 'standard' of exhibition ceramics (*kaijō tōgei*). If, on the other hand, a submission was 'different' from the same potter's previous work (as well as from other submissions to the exhibition being juried), it became immediately worthy of selection. In none of these instances did the judges engage with a submission in itself.

Relational evaluation could also be seen in the assessments at the end of each round of voting of individual pots which were candidates for the Princess Chichibu Prize. In other words, jury members were intent not upon judging inherent qualities that would enable them to decide the 'best pot' in the exhibition, but upon finding a 'winning pot' that depended on *produced contrasts*.[37] In this they faced the unenviable task of comparing "incommensurate flaws."[38] The fact that jury members were asked to award prizes on the

244 ▣ **CHAPTER 11**

basis of relative, rather than absolute, performance[39] underlines the fact that competitive exhibitions like the JCAE are tournaments during which different sets of values engage in ensemblages of worth to decide the winner.[40] Because judges' reactions were general, rather than related to specific qualities of a work on display, and because they seemed disinclined to 'explain' the sources of their subjective reactions to each pot, we should, perhaps, recognize that their task was to *recommend* rather than to *evaluate*.[41] In this respect, they were like fashion magazines, which propose new fashion styles to their readers every season, rather than evaluate them.

Nevertheless, the "central rules of deliberation" outlined by Lamont appear to hold good for the jurying of Japanese ceramics.[42] The JCAE is thus not an isolated ethnographic case, for it allows us to make comparisons across both cultural boundaries and product ranges. A standard of reciprocity prevailed among jury members who were disposed towards producing a consensual decision and thus realizing the common good, even though their attempts at persuasion tended to be along procedural rather than aesthetic lines and did not provide "opportunity for full and equal voice" because of age and interpersonal relations.[43] It was *personal* deference and respect, therefore, rather than deference for expertise and respect of disciplinary sovereignty, that gave rise to collegiality and provided "the oil that keeps the wheels of deliberation turning when panellists otherwise might not be willing to accommodate one another."[44]

Finally, as an act of consecration, the JCAE had to fulfil four conditions. The organization awarding the honour (the Mainichi Newspaper Company) had to have cultural authority; it also had to adhere to rigorous procedures when selecting prize recipients; the main award (the Princess Chichibu Cup) needed to be selective, in the sense that only a very small proportion of potential recipients could receive it; and, crucially, the organization had to be able to identify objective differences that clearly demarcated potters and pots that were consecrated from those that were not.[45]

Now, as with the Baseball Hall of Fame analysed by Allen and Parsons, the JCAE met the first three criteria, but fell short on the fourth. The social position of jury members gave the awarding organization cultural authority: an authority which Mainichi strengthened by publishing a frank account of what had happened during the jury's voting for the Princess Chichibu Cup, which, by being awarded every second year, is extremely selective. But voting patterns made it clear that jurors could not identify objective differences that would mark off one pot from its competitors and so make it obviously worthy of the Princess Chichibu Cup on the basis

THE POLITICS OF EVALUATION 245

of agreed 'merit.' As a result, other criteria had to be brought into play to justify final selection of Imaemon's submission. In this respect, the jurying process did *not* assert that personalistic ties or prior judgements were irrelevant. Rather, the fact that judges made it their business to be aware of who had submitted what and often made their selections on the basis of personal ties (based on long-term 'loyalty') encouraged neither fairness in jurying nor the necessary transformation of contestants into strangers to allow their work to be judged on a level playing field.[46]

Nevertheless, at the same time, ceramics exhibition awards do offer a basis for judgements about possible future achievement.[47] Being awarded the Princess Chichibu Cup has tended to have further consequences in terms of 'cumulative recognition' for those concerned. Of the 21 winners of the prize since the inception of the JCAE, four (including Imaemon XIII) have since been designated the holders of Important Intangible Cultural Properties. The "meritocratic principles" invoked in the jurying process, therefore, are seemingly justified and reinforced by the later bestowal of the highest award possible to a potter in Japan. This in turn legitimizes the JCAE itself, together with its jurying process, judges, prize bestowers, and sponsoring organization. Encounters that may have started out being in some way 'creative' thus end up as institutionalising and institutionalised.

The fact that the fourth condition—the identification of objective difference and accompanying clear demarcation of consecrated from non-consecrated—was *not* met in my account of jurying processes at the JCAE explains, perhaps, why it is so difficult for scholars to study jurying processes in situ. Those who hand out awards and prizes *must* keep the processes of consecration secret in a black box if they are to maintain the legitimacy of those in whose trust they are placed. Otherwise it will become clear that the Emperor, while not entirely without clothes, may be somewhat improperly dressed for the occasion.

CODA

In this book, I have had the temerity to grapple with the slippery concept of 'creativity' and to show through several ethnographic accounts how it is, or is not, used in different forms of cultural production. By examining ceramics, advertising, and fashion magazines, primarily as they are conceived, produced, and appreciated in Japan, I have taken the proverbial bit between the teeth and compared Japanese creative workers' actual practices with theorizing that has taken place almost entirely in an American and European academic tradition. This has led to one or two slightly surprising results as particular cultural and industry differences in emphases emerge. But, all in all, the field on which people play their creative game in Japan doesn't seem to be *that* different from other fields in other lands. The rules they abide by are more or less the same, as are their goals (and goalposts), although Japanese players tend, perhaps, to be better coordinated as a team (albeit with individuals still competing among themselves).

The main theoretical argument about what constitutes the creative act—derived from the work of Arthur Koestler as well as that of anthropologists such as Elizabeth Hallam, Tim Ingold, and John Liep—has been shown to stand up well in Japanese contexts of cultural production. What Koestler calls "bisociation" is the mark of creativity in such varied activities as making pottery, coming up with an advertising campaign idea, and editing fashion magazines. This often involves improvisations that result from 'thinking aside'—a temporary setting aside of controlling reason in favour of other codes that afford "the underground games of the mind"[1]—and give rise to perceptions of 'originality' (or 'difference'). I also noted that the idea of creativity-as-bisociation might be applied not only to the actual making of a film or fashion collection, but also to its conception, appraisal, and promotion. It was the initial bringing together of hitherto unassociated frames of reference in the planning of my pottery exhibition, for example, that then afforded further technical and aesthetic bisociations when I got down to making my pots.

And yet, I also suggested that Japanese conceptions of 'creativity' are, perhaps, a little different from those generally accepted in Europe and North America. In particular, I argued against the notion of 'inspiration' proposed by Boltanski and Thévenot, but rather for one of 'detachment' in Japan. Ultimately, however, as the book progressed, the reader (I'm talking about you) became aware of the fact, as with many 'things Japanese,' the difference is quite subtle. While one located the source of creativity in the *individual*, the other did so in the *relationship* between individual maker and the thing being made. According to Western theorists, creators are 'inspired'; in other words, creativity stems from an inner quality that is present in some individuals (who are 'creative'), but not in others (who are not). This inspiration affords the making of particular products, which are then revered because (with nicely circular reasoning) they are the work of 'creative' persons. At this point, they somehow take on an inner soul (or *animus*) of their own so that people find it virtually impossible to distinguish between a product and the person or persons who made it. This kind of 'animism'—a good old anthropological trope that endows non-human entities with human attributes—itself affords and sustains a form of consumerism which relies upon, and is sustained by, a system of branding.[2]

In Japan, however, creative people are not seen as receiving 'inspiration' as such. Rather, they work to put their 'heart' into cultural products. This they achieve through long hours of repetition and hard work, and when they do so, they succeed in being 'detached' from the results of their work, since 'detachment' means literally having 'no heart.' And yet, the maker's heart is perceived to have entered the thing that s/he has made. People in Japan, too, see pots, calligraphy, or flower arrangement as being imbued with animate qualities; they, too, cannot stop themselves from confusing products with the perceived 'spirituality' of the people who make them, which is why they, too, live in and make their own contributions to a world of brands. The difference, if there is one, is that in general, cultural producers in Japan believe that (their version of) creativity derives primarily, perhaps even solely, from discipline, training, hard work, and practice: from 'putting their heart into' something. Although this attitude may also be found among some cultural producers in Europe and North America who are less prone than others to mystifying their work, there is still a general, ill-defined notion in those parts of the world that creativity is somehow inborn: a gift, rather than graft.

And yet in both Japanese and Western worlds 'interiority' comes to be associated with creativity: spiritually, socially, and symbolically. We saw how the studio used for an advertising campaign was marked by inner depth and outer surface, and how different personnel were distributed between these two axes, with creative people located first and foremost in the 'depth' (*oku*). Not only this, but creativity was seen as taking place within a bounded social group. It was the fact that fashion magazines addressed the 'fashion village' as well as a targeted readership and advertising clients that enabled it to be 'creative' when it came to producing its monthly fashion stories.

Of course, how, or whether, creativity comes to be recognized as such ultimately has little to do with the cultural producer or performer. As Koestler remarks, our appreciation of an artwork or cultural product is hardly ever a unitary act. For the most part, it results from "two or more simultaneous processes which interfere with and tend to distort each other."[3] We saw this at work more or less consciously when jury members selected a porcelain bowl by a thirteenth-generation overglaze ceramicist, rather than an abstract 'lump of clay' by an unknown schoolteacher, as winner of the Princess Chichibu Cup. We saw it also being used expressly when a creative director made an association between a rock star, popular among high school and university students, and a somewhat staid life insurance company. I know that some of my own pots sold because I was labelled "the second Leach" by local media journalists covering my exhibition. As Koestler nicely put it, "each time we think we are making a purely aesthetic judgement according to our lights, the stage-lights interfere."[4]

These stage-lights I have outlined as forming ensemblages of worth, each of whose values come to bear in one way or another on the conception, manufacture, appreciation, sale, and use of cultural products. These values themselves are afforded by materials, techniques, and social and organizational relations of one sort or another, as well as by aesthetic styles, genres, and brand images, and the situational contexts in which they all take place. Different players tend to emphasize different affordances and values: a photographer his social network, a potter her clay and glazes, the marketing department its company's brand image, a collector an artist's name, as well as the price asked of an artwork; and so on and so forth. Even aesthetic specialists such as critics are unable to limit themselves to judgements based entirely upon appreciative values. We shouldn't need a financial crisis, therefore, to remind us that what people say and what they do are often different matters and that, in this respect, evaluations and valuations of worth are almost always in some ways fraudulent.

What else? I argued that cultural products are almost invariably structured, both in their conception and performance, in terms of two competing mechanisms: anchorage and flow. Each of these is necessary for the other to function effectively. Indeed, bisociations depend upon the anchorage of two different planes of reference. And yet it is because of their concern with craftsmanship that creative workers in Japan talk so consistently of 'flow' (*nagare*) as a structuring device for their work. In jazz performances, 'group flow'—in the guise of improvisations that achieve a 'groove'—becomes the overriding aim. It is when people working together 'lock in' to one another that we can talk about 'ensembling.' Just as ensemblages of worth consist of felicitous combinations of different values, so does ensembling itself consist of a felicitous gathering of like-minded people collaborating with focused concentration. Cognitive psychologists have picked up on this to argue that herein lies creativity. I counter-argued that, while improvisations may allow the association of unexpected planes, 'group flow' is not a necessary condition for creativity. Although it may provide jazz musicians, an advertising campaign's production team, or all those working to put together a catwalk show with satisfaction and rationalised justification for doing the work that they do, 'group flow' also has to be recognised as such by audiences outside production for it to be accepted as 'creative.' This doesn't always come about. Work done in the 'right' way, therefore, doesn't necessarily produce 'good' work, however much we might wish it.

The Worth of Names

One other thing that occasionally reared its head from time to time in people's discussions of their work was the system of names prevalent in different forms of cultural production. Creative industries routinely create and make use of the reputations of individual actors, works, genres (often in the form of brands), and organizations. Indeed, it may well be these, rather than any common form of social organization, production methods, or value chain, that bind together different industries of fashion, film, publishing, and so on under the single denomination of 'creative industries.' Like art worlds, they single out from the mass of more or less similar work done by more or less interchangeable people a few works and a few makers of works of special worth. They reward that special worth with esteem and, frequently but not necessarily, in more material ways too. They use reputations, once made, to organize other activities, treating things and people with distinguished reputations differently from others.[5]

Although Rilke has nicely defined fame as "the sum of the misunderstandings which are formed around one name,"[6] we may see a theory of reputation for the creative industries as residing in the existence of specially talented people who create products that are recognised as being innovative, *different*, and thus exceptional. This is so because they exhibit a profound

250 ▣ **CODA**

understanding of the genre (art, fashion, soap, or thriller) in which they work, and/or stimulate the sale of cultural goods. The latter not only better the lives of those who consume them. They also exhibit special qualities which testify to their maker's (or makers') special talents, while—with an aesthetically pleasing circularity noted above—the already-known talents of the maker testify to the special qualities of the creative product itself.[7]

Even though there are differences here, too, among the various creative industries,[8] reputations *matter* to all concerned. They matter in particular because they help define and sustain the different fields of art, architecture, publishing, theatre, and so on, and the aesthetic evaluations that take place therein (as well as their ensuing valuations). Awards systems, such as the one I described for Japanese ceramics in Chapter 10, make use of reputations to perform a sociocultural function. They select either certain forms of cultural production that they regard as socially valuable (the Gold Dagger Award for best crime novel of the year, or the Astrid Lindgren Children's Prize in publishing, for example), or the producers thereof (the Nobel Prize awarded to selected authors for their lifetime contribution to literature). By selecting certain books or films, but not others, award systems build a *canon* of works in a particular cultural field. They create symbolic capital.

But prizes also have an economic function, since they are one of several marketing mechanisms used by creative industries to promote their products. They can bring relatively unknown film directors, artists, and musicians to public recognition, as well as enhance the reputation of those already established in their separate fields. This in turn affords directors the opportunity to make a 'big budget' film next time round, artists to raise the price of their canvases, and musicians to charge higher performance fees (as well as play in bigger and 'better' venues). They also turn the attention of the media to films, art, and music, thereby supporting their consumption more generally. They serve, in short, an "economy of prestige."[9]

The fact that reputations enable and sustain an ongoing exchange between cultural, symbolic, and economic capital suggests the proposition that contemporary economies function according to a logic of names. Some of us drive a BMW (if you happen to be a Japanese celebrity's manager, at any rate), wear Chanel No. 5 perfume, and drink grand cru wines (others prefer a battered Mini, Dior Addict, and a bottle of plonk). We might wear Doc Marten boots or an Yves Saint Laurent gown. In the office, we may well use Scotch tape and (if you're Japanese) a Hotchkiss stapler, at home a Hoover. Names are consistently confused in our everyday conversations.

Sometimes we use people's names (a Cardigan, Sandwich, or, in some languages, Röntgen), at other times companies' names (a Jaguar or Burberry), to talk about products. We also use abbreviations (a Coke or a Mac), even metaphors (Golden Arches), and substitute a brand name for the thing itself (a Macintosh or Walkman).[10] Names are found in three distinct interlocking social spheres: of people (celebrities, personalities, stars, CEOs), products (brands), and organisations (corporations, government bodies, and international organizations like NATO and UNESCO). In the world of reputation, "the relation of worth is a relation of identification."[11] Advertisers make use of names to give 'personalities' to inanimate things and to forms of social organisation, thereby reinforcing the 'animism' that we have initiated by inducing a maker's human qualities in the objects s/he makes.

Names tend to take on particular importance in two ways in fields of cultural production. First, we find an active use and dissemination of names as part of the promotional strategies of advertising (which thus aims to enhance reputations rather than sell products directly)[12] and different forms of popular culture. In the fashion industry, for example, the names of fashion designers and the houses they work for, of photographers and their assistants, of models, stylists, and hairdressers, as well as of fashion magazine personnel, are a crucial site for the functioning of the field as a whole. Each name strives to 'make its mark' in a struggle for power and so legitimise fashion's "categories of perception and appreciation."[13]

Second, the primary means of linking organisations (corporations) to the products that they sell is through celebrities of one sort or another, as we saw with Watanabe Misato and MLI in Chapter 4. Celebrities constitute a 'world of fame' in which opinion—and not any specific professional quality—establishes equivalence. The worth of each being depends on the opinion of others, so that organizations try to take advantage of the fact that "fame establishes worth."[14] Designers and fashion houses take a lot of time and trouble preparing special clothes (which may not be worn) for actors and actresses attending the American film industry's annual Academy Awards (known popularly as the Oscars). Jewellers will also lend coveted necklaces and earrings to actresses for the evening, on the basis that they may be caught for a moment or two in the glare of network television coverage of the occasion.[15]

Names, then, satisfy an intellectual demand for order, involving a long-term accumulation of social and cultural capital that is then converted into economic capital and back again. Celebrities serve not just as "cultural intermediaries,"[16] but as *mediators,* in that the effects wrought by how they "transform, translate, distort, and modify the meaning or the elements they are supposed to carry" are unpredictable.[17] Like animals and plants in a totemistic system, celebrities are deemed to be useful or interesting because they are first of all known, rather than known as a result of their usefulness.[18] In this sense, celebrities, too, *afford.* Initiating evaluations and valuation, and operating in a particular commercial field, they are "the crucial element in a mixed economy" that we might well call a *name economy.*[19] But they also link different fields of popular culture, as when, at the height of her fame, supermodel Naomi Campbell made forays into film, music videos, recording, publishing, and the Fashion Café, as well as the by-now customary crossover between runway performances and fashion magazine spreads. At the same time, Campbell had to compete with other models of her generation who were simultaneously trying to make their marks in different ways (Helena Christensen, for example, pursued her career as a photographer and magazine creative director, and launched her own clothing line, while also appearing in the usual music videos and films). It is the struggle among names that maintains a structured difference, synchronically and diachronically, within and between the different creative industries and fields of cultural production in which they operate.

The name economy rests uneasily upon, and is sustained by, instabilities arising out of the triangular relationship between creativity, celebrities, and symbolic markets. Creativity has 'beauty' (*bi*) as its higher common principle, but beauty is 'beyond price.' Nevertheless, as we saw with my pottery exhibition, prices must be attached to creative products, even though cultural producers are convinced that creativity is not commercial. One way out of this conundrum is for them to be 'celebrated' as 'artists' and so to allow the world of detachment or inspiration to be merged with that of fame. However, precisely because confirmation of the former "depends on the certainty of an intimate conviction," and that of the latter on the opinions of others,[20] this leads merely to a new conundrum that pits personal evaluation against multiple evaluations by others. The challenge, as I have argued in this book, is how best to create, sustain, and represent equivalence between beauty, fame and price. For this, these worlds of worth often call upon the 'domestic' world (in the form of a fashion 'house,' the fashion 'village,' or fashion magazine 'family'), whose bonds of mutual trust help fix the reputations of both creators and created works, as well as prices. Together they prevent rapid fluctuations in market evaluations and valuations.[21]

The Worth of Scholarship

In writing this book I have participated in a tournament of names, albeit those found only in the 'small world' of academia. The subjects selected, research methods adopted, scholars referred to, and arguments made all play off against other books and articles already published, read, reviewed, and cited. Together, they contribute to and sustain a higher common principle of 'scholarship', a system of references which reveals where the author wishes to position himself and joust, in the middle, outside, or on the edge of one or more disciplinary boxes (in this case, anthropology, art and aesthetics, economic sociology, 'Japanology', and the sociology of valuation and evaluation).

Given that references themselves have now been co-opted to form a control mechanism founded on citations, scholarship is in danger of becoming no more than a system of names repeated ad infinitum in articles in academic journals, those harbingers of intellectual conformity and lucrative sources of profit for publishing companies. Books, for the moment at least, defy such measurement. Unlike journals, they also afford their authors space for experiment, improvisation, and the association of hitherto unassociated spheres of thought. Yet we are told by our masters (and mistresses) to publish in journals since it is these, plus their accompanying rankings, impact factors, and h-indices, that will make or break our academic careers. At the same time, like my potter friends in Japan, we know (if we're honest) that 'talent' and skill at our chosen task only get us halfway up the ladder to success; the rest depends on (among other things) timing, serendipity, knowing the right people, and coming up with an appropriate sound-bite from time to time to advertise our existence. We cannot afford to overlook affordances.

So far, like lap dogs, most of us have lain on our backs and accepted the administrative nonsense that is foisted upon us. Maybe this is a particularly prominent feature of European, rather than North American, universities and business schools, but it seems that academic staff have had little option but to do as they're told. In particular, junior and mid-level scholars are not in a position to stand up for ideas or actions that go against the administrative grain. But those of us who have made it to the top through some ensemblage of ability, personality, and circumstance, have a duty, I think, to take a stand on what we believe is right and against what we think is wrong. We may be wrong in what we think is right, or right in what we think is wrong, but it is our duty as scholars to engage in dialogue, often so woefully lacking in institutions of higher learning.

Like those whom I respect in the academic worlds, I myself believe in scholarship as an exchange of ideas, and not in the empty parroting of other scholars' names. I believe in books, for it is books, not journal articles, which introduce new knowledge. I believe in an interdisciplinary approach to scholarship, and not in the mutual back-slapping antics of a disciplinary in-group whose members quote only one another (with the occasional addition from outside the group as a mark of 'distinction') as they hitchhike along a path to marginal fame. I do not believe in a 'Japanese' (or South Asian, West African, Amazonian, or other regional-based) anthropology, but in what 'things Japanese' can contribute theoretically to the discipline as a whole. Similarly, I am not yet convinced of the necessity for a 'business' anthropology as such, since what counts for me is the application of general anthropological theories to the analysis of business organizations and trading relations (in the manner that I have applied them in this book). Such beliefs form the backbone of common sense about what it is we scholars should be doing. I would add, however, that I do not believe in the pedestrian formalism of academic journals masquerading as founts of knowledge. Nor do I believe in the use of citations as an evaluation of 'quality' and valuation of 'worth.'

Beliefs, of course, do not necessarily end up as practices. I am not convinced, for example, that I have not participated in a bit of empty parroting here and there during the course of writing this monograph. Nor am I absolutely sure at what point inter-, as opposed to multi-, disciplinary scholarship can be said to take place, and whether such a point has been reached in this book. But I've tried. And that, at least, is a beginning. Hopefully, it will prompt others more able than myself to cast aside all those pseudo-intellectual traditions that rely on founding fathers, dons, and unholy boasts, and to move into the rarified air of 'thinking aside.' We need, I believe, more creative engagements with scholarship 'on the edge': a belief that merely echoes the tensions between detachment (and inspiration), fame, and the market described throughout this business of writing creativity.

NOTES

Overture

1 Koestler, *The Act of Creation.* London: Pan, 1970, p. 182.

2 Koestler, pp. 121–3, 201–2.

3 Dornfeld, *Producing Public Television, Producing Public Culture.* Princeton, NJ: Princeton University Press, 1998, p. 14.

4 Condon and Ogston, "A segmentation of behaviour." *Journal of Psychiatric Research* 5, 1967; Sawyer, *Group Creativity,* New Jersey: Lawrence Erlbaum Associates, 2003.

5 O'Donnell, *Making Ensemble Possible,* Ph.D. Dissertation in the Doctoral School of Organisation and Management Studies, Copenhagen Business School, 2013a, p. 15; Sawyer, "Group creativity." *Psychology of Music* 34, pp. 157–61.

6 Lévi-Strauss, *The Savage Mind.* London: Weidenfeld and Nicolson, 1966, p. 22.

7 Lamont, "Towards a comparative sociology of valuation and evaluation." *Annual Review of Sociology* 38, 2012.

8 E.g., Amabile, "How to kill creativity." *Harvard Business Review,* September–October 1998, pp. 77–87.

9 E.g., Jeffcut and Pratt, "Managing creativity in the cultural industries." *Creativity and Innovation Management,* 2003.

10 Levitt, "Creativity is not enough." *The Best of HBR,* August 2002, pp. 137–44.

11 Liep, "Introduction." In Liep (ed.), *Locating Cultural Creativity.* London: Pluto, 2001, p. 1.

12 Boden, "What is creativity?" In Boden (ed.), *Dimensions of Creativity.* Cambridge, MA: MIT Press, 1994; Moeran and Christensen (eds.), *Exploring Creativity.* Cambridge: Cambridge University Press, 2013.

13 Dornfeld, p. 16.

14 For a delineation of this emergent sub-field of anthropology, see Jordan, *Business Anthropology* (2nd ed.), Long Grove, IL: Waveland, 2013, as well as the Open Access *Journal of Business Anthropology* at www.cbs.dk/jba.

15 Rohlen, *For Harmony and Strength.* Berkeley & Los Angeles: University of California Press, 1974; Dore, *British Factory-Japanese Factory.* Berkeley & Los Angeles: University of California Press, 1973; Clark, *The Japanese Company.* New Haven and London: Yale University Press, 1979; Moeran, *A Japanese Advertising Agency.* Richmond, UK: Curzon, 1996; Bestor, *Tsukiji.* Berkeley & Los Angeles: University of California Press, 2004.

16 Law, "Actor network theory and material semiotics." In Turner (ed.), *The New Blackwell Companion to Social Theory.* Oxford: Basil Blackwell, 2009, p. 141.

17 See Çalişkan and Callon, "Economization, part 1." *Economy and Society* 38, 2009; Latour, *Reassembling the Social.* Oxford: Oxford University Press, 2005, pp. 5–8.

18 Çalişkan and Callon; Latour; Callon, "The embeddedness of economic markets in economics." In Callon (ed.), *The Laws of the Markets.* Oxford: Blackwell, 1998.

19 Becker and Strauss, "Careers, personality, and adult socialization." *American Journal of Sociology* 62, 1956.

256 ▣ **NOTES**

20 Negus and Pickering, *Creativity, Cultural Value and Communication*. London: Sage, 2004, pp. 46–9.

21 E.g., Florida, *The Rise of the Creative Class*. New York: Basic Books, 2002, p. 5.

22 Hauser, *The Sociology of Art*. London: Routledge & Kegan Paul, 1982, p. 18.

23 Latour, p. 46.

24 Latour, p. 46.

25 Negus and Pickering, p. vi.

26 Sennett, *The Craftsman*. London: Allen Lane, 2008, p. 290. Gell notes the existence of a more "quietist" mode of creativity found in Japanese and Indian tantric art forms (*Art and Agency*. Oxford: Clarendon Press, 1998, p. 30).

27 Hauser, p. 19.

28 Caves, *Creative Industries*. Cambridge, MA: Harvard University Press, 2000.

29 E.g., Howkins, *The Creative Economy*. Harmondsworth: Penguin, 2002; Hesmondhalgh, *Cultural Industries*. London: Sage, 2002, pp. 12-14.

30 Csikszentmihalyi, *Creativity*. New York: HarperCollins, 1996, pp. 27–8.

31 Liep, p. 2.

32 Assuming that there is nothing new on earth, Francis Bacon argued that "all novelty is but oblivion" (Borges, *Collected Fictions*. London: Penguin, 1998, p. 183).

33 Ingold and Hallam, "Creativity and cultural improvisation." In *Creativity and Cultural Improvisation*. Oxford: Berg, 2007, pp. 2–3; Sennett, *Together*. London: Allen Lane, 2012, p. 214.

34 Barrett, "Creativity and improvisation in jazz and organizations." *Organization Science* 9, 1998, pp. 605.

35 Barrett, pp. 606–8.

36 Ingold and Hallam, pp. 2–3.

37 Sawyer, 2006, p. 157.

38 Becker, "The work itself." In H. S. Becker, R. R. Faulkner, and B. Kirshenblatt-Gimblett (eds.), *Art from Start to Finish*. Chicago and London: University of Chicago Press, 2006, p. 24.

39 Becker, pp. 25-6.

40 Caves, op. cit.

41 Becker, *Art Worlds*. Berkeley & Los Angeles: University of California Press, 1982, p. 26.

42 Koestler, pp. 144–77. De Bono advocates "lateral thinking." (De Bono, *Serious Creativity*. New York: HarperCollins, 1992.)

43 Csikszentmihalyi, 1996, pp. 79-80.

44 Koestler, p. 108.

45 Koestler, p. 119.

46 Koestler, p. 178.

47 Koestler, p. 198.

48 Hauser, 1982, p. 478.

49 Becker, pp. 201, 226.

50 See, for example, Eco, "James Bond." *Communications* 8, 1966, pp. 77–93.

51 Zeliger, *Economic Lives*. Princeton, NJ: Princeton University Press, 2011.

52 Bourdieu, *The Field of Cultural Production*. Cambridge: Polity, 1993, p. 53.

Chapter 1

1   Gibson, "The theory of affordances." In R. Shaw and J. Bransford (eds.), *Perceiving, Acting and Knowing*. Hillsdale, NJ: Lawrence Erlbaum, 1997.

2   See, for example, Moeran, *Ethnography at Work*. Oxford: Berg, 2006, pp. 79–100; and Moeran and Christensen, "Introduction." In Moeran and Christensen (eds.). *Exploring Creativity*, 2013.

3   For example, Norman, *The Design of Everyday Things*. New York: Basic Books, 1990.

4   Cf. Negus and Pickering, p. 68; Latour, 2005, p. 72.

5   Norman, "Affordance, conventions, and design." *Interactions*, 1999; Hartson, "Cognitive, physical, sensory, and functional affordances in interaction design." *Behaviour and Information Technology* 22, pp. 316–22.

6   Sennett, *Together*. London: Allen Lane, 2012, p. 214.

7   Koestler, p. 382, 406.

8   Zeliger, *Economic Lives*. Princeton & Oxford: Princeton University Press, 2011, p. 304.

9   Zeliger, p. 307.

10 See Becker, *Art Worlds*, pp. 40–67.

11 Bourdieu, *The Field of Cultural Production*. Cambridge: Polity, 1993.

12 Bourdieu, 1993, p. 64.

13 Bourdieu, *The Logic of Practice*. Cambridge: Polity, 1990, p. 53.

14 Bourdieu, 1993, p. 30.

15 Law, 2009, p. 147.

16 Law, "On the methods of long distance control." In Law (ed.), *Power, Action, Belief*. London: Routledge & Kegan Paul, 1986; Callon, "Some elements of a sociology of translation." In Law (ed.), 1986; Latour, 2005, p. 217.

17 Çalişkan and Callon, 2009, p. 386.

18 Menger, "Profiles of the unfinished." In Becker, Faulkner, and Kirshenblatt-Gimblett (eds.), *Art from Start to Finish*. Chicago: University of Chicago Press, 2006, p. 63.

19 Friedman, "The iron cage of creativity." In Liep (ed.), *Locating Cultural Creativity*. London: Pluto, 2001.

20 Becker, p. 29.

21 Ingold, "Materials against materiality." *Archaeological Dialogues* 14, 2007, pp. 13–4.

22 Koestler, *The Act of Creation*. London: Pan, 1970, p. 38.

23 For an account of camera and other techniques used in the *Paranormal* films, see Bordwell, "Observations on film art." http://www.davidbordwell.net/blog/2012/11/13.

24 This is the main difference between the anthropological approaches to material culture by Tim Ingold (2007), on the one hand, and Danny Miller, on the other. (See Miller, "Stone age or plastic age?" *Archaeological Dialogues* 14, 2007, pp. 23–7.)

25 Koestler, pp. 122–3.

26 Sennett, *The Craftsman*. London: Allen Lane, 2008, p. 127.

27 Pollak, "The performance of the wooden printing press." *The Library Quarterly* 42, 1972, p. 220.

28 Hutter, pp. 65–7, 69–70.

29 For an extended discussion of spatial affordance and the interplay between vision and sound in musical performance, see O'Donnell, "Reconceiving constraint as possibility in a music ensemble." In Moeran and Christensen, 2013b.

30 Moeran, "Framing values." In Nakamaki and Sedgwick (eds.), *Business and Anthropology*. Osaka: National Museum of Ethnology, 2007, pp. 7–23.

31 Csaba and Ger, "Patina meets fashion." In Moeran and Christensen, 2013b.

32 Garcia-Parpet, "Symbolic value and the establishment of prices." In Beckert and Aspers (eds.), *The Worth of Goods*. Oxford: Oxford University Press, 2011, p. 125.

33 Bourdieu, 1993.

34 Haeger and Storchmann, "Prices of American Pinot Noir wines." *Agricultural Economics* 35, 2006, p. 69.

35 Demossier, *Wine Drinking Culture in France*. Cardiff: University of Wales Press, 2010, pp. 43–4.

36 Christensen and Strandgaard Pedersen, "Restaurant rankings in the culinary field." In Moeran and Christensen (eds.), 2013b, p. 239.

37 Haeger and Storchmann, p. 69.

38 Caves, *Creative Industries*. Cambridge, MA: Harvard University Press, 2000, p. 3.

39 Mathieu and Bertelsen, "Evaluation in film festival prize juries." In Moeran and Christensen, 2013b.

40 Dornfeld, *Producing Public Television, Producing Public Culture*. Princeton, NJ: Princeton University Press, 1998, pp. 146–7.

41 Hower, T*he History of an Advertising Agency*. Cambridge, MA: Harvard University Press, 1939, p. 388.

42 Vangkilde, "In search of a creative concept in HUGO BOSS." In Moeran and Christensen, 2013b.

43 Hauser, p. 400.

44 Hauser, p. 30.

45 Mears, *Pricing Beauty*. Berkeley & Los Angeles: University of California Press, 2011, p. 119.

46 O'Donnell, *Making Ensemble Possible*, 2013a, p. 198.

47 Maitland, "Creativity." *The Journal of Aesthetics and Art Criticism* 34, 1976, p. 406.

48 Childress, "What's the matter with *Jarrettsville?*" In Moeran and Christensen, 2013b.

49 Alačovska, *Genre and Autonomy in Cultural Production*. Copenhagen: Copenhagen Business School, 2013a.

50 As Mears notes of fashion modelling: "the object is not just to book a job but to rebook a job" (2011, p. 112).

51 Alačovska, "Creativity in the brief." In Moeran and Christensen, 2013b.

52 Vangkilde, 2013.

53 Fiske, *Television Culture*. London: Methuen, 1987, p. 109.

54 Dornfeld, p. 91.

55 Moeran, *A Japanese Advertising Agency*. London: Curzon, 1996, pp. 158–9.

56 Throughout this book, I have adopted the customary usage of writing Japanese names in the way in which they are used in Japan: that is to say, surname first and first name second.

57 Mears, p. 109.

58 Becker, p. 78.

59 Mathieu and Bertselsen in Moeran and Christensen, 2013b.

60 Fukuda, "Seiyaku wa kōkoku no haha desu." In Amano (ed.), *Kōkoku no Dai-Nyūmon*. Tōkyō: Madora Shuppan, 1992, p. 147.

61 Becker, p. 77.

62 Towse, "Market value and artists' earnings." In Klamer (ed.), *The Value of Culture*. Amsterdam: Amsterdam University Press, 1996, p. 99.

63 Caves, pp. 6–7.

64 Becker, pp. 81–2.

65 Mears, "Pricing looks." In Beckert and Aspers (eds.), *The Worth of Goods*. Oxford: Oxford University Press, 2011.

66 Baxandall, *Painting and Experience in Fifteenth Century Italy*. Oxford: Oxford University Press, 1972.

67 Thompson, *The $12 Million Stuffed Shark*. London: Aurum, 2008.

68 Moeran, 1996, p. 156.

69 Csaba and Ger, 2013.

70 Moeran, "Promoting culture." In Moeran (ed.), *Asian Media Productions*. London: Curzon, 2001, pp. 270–1.

71 Çalişkan and Callon, "Economization, part 1." *Economy and Society* 38, 2009, p. 387; Barry and Slater, "Technology, politics and the market." *Economy and Society* 31, 2002, p. 292.

72 Moeran, *Folk Art Potters of Japan*, 1997.

73 Moeran, "Materials, skills and cultural resources." *Journal of Modern Crafts* 1, 2008.

74 Hutter, "Creating artistic from economic value." In Hutter and Throsby (eds.) *Beyond Price*. Cambridge: Cambridge University Press, 2008, pp. 67–9.

75 Hutter, p. 64.

76 Hutter, pp. 62–5.

77 A harpsichord, however, has a versatility not afforded the pianoforte; it can be tuned to virtually any musical tradition—Arabic, Indian, Western—with eight to twelve notes, quarter notes, and half notes, respectively. (Personal communication, Maya Moeran.)

78 Becker, 1982, pp. 40–1.

79 Becker, p. 26.

80 Latour, "On actor-network theory." *Soziale Welt* 47, 1996.

81 Callon, "The economy of qualities." *Economy and Society* 31, 2002.

Chapter 2

1 Latour, 2005, p. 87.

2 Bourdieu, *The Field of Cultural Production*. Cambridge: Polity, 1993, pp. 74–6.

3 Bourdieu, pp. 67–9.

4 In this respect, as an outsider to the ceramic art world, I was deemed to be 'safe.' See also Moeran, *The Business of Ethnography*. Oxford: Berg, 2005, pp. 135–48.

5 Goffman, *The Presentation of Self in Everyday Life*. New York: Anchor, 1959, pp. 109–40.

6 Bourdieu, p. 81.

260 ▣ NOTES

7 That Miyamoto should have even considered allowing an amateur like myself to hold his own one-man exhibition revealed, even though it was closed in, the fluid nature of the contemporary ceramic art world in Japan at that time (cf. Rosenberg, "The art establishment." In Albrecht, Barnett, and Griff [eds.], *The Sociology of Art and Literature,* London: Duckworth, 1970, p. 388).

8 Moeran, *Folk Art Potters of Japan.* London: Curzon, 1997.

9 Wacquant, "The pugilistic point of view." *Theory and Society* 24, 1995, p. 494.

10 I owe a great debt of gratitude to Kajiwara Jirō who, over a period of two years, selflessly gave me his time and did his utmost to set up contacts for me in my study of the ceramic art world in Japan, while also allowing me to throw pots on one of his spare wheels. A similar thank you goes to Miyamoto Fusa who, together with Reisuke (alas, now deceased), looked after me and my research interests in numerous other ways.

11 Bourdieu, pp. 120–25.

12 And, he might have added, good for the Mainichi newspaper's reputation!

13 Becker, p. 24.

14 Bourdieu, pp. 76–7.

15 Bakhtin, *Rabelais and his World.* Bloomington, IN: Indiana University Press, 1984, pp. 4–12.

16 Koestler, p. 160.

17 This was the direct result of the decision to hold my show at the same time as the Traditional Crafts Exhibition, and reveals an unanticipated consequence of the adoption of one particular (temporal) affordance over another.

18 Vollard, *Recollections of a Picture Dealer.* New York: Dover, 1978, p. 62.

19 Boltanski and Thévenot, *On Justification.* Princeton: Princeton University Press, 2006, p. 160.

20 Such questions helped me immensely during the rest of my research in the field.

21 Pye, *The Nature and Art of Workmanship.* London: Herbert Press, 1995, p. 20.

22 So well, in fact, that Tanaka Hajime later incorporated the chattering design as a standard example of his own pottery style. Similarly, Kajiwara Jirō for a while adopted my triangle design for his own square dishes in Koishiwara.

23 Caves, *Creative Industries.* Cambridge MA: Harvard University Press, 2000.

24 In the end, I decided to keep the bird tray (I am glad I did so and still have it). The collector concerned boycotted my exhibition and bought nothing as a result.

25 The Ura-Senke school of tea was the most prominent at the time of my research.

26 Thompson, *The $12 Million Stuffed Shark.* London: Aurum, 2008, pp. 210–11.

27 Thompson, p. 209.

28 Velthuis, *Talking Prices.* Princeton, NJ: Princeton University Press, 2005, pp. 158–9.

29 In those heady days of 1982, when the exhibition took place, the dollar-yen exchange rate was US$1 = ¥248.

30 To gauge how this top price of $400 compared with prices charged by other potters in Japan, let me add that Kajiwara Jirō in Koishiwara would have priced a similarly sized stoneware pot at about $600 and Tanaka Hajime a porcelain dish at $800, while a comparable Imaemon XIII overglaze enamel porcelain bowl would have been on offer at between $1,600 and $2,000. Stoneware tea bowls by Arakawa Toyozō, the holder of an Important Intangible Cultural Property (*jūyō mukei bunkazai*), on the other hand, were retailing at approximately $24,000 in the same year.

31 Thompson, p. 208.

32 This is most obvious, perhaps, in TV talk shows where guests and producers engage in highly routinized emotional labour as they search for "the money shot" (Grindstaff, *The Money Shot*. Chicago: University of Chicago Press, 2002, pp. 115–45).

33 Moeran, pp. 209–20.

34 Bernard Leach (1887–1979) was an English potter who spent the first four years of his life in Japan and then went to live there as an adult from 1909 to 1920 (with a year's break in Beijing in 1914). He was instrumental in bringing William Morris's ideas to Japan and became a close friend of Yanagi Sōetsu, founder of the Japanese folk art (or *mingei*) movement. Leach's work is regarded extremely highly in Japan and fetches a high price there.

35 Thompson, p. 40.

Chapter 3

1 Karpik, *Valuing the Unique*. Princeton: Princeton University Press, 2010.

2 Hutter, "Infinite surprises." In Beckert and Aspers, 2011, p. 201.

3 Boltanski and Thévenot, *On Justification*. Princeton: Princeton University Press, 1991.

4 Karpik, pp. 10–13.

5 Gibson, *The Ecological Approach to Visual Perception*. Boston: Houghton Mifflin, 1979, p. 127.

6 Latour, 2005, p. 114.

7 Lamont, "Towards a comparative sociology of valuation and evaluation." *Annual Review of Sociology* 38.

8 Boltanski and Thévenot, p. 159.

9 Boltanski and Thévenot, pp. 160–4.

10 Boltanski and Thévenot, p. 141.

11 Witness, "the value, or worth, of a man is as of all other things, his price" (Hobbes, Leviathan, 1651, p. 31).

12 See Beckert and Aspers, *The Worth of Goods*. Oxford: Oxford University Press, 2011, p. 6.

13 Boltanski and Thévenot, p. 142.

14 Graeber, *Towards an Anthropological Theory of Value*. New York: Palgrave, 2001, p. 3.

15 Latour, *Reassembling the Social*. Oxford: Oxford University Press, 2006, p. 6.

16 Such arguments focus on formalist and substantivist properties of different types of economy, which, for the sake of brevity, I will not enter into here. (See Wilk, *Economies and Cultures*. Boulder, CO: Westview, 1996; Çalişkan and Callon, "Economization, part 1." *Economy and Society* 38, 2009, pp. 372–8.)

17 Slater and Tonkiss, *Market Society*. Cambridge: Polity, 2001, p. 49. See also Debreu, *A Theory of Value*. New Haven and London: Yale University Press, 1959.

18 Throsby, pp. 19–20.

19 Stark, "For a sociology of worth." Working Paper Series, Center on Organizational Innovation, Columbia University, New York, 2000.

20 Stark, pp. 2–3.

21 White, "Where do markets come from?" *American Journal of Sociology* 87, 1981; Boltanski and Thévenot, 2006.

262 ◎ **NOTES**

22 Hutter and Throsby, "Value and valuation in art and culture: introduction and overview." In Hutter and Throsby (eds.), *Beyond Price*. Cambridge: Cambridge University Press, 2008, p. 1.

23 See, for example, Granovetter, "Economic actions and social structure." *American Journal of Sociology* 91, 1985.

24 Throsby, pp. 28–29.

25 Frey, *Art & Economics*. Berlin: Springer, 2003.

26 Throsby, pp. 19, 24, 28.

27 Graeber, 2001; Appadurai (1986: 21ff.), too, refers to a "tournament of value" in the singular.

28 Herrnstein-Smith, *Contingencies of Value*. Cambridge, MA: Harvard University Press, 1988, p. 127.

29 Hitlin and Piliavin, "Values." *Annual Review of Sociology* 30, 2004, pp. 359–60.

30 Stark, p. 5. For Stark, it is this that will save economic sociology from being no more than the study of business.

31 Bourdieu, 1993.

32 Lampel and Nadavulakere, "Classics foretold?" *Cultural Trends* 18, 2009, p. 239.

33 For example, Nozick, *Philosophical Explanation*. Cambridge, MA: Belknap Press, 1981.

34 Cf. Adorno, *Aesthetic Theory*. London: Routledge, 1984.

35 Hauser, *The Sociology of Art*. London: Routledge & Kegan Paul, 1982, p. 314.

36 Throsby, pp. 30–1.

37 Throsby, p. 27.

38 Likewise, by positing a "theory of value," economists themselves make a claim to objective validity of the standards, norms, and judgements that they use in their theorizing.

39 Throsby, pp. 32–3.

40 de Saussure, *Course in General Linguistics*. London: Duckworth, 1983.

41 Simmel, *The Philosophy of Money*. London: Routledge & Kegan Paul, 1978, p. 60.

42 Zelizer, "Human values and the market." *American Journal of Sociology* 84, 1978, p. 591.

43 Schucking, *The Sociology of Literary Taste*. Chicago: University of Chicago Press, 1974, p. 53. In his study of the scholarly publishing in the United States in the early 1980s, Powell also notes that "it is common knowledge that unsolicited manuscripts have very slim chances of being published" (Powell, *Getting into Print*, Chicago: Chicago University Press, 1985, p. 89). This in part explains the rise and power of the literary "super-agent" (Thompson, *Merchants of Culture*, Cambridge: Polity Press, 2010, pp. 84–99).

44 Hauser, *The Sociology of Art*. London: Routledge & Kegan Paul, 1984, p. 509.

45 Rosenberg, p. 391.

46 Becker, p. 46.

47 Becker, p. 46.

48 Schucking, p. 71.

49 Thompson, 2008, p. 41. The same can be said, of course, of an academic world, the difference being that 'buzz' generates higher personal income, rather than product price per se.

NOTES 263

50 Karpik, 2009, p. 134. My informants anticipated by some three decades the identical tripartite distinction made by Lucien Karpik in his study of uncertainties of the "authenticity regime."

51 In Hutter and Shusterman's terminology (p. 199), "art-technical" value.

52 Cf. Becker 1982.

53 For similar examples of the uses to which Cezanne's paintings were once put by their owners, see Vollard, p. 185.

54 Karpik, p. 69.

55 Karpik, p. 35.

56 Variations are possible. An art dealer, for example, often 'places' a painting or other artwork with a collector who expresses reservations about it (in terms of either price or 'artistic' value). By allowing him to keep it at home for a while, the dealer hopes to erase the difference each of them places on the symbolic and/or commodity exchange value of the work in question and so effect a sale.

57 Hutter and Shusterman, p. 200.

58 Bourdieu, p. 30.

59 I include models among 'things' because of the way in which their bodies are treated as commodities in photographic shoots and catwalk shows.

60 The disadvantage, perhaps, is that it ignores individual or affective values (stemming from what Bourdieu would term habitus), although it could be argued that the latter are in fact socially constructed and therefore an integral part of social values.

61 Anand and Jones, "Tournament rituals, category dynamics, and field configuration." *Journal of Management Studies* 45, 2008, pp. 1049–51.

62 This task is made easier by the fact that various publications regularly establish hierarchies for corporations (by means of sumō wrestler rankings), based on annual turnover and profit, number of employees, senior management's education background, and so on. Similar data—contributing to Richard Caves's "A list/B list" property—are available for artists and artist craftsmen.

63 Ginsburgh and Weyers, "Quantitative approaches to valuation in the arts, with an application to movies." In Hutter and Throsby (eds.), *Beyond Price*. Cambridge: Cambridge University Press, 2008.

64 Boltanski and Thévenot (pp. 293–4) argue that "the initiatory relation" of master to apprentice involves a compromise between "inspired" and "domestic" worlds of worth.

65 Moeran, 1997, p. 199.

Chapter 4

1 Boltanski and Thévenot, 2006, pp. 159–64.

2 Boltanski and Thévenot, p. 160.

Chapter 5

1 Koestler, p. 96.

2 Goffman, *Frame Analysis*. Boston: Northeastern University Press, 1986; Becker, p. x.

3 Moeran, *A Japanese Advertising Agency*. London: Curzon, 1996, p. 27.

4 Douglas and Isherwood, *The World of Goods*. New York: Basic Books, 1979, p. 72; Moeran, pp. 126–130.

264 ▣ NOTES

5   Hower, *The History of an Advertising Agency.* Cambridge, MA: Harvard University Press, 1939.

6   Young, *How to Become an Advertising Man.* Lincolnwood, IL: NTC Business Books, 1991 (1963); Hopkins, *My Life in Advertising & Scientific Advertising.* Lincolnwood, IL: NTC Business Books, 1998.

7   See, for example, Ogilvy, *Confessions of an Advertising Man.* New York: Atheneum, 1963; and *Ogilvy on Advertising.* London: Guild Publishing, 1983.

8   Arlen, *Thirty Seconds.* Harmondsworth: Penguin, 1979; Mayer, *Madison Avenue, U.S.A.* Lincolnwood, IL: NTC Business Books, 1991; Rothenberg, *Where the Suckers Moon.* New York: Vintage, 1994; Goldman, *Conflicting Accounts.* New York: Simon & Schuster, 1997.

9   Lien, *Marketing and Modernity.* Oxford: Berg, 1997; Moeran, 1996, p. 27; Miller, *Capitalism.* Oxford: Berg, 1997; Kemper, *Buying and Believing.* Chicago: Chicago University Press, 2001; Mazzarella, *Shoveling Smoke.* Durham: Duke University Press, 2003.

10 McCreery, "Creating advertising in Japan." In Moeran (ed.), *Asian Media Productions.* London: Curzon, 2001; Malefyt, "Models, metaphors and client relations." In Malefyt and Moeran (eds.), *Advertising Cultures.* Oxford: Berg, 2003; Morais, "Conflict and confluence in advertising meetings." *Human Organization* 66, 2007; Malefyt and Morais, *Advertising and Anthropology,* Oxford: Berg, 2012.

11 Caves, pp. 6–7.

12 Moeran, 1996, pp. 116–65.

13 Quinn, "The account executive in an advertising agency." In Jones (ed.), *The Advertising Business.* Thousand Oaks, CA: Sage, 1990.

14 Cf. Caves, p. 106.

15 Grabher, "The project ecology of advertising." *Regional Studies* 36, 2002.

16 Grabher, p. 249.

17 Moeran, pp. 42–8.

18 In Japan, an advertising agency's creative team usually consists of a copywriter and art director who work under the guidance of a creative director. When a campaign includes a television commercial, the creative director usually takes command of shooting; the art director tends to be in control of print advertising.

19 Aspers, *Markets in Fashion.* Stockholm: City University Press, 2001, pp. 58–101.

20 Goffman, p. 85.

21 The data that follow were gathered during participant observation in five studio ad campaign shoots held in Tokyo in 1990 and again in 2002. All of them involved a model or celebrity who also appeared in fashion magazines, for whom all the photographers also on occasion worked. The analysis that follows reflects this aspect of these advertising campaigns.

22 Goffman, p. 21.

23 Moeran, "A tournament of value: strategies of presentation in Japanese advertising." *Ethnos* 54, 1993.

24 Malefyt, 2003.

25 Goffman, p. 21.

26 Goffman, p. 22.

27 Goffman, pp. 124–9.

28 Goffman, p. 499.

29 The stylist usually has a row of clothes on hangers available for use in or near the beauty room.

30 For the record, I should point out here that all the photographers and art directors encountered in the five studio shoots I attended in Japan were men, hence my use of the masculine pronoun.

31 On location, the minibus.

32 For further discussion and analysis of situational frames in Japanese business settings, see Moeran (2005, pp. 63–65). Dale and Burrell (2008) also discuss the conceptualization of space in organizational contexts, but tend to focus on fixed constructions rather than on the kind of recurring reconstructions of space analysed here.

33 In this instance, creativity lay in the bisociation of hair and food (eating utensil), thereby affording the model a second 'mouth' which, together with her real mouth, could be said to have emphasized what lay between them: her eyes and the contact lenses being advertised.

34 Becker, p. 91.

35 Negus and Pickering, *Creativity, Communication and Cultural Value*. London: Sage, 2004, p. 19.

36 Sawyer, 2006, p. 159.

37 Grabher, p. 254; Aspers, pp. 60–70.

38 Becker, p. 359.

39 Interview, Ishizaki Michihiro, art director, November 2002.

40 Bourdieu, *The State Nobility*. Cambridge: Polity, 1996b, p. 360.

41 Aspers, p. 62; Moeran, 2005, pp. 118–9, 124–5.

42 Bourdieu, 1993, p. 81.

43 Bourdieu, 1993, pp. 50–1.

44 Goffman, *The Presentation of Self in Everyday Life*. New York: Anchor, 1959, p. 83.

45 Goffman, 1959, p. 88.

46 Boltanski and Thévenot, 2006, p. 278.

47 Goffman, 1986, pp. 378–9.

48 Goffman, 1959, p. 92.

49 Marshall, *Principles of Economics*. London: Macmillan, 1961, p. 271.

50 Goffman, 1959, p. 95.

51 Dornfeld, p. 69.

52 Bourdieu, 1993, p. 176.

53 Bourdieu, 1993, p. 42.

54 Caves, p. 119.

55 Baxandall, *Painting and Experience in Fifteenth Century Italy*. Oxford: Oxford University Press, 1972, p. 1.

56 Cf. Bourdieu 1993, pp. 58, 61, 119.

57 Witness Ishii's counterposing the idea of 'rebirth' (in Misato's music) against MLI's 'stiff', 'gloomy', and 'stuck-up' reputation, and her 'way of life' with the fact that his client was a life insurance company.

58 Bogart, *Artists, Advertising, and the Borders of Art*. Chicago: University of Chicago Press, 1995, p. 135.

266 ▣ **NOTES**

59 Bogart, 1995, pp. 136–7.

60 Bogart, 1995, p. 66.

61 Becker, pp. 81–6.

62 This mirrors the situation facing the account manager vis-à-vis the client and his account team, as well as the account team vis-à-vis its creation of an ad campaign that will please both client and targeted consumers.

63 Rosenblum, "Style as social process," *American Sociological Review* 43, 1978, p. 428.

64 Bourdieu, 1993, p. 61.

65 Rosenblum, p. 429.

66 Aspers (pp. 82, 86) notes that in Sweden, too, it is the fashion photographer who decides who will be part of the production team and employs the stylist, hairdresser, and makeup artist.

67 Such respect extends to creative-client relations, unlike in the United States (cf. Jackall and Hirota, *Image Makers*. Chicago: University of Chicago Press, 2000, pp. 95–96).

68 Rosenblum, p. 430.

69 Rosenblum, p. 430.

70 Rosenblum, p. 431.

71 Rosenblum, p. 84.

72 Portfolios are also used by models, makeup artists, stylists, and assistants of one kind or another (Aspers, p. 70), as well as by art directors, copywriters, and others in the advertising industry. In academia, the function of the portfolio is performed by the curricululm vitae (CV).

73 Interview, Nicky Kohler, November 2002.

74 Aspers, p. 94.

75 Interview, Miyahara Muga, Tokyo, November 2002.

76 Rosenblum, p. 111.

77 Becker, pp. 29–30.

78 Dornfeld, p. 79.

79 Negus and Pickering, p. 68.

80 Dornfeld, p. 81.

81 Dornfeld, p. 78.

82 Caves, pp. 4–5.

83 Boltanski and Thévenot, p. 160.

84 "Subjection to *money* (venality) is among the forms of bondage from which one must free oneself to be in the right state to receive inspiration" (or, in my formulation, to be detached). Boltanski and Thévenot, p. 239.

85 Ingold and Hallam, 2007.

Chapter 6

1 The exception was Ferguson, *Forever Feminine*. London: Heinemann, 1983.

2 See, for example, McCracken, *Decoding Women's Magazines*. Basingstoke: Macmillan, 1993; Hermes, *Reading Women's Magazines*. Cambridge: Polity, 1995.

3 Marcus, "Ethnography in/of the world system." *Annual Review of Anthropology* 25, 1995; Moeran, 2005, pp. 198–9.

NOTES ▢ 267

4 Wacquant, 1995.

5 I am not the only one to fail in this task. Gough-Yates (*Understanding Women's Magazines*. London: Routledge 2003, pp. 21–23) recounts similar difficulties in her attempts to conduct ethnography among British women's magazines. My impression is that I was treated far better. No interviews were summarily cancelled; no interview lasted less than an hour, and most went up to and beyond two hours. I am extremely grateful to all those concerned for their goodwill, time, and patience in answering my frequently naïve questions.

6 I should add that I have benefited enormously from my year's fieldwork in a Japanese advertising agency where I spent considerable time learning about media organizations' activities (Moeran, 1996).

7 Beetham, *A Magazine of Her Own*. London: Routledge, 1996, pp. 1–5.

8 Marchand, *Advertising the American Dream*. Berkeley & Los Angeles: University of California Press, 1985, p. 48.

9 McKay, *The Magazines Handbook*. London: Routledge, 2000, p. 190.

10 See also Grindstaff on television (*The Money Shot*. Chicago: Chicago University Press, 2002, p. 33). As Virgil Thomson once noted for music, "the Public doesn't exist except as a statistical concept" (quoted in Rosenberg and Fliegel, 1970, p. 500).

11 Caves, *Creative Industries: Contracts between Art and Commerce*. Harvard University Press, 2000.

12 Davis, *Fashion, Culture, and Identity*. Chicago: University of Chicago Press, 1995, pp. 146–9.

13 Entwistle, *The Fashioned Body*. Cambridge: Polity, 2000, p. 236.

14 Entwistle, p. 237.

15 Entwistle, p. 238.

16 Needless to say, perhaps, magazines make seasonal adaptations, depending on their place of publication. 'Light' months, like January or June in Hong Kong, are said to afford more 'creativity' in terms of topic selection (interview, Xaven Mak, editor of *Harper's Bazaar*, Hong Kong, May 10, 2001).

17 McKay, p. 122.

18 Alačovska, 2013b, pp. 174–80.

19 Interview, Itō Misao, editor-in-chief, *Harper's Bazaar* Japan, November 19, 2002. See also Aspers, 2001, p. 7.

20 Interview, Watanabe Mitsuko, Fashion Features Director, *Vogue Nippon*, September 21, 2004.

21 *Vogue* USA, March 2005, described on its cover as "The Power Issue."

22 Mears, *Pricing Beauty*. Berkeley & Los Angeles: University of California Press, 2011, pp. 71–120.

23 Another reason cited for such differences was "localization." It was claimed that local issues of *Elle*, for example, did not translate photo captions for this reason, and made use of as much local editorial content as possible in its different issues. (Interview, Philip Guelton, Hachette Filippacci, January 29, 1998.)

24 The description given here builds on that provided by Aspers (2001, pp. 17–18), but differs in one or two important respects such as the role of the photographer in the final appearance of a fashion story in a magazine.

268 ▣ NOTES

25 Interview, Matsuzawa Shōko, deputy editor-in-chief, *Elle Japon*, November 22, 2002.

26 Interview, Fujimoto Yasushi, creative director, *Vogue Nippon*, September 22, 2004.

27 Moeran, 1996, pp. 227–9; McKay, p. 143.

28 Like art gallery openings (Plattner, 1996, p. 145), collections are essentially occasions created to manage business and social relations.

29 A fashion editor is responsible for creating a distinctive fashion well, for coordinating the personnel involved in a story's production, and for editing the photographs. The job of a stylist, on the other hand, is "to put the 'right' clothes on the models, steam the clothes, and make sure that the right clothes are chosen, picked up and returned. The stylist, in short, takes care of everything related to the clothes" (Aspers, p. 83).

30 Interview, Tsukamoto Kaori, fashion director, *Vogue Nippon*, November 20, 2002.

31 Interview, Watanabe Mitsuko.

32 *Elle* Hong Kong, "First Look," March 2005.

33 *Vogue Nippon,* April 2005.

34 *Vogue* UK, March 2005.

35 *Vogue* USA, March 2005.

36 Compare, for example, "Myth and Magic" (*Vogue Nippon*) with "Deluxe & Relaxed" (*Harper's Bazaar* Japan) and "Spring Chic is My Way-ism" (*Elle Japon,* all April 2005).

37 Interview, Matsuzawa Shōko.

38 Hauser, 1982, p. 433.

39 McCracken, 1993.

40 Interview, Olivia Wong, editorial director, *Marie Claire* Hong Kong, April 27, 2001.

41 E.g., Winship, *Inside Women's Magazines,* London and New York: Pandora, 1987, pp. 38–41.

42 Interview, Saitō Kazuhiro, editor-in-chief, *Vogue Nippon*, September 21, 2004.

43 Boltanski and Thévenot, 2006, pp. 178–85.

44 Painters and sculptors also deal with multiple, more or less distinct, publics (Rosenberg and Fliegel, 1970).

45 *Elle* France, March 9, 1998.

46 *Vogue* UK, October 2000.

47 "Bigger is Better," *Elle* UK, June 2002; "Mode no shuyaku ni henshin shita, sweat," *Figaro Japon,* April 2001; "Fashion Week," *Harper's Bazaar* USA, February 2002.

48 *Vogue* USA, March 2005.

49 *Vogue* UK, October 2000.

50 *Harper's Bazaar* USA, December 2001.

51 Winship, p. 9.

52 *Harper's Bazaar* USA, March 1998.

53 *Vogue* UK, October 2000.

54 *Marie Claire* UK, February 2002.

55 In contra-distinction, the left, or verso, page moves and is therefore not readily focused on by readers. (Interview, Alex Fung, Hong Kong Polytechnic University Design School, May 2001.)

NOTES ▣ 269

56 See Csikszentmihalyi, 1996; Sawyer, "Group creativity." *Psychology of Music* 34, 2006.

57 Barthes, *Image Music Text*. London: Fontana, 1977.

58 Interview, Saitō Kazuhiro.

Chapter 7

1 Powdermaker, *Hollywood, the Dream Factory*. Boston: Little, Brown, 1950, p. 285.

2 Bielby and Bielby, "All hits are flukes." *American Journal of Sociology,* 1994; Karpik, *Valuing the Unique,* 2010, p. 223.

3 Boltanski and Thévenot, 2006, p. 294.

4 In ad agencies and film studios, the corresponding divide is between accounts and creative on the one hand, and director and producer on the other.

5 Dornfeld, p. 149.

6 Dornfeld, p. 150.

7 Moeran, 1996, Chapters 3 and 4.

8 Mears, 2011, p. 89.

9 Bourdieu, 1993, p. 141.

10 Moulin, *The French Art Market*. New Brunswick and London: Rutgers University Press, 1987, p. 76; Plattner, "A most ingenious paradox." *American Anthropologist* 100, 1998, pp. 486–7.

11 Blumer, "Fashion." *Sociological Quarterly* 10, 1969, p. 290. The history of fashion, like fashion criticism, tends towards a doctrine of clothing genres and techniques and, in this respect, resembles the history of art and art criticism (Hauser, 1982, p. 429).

12 Hauser, p. 431. We find here that "the dialectics of pretension and distinction that is the basis of the transformations of the field of production reappears in the field of consumption" (Bourdieu 1993, p. 135).

13 Davis, 1995, p. 126.

14 Bourdieu, 1993, p. 138.

15 Entwistle, 2000, p. 237.

16 Hauser, p. 468.

17 As Bourdieu (p. 138) acidly points out: "if you're a fashion journalist, it is not advisable to have a sociological view of the world."

18 Entwistle, p. 237.

19 Bourdieu, 1993.

20 Karpik, pp. 96–128, 218.

21 Bourdieu, 1996a, pp. 142–59.

22 Bourdieu, pp. 10–15, 44–6, 55–6.

23 Boltanski and Thévenot, pp. 196–7.

24 Boltanski and Thévenot, pp. 133–79.

25 Boltanski and Thévenot, p. 144.

26 Boltanski and Thévenot, pp. 160–1.

27 Boltanski and Thévenot, p. 161. We may here substitute the words "collections" for "works," "fashion designers" for "creators," and "As Seen" pages for "People columns."

28 Boltanski and Thévenot, pp. 165–6.

29 Boltanski and Thévenot, p. 183.

30 Boltanski and Thévenot, p. 60.

270 ▣ **NOTES**

31 Aspers, 2001.

32 Callon, *The Laws of the Markets*. Oxford: Blackwell/The Sociological Review, 1998.

33 Beckert and Aspers, *The Worth of Goods*. Oxford: Oxford University Press, 2011.

34 Mears, p. 29.

35 Mears, p. 38.

36 A similar job and status division pervades the world of stoneworkers in England, where the carving of lettering for gravestones provides a more or less regular, bread-and-butter income for "letterers," while irregular sculptural work of all kinds is carried out by "stone carvers" or "sculptors." (Personal communication, Alyosha Moeran.)

37 Mears, p. 39.

38 Entwistle, *The Aesthetic Economy of Fashion*. Oxford: Berg, 2009.

39 Fairchild, *Chic Savages*. New York: Simon & Schuster, 1989, p. 146.

40 Aspers, Chapter 3.

41 Interview, Guillaume Bruneau, art director, *Elle* USA, November 26, 2001.

42 Boltanski and Thévenot, p. 200.

43 Bourdieu, 1996a, Chapter 3.

Chapter 8

1 It was a custom to use working people's names for designs made at Aluminia, one of Royal Copenhagen's factories. A green-glazed ware was called "Sigurt," for example, and another blue-glazed product line, "Sonja."

2 Nowadays almost all production of Royal Copenhagen wares takes place in Thailand. The old porcelain factory site has been redeveloped and occupied in part by the Copenhagen Business School, where I work; my office overlooks the old tunnel kiln, now tastefully converted into a canteen and student study area. It seems I can't get away from pottery!

3 I was, alas, unable to contact and interview management personnel from those days, something that may well tinge the analysis that follows.

4 This temperature is slightly below that reached by stoneware potters in Koishiwara (1180 degrees), but not as high as that of porcelain (around 1300 degrees).

Chapter 9

1 Appadurai, *The Social Life of Things*. Cambridge: Cambridge University Press, 1986.

2 Çaliṣkan and Callon, 2009, p. 386.

3 Richard Sennett, *The Craftsman*. London: Allen Lane, 2008, p. 21.

4 Cutler, "The right hand's cunning." *Speculum* 72, 1997, pp. 985–6.

5 Lave and Wenger, *Situated Learning*. Cambridge: Cambridge University Press, 1991.

6 Sennett, p. 20, 58.

7 Sennett, p. 76.

8 DeCoker, "Seven characteristics of a traditional approach to learning." In Singleton (ed.), *Learning in Likely Places*. Cambridge: Cambridge University Press, 1998.

9 Herrigel, *Zen in the Art of Archery*. London: Routledge & Kegan Paul, 1953.

10 Ueda, Zeami, *Basho, Yeats, Pound*. The Hague: Mouton, 1965, p. 13; Tsubaki, "Zeami and the transition of the concept of yūgen." *Journal of Aesthetics and Art Criticism* 30, 1971.

11 Morris, "Useful work versus useless toil" in *Selected Writings and Designs*. Harmondsworth: Pelican, 1962, p. 118.

12 Schwartz, *The Culture of the Copy*. New York: Zone Books, 1996, p. 215.

13 Sennett, p. 238.

14 Blackwell and Seabrook, *Talking Work*. London: faber and faber, 1996, p. 28.

15 Blackwell and Seabrook, p. 143.

16 A promise made also to consumers by advertising. Cf. Williams, "Advertising," 1980.

17 Sennett, p. 40.

18 Sennett, p. 41.

19 Blackwell and Seabrook, pp. 191–2. See also Sennett, pp. 106–8. How ironic that the old ways based on "handicrafts" should be replaced by a machine-based "manufactory"!

20 Pålsson, "Enskilment at sea." *Man* (N.S.) 29, 1994, p. 910.

21 Pålsson, p. 916.

22 Blackwell and Seabrook, p. 38.

23 Haase, "Learning to be an apprentice," in Singleton (ed.), *Learning in Likely Places*. Cambridge: Cambridge University Press, 1991, p. 108.

24 Sennett, p. 79, 123.

25 Claude Lévi-Strauss, *The Jealous Potter*. Chicago: University of Chicago Press, 1988, p. 176.

26 Lévi-Strauss, 1988, p. 50.

27 Ursula Munch-Petersen, "En prøveproduktion i fajance 1991." In *Hverdagsstel Munch-Petersen Fajance fra Royal Copenhagen*. København: Royal Copenhagen A/S, 1991.

28 Teresa Nielsen, *Ursula Munch-Petersen*. København: Rhodos, 2004, p. 145.

29 Figueroa, William, 'Ursula Munch-Petersen.' http://www.williamfigueroa.com/ArtAndDesignCollections/UrsulaMunchPetersen/ursula.html, accessed May 18, 2011.

30 Sennett, 2008, pp. 120–141.

31 Sennett, p. 44.

32 Sennett, p. 45.

33 Sennett, p. 9.

34 Hauser, 1982, p. 21.

35 Sennett, p. 54.

36 Hauser, p. 31.

37 Hauser, p. 433.

38 Becker, 1982, p. 236.

39 Becker, 1982, p. 244.

40 Zafón, *The Angel's Game*. Translated by Lucia Graves. London: Weidenfeld & Nicholson, 2009, p. 139.

41 Jackson, *The Politics of Storytelling*. Copenhagen: Museum Tusculanum Press, 2002, pp. 14–15.

42 Benjamin, *Illusions*. New York: Schoken, 1968, p. 92.

43 Pålsson, p. 901.

44 Ingold, "Bringing things to life," 2010, p. 9.

45 Some manufacturers try to offset quality variations in their annual purchases by mixing a particular ingredient in such a way that they use a combination of three years' supplies at any one time.

46 Cloves, for example, have to be separated entirely from benzoin, with one being added at the beginning, and the other at the end, of the blending process.

47 Csikszentmihalyi, *Creativity*. New York: HarperCollins, 1996, pp. 118–23.

48 Csikszentmihalyi, *Flow*. New York: Harper & Row, 1990; Sawyer, "Group creativity." *Psychology of Music,* 2006.

49 Berliner, *Thinking in Jazz*. Chicago: University of Chicago Press, 1994, p. 190.

50 The following paragraphs pick up on Barrett's analysis of creativity and improvisation in jazz and organizations (1998, pp. 607–17).

51 Barrett, 1998, p. 613.

52 Cf., Sawyer, 2003, Chapter 2.

53 O'Donnell, *Making Ensemble Possible*, 2013a, p. 199.

54 Barrett, 1998, p. 614.

55 Sudnow, *Ways of the Hand*. Cambridge, MA: MIT Press, 2001, p. 77.

Chapter 10

1 Goode, *The Celebration of Heroes*. Berkeley & Los Angeles: University of California Press, 1978, pp. 41–65; English, *The Economy of Prestige*. Cambridge, MA: Harvard University Press, 2005.

2 Japan specialists will know that "cup" is, perhaps, not an absolutely accurate translation of *hai,* which refers to a celebratory drink of *sake,* but in this context, it seems the most appropriate.

3 Lampel and Meyer, "Field-configuring events as structuring mechanisms." *Journal of Management Studies* 45, 2008.

4 Moeran, "One man exhibition in Japan." In Ben-Ari, Moeran, and Valentine (eds.), *Unwrapping Japan*. Manchester: Manchester University Press, 1990.

5 Havens, *Artist and Patron in Post-War Japan*. Princeton: Princeton University Press, 1982.

6 Asano, *Asahi no Tenrankai: Sono Kako to Mirai*. Tōkyō: Asahijin, 1981.

7 Moeran, "The art world of contemporary Japanese ceramics." *Journal of Japanese Studies* 13, 1987.

8 Allix, "The geography of fairs." *Geographical Review* 12, 1922, p. 540; Braudel, *The Wheels of Commerce*. Berkeley & Los Angeles: University of California Press, 1992, p. 92; Moeran and Strandgaard Pedersen, 2011, pp. 4–5.

9 It should be recognized that these exhibitions constituted the 'network' in 1981, and that several changes have taken place since then. The Asahi Ceramics Exhibition (*Asahi Tōgeiten*), for example, came to an end after its 41st showing, in 2004.

10 In all, about a dozen foreign potters, working in such pottery centres as Mashiko, Shigaraki, and Bizen, used to submit their work.

11 In 1981, the Functional Pottery Section replaced the former Folk Arts Section (*mingei bumon*), which had been receiving fewer and fewer submissions in previous years. By including the word 'craft' in its description, the organizers hoped to boost potters' interest in this third section of the exhibition.

12 At the time of my research, Chichibu no Miya (Princess Chichibu) was the sister-in-law of then Emperor Shōwa (Hirohito), and an aficionado of pottery, which she was reputed to make in her spare time at the Imperial family's residence in Gotemba. She was also Honorary Patron of the JCAE.

13 The JCAE Prize was instituted in place of a prize originally sponsored by the Japan Foundation (*Kokusai Kōryū Kikin-shō*), which, for reasons connected with the fact that the exhibition no longer travelled abroad, withdrew its support in 1979. Further changes have since occurred in the allocation of prizes, as well as in their naming and number. From the thirteenth exhibition in 1995, the first prize has been split, between the *Chichibu no Miya-hai* and the runner-up *Nihon Tōgeiten-shō*. In 1987, the *Gaimu Daijin-shō* was withdrawn, and replaced by two *Mainichi Shinbunsha-shō*, prizes, and 10 years later the *Monbu Daijin* Prize was reduced in importance to an 'encouragement' prize (*Monbu Daijin Shōrei-shō*). In 2005, however, the last reverted to its original status with a change of ministry name (*Monbu Kagaku Daijin-shō*). In 2009, three 'special' prizes were added to the list of awards.

14 Potters were charged a processing fee of ¥4,000 a pot, together with transportation charges.

15 Mathieu and Bertelsen, "Evaluation in film festival prize juries." In Moeran and Christensen (eds.), *Exploring Creativity*, 2013.

16 See, for example, Glejser and Heyndels, "Efficiency and inefficiency in the ranking of competitions." *Journal of Cultural Economics* 25, 2001; Ginsburgh and van Ours, "Expert opinion and compensation." *American Economic Review* 93, 2003.

17 Wilk, "The local and the global in the political economy of beauty." *Review of International Political Economy* 2, 1995.

18 English, 2005, pp. 334–45; Merton, "The Matthew effect in science." *Science* (N.S.) 159, 1968.

19 A grand total of about 240 pots was judged appropriate for the space set aside for the JCAE by the Tokyo branch of Daimaru Department Store.

20 Cf. Lamont, *How Professors Think.* Cambridge, MA: Harvard University Press, 2009, pp. 29, 43–5.

21 To preserve their anonymity, I have given fictitious names to all individual judges mentioned here.

Chapter 11

1 English, 2005, p. 1.

2 English, pp. 189–90.

3 English, p. 212.

4 English, p. 50.

5 Goode, *The Celebration of Heroes.* Berkeley & Los Angeles: University of California Press, 1978.

6 See, for example, Belk, "Awards, rewards, prizes, and punishments." *Advances in Consumer Research* 22, 1995; Nelson et al, 2001; Ginsburgh, "Awards, success, and aesthetic quality in the arts." *The Journal of Economic Perspectives* 17, 2003; English, 2005; Deuchert, Adjamah and Pauly, "For Oscar glory or Oscar money?" *Journal of Cultural Economics* 29, 2005; Boyle and Chiou, "Broadway productions and the value of a Tony Award." *Journal of Cultural Economics* 33, 2009.

274 ▢ NOTES

7   English, 2005; Best, "Prize proliferation." *Sociological Forum* 23, 2008; Squires, "A common ground?" *The Public* 11, 2004; Gemser and Wijnberg, "The economic significance of industrial design awards." *Design Management Journal* 2, 2002; Magnus, "Employee recognition." *Personnel Journal* 60, 1981.

8   Bourdieu, 1993, 1996a.

9   English, "Winning the culture game." *New Literary History* 33, 2002; Mack, "Accounting for taste." *Harvard Journal of Asiatic Studies* 64, 2004; Norris, "The Booker Prize." *Journal for Cultural Research* 10, 2006; Squires, "Book marketing and the Booker Prize." In Matthews and Moody (eds.), *Judging a Book by Its Cover.* Aldershot/Burlington: Ashgate, 2007.

10   De Valck, *Film Festivals.* Amsterdam: Amsterdam University Press, 2007; De Valck and Soeteman, "And the winner is. . . ." *International Journal of Cultural Studies* 13, 2010.

11   Karpik, *Valuing the Unique,* 2010.

12   Karpik, 2010, p. 168–9.

13   Karpik, 2010, p. 169.

14   Karpik, 2010, p. 170.

15   Albrecht, Barnett, and Griff, *The Sociology of Art & Literature.* London: Duckworth, 1970, p. 431.

16   Hauser, *The Sociology of Art,* p. 471.

17   Rosenberg and Fliegel, "The artist and his publics." 1970, p. 501.

18   The four tasks that follow are based on Karpik, 2010, p. 137.

19   Japanese pottery critics have not been alone in this task. Marion Demossier gives an intriguing account of the development of different discourses of taste in French oenological writings and media outputs during the 1970s. Here, too, specialists have stepped in to define quality, based on a consensual and negotiated process involving wine growing regions, denomination of origin, villages, wine growers, and cooperatives. (Demossier, *Wine Drinking Culture in France,* 2010, Chapter 4.)

20   Lamont, 2009.

21   Boltanski and Thévenot, 2006, p. 141.

22   Some weeks later, Murata explained what Imai was hinting at when he told me how Imaemon had changed the blue *dami* underwash on the vase to a *fukizumide* charcoal grey and had painted a standard, traditional design of pink flowers, rather than red. This was, in Murata's words, "stretching tradition to the limit."

23   Boltanski and Thévenot, p. 141.

24   Hauser, p. 474.

25   Rosenberg and Fliegel, p. 513.

26   It was suggested that in Tokyo and Kyoto potters tended to gather around leading potters like Tamura Kōichi and Fujimoto Nōdō who, as professors at the leading art schools, had formed around them factions of their former students. Rural-based potters attached themselves to critics precisely because they came from these centres and knew what was going on there.

27   Lamont, p. 128.

28   See Mack, p. 317.

29   Nakane, *Tate Shakai no Ningen Kankei.* Tōkyō: Kōdansha Gendai Shinsho, 1967.

NOTES ▣ 275

30 Best, p. 7.

31 Goode, p. 152.

32 English, 2002, p. 116. See also Albrecht, *The Sociology of Art and Literature*. London: Dutton, 1970, p. 431.

33 Cf. Mack, p. 293.

34 Malinowski, *Argonauts of the Western Pacific*. London: G. Routledge and Sons, 1922.

35 Godelier, "What Mauss did not say." In Werner and Bell (eds.), *Values and Valuables*. Walnut Creek, CA: AltaMira, 2004, p. 15.

36 Cf. Becker, 1982, p. 14.

37 Mathieu and Bertelsen, 2013, p. 221.

38 Lamont, 2009, p. 47.

39 Nelson, Donihue, Waldman, and Wheaton, "What's an Oscar worth?" *Economic Inquiry* 39, 2001, p. 14.

40 Moeran, "The book fair as a tournament of values." *Journal of the Royal Anthropological Institute* (N.S.) 16, 2010; Moeran and Strandgaard Pedersen, 2011, pp. 9–16.

41 Cf. Lang, "Mass, class, and the reviewer." In Foster and Blau (eds.), *Art and Society*. New York: SUNY, 1989, pp. 193–4.

42 Lamont, pp. 116–20.

43 Lamont, p. 117.

44 Lamont, p. 120.

45 Allen and Parsons, "The institutionalization of fame." *American Sociological Review* 71, 2006, pp. 810–11.

46 Goode, p. 154.

47 Goode, p. 164.

Coda

1 Koestler, 1970, p. 182.

2 Vangkilde, "In search of a creative concept in HUGO BOSS." In Moeran and Christensen (eds.), 2013, pp. 75–6.

3 Koestler, 1970, p. 407.

4 Koestler, 1970, p. 411.

5 Becker, 1982, p. 352.

6 Hauser, 1982, p. 534.

7 Becker, pp. 352–3.

8 Moeran and Christensen, 2013a, pp. 33–4.

9 Squires, "Book marketing and the Booker Prize," 2007, p. 92; English, 2005.

10 "To make oneself known, it is a good idea to have a *name,* or, for products, a *brand name*" (Boltanski and Thévenot, 2006, p. 180).

11 Boltanski and Thévenot, p. 181.

12 Boltanski and Thévenot, p. 155.

13 Bourdieu, 1993, p. 106.

14 Boltanski and Thévenot, p. 179.

NOTES

15 Occasionally, the limelight can be slightly embarrassing, as when one million dollars' worth of Chopard jewellery (to be distributed to film stars) was stolen from an employee's hotel room during the 2013 Cannes Film Festival.

16 Bourdieu, *Distinction*. London: Routledge & Kegan Paul, 1984, pp. 354–65.

17 Latour, 2005, pp. 39, 59.

18 Lévi-Strauss, 1966, p. 15.

19 Skov, *Stories of World Fashion and the Hong Kong Fashion World*. University of Hong Kong, 2000, p. 158.

20 Boltanski and Thévenot, p. 247.

21 Boltanski and Thévenot, pp. 322–3.

REFERENCES

Adorno, T. 1984 *Aesthetic Theory*. London: Routledge.

Alačovska, A. 2013a Genre and Autonomy in Cultural Production: The Case of Travel Guidebook Production. Ph.D. dissertation, Doctoral School of Organisation and Management Studies, Copenhagen Business School. Ph.D. Series 21.2013.

_____. 2013b "Creativity in the brief: travel guidebook writers and good work." In B. Moeran and B. T. Christensen (eds.), *Exploring Creativity: Evaluative Practices in Innovation, Design, and the Arts*. Cambridge: Cambridge University Press.

Albrecht, M., Barnett, J. and M. Griff (eds.) 1970 *The Sociology of Art & Literature: A Reader*. London: Duckworth.

Allen, M. P., and N. L. Parsons 2006 "The institutionalization of fame: achievement, recognition, and cultural consecration in baseball." *American Sociological Review* 71(5):808–25.

Amabile, T. M. 1998 "How to kill creativity." *Harvard Business Review* September–October. Reprint 98501:77–87.

Anand, N., and B. Jones 2008 "Tournament rituals, category dynamics, and field configuration: the case of the Booker Prize." *Journal of Management Studies* 45(6):1036–60.

Appadurai, A. (ed.) 1986 *The Social Life of Things*. Cambridge: Cambridge University Press.

Arlen, M. J. 1979 *Thirty Seconds*. Harmondsworth: Penguin.

Asano Shōichi 1981 *Asahi no Tenrankai: Sono Kako to Mirai*. Tōkyō: Asahijin.

Bakhtin, M. 1984 *Rabelais and his World*. Trans. Helene Iswolsky. Bloomington, IN: Indiana University Press.

Barrett, F. 1998 "Coda: creativity and improvisation in jazz and organizations: implications for organizational learning." *Organization Science* 9(5):605–22.

Barry, A., and D. Slater 2002 "Technology, politics and the market: an interview with Michel Callon." *Economy and Society* 31(2):285–306.

Barthes, R. 1977 *Image Music Text*. London: Fontana.

Baudrillard, J. 1981 *For a Critique of the Political Economy of the Sign*. Trans. with an introduction by Charles Levin. New York: Telos.

_____. 1996 *The System of Objects*. Trans. J. Benedict. London and New York: Verso.

_____. 1998 *The Consumer Society: Myths and Structures*. London: Sage.

Baxandall, M. 1972 *Painting and Experience in Fifteenth Century Italy*. Oxford: Oxford University Press.

Becker, H. S. 1982 *Art Worlds*. Berkeley & Los Angeles: University of California Press.

_____. 2006 "The work itself." In H. S. Becker, R. R. Faulkner and B. Kirshenblatt-Gimblett (eds.), *Art from Start to Finish: Jazz, Painting, Writing, and Other Improvisations*. Chicago and London: University of Chicago Press.

Becker, H. S., and A. L. Strauss 1956 "Careers, personality, and adult socialization." *American Journal of Sociology* 62(3):253–63.

278 ▫ **REFERENCES**

Beckert, J., and P. Aspers (eds.) 2011 "Introduction: value in markets." In J. Beckert and P. Aspers (eds.), *The Worth of Goods*. Oxford: Oxford University Press.

Beetham, M. 1996 *A Magazine of Her Own*. London: Routledge.

Benjamin, W. 1968 *Illusions*. Edited and with an introduction by Hannah Arendt. New York: Schoken.

Best, J. 2008 "Prize proliferation." *Sociological Forum* 23(1):1–27.

Bestor, T. 2004 *Tsukiji: The Fish Market at the Center of the World*. Berkeley & Los Angeles: University of California Press.

Bielby, W., and D. Bielby 1994 "'All hits are flukes': institutionalized decision making and the rhetoric of network prime-time program development." *American Journal of Sociology* 99(5):1287–313.

Blackwell, T., and J. Seabrook 1996 *Talking Work: An Oral History*. London: faber and faber.

Blumer, H. 1969 "Fashion: from class differentiation to collective selection." *Sociological Quarterly* 10:275–91.

Boden, M. 1994 "What is creativity?" In Boden, M. (ed.), *Dimensions of Creativity*. Cambridge, MA: MIT Press.

Bogart, M. H. 1995 *Artists, Advertising, and the Borders of Art*. Chicago: University of Chicago Press.

Bohdanowicz, J., and L. Clamp 1994 *Fashion Marketing*. London and New York: Routledge.

Boltanski, L., and L. Thévenot 2006 *On Justification: Economies of Worth*. Trans. Catherine Porter. Princeton, NJ: Princeton University Press.

Boorstin, D. 1963 *The Image*. Harmondsworth: Pelican.

Bordwell, D. 2012 "Return to paranormalcy." Available at http://www.davidbordwell. net/blog/2012/11/13/return-to-paranormalcy/ (accessed 24/01/2013).

Borges, J. 1998 *Collected Fictions*. Trans. Andrew Hurley. London: Penguin.

Bourdieu, P. 1984 *Distinction: A Social Critique of the Judgement of Taste*. London: Routledge & Kegan Paul.

_____. 1990 *The Logic of Practice*. Cambridge: Polity.

_____. 1993 *The Field of Cultural Production: Essays on Art and Literature*. Edited and introduced by Randal Johnson. Cambridge: Polity.

_____. 1996a *The Rules of Art: The Genesis and Structure of the Literary Field*. Trans. S. Emanuel. Cambridge: Polity.

_____. 1996b *The State Nobility: Elite Schools in the Field of Power*. Cambridge: Polity.

Boyle, M., and L. Chiou 2009 "Broadway productions and the value of a Tony Award." *Journal of Cultural Economics* 33:49–68.

Brown, S. 1995 *Postmodern Marketing*. London and New York: Routledge.

Bunkachō n.d. "Jūyō mukei bunkazai 'Ontayaki' kensa kijun." Unpublished document supplied by Hita City Government, April 2005.

Çalişkan, K., and M. Callon 2009 "Economization, part 1: shifting attention from the economy towards processes of economization." *Economy and Society* 38(3):369–98.

Callon, M. 1986 "Some elements of a sociology of translation: domestication of the scallops and the fishermen of Saint Brieuc Bay." In J. Law (ed.), *Power, Action, Belief*. London: Routledge & Kegan Paul.

Callon, M. 1998 "The embeddedness of economic markets in economics." In M. Callon (ed.), *The Laws of the Markets*. Oxford: Blackwell.

_____. (ed.) 1998 *The Laws of the Markets*. Oxford: Blackwell/The Sociological Review.

_____. 2002 "The economy of qualities." *Economy and Society* 31(2):194–217.

Caves, R. 2000 *Creative Industries: Contracts between Art and Commerce*. Cambridge MA: Harvard University Press.

Childress, C. C. 2013 "What's the matter with Jarrettsville? Genre classification as an unstable and opportunistic construct." In B. Moeran and B. T. Christensen (eds.), *Exploring Creativity: Evaluative Practices in Innovation, Design, and the Arts*. Cambridge: Cambridge University Press.

Christensen, B. T., and J. Strandgaard Pedersen 2013 "Restaurant rankings in the culinary field." In B. Moeran and B. T. Christensen (eds.), *Exploring Creativity: Evaluative Practices in Innovation, Design, and the Arts*. Cambridge: Cambridge University Press.

Clark, R. 1979 *The Japanese Company*. New Haven and London: Yale University Press.

Condon, W. S., and W. D. Ogston 1967 "A segmentation of behavior." *Journal of Psychiatric Research* 5:221–35.

Costa, J. A., and G. J. Bamossy (eds.) 1995 *Marketing in a Multicultural World: Ethnicity, Nationalism, and Cultural Identity*. London: Sage.

Csaba, F. H., and G. Ger 2013 "Patina meets fashion: on the evaluation and devaluation of oriental carpets." In B. Moeran and B. T. Christensen (eds.), *Exploring Creativity: Evaluative Practices in Innovation, Design, and the Arts*. Cambridge: Cambridge University Press.

Csikszentmihalyi, M. 1996 *Creativity: Flow and the Psychology of Discovery and Invention*. New York: HarperCollins.

Cutler, A. 1997 "The right hand's cunning: craftsmanship and the demand for art in late antiquity and the early middle ages." *Speculum* 72(4):971–94.

Dale, K., and G. Burrell 2008 *The Spaces of Organisation & the Organisation of Space: Power, Identity & Materiality in Work*. Basingstoke: Palgrave Macmillan.

Davis, F. 1995 *Fashion, Culture, and Identity*. Chicago: University of Chicago Press.

de Bono, E. 1992 *Serious Creativity: Using the Power of Lateral Thinking To Create New Ideas*. New York: HarperCollins.

de Saussure, F. 1983 *Course in General Linguistics*. Trans. and annotated by Roy Harris. London: Duckworth.

de Valck, M. 2007 *Film Festivals: From European Geopolitics to Global Cinephilia*. Amsterdam: Amsterdam University Press.

de Valck, M., and M. Soeteman 2010 "'And the winner is…' What happens behind the scenes of film festival competitions." *International Journal of Cultural Studies* 13(3):290–307.

Debreu, G. 1987 (1959) *A Theory of Value: An Axiomatic Analysis of Economic Equilibrium*. New Haven and London: Yale University Press.

DeCoker, G. 1998 "Seven characteristics of a traditional Japanese approach to learning." In J. Singleton (ed.), *Learning in Likely Places: Varieties of Apprenticeship in Japan*. Cambridge: Cambridge University Press.

Demossier, M. 2010 *Wine Drinking Culture in France: A National Myth or a Modern Passion?* Cardiff: University of Wales Press.

280 ▣ REFERENCES

Deuchert, E., Adjamah, K., and F. Pauly 2005 "For Oscar glory or Oscar money? Academy Awards and movies success." *Journal of Cultural Economics* 29:159–76.

Dore, R. P. 1973 *British Factory-Japanese Factory.* Berkeley & Los Angeles: University of California Press.

Dornfeld, B. 1998 *Producing Public Television, Producing Public Culture.* Princeton, NJ: Princeton University Press.

Douglas, M., and B. Isherwood 1979 *The World of Goods: Towards an Anthropology of Consumption.* New York: Basic Books.

Eco, U. 1966 "James Bond: une combinatoire narrative." *Communications* 8(8):77–93.

English, J. 2002 "Winning the culture game: prizes, awards, and the rules of art." *New Literary History* 33(1):109–35.

English, J. 2005 *The Economy of Prestige: Prizes, Awards, and the Circulation of Cultural Value.* Cambridge, MA: Harvard University Press.

Entwistle, J. 2000 *The Fashioned Body: Fashion, Dress and Modern Social Theory.* Cambridge: Polity.

_____. 2009 *The Aesthetic Economy of Fashion.* Oxford: Berg.

Ewen, S. 1996 *PR: A Social History of Spin.* New York: Basic Books.

Fairchild, J. 1989 *Chic Savages.* New York: Simon & Schuster.

Ferguson, M. 1983 *Forever Feminine: Women's Magazines and the Cult of Femininity.* London: Heinemann.

Fine, G. A. 1996 *Kitchens: The Culture of Restaurant Work.* Berkeley & Los Angeles: University of California Press.

Fiske, J. 1987 *Television Culture.* London: Methuen.

Florida, R. 2002 *The Rise of the Creative Class . . . And How It's Transforming Work, Leisure, Community, and Everyday Life.* New York: Basic Books.

Friedman, J. 2001 "The iron cage of creativity: an exploration." In J. Liep (ed.), *Locating Cultural Creativity.* London: Pluto.

Frey, B. 2003 *Art & Economics: Analysis & Cultural Policy* (second edition). Berlin: Springer.

Fukuda T. 1992 "Seiyaku wa kōkoku no haha desu." In Y. Amano (ed.) *Kōkoku no Dai-Nyūmon: Kōkoku Hihyō-hen.* Tōkyō: Madora Shuppan.

Garcia-Parpet, M.-F. 2011 "Symbolic value and the establishment of prices: globalization of the wine market." In J. Beckert and P. Aspers (eds.), *The Worth of Goods: Valuation and Pricing in the Economy.* Oxford: Oxford University Press.

Gell, A. 1998 *Art and Agency.* Oxford: Clarendon Press.

Gemser, G., and N. M. Wijnberg 2002 "The economic significance of industrial design awards: a conceptual framework." *Design Management Journal* 2(1):61–71.

Gibson, J. 1977 "The theory of affordances." In R. Shaw and J. Bransford (eds.), *Perceiving, Acting and Knowing.* Hillsdale, NJ: Lawrence Erlbaum.

_____. 1979 *The Ecological Approach to Visual Perception.* Boston: Houghton Mifflin.

Giddens, A. 1993 *Sociology* (second edition). Cambridge: Polity.

Ginsburgh, V. 2003 "Awards, success, and aesthetic quality in the arts." *The Journal of Economic Perspectives* 17(2):99–111.

Ginsburgh, V., and J. C. van Ours 2003 "Expert opinion and compensation: evidence from a musical competition." *American Economic Review* 93:289–96.

Ginsburgh, V., and S. Weyers 2008 "Quantitative approaches to valuation in the arts, with an application to movies." In M. Hutter and D. Throsby (eds.), *Beyond Price: Value in Culture, Economics, and the Arts.* Cambridge: Cambridge University Press.

Godelier, M. 2004 "What Mauss did not say: things you give, things you sell, and things that must be kept." In C. Werner and D. Bell (eds.), *Values and Valuables: From the Sacred to the Symbolic.* Walnut Creek, CA: AltaMira.

Goffman, E. 1959 *The Presentation of Self in Everyday Life.* New York: Anchor.

_____. 1986 [1974] *Frame Analysis: An Essay on the Organization of Experience.* Boston: Northeastern University Press.

Goldman, K. 1997 *Conflicting Accounts: The Creation and Crash of the Saatchi & Saatchi Advertising Empire.* New York: Simon & Schuster.

Goode, W. J. 1978 *The Celebration of Heroes: Prestige as a Social Control System.* Berkeley & Los Angeles: University of California Press.

Gough-Yates, A. 2003 *Understanding Women's Magazines: Publishing, Markets and Readerships.* London: Routledge.

Grabher, G. 2002 "The project ecology of advertising: tasks, talents, and teams." *Regional Studies* 36(3):245–62.

Graeber, D. 2001 *Toward an Anthropological Theory of Value.* New York: Palgrave.

Granovetter, M. 1985 Economic actions and social structure: the problem of embeddedness. *American Journal of Sociology* 91(3):481–510.

Grindstaff, L. 2002 *The Money Shot: Trash, Class, and the Making of TV Talk Shows.* Chicago: University of Chicago Press.

Haase, B. 1998 "Learning to be an apprentice." In J. Singleton (ed.), *Learning in Likely Places: Varieties of Apprenticeship in Japan.* Cambridge: Cambridge University Press.

Haeger, J., and K. Storchmann 2006 "Prices of American Pinot Noir wines: climate, craftsmanship, critics." *Agricultural Economics* 35:67–78.

Hannerz, U. 1982 *Cultural Complexity.* New York: Columbia University Press.

Hartson, H. 2003 "Cognitive, physical, sensory, and functional affordances in interaction design." *Behaviour and Information Technology* 22(5):315–38.

Haug, W. 1986 *Critique of Commodity Aesthetics: Appearance, Sexuality and Advertising in Capitalist Society.* Trans. Robert Bock. Cambridge: Polity.

Hauser, A. 1982 *The Sociology of Art.* Trans. Kenneth J. Northcott. London: Routledge & Kegan Paul.

Havens, T. 1982 *Artist and Patron in Post-War Japan.* Princeton, NJ: Princeton University Press.

Hermes, J. 1995 *Reading Women's Magazines: An Analysis of Everyday Media Use.* Cambridge: Polity.

Herrigel, E. 1953 *Zen in the Art of Archery.* London: Routledge & Kegan Paul.

Herrnstein-Smith, B. 1988 *Contingencies of Value: Alternative Perspectives for Critical Theory.* Cambridge, MA: Harvard University Press.

Hesmondhalgh, D. 2002 *The Cultural Industries.* London & Thousand Oaks, CA: Sage.

Hine, T. 1995 *The Total Package: The Evolution and Secret Meanings of Boxes, Bottles, Cans and Tubes.* Boston: Little, Brown and Company.

282 ▢ REFERENCES

Hitlin, S., and J. A. Piliavin 2004 "Values: reviving a dormant concept." *Annual Review of Sociology* 30:359–93.

Hobbes, T. 1651 *Leviathan.* Available at: http://gluksmann.de/Links_A_E/Hobbes_Leviathan_pdf.

Hopkins, C. C. 1998 *My Life in Advertising* & *Scientific Advertising.* Lincolnwood, IL: NTC Business Books.

Hower, R. M. 1939 *The History of an Advertising Agency.* Cambridge, MA: Harvard University Press.

Howkins, J. 2002 *The Creative Economy: How People Make Money from Ideas.* Harmondsworth: Penguin.

Hutter, M. 2008 "Creating artistic from economic value: changing input prices and new art." *In* M. Hutter and D. Throsby (eds.), *Beyond Price: Value in Culture, Economics, and the Arts.* Cambridge: Cambridge University Press.

———. 2011 "Infinite surprises: stabilization of value in the creative industries." *In* J. Beckert and P. Aspers (eds.), *The Worth of Goods.* Oxford: Oxford University Press.

Hutter, M. and R. Shusterman 2006 "Value and the valuation of art in economic and aesthetic theory." *In* V. Ginsburgh and D. Throsby (eds.), *Handbook of the Economics of Art and Culture.* Amsterdam: Elsevier North Holland.

Hutter, M. and D. Throsby (eds.) 2008 *Beyond Price: Value in Culture, Economy and the Arts.* Cambridge: Cambridge University Press.

Ingold, T. 2007 "Materials against materiality." *Archaeological Dialogues* 14(1):1–16.

———. 2010 "Bringing things to life: creative entanglements in a world of materials." Working Paper #15. Manchester: Realities.

Ingold, T., and E. Hallam 2007 "Creativity and cultural improvisation: an introduction." *In* E. Hallam and T. Ingold (eds.), *Creativity and Cultural Improvisation.* ASA Monographs 44. Oxford: Berg.

Jackall, R., and J. M. Hirota 2000 *Image Makers: Advertising, Public Relations, and the Ethos of Advocacy.* Chicago: University of Chicago Press.

Jackson, M. 2002 *The Politics of Storytelling: Violence, Transgression and Intersubjectivity.* Copenhagen: Museum Tusculanum Press.

Jeffcut, P., and A. Pratt 2003 "Managing creativity in the cultural industries." *Creativity and Innovation Management* 11(4):225–33.

Jordan, A. 2013 *Business Anthropology* (second edition). Long Grove, IL: Waveland.

Karpik, L. 2010 *Valuing the Unique: The Economics of Singularities.* Princeton, NJ: Princeton University Press.

Kemper, S. 2001 *Buying and Believing: Sri Lankan Advertising and Consumers in a Transnational World.* Chicago: Chicago University Press.

Koestler, A. 1970 *The Act of Creation.* London: Pan.

Lamont, M. 2009 *How Professors Think: Inside the Curious World of Academic Judgment.* Cambridge, MA: Harvard University Press.

———. 2012 "Towards a comparative sociology of valuation and evaluation." *Annual Review of Sociology* 38:201–21.

Lampel, J., and A. Meyer 2008 "Field-configuring events as structuring mechanisms: how conferences, ceremonies, and trade shows constitute new technologies, industries, and markets." *Journal of Management Studies* 45(6):1025–35.

Lampel, J., and S. Nadavulakere 2009 "Classics foretold? Contemporaneous and retrospective consecration in the UK film industry." *Cultural Trends* 18(3):239–48.

Lang, K. 1989 "Mass, class, and the reviewer." *In* R. Foster and J. Blau (eds.), *Art and Society: Readings in the Sociology of Art*. New York: SUNY Press.

Latour, B. 1996 "On actor-network theory: a few clarifications." *Soziale Welt* 47(4):369–81.

_____. 2005 *Reassembling the Social: An Introduction to Actor-Network-Theory*. Oxford: Oxford University Press.

Latour, B., and S. Woolgar 1986 (1979) *Laboratory Life: The Construction of Scientific Facts*. Princeton, NJ: Princeton University Press.

Lave, J., and E. Wenger 1991 *Situated Learning: Legitimate Peripheral Participation*. Cambridge: Cambridge University Press.

Law, J. 1986 "On the methods of long distance control: vessels, navigation, and the Portuguese route to India." *In* J. Law (ed.), *Power, Action, Belief*. London: Routledge & Kegan Paul.

_____. 2009 "Actor network theory and material semiotics." *In* B. Turner (ed.), *The New Blackwell Companion to Social Theory*. Oxford: Blackwell.

Leach, B. 1978 *Beyond East and West: Memoirs, Portraits, and Essays*. London: faber & faber.

Lévi-Strauss, C. 1966 *The Savage Mind*. London: Weidenfeld & Nicolson.

_____. 1988 *The Jealous Potter*. Trans. Bénédicte Chorier. Chicago, IL: University of Chicago Press.

Levitt, T. 2002 "Creativity is not enough." *The Best of HBR: The Innovative Enterprise*. Reprint R0208K:137–44.

Lien, M. 1997 *Marketing and Modernity*. Oxford: Berg.

Liep, J. 2001 "Introduction." *In* J. Liep (ed.), *Locating Cultural Creativity*. London: Pluto.

Lowenthal, L. 1968 *Literature, Popular Culture and Society*. Palo Alto, CA: Pacific Books.

Mack, E. 2004 "Accounting for taste: the creation of the Akutagawa and Naoki Prizes for literature." *Harvard Journal of Asiatic Studies* 64(2):291–340.

Magnus, M. 1981 "Employee recognition: a key to motivation." *Personnel Journal* 60:103–7.

Maitland, J. 1976 "Creativity." *The Journal of Aesthetics and Art Criticism* 34(4):397–409.

Malefyt, T. de Waal 2003 "Models, metaphors and client relations: the negotiated meanings of advertising." *In* T. de Waal Malefyt and B. Moeran (eds.), *Advertising Cultures*. Oxford: Berg.

Malefyt, T. De Waal, and R. J. Morais 2012 *Advertising and Anthropology: Ethnographic Practice and Cultural Perspectives*. Oxford: Berg.

Marchand, R. 1985 *Advertising the American Dream*. Berkeley & Los Angeles: University of California Press.

Marchand, Roland 1998 *Creating the Corporate Soul: The Rise of Public Relations and Corporate Imagery in American Big Business*. Berkeley and Los Angeles: University of California Press.

Marcus, G. 1995 "Ethnography in/of the world system: the emergence of multi-sited ethnography." *Annual Review of Anthropology* 25:95–117.

Marshall, A. 1961 *Principles of Economics*. London: Macmillan.

Mathieu, C., and M. Bertelsen 2013 "Evaluation in film festival prize juries." *In* B. Moeran and B. T. Christensen (eds.), *Exploring Creativity: Evaluative Practices in Innovation, Design, and the Arts*. Cambridge: Cambridge University Press.

Mayer, M. 1991 *Madison Avenue, U.S.A.* Lincolnwood, IL: NTC Business Books.

Mazzarella, W. 2003 *Shoveling Smoke: Advertising and Globalization in Contemporary India*. Durham, NC: Duke University Press.

McCracken, E. 1993 *Decoding Women's Magazines: From Mademoiselle to Ms.* Basingstoke, UK: Macmillan.

McCreery, J. L. 2001 "Creating advertising in Japan: a sketch in search of a principle." *In* B. Moeran (ed.), *Asian Media Productions*. London: Curzon.

McKay, J. 2000 *The Magazines Handbook*. London: Routledge.

Mears, A. 2011 *Pricing Beauty: The Making of a Fashion Model*. Berkeley & Los Angeles: University of California Press.

Menger, P.-M. 2006 "Profiles of the unfinished: Rodin's work and the varieties of incompleteness." *In* H. S. Becker, R. R. Faulkner, and B. Kirshenblatt-Gimblett (eds.), *Art from Start to Finish: Jazz, Painting, Writing, and Other Improvisations*. Chicago and London: University of Chicago Press.

Miller, D. 1997 *Capitalism: An Ethnographic Approach*. Oxford: Berg.

_____. 2007 "Stone age or plastic age?" *Archaeological Dialogues* 14:23–7.

Miller, M. 1981 *The Bon Marché: Bourgeois Culture and the Department Store, 1869-1920*. Princeton, NJ: Princeton University Press.

Moeran, B. 1984 *Lost Innocence: Folk Craft Potters of Onta, Japan*. Berkeley & Los Angeles: University of California Press.

_____. 1985 *Ōkubo Diary: Portrait of a Japanese Valley*. Stanford, CA: Stanford University Press.

_____. 1987 "The art world of contemporary Japanese ceramics." *Journal of Japanese Studies* 13(1):27–50.

_____. 1990 "One man exhibition in Japan." *In* E. Ben-Ari, B. Moeran, and J. Valentine (eds.), *Unwrapping Japan*. Manchester: Manchester University Press.

_____. 1993 "A tournament of value: strategies of presentation in Japanese advertising." *Ethnos* 54(1–2):73–93.

_____. 1996 *A Japanese Advertising Agency: An Anthropology of Media and Markets*. London: Curzon.

_____. 1997 *Folk Art Potters of Japan*. London: Curzon.

_____. 1998 "The birth of the Japanese department store." *In* K. MacPherson (ed.), *Asian Department Stores*. London: Curzon.

_____. 2001 "Promoting culture: the work of a Japanese advertising agency." *In* B. Moeran (ed.), *Asian Media Productions*. London: Curzon.

_____. 2005 *The Business of Ethnography*. Oxford: Berg.

_____. 2006 *Ethnography at Work*. Oxford: Berg.

_____. 2008 "Materials, skills and cultural resources: Onta folk art pottery revisited." *Journal of Modern Crafts* 1(1):35–54.

_____. 2009 "The organization of creativity in Japanese advertising production." Managing in the Creative Industries: Managing the Motley Crew (special issue). *Human Relations* 62(7):963–85.

REFERENCES　285

Moeran, B. 2010 "The book fair as a tournament of values." *Journal of the Royal Anthropological Institute (N.S.)* 16:138–54.

_____. 2013 "Framing values: symbolic space in the display of art works." *In* H. Nakamaki and M. Sedgwick (eds.), *Business and Anthropology: A Focus on Sacred Space.* Senri Ethnological Studies 82. Osaka: National Museum of Ethnology.

Moeran, B., and B. T. Christensen (eds.) 2013 *Exploring Creativity: Evaluative Practices in Innovation, Design, and the Arts.* Cambridge: Cambridge University Press.

Moeran, B., and J. Strandgaard Pedersen (eds.) 2011 *Negotiating Values in the Creative Industries: Fairs, Festivals, and Competitive Events.* Cambridge: Cambridge University Press.

Morais, R. J. 2007 "Conflict and confluence in advertising meetings." *Human Organization* 66(2):150–59.

Morris, W. 1962 "Useful work versus useless toil." *In* A. Briggs (ed.), *Selected Writings and Designs.* Harmondsworth: Pelican.

Moulin, R. 1987 *The French Art Market: A Sociological View* [trans. Arthur Goldhammer]. New Brunswick and London: Rutgers University Press.

Munch-Petersen, U. 1991 "En prøveproduktion i fajance 1991." In *Hverdagsstel Munch-Petersen Fajance fra Royal Copenhagen.* København: Royal Copenhagen A/S.

Myers, F. (ed.) 2001 *The Empire of Things.* Santa Fe, NM: School of American Research Press.

Negus, K., and M. Pickering 2004 *Creativity, Communication and Cultural Value.* London: Sage.

Nelson, R. A., Donihue, M. R., Waldman, D. M., and C. Wheaton 2001 "What's an Oscar worth?" *Economic Inquiry* 39(1):1–16.

Nielsen, T. 2004 *Ursula Munch-Petersen.* København: Rhodos.

Norman, D. 1990 *The Design of Everyday Things.* New York: Basic Books.

_____. 1999 "Affordance, conventions, and design." *Interactions* (May–June):38–42. Available at http://webhome.cs.uvic.ca (accessed 19/12/2012).

Norris, S. 2006 "The Booker Prize: a Bourdieusian perspective." *Journal for Cultural Research* 10(2):139–58.

Nozick, R. 1981 *Philosophical Explanation.* Cambridge, MA: Belknap Press.

Odagiri A. 1992 "Business o game ni suru." *In* Y. Amano (ed.), *Kōkoku no Dai-Nyūmon: Kōkoku hihyō-hen.* Tōkyō: Madora Shuppan.

O'Donnell, S. 2013a *Making Ensemble Possible: How Special Groups Organize for Collaborative Creativity in Conditions of Spatial Variability and Distance.* Ph.D. dissertation, Doctoral School of Organisation and Management Studies, Copenhagen Business School, Denmark. Ph.D. Series 7.2013.

_____. 2013b "Reconceiving constraint as possibility in a music ensemble." *In* B. Moeran and B. T. Christensen (eds.), *Exploring Creativity: Evaluative Practices in Innovation, Design, and the Arts.* Cambridge: Cambridge University Press.

Ogilvy, D. 1963 *Confessions of an Advertising Man.* New York: Atheneum.

_____. 1983 *Ogilvy on Advertising.* London: Guild Publishing.

Pálsson, G. 1994 "Enskilment at sea." *Man (N.S.)* 29(4):901–27.

Peterson, R. 1997 "Revitalizing the culture concept." *American Review of Sociology* 5:137–66.

REFERENCES

Plattner, S. 1996 *High Art Down Home: An Economic Ethnography of a Local Art Market*. Chicago, IL: University of Chicago Press.

———. 1998 "A most ingenious paradox: the market for contemporary fine art." *American Anthropologist* 100(2):482–93.

Pollak, M. 1972 "The performance of the wooden printing press." *The Library Quarterly* 42(2):218–64.

Powdermaker, H. 1950 *Hollywood, the Dream Factory: An Anthropologist Looks at the Movies*. Boston: Brown, Little.

Powell, W. 1985 *Getting into Print*, Chicago, IL: Chicago University Press.

Pye, D. 1995 (1968) *The Nature and Art of Workmanship*. London: Herbert Press.

Quinn, J. 1999 "The account executive in an advertising agency." *In* J. P. Jones (ed.), *The Advertising Business*. Thousand Oaks, CA: Sage.

Rohlen, T. 1974 *For Harmony and Strength*. Berkeley & Los Angeles: University of California Press.

Rosenberg, B., and N. Fliegel 1970 "The artist and his publics: the ambiguity of success." *In* M. Albrecht, J. Barnett, and M. Griff (eds.), *The Sociology of Art and Literature*. London: Duckworth.

Rosenberg, H. 1970 "The art establishment." *In* M. Albrecht, J. Barnett, and M. Griff (eds.), *The Sociology of Art and Literature*. London: Duckworth.

Rosenblum, B. 1978 "Style as social process." *American Sociological Review* 43:422–38.

Rothenberg, R. 1994 *Where the Suckers Moon: The Life and Death of an Advertising Campaign*. New York: Vintage.

Sawyer, R. Keith 2003 *Group Creativity: Music, Theatre, Collaboration*. Hillsdale, NJ: Lawrence Erlbaum Associates.

———. 2006 "Group creativity: musical performance and collaboration." *Psychology of Music* 34(2):148–65.

Schmitt, B., and A. Simonson 1997 *Marketing Aesthetics: The Strategic Management of Brands, Identity, and Image*. New York: Free Press.

Schucking, L. 1974 *The Sociology of Literary Taste*. Trans. Brian Battershaw. Chicago, IL: University of Chicago Press.

Schudson, M. 1984 *Advertising: The Uneasy Persuasion*. New York: Basic Books.

Schwartz, H. 1996 *The Culture of the Copy: Striking Likenesses, Unreasonable Facsimiles*. New York: Zone Books.

Schwartz, S. H. 1994 "Are there universal aspects in the structure and content of human values?" *Journal of Social Issues* 50:19–45.

Schwartz, S. H., and W. Bilsky 1987 "Towards a psychological structure of human values." *Journal of Personal Social Psychology* 53:550–62.

Sennett, R. 2008 *The Craftsman*. London: Allen Lane.

———. 2012 *Together: The Rituals, Pleasures and Politics of Cooperation*. London: Allen Lane.

Simmel, G. 1978 *The Philosophy of Money*. Trans. T. Bottomore and D. Frisby. London: Routledge & Kegan Paul.

Skov, L. 2000 *Stories of World Fashion and the Hong Kong Fashion World*. Ph.D. dissertation, University of Hong Kong.

Slater, D., and F. Tonkiss 2001 *Market Society*. Cambridge: Polity.

Spates, J. 1983 "The sociology of values." *Annual Review of Sociology* 9:27–49.

Squires, C. 2004 "A common ground? Book prize culture in Europe." *The Public* 11(4):37–48.

_____. 2007 "Book marketing and the Booker Prize." *In* N. Matthews and N. Moody (eds.), *Judging a Book by Its Cover: Fans, Publishers, Designers, and the Marketing of Fiction*. Aldershot/Burlington: Ashgate.

Stark, D. 2000 "For a sociology of worth." Working Paper Series, Center on Organizational Innovation, Columbia University, New York. Available at http://www.coi.columbia.edu/pdf/stark_fsw.pdf.

Sudnow, D. 2001 *Ways of the Hand*. Cambridge, MA: MIT Press.

Terakawa Yasurō 1996 *Kuni no Jūyō Mukei Bunkazai ni Shitei Sareta Ontayaki to Gijutsu Honzonkai ni tsuite*. Hita: Private Publication.

Terakawa Yūki 1967 *Ōitaken no Kōgei Sangyō*. Oita: Oita Prefectural Government.

Thompson, D. 2008 *The $12 Million Stuffed Shark: The Curious Economics of Contemporary Art and Auction Houses*. London: Aurum.

Thompson, J. 2010 *Merchants of Culture*. Cambridge: Polity Press.

Throsby, D. 2001 *Economics and Culture*. Cambridge: Cambridge University Press.

Tomimoto Kenkichi 1981 "Uiriamu Morisu no hanashi." *In* Tomimoto Kenkichi, *Tomimoto Kenkichi Chosakushū*. Tokyo.

Towse, R. 1996 "Market value and artists' earnings." *In* A. Klamer (ed.) *The Value of Culture: On the Relationship between Economics and Art*. Amsterdam: Amsterdam University Press.

Tsubaki, A. 1971 "Zeami and the transition of the concept of *yūgen*." *Journal of Aesthetics and Art Criticism* 30(1):35–57.

Ueda, M. 1965 *Zeami, Basho, Yeats, Pound: A Study in Japanese and English Poetics*. The Hague: Mouton.

Usunier, J.-C. 2000 *Marketing Across Cultures* (third edition). Harlow: Prentice Hall.

Vangkilde, K. T. 2013 "In search of a creative concept in HUGO BOSS." *In* B. Moeran and B. T. Christensen (eds.), *Exploring Creativity: Evaluative Practices in Innovation, Design, and the Arts*. Cambridge: Cambridge University Press.

Velthuis, O. 2005 *Talking Prices: Symbolic Meanings of Prices on the Market for Contemporary Art*. Princeton, NJ: Princeton University Press.

Vollard, A. 1978 *Recollections of a Picture Dealer*. New York: Dover.

Wacquant, L. 1995 "The pugilistic point of view: how boxers think and feel about their trade." *Theory and Society* 24(4):489–535.

Wernick, A. 1991 *Promotional Culture: Advertising, Ideology and Symbolic Expression*. London: Sage.

White, H. 1981 "Where do markets come from?" *American Journal of Sociology* 87(3):517–47.

Wilk, R. 1995 "The local and the global in the political economy of beauty: from Miss Belize to Miss World." *Review of International Political Economy* 2(1):117–34.

_____. 1996 *Economies and Cultures: Foundations of Economic Anthropology*. Boulder, CO: Westview.

Williams, R. 1980 "Advertising: the magic system." *In* R. Williams, *Problems in Materialism and Culture*. London: Verso.

REFERENCES

Williams, R. M. Jr. 1979 "Change and stability in values and value systems: a sociological perspective." *In* M. Rokeach (ed.), *Understanding Human Values: Individual and Societal*. New York: Free Press.

Winship, J. 1987 *Inside Women's Magazines*. London and New York: Pandora.

Young, J. Webb 1991 [1963] *How to Become an Advertising Man*. Lincolnwood, IL: NTC Business Books.

Zafón, C. Ruiz 2009 *The Angel's Game*. Trans. Lucia Graves. London: Weidenfeld & Nicholson.

Zaloom, C. 2006 *Out of the Pits: Traders and Technology from Chicago to London*. Chicago, IL: The University of Chicago Press.

Zelizer, V. 1978 "Human values and the market: the case of life insurance and death in nineteenth-century America." *American Journal of Sociology* 84(4):591–610.

_____. 2011 *Economic Lives: How Culture Shapes the Economy*. Princeton, NJ: Princeton University Press.

INDEX

A

actor-network 38, 59
    (*see also* network)
adversaries in collusion 63, 242
advertising 16, 31, 43, 46, 53, 54, 120, 142, 145, 147, 148, 153
    and fashion magazines 158-61, 165
    production 101-21, 215
    production team 30, 102, 111, 112, 119, 120, 123, 124-34, 137, 139, 213, 219, 249, 266n
advertising world 17, 120, 121-3, 125, 139, 214
aesthetic(s) 21, 30, 49, 50, 60, 61, 72, 76, 79, 81, 88, 119, 137, 142, 165, 166, 170, 172, 173-4, 208, 219, 246, 253
    affordance 48, 138
    and design 178, 182
    discourse/language 38, 91, 168, 235-6, 237-8 (*see also* evaluation)
    economy 32, 172-6
    ideals 17, 24, 39, 54, 61, 94, 101, 182
    (*see also* value)
affordance 17-18, 29-30, 32, 35, 36, 60, 73, 82, 83, 101, 120, 138, 173, 248, 253
    circuits of 29, 30, 35-59, 83, 84, 89, 90, 93, 96, 121, 219
    economic 44, 46, 53-55, 56, 122, 201
    representational 44, 47-51, 53, 56, 58, 122
    social 51-3, 122, 143, 153
    spatial 42-5, 57, 126
    techno-material 39-42, 44, 53, 56, 119, 122, 175
    temporal 45-7, 54, 57, 68, 122, 126, 146, 147-8, 153
    (*see also* ensemblage)
anchorage 209, 215, 216, 248
    and flow 32, 157-61, 163-4, 248
apprentice 55, 56, 70, 99, 155, 201, 210, 223, 231, 263n
    -ship 71, 201-2
    (*see also* training)
art world 28, 52, 65, 78, 81, 83, 92-3, 95, 96, 120, 125, 165
    ceramic 12, 17, 38, 62-3, 67, 71, 82, 84, 90, 92, 93, 102, 143, 174, 219-21, 234, 239, 260n
assemblage 18, 38, 57, 88
    (*see also* ensemblage)

B

Becker, Howard 23, 25, 65, 120, 165, 209
bisociation 3, 50, 69, 109, 119, 120, 246, 265n

Boltanski, Luc and Laurent Thévénot 84, 86, 101, 102, 154, 246

Bourdieu, Pierre 31, 32, 37, 39, 44, 62, 65, 97, 130, 165, 168, 176, 233

business anthropology 17, 18, 85, 88, 254

C

capital
    conversion of 37, 54, 65
    cultural 62, 65, 70, 97, 129, 250, 252
    economic 65, 97, 129, 250, 252
    educational 97
    fashion 36, 165
    forms of 37, 62, 97, 233
    social 70, 83, 97, 129, 173
    symbolic 37, 70, 83, 97, 130, 173, 250

celebrity 51, 53, 73, 103, 109, 119, 124, 125-6, 133, 141, 166, 170, 174, 213, 214, 250, 265n
    (*see also* name economy)

ceramics *see* faience, porcelain, pottery, stoneware

clay 25, 33, 41-2, 44, 45, 48, 55-7, 64, 69, 71, 72, 73-4, 93, 100, 164, 178, 187, 188, 191, 197, 202, 216, 231, 235, 239, 248
    and glazes 182-6
    as good to think 202-10
    (*see also* glaze, material)

convention 16, 23, 28, 36, 39-41, 46, 47, 48, 49, 57, 58, 83, 92, 94, 95, 120, 130, 137, 173, 209, 218

craftsman 33, 77, 101, 194, 195, 198
    artist 62, 84, 95

craftsmanship 33, 95, 164, 200-16
    (*see also* creativity)

creative
    brief 27, 30, 108-13, 119, 120
    director 16, 50, 103, 104, 109, 110, 119, 122, 124, 125, 126, 133, 134, 161, 214, 248, 252, 264n
    market 168-71
    practice 13, 16, 21, 28, 47, 121
    process 15, 17, 18, 21, 22, 25, 26, 27, 29, 35, 59, 60, 61, 101, 130, 164, 176, 178
    product 17, 22, 23, 24, 28, 30, 32, 40, 45, 47, 49, 50, 51, 61, 82, 85, 88, 89, 91, 102, 121, 144, 213, 216, 219, 223, 233, 250, 252
    work 18, 21, 24, 25, 26, 27, 28, 31, 38, 40, 43, 47, 51, 52, 53, 58, 61, 96, 101, 102, 125, 132, 139, 153, 168, 171, 213, 214, 222
        conception of 119
    worker 31, 35, 246, 249
    world 17-18, 29, 58, 98, 129, 173, 233
    (*see also* creative industry, encounter, engagement)

creative industry 23, 25, 29, 31, 33, 34, 36, 37, 38, 39, 49, 53, 60, 65, 121, 122, 145, 156, 157, 162, 171, 177, 206, 232, 234, 249, 252

and intellectual property 37, 48

economic properties of 45, 82, 145, 146, 154, 164, 213 (*see also* motley crew, nobody knows)

personnel 32, 51, 52, 168, 250

political discourse of 18-21

terminology 13

creativity 13, 18, 21-5, 27, 35, 37, 47, 49, 50, 52, 53, 54, 59, 60, 64, 83, 84, 90, 101, 116, 121, 135, 161, 162, 232, 247, 252

and affordances 29, 73, 103, 138, 148

and business 15, 16, 20, 28, 29, 133

and constraints 35, 38, 137, 138

and craftsmanship 33, 164, 200, 216

and flow 33, 159, 210-6, 249

and interiority 154, 247-8

and power 139-40

as magic 15, 172

audiences of 142-4, 168

definitions of 13-15, 19

in Japan 101-3, 136-7, 176, 214, 247-8

iron cage of 38, 49

management of 16, 38, 138-9

organization of 17, 31, 38, 102, 119-40

(*see also* detachment, flow, improvisation, innovation, inspiration, trust)

critic 26, 34, 51, 62, 68, 70, 71, 76, 91, 94, 99, 101, 120, 146, 165, 168, 169, 219, 220, 223, 241, 242-3, 248, 274n

functions of 234-9

power of 238-9, 242

cultural economics 86

cultural production 13, 15, 19, 22, 23, 24, 25, 27, 28, 29, 32, 35, 36, 39, 40, 51, 52, 55, 58, 59, 60, 82, 102, 119, 120, 138, 143, 157, 162, 163, 171, 205, 213-4, 246, 249, 250

field of 34, 37, 44, 47, 97, 139, 165, 172, 251, 252

restricted and large scale 32, 233-4

D

Daimaru Department Store 217, 218, 221, 242, 273n

department store 30, 33, 39, 43, 68, 69, 70, 78, 80, 81, 92, 94, 98-9, 142, 144, 146, 217, 234, 237, 242

and art worlds 62-5, 220-1, 242-3

exhibitions 71, 81, 83, 125

rankings 62, 98-8, 169, 221, 222

292 ▣ **INDEX**

design 15, 17, 26, 33, 35, 37, 51, 60, 147, 198, 199, 209, 216, 224
  and ceramics 177-99, 231
  and decoration 73, 74-5, 93, 177,193, 215, 235
  and form 44, 71-2, 78, 186-91, 207, 235
  aesthetics 182
  Council 20
  golf course 40-1, 204
  magazine 26, 160
designer 16, 20, 21, 23, 27, 38, 51, 148, 168, 190, 195, 207
  fashion 16, 20, 27, 28, 32, 36, 46, 47, 49, 61, 97, 116, 139, 142, 146, 150-1, 154, 155, 165,
    166-7, 171, 173, 174-5, 251
detachment (mushin) 101-2, 139, 154, 176, 210, 215-6, 235, 246-7, 252, 254

E

economics 85-6
editorial moment 25-8, 178
encounter 15, 103, 129-32, 139, 144, 165, 171, 177, 204, 219, 221, 236, 245
creative 60, 120, 182, 221, 223, 232
engagement 13, 15, 26, 39,60, 73, 95, 103, 129, 144, 178, 182, 205, 223, 225, 233
  creative 15-18, 73, 74, 83, 93, 101, 166, 167, 221, 254
ensemblage 22, 27, 49, 51, 59, 61, 174, 254
  of affordances 18, 30, 42, 55, 84, 93
  of values 89, 90, 133, 216
  of worth 30, 60, 82-100, 101, 121, 151, 162, 169, 174, 176, 219, 221, 232, 233, 244, 248, 249
ensemble 22, 41, 43, 133
  (*see also* flow)
ethnographic 28
  account 29, 30, 31, 33, 126, 246
  approach 17, 24
  material 24, 30
  study 17, 60, 102, 244
ethnography 29, 167n
  (*see also* participant observation)
evaluation 15, 18, 24, 25, 26-8, 33, 46, 51, 59, 60, 67, 68, 78, 91, 96, 99, 135, 167, 178, 200,
    207, 210, 214, 216, 223, 254
  aesthetic 62, 67, 94, 97, 99, 236, 239, 241, 248, 250
  criteria for 78-9, 80, 82
  definition of 84-5
  language of 235-9 (*see also* aesthetic)
  politics of 34, 232-45
  valuation and 30, 34, 36, 84, 88, 168, 169, 200, 248, 252, 253
    sociology of (SVE) 84, 85
  (*see also* aesthetic[s], editorial moment, jury, value, worth)

INDEX ◙ 293

exhibition 15, 25, 39, 45, 51, 91, 93, 98, 99, 119, 125, 142, 163, 169, 178, 182, 186, 191, 192, 200, 203

framing 64-7, 94, 120

Japan Ceramic Art Exhibition (Nihon Tōgeiten) 33, 217-31

jurying 34, 239-45

Traditional Crafts Exhibition (Dentō Kōgeiten) 68, 94

types of 44, 50, 62, 221, 238

(*see also* department store, pottery, price, prize, recommendation)

F

faience 33, 48, 54-5, 59, 177, 182-3, 206, 207, 208, 209

fashion magazine 25, 29, 31, 32, 37, 39, 48, 52, 61, 141-61, 168, 169, 170, 172, 246, 248, 265n

and fashion 136-7, 144, 145-53, 165-8

readerships 153-7

flow 32, 58, 150, 160, 161, 163-4, 202, 226, 248, 249

creativity and 210-6

group 15, 129, 213-6, 249

(*see also* anchorage, ensemble)

frame 14, 18, 38, 54, 94, 125, 138, 245, 265n

analysis 121, 125, 126, 129

-based fieldwork 143-4

creative process and 60, 61, 64-71, 131-2

G

genre 15, 16, 17, 23, 24, 27, 32, 33, 34, 38, 39, 41, 47, 48-50, 53, 57, 58, 61, 69, 72, 73-4, 77, 78, 90, 95, 164, 208, 213, 234, 235, 248, 249, 250, 269n

(*see also* mingei, Royal Copenhagen)

glaze 25, 33, 42, 48, 56, 57, 64, 68, 73, 93-4, 100, 178, 180, 182-6, 189, 191, 192, 195, 197, 198, 200, 202, 207, 235, 236, 248

over 50, 70, 73, 217, 218, 231, 248, 261n

(*see also* clay, material)

Gutenberg 14, 40

H

habitus (disposition) 37, 38, 52, 85, 134, 176, 263n

I

Imaizumi Imaemon XIII 50-1, 60, 70-1, 79, 84, 85, 90, 91, 218, 230-1, 236, 238, 239, 244, 245, 261n

Important Intangible Cultural Property (jūyō mukei bunkazai) 57, 62, 70, 97, 217, 220, 245, 261n

improvisation 21, 23, 24, 25, 30, 31, 33, 36, 72, 83, 119, 128, 139, 210, 213-4, 215-6, 246, 249, 253, 272n

and creativity 23, 25, 36, 128, 213, 215, 216, 249

collaborative 25, 213

cultural 31, 139

jazz 213, 215, 249

(*see also* creativity)

incense 210-3

innovation 16, 19, 22, 23, 25, 50, 56, 63, 167, 207

inspiration 19, 40, 87, 101, 246, 247, 252, 254

inspired world 84, 93, 101-2

J

Japan Ceramic Art Exhibition (nihon tōgeiten) 33, 217, 218, 221-3, 224, 225, 227, 235, 236, 237, 239, 273n

jurying of 240-5

(*see also* exhibition, jury)

jury 34, 46, 217, 218, 222, 223-5, 233, 235, 237

and evaluation 235-6, 239-45

and prize awarding 225-231

(*see also* evaluation, Japan Ceramic Art Exhibition, prize)

K

Kajiwara Jirō 64, 71, 72, 83, 203, 260n, 261n

Karpik, Lucien 82, 168-9, 170-1, 234

Koestler, Arthur 13, 24, 25, 119, 246, 248

Koishiwara 55-6, 64, 68, 69, 73, 74, 77, 95, 215, 260n, 261n

L

Lamont, Michèle 84, 236, 240, 244

M

Mainichi Newspaper 64, 65-6, 91, 217, 218, 221-2, 223, 224, 226, 228, 230, 237, 241-2, 244, 260n, 273n

market 17, 27, 28, 32, 36, 44, 45, 47, 55, 68, 76, 77, 83, 86, 121, 145, 152, 164, 167, 168, 169, 173, 195, 201, 234, 243, 253, 254

aesthetic 32, 172, 173, 174, 175, 176

demand 53, 56

economic 32, 172, 175

mass 82, 172

network 170-2

of singularities 96, 168

prestige 217

symbolic 32, 162, 172-6, 233, 252

marketing 16, 27, 38, 50, 62, 69, 122, 123, 125, 138, 157, 165, 178, 184, 190, 192, 194, 200, 208, 219, 232, 248, 250

material 13, 14, 16, 17, 22, 24, 28, 38, 39-42, 46, 48, 52, 54, 55, 57, 58, 61, 74, 80, 83, 88, 93-4, 101, 133, 136, 150, 151, 160, 182, 204, 207, 208, 210-3, 248

(*see also* affordance, clay, glaze, values)

INDEX 🔲 295

Meiji Life Insurance (*meiji seimei*) 103, 104, 105, 107, 108-9, 111, 114, 115, 116, 117, 118, 119, 120, 121, 124, 125, 126, 251, 266n

mingei 56, 73, 169, 179, 222, 229, 261n, 272n
　(*see also* genre, stoneware)

motley crew 19, 52, 102, 103, 122, 123, 124, 129, 132, 137, 138, 140, 146
　(*see also* creative industry, production team)

Munch-Petersen, Ursula 33, 54, 177-80, 181, 182, 183, 186, 192, 193, 194, 195, 196, 200, 202, 206, 207, 208, 209, 210, 220

N

name economy 34, 51, 157, 252-3
　(*see also* celebrity, reputation)

network 17, 24, 37, 38, 62, 81, 97, 130, 168, 169, 209, 221, 223, 240, 248
　-based fieldwork 143
　market 170-1
　of people cooperating 52, 65, 121, 65
　practitioner 171-2
　(*see also* actor-network)

nobody knows 24, 82, 146, 162, 213
　(*see also* creative industry)

O

Onta 56-7, 73, 100

Oscar 26, 46, 98, 251

P

participant observation 21, 33, 64, 143, 264n
　(*see also* ethnography)

perfume 45, 46, 156, 210-1, 250
　perfumer 32
　(*see also* incense)

porcelain 25, 40, 42, 48, 55, 68-9, 70, 73-4, 78-9, 83, 90, 93, 95, 99, 119, 164, 168, 177, 182, 188, 194, 198, 207, 209, 217, 218, 230, 236, 239, 248, 261n
　Royal Porcelain Factory 177, 179, 180, 181, 182, 197, 198, 199

pottery 29, 33, 37, 39, 42, 44, 55-7, 64, 69, 70, 71, 72-3, 76, 80, 91, 95, 142, 144, 169, 177-9, 182, 184, 194, 201, 211, 215, 216, 217, 220, 222, 224-5, 229, 235, 237, 246, 272n
　critics 146, 234, 274n
　exhibition 25, 30, 45, 51, 60, 63, 64-81, 82, 83, 84, 89, 98, 101, 102, 120, 143, 164, 168, 205, 219, 246, 252
　style 100, 260n
　(*see also* critic, exhibition, faience, porcelain, stoneware, terroir)

power 16, 24, 31, 33, 37, 41, 51, 54, 76, 92, 97, 132, 138, 149, 151, 167, 196, 209, 210, 251, 262n
　field of 38
　(*see also* creativity, critic)

price 26, 30, 34, 40, 44, 54-5, 61, 71, 80-1, 82, 83, 84, 86-8, 93, 95, 96, 97, 99, 100, 145, 150, 159, 168, 169, 198, 216, 217, 229, 243, 248, 250, 252-3, 261n, 263n

prize 26, 33-4, 46, 50-1, 70, 79, 99, 169, 179, 217-9, 220, 222-5, 232-4, 235, 241-3, 244, 245, 250, 273n

Nobel 26, 250

Princess Chichibu Cup (chichibu no miya hai) 26, 51, 218, 223, 225, 226, 227, 228, 229, 231, 233, 234, 235, 236, 244, 245, 248

process of awarding 225-31, 236

production-consumption 26, 40, 87, 121, 145, 146, 166-7, 173, 211, 216, 242, 269n

R

recommendation (suisenbun) 69-71, 91, 92, 218, 238

regime of economic coordination 168, 169

authenticity 169-70, 234, 237, 263n

expert-opinion 170, 234

mega- 169-70

reputation 31, 34, 44, 52, 65, 76, 77, 80, 92, 129, 134, 157, 171, 231, 238, 240, 249, 260n, 266n

(*see also* name economy)

Royal Copenhagen 33, 54-5, 177-99, 180, 206-9

as brand 190, 194-5

(*see also* genre)

S

singularity 38, 82, 84, 95, 96, 171

market of 168

skill 13, 24, 25, 30, 3, 39, 40, 48, 52, 57, 60, 69, 95, 119, 133, 156, 173, 194, 199,208, 210, 214, 253

embodied 33, 200-6

social 130, 220

technical 19, 71, 72, 95

(*see also* apprentice, training)

space of possibles 31, 37, 121, 132-7, 140

spontaneity 13, 19, 83, 84, 213

(*see also* creativity, improvisation)

stoneware 25, 42, 48, 64, 68-9,71, 73, 74, 77, 78, 82, 93, 95, 97, 99, 119, 164, 183, 207, 239, 261n

(*see also* faience, *mingei,* porcelain, pottery)

studio 26, 31, 43, 54, 106, 107, 112, 115, 120, 121, 123, 129, 130, 131, 132, 135, 138, 139, 140, 144, 151, 154, 171, 206, 215, 247

film 162, 163, 269n

pottery 180, 187

recording 213

shoot 23, 43, 125, 126, 168, 264n

spatial organization of 124-8, 132

symbolic 21, 37, 43, 78, 98, 100, 131, 132, 138, 170, 172, 179, 242, 247

    market 32, 145, 162, 172-6, 233, 252

    resources 37, 97

    space 31, 43, 120, 127, 128, 129, 132

    value 86, 96, 98, 156, 234

    (*see also* capital, ensemblage, value, worth)

T

Tamaya Department Store 65, 66, 67, 68, 78, 80, 81, 91 ,92, 94, 142, 221

terroir

    and pottery kilns 169, 274n

    and wine 44-5

    Nordic 44

    (*see also* wine)

training 20, 94, 113, 129-30, 178, 197, 201-2, 247

    (*see also* apprentice, skill)

trust 36, 130, 139, 168, 173, 253

    and creative work 25, 31, 65, 132, 171-2, 214, 215

V

value 17, 18, 27, 28, 30, 32, 43, 45, 47, 60, 62, 84-5, 89, 90, 95, 97, 101, 120, 138, 144, 172, 174, 175, 182, 229, 232, 233, 244, 248, 249, 263n

    aesthetic 30, 62, 86, 90, 93, 97, 165, 167, 173, 178, 190, 223 (*see also* aesthetic[s])

    affective 236n

    appreciative 89, 90-1, 96, 98, 99, 100, 173, 176, 177, 192, 194, 198, 223, 235, 237, 248

    chain 144, 159, 166, 176, 249

    commodity-exchange 30, 93, 95, 96, 97, 98, 162, 169, 174, 190

    cultural 18, 88, 89

    economic 30, 93, 96, 177, 190, 198

    human 196

    intrinsic 87, 88

    market 77

    material 89, 198

    monetary 84, 87

    situational 94-5, 96, 97, 98, 99, 176

    social 30, 88, 89, 91-3, 96, 97, 98, 99, 176, 192, 198, 237, 263n

    spatial 30, 89

    symbolic-exchange 30, 32, 90, 95, 96, 97, 98, 162, 169, 174, 176, 263n

    technical 93-4, 96, 97, 98, 99, 176, 182

    temporal 30, 89

    theory of 85-9

    use 30, 95, 96, 97, 99-100, 176

    (*see also* symbolic, worth)

W

Watanabe Misato 103-7, 109-110, 111-7, 118, 121, 124, 126, 251, 266n

wine 14, 40, 44-5, 91, 168, 169, 170, 232, 235, 250, 274n

    (*see also* terroir)

worth 15, 17, 26, 30, 32, 84, 86, 87-8, 91, 94, 98, 99, 102, 170, 175, 223, 233, 248

    anthropology of 18

    ensemblage of 30, 60, 82-100, 101, 121, 151, 162, 169, 174, 176, 219, 221, 232, 233, 244, 248, 249

    of names 249-53

    of scholarship 253-5

    sociology of 87

    world of 82, 89, 93, 102, 252

ABOUT THE AUTHOR

Brian Moeran has had a chequered career. Would-be helicopter pilot in Her Britannic Majesty's Royal Navy back in the early 1960s, he got out in time to avoid killing people and became a television comedian in Japan instead. When people started dying of laughter, he turned anthropologist, and for the past 30 years has been writing about pottery, advertising, women's fashion magazines, book publishing, and smell—primarily, but not exclusively, in Japan. He now does his best to prevent people from dying of boredom, but cannot guarantee to have been always successful. He has been around long enough to be appointed professor of this and that at well-known academic institutions in England, Denmark, and Hong Kong, but probably his single greatest achievement has been the fact that he once hitchhiked from Aachen to Athens two hours faster than the train. Will the *Guinness Book of World Records* please take note?